Delicious IN DUNGEON

RYOKO KUI

8

Delicious IN DUNGEON

8

Contents

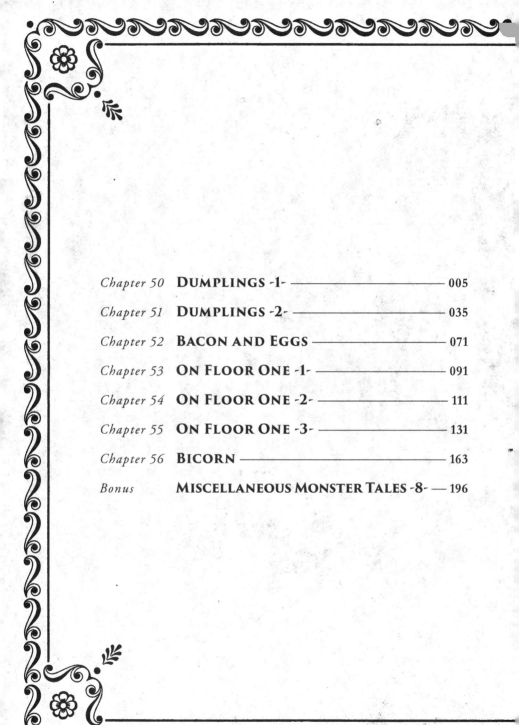

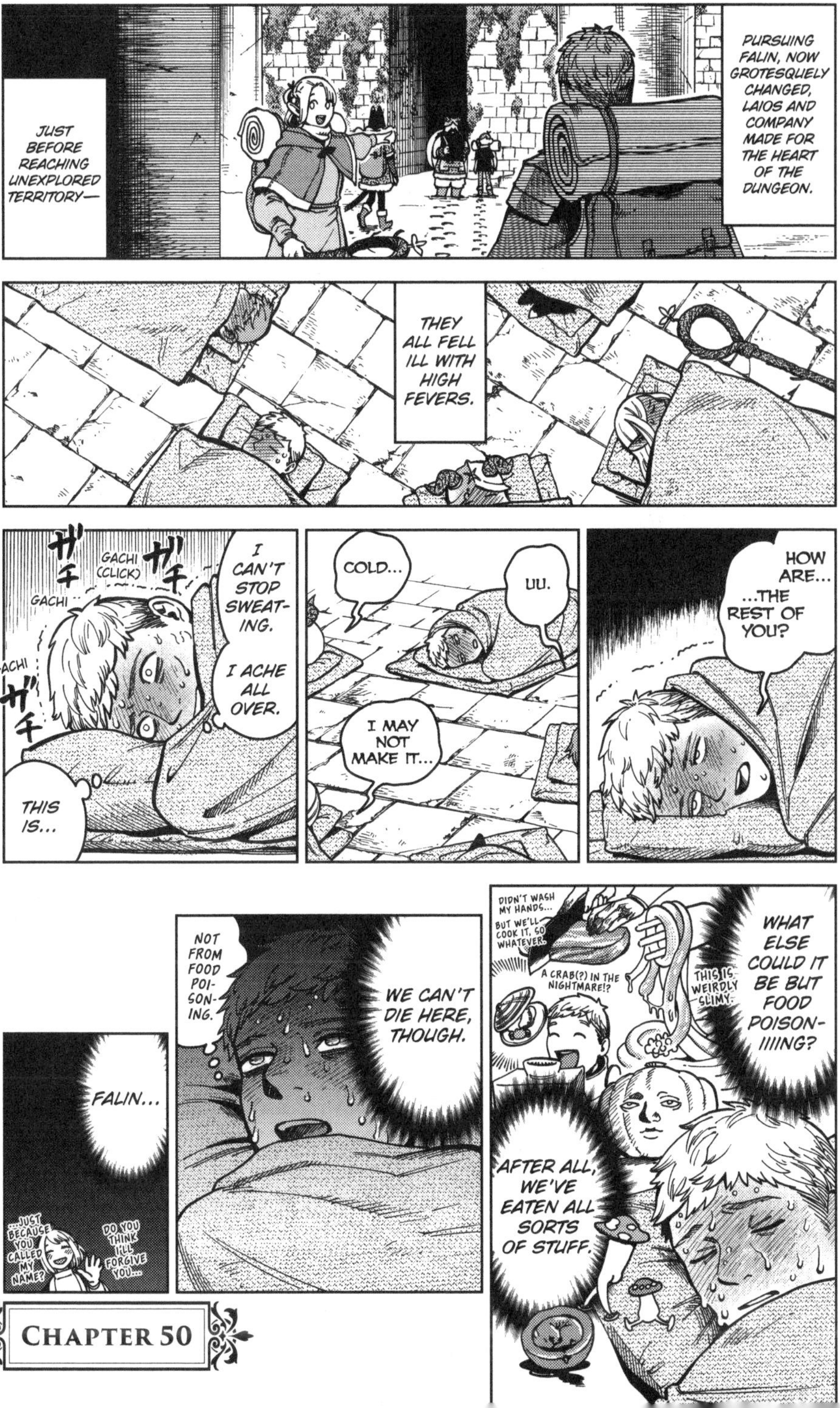
PURSUING FALIN, NOW GROTESQUELY CHANGED, LAIOS AND COMPANY MADE FOR THE HEART OF THE DUNGEON.
JUST BEFORE REACHING UNEXPLORED TERRITORY—
THEY ALL FELL ILL WITH HIGH FEVERS.
HOW ARE... ...THE REST OF YOU?
UU.
COLD...
I MAY NOT MAKE IT...
I CAN'T STOP SWEATING.
I ACHE ALL OVER.
GACHI (CLICK)
GACHI
GACHI
THIS IS...
WHAT ELSE COULD IT BE BUT FOOD POISON-IIIING?
DIDN'T WASH MY HANDS... BUT WE'LL COOK IT, SO WHATEVER.
THIS IS WEIRDLY SLIMY.
A CRAB(?) IN THE NIGHTMARE!?
AFTER ALL, WE'VE EATEN ALL SORTS OF STUFF.
WE CAN'T DIE HERE, THOUGH.
NOT FROM FOOD POISONING.
FALIN...
DO YOU THINK I'LL FORGIVE YOU...
...JUST BECAUSE YOU CALLED MY NAME?

Chapter 50

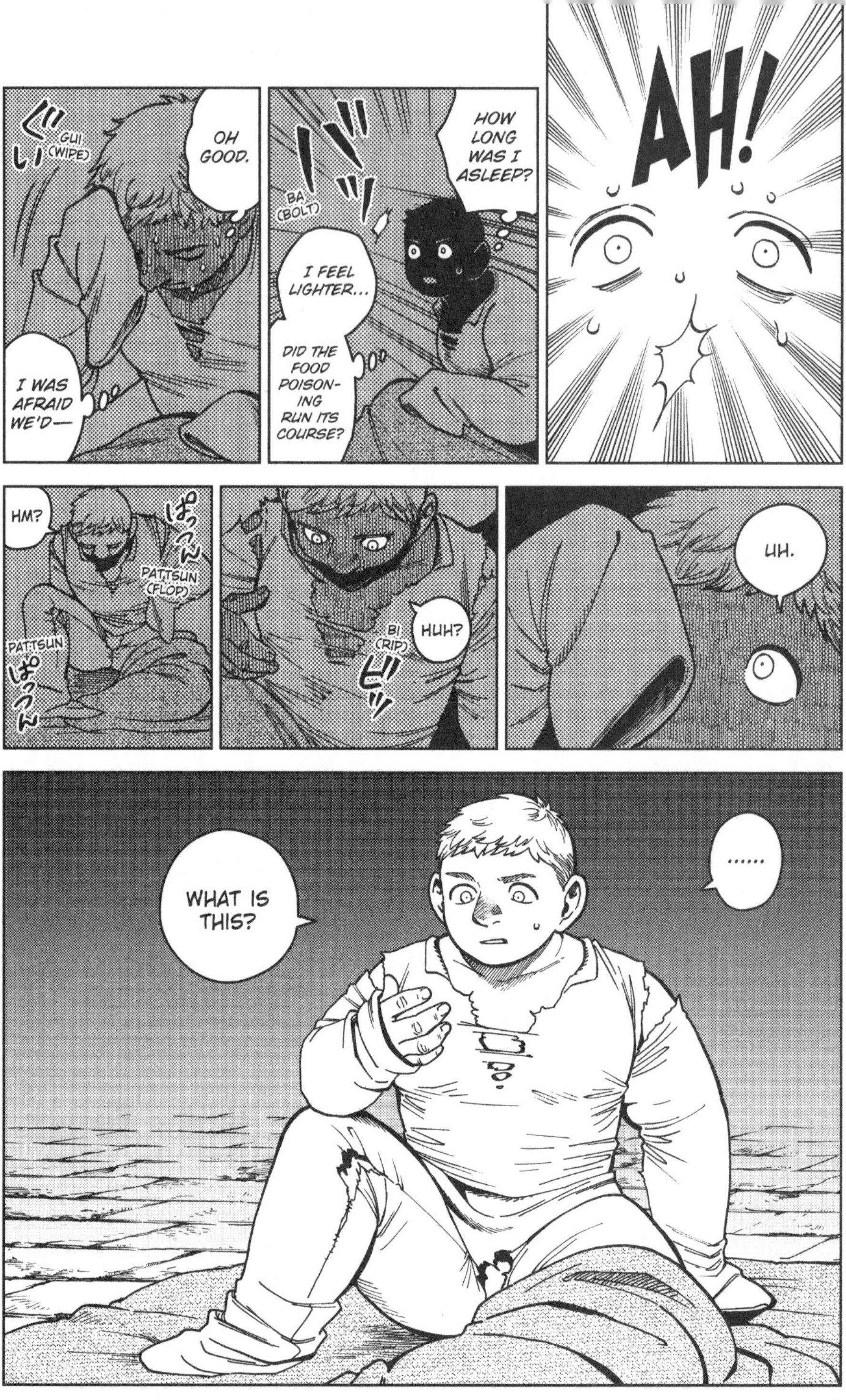
AH!
HOW LONG WAS I ASLEEP?
バッ
BA (BOLT)
I FEEL LIGHTER...
DID THE FOOD POISONING RUN ITS COURSE?
OH GOOD.
ぐい
GUI (WIPE)
I WAS AFRAID WE'D—
UH.
HUH?
ビッ
BI (RIP)
ぱっつん
PATTSUN (FLOP)
HM?
PATTSUN
ぱっつん
......
WHAT IS THIS?

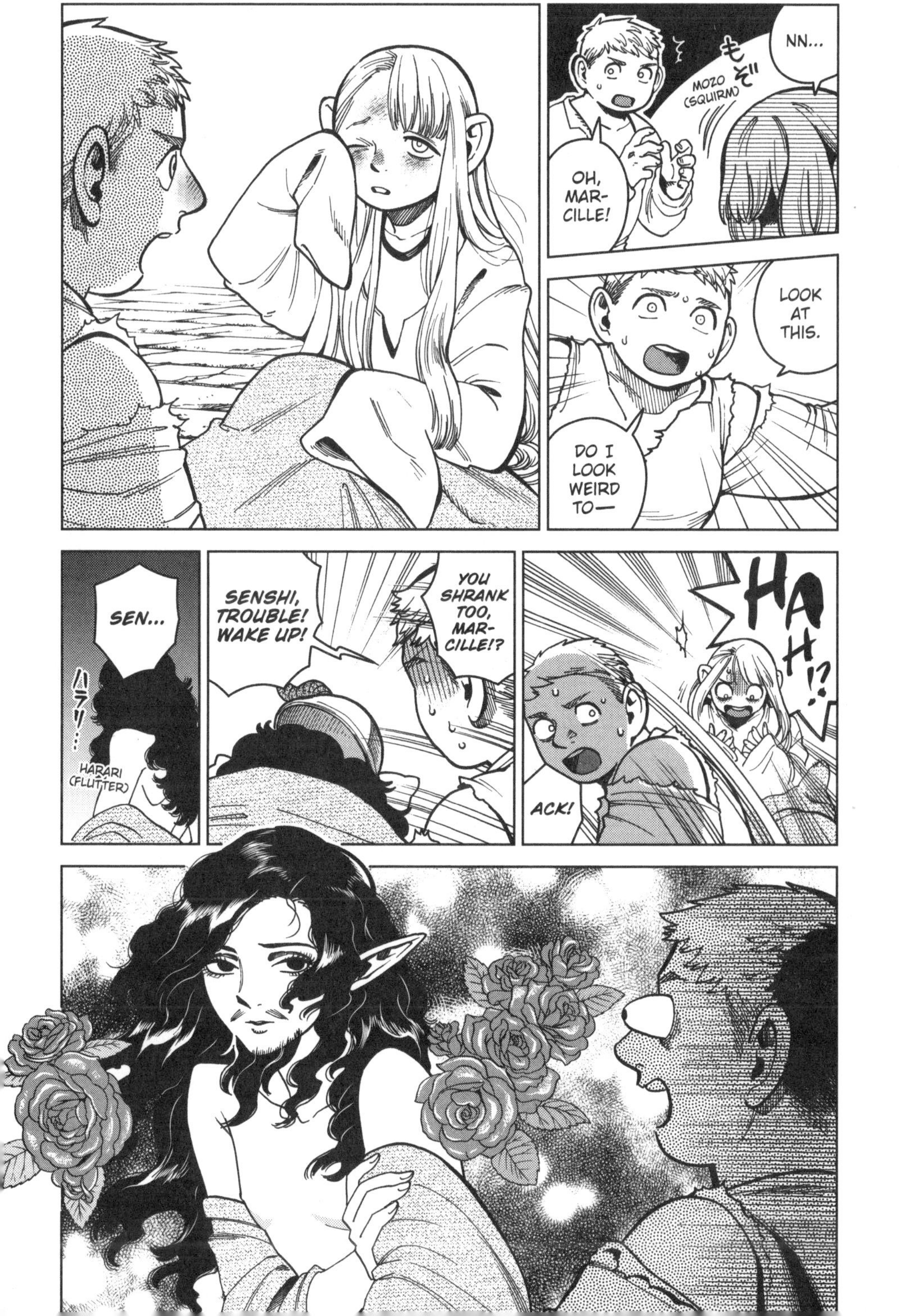
NN...
もぞ
MOZO (SQUIRM)
OH, MAR-CILLE!
LOOK AT THIS.
DO I LOOK WEIRD TO—
HAH!?
ACK!
YOU SHRANK TOO, MAR-CILLE!?
SENSHI, TROUBLE! WAKE UP!
SEN...
ハラリ…
HARARI (FLUTTER)

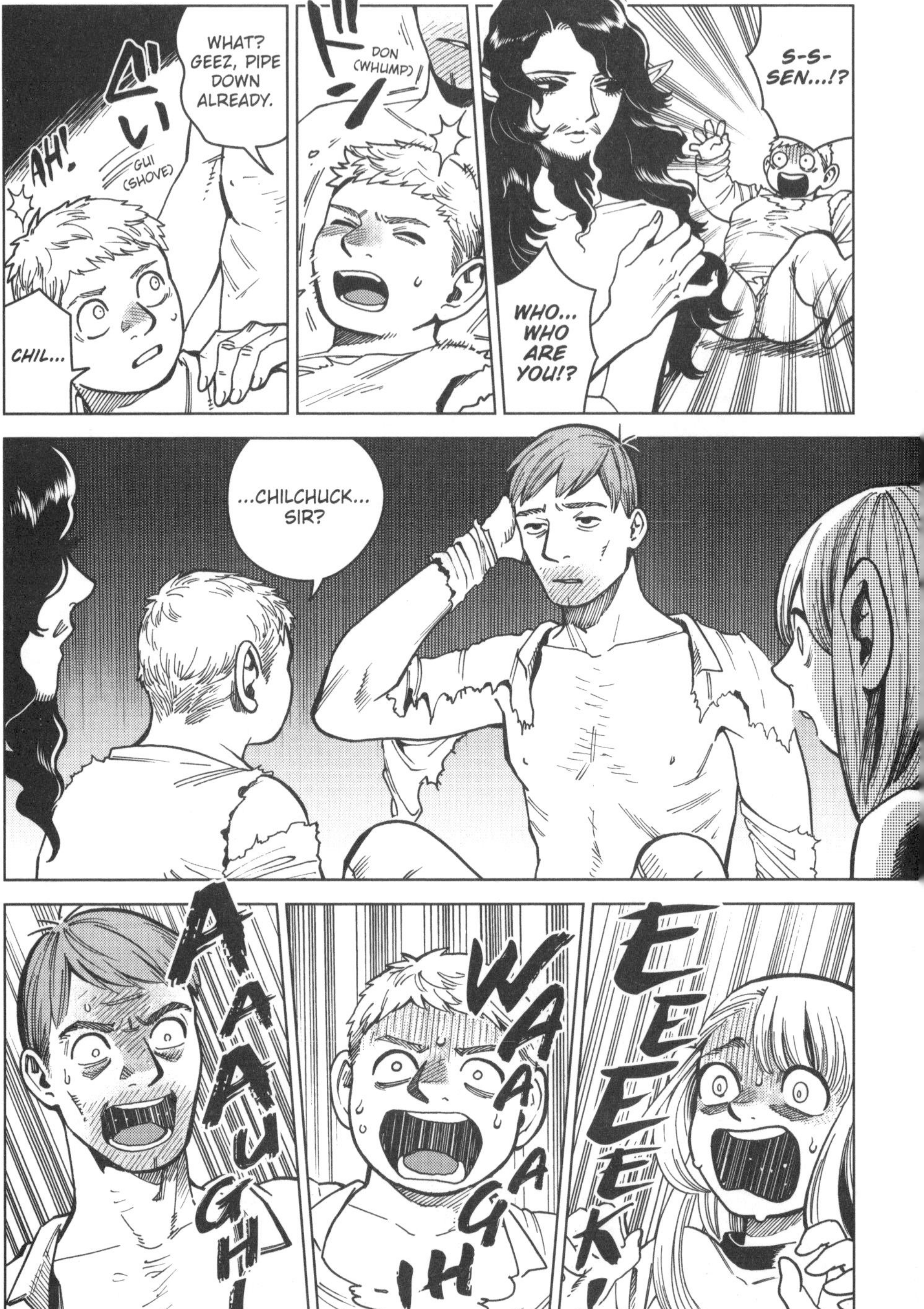
S-S-SEN...!?
WHO... WHO ARE YOU!?
DON (WHUMP)
WHAT? GEEZ, PIPE DOWN ALREADY.
GUI (SHOVE)
AH!
CHIL...
...CHILCHUCK... SIR?
EEEEEK!!
WAAAAGH!!
AAAAUGH!!

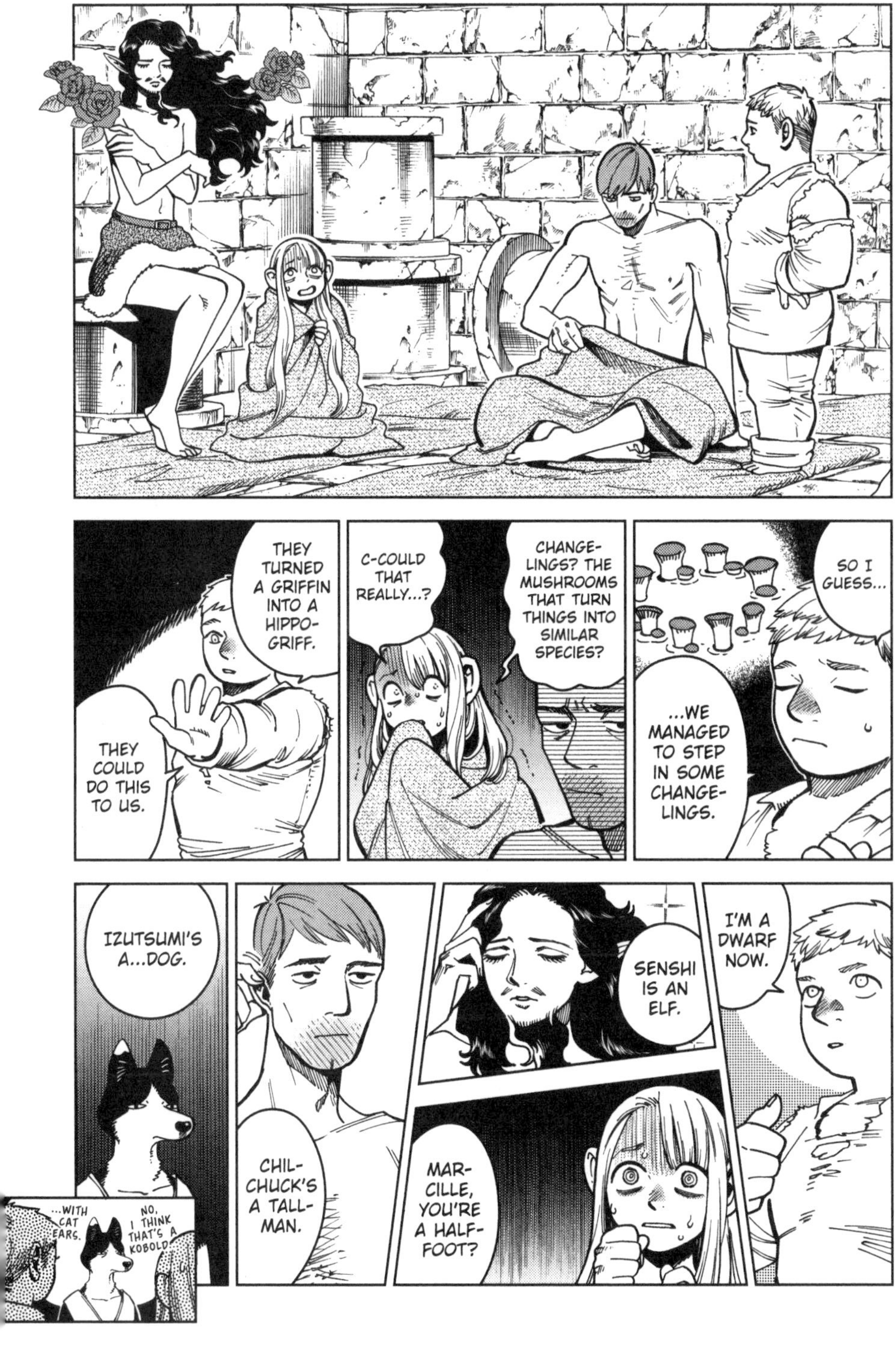
SO I GUESS...
...WE MANAGED TO STEP IN SOME CHANGE-LINGS.
CHANGE-LINGS? THE MUSHROOMS THAT TURN THINGS INTO SIMILAR SPECIES?
C-COULD THAT REALLY...?
THEY TURNED A GRIFFIN INTO A HIPPO-GRIFF.
THEY COULD DO THIS TO US.
I'M A DWARF NOW.
SENSHI IS AN ELF.
MAR-CILLE, YOU'RE A HALF-FOOT?
CHIL-CHUCK'S A TALL-MAN.
IZUTSUMI'S A...DOG.
...WITH CAT EARS.
NO, I THINK THAT'S A KOBOLD.

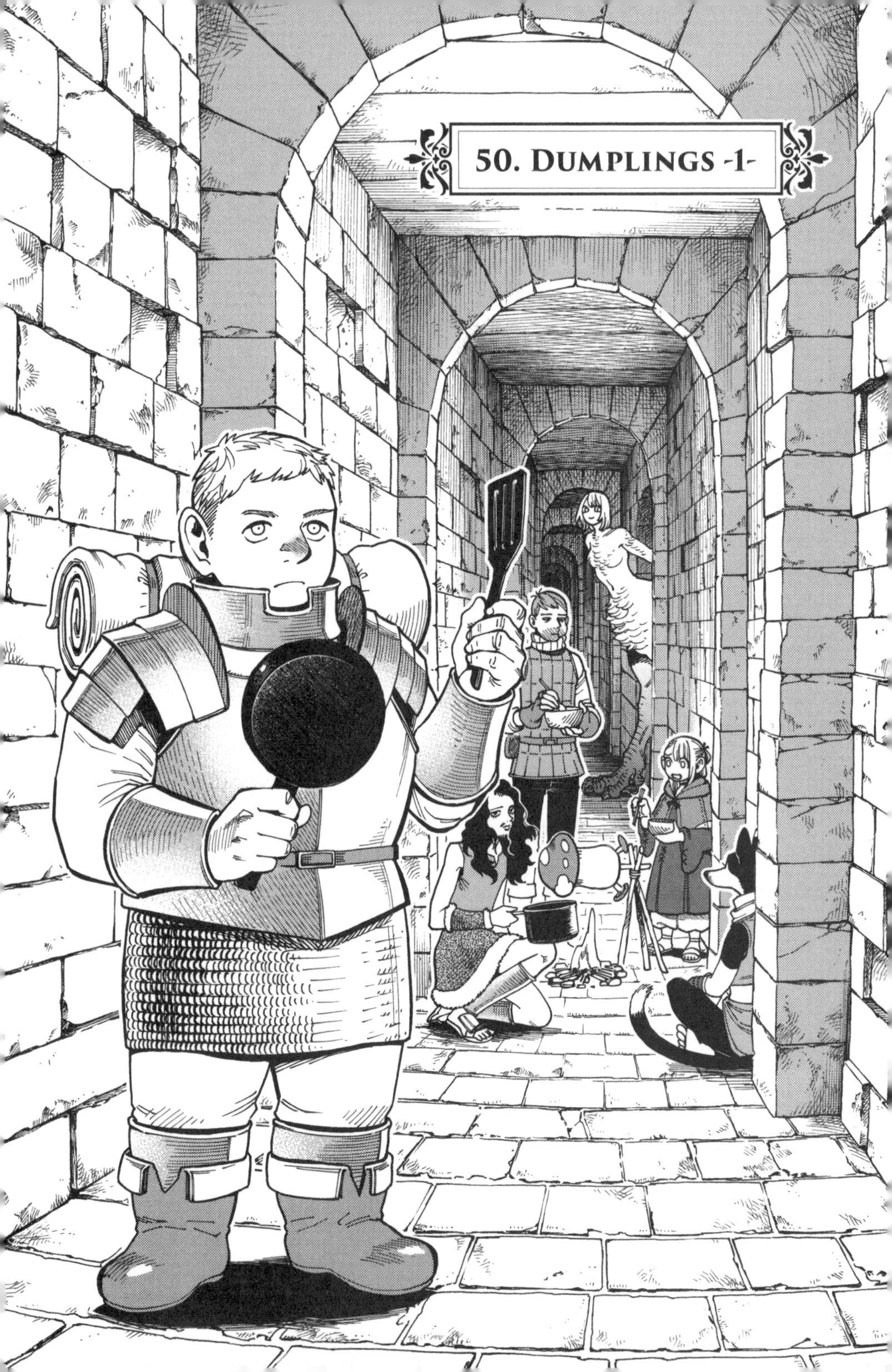
50. Dumplings -1-

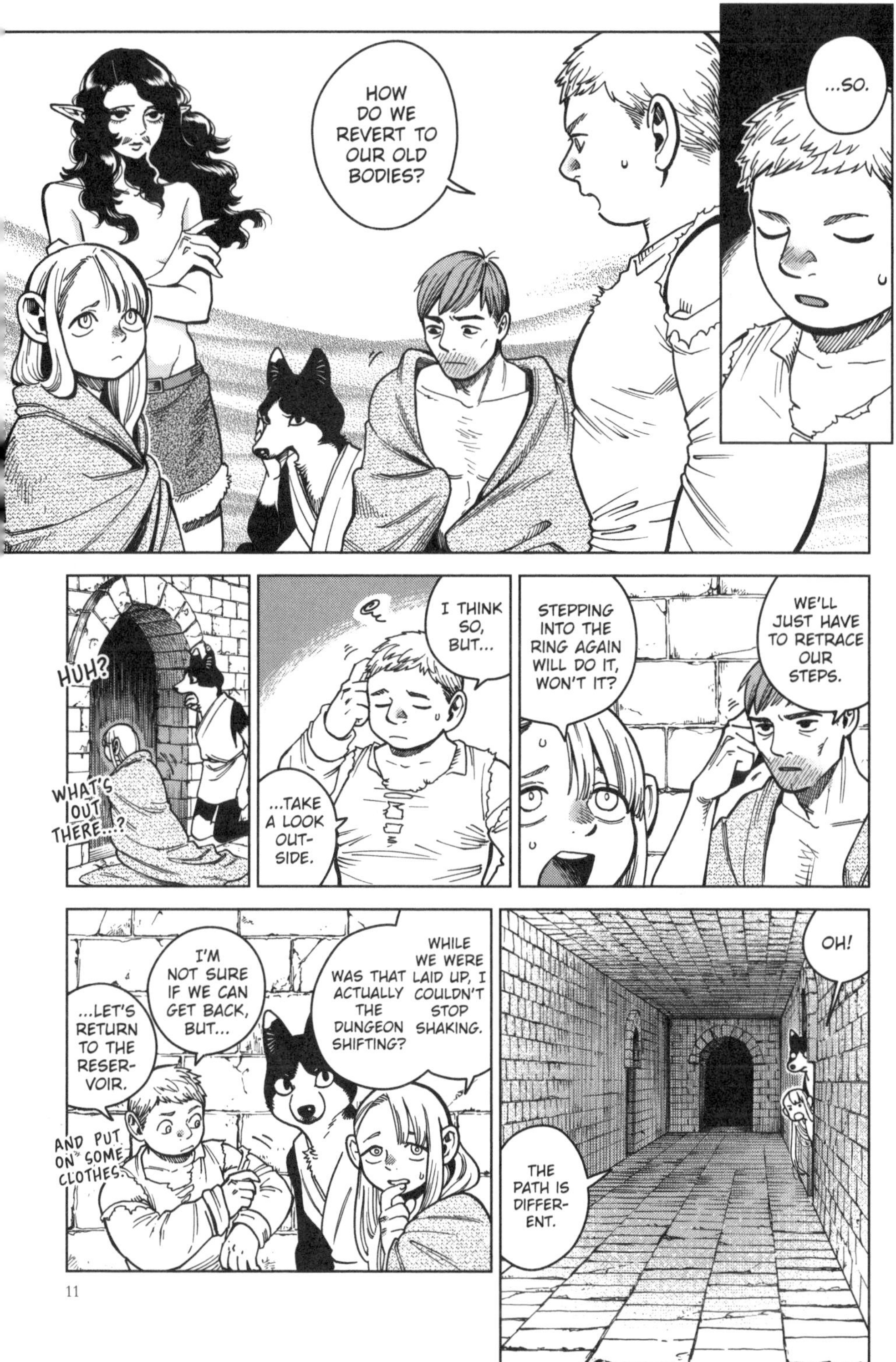
...SO.
HOW DO WE REVERT TO OUR OLD BODIES?
WE'LL JUST HAVE TO RETRACE OUR STEPS.
STEPPING INTO THE RING AGAIN WILL DO IT, WON'T IT?
I THINK SO, BUT...
...TAKE A LOOK OUTSIDE.
HUH?
WHAT'S OUT THERE...?
OH!
THE PATH IS DIFFERENT.
WHILE WE WERE LAID UP, I COULDN'T STOP SHAKING.
WAS THAT ACTUALLY THE DUNGEON SHIFTING?
I'M NOT SURE IF WE CAN GET BACK, BUT...
...LET'S RETURN TO THE RESERVOIR.
AND PUT ON SOME CLOTHES.

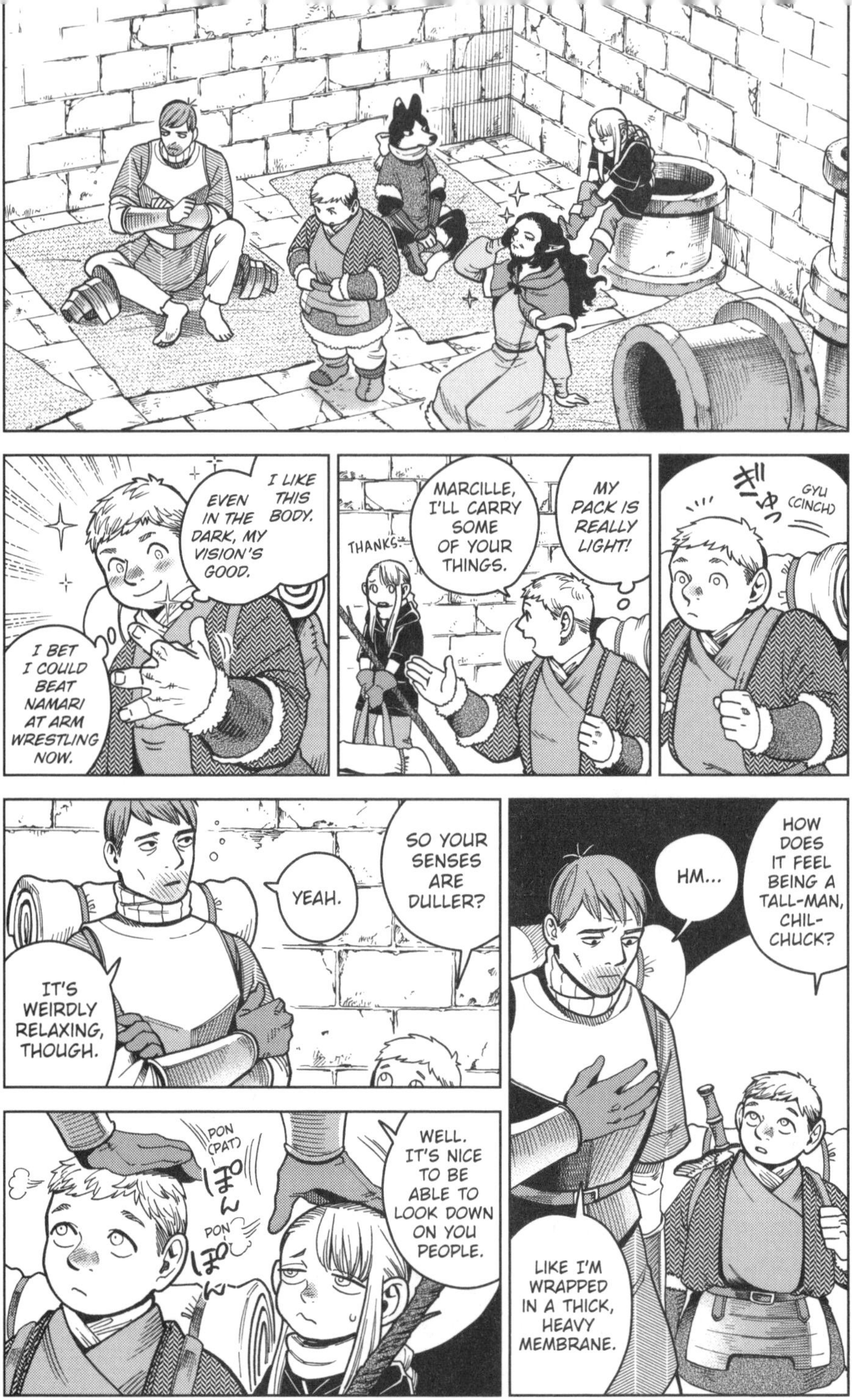
ぎゅっ
GYU (CINCH)
MY PACK IS REALLY LIGHT!
MARCILLE, I'LL CARRY SOME OF YOUR THINGS.
THANKS.
I LIKE THIS BODY.
EVEN IN THE DARK, MY VISION'S GOOD.
I BET I COULD BEAT NAMARI AT ARM WRESTLING NOW.
HOW DOES IT FEEL BEING A TALL-MAN, CHIL-CHUCK?
HM...
LIKE I'M WRAPPED IN A THICK, HEAVY MEMBRANE.
SO YOUR SENSES ARE DULLER?
YEAH.
IT'S WEIRDLY RELAXING, THOUGH.
WELL. IT'S NICE TO BE ABLE TO LOOK DOWN ON YOU PEOPLE.
PON (PAT)
ぽん
PON
ぽん

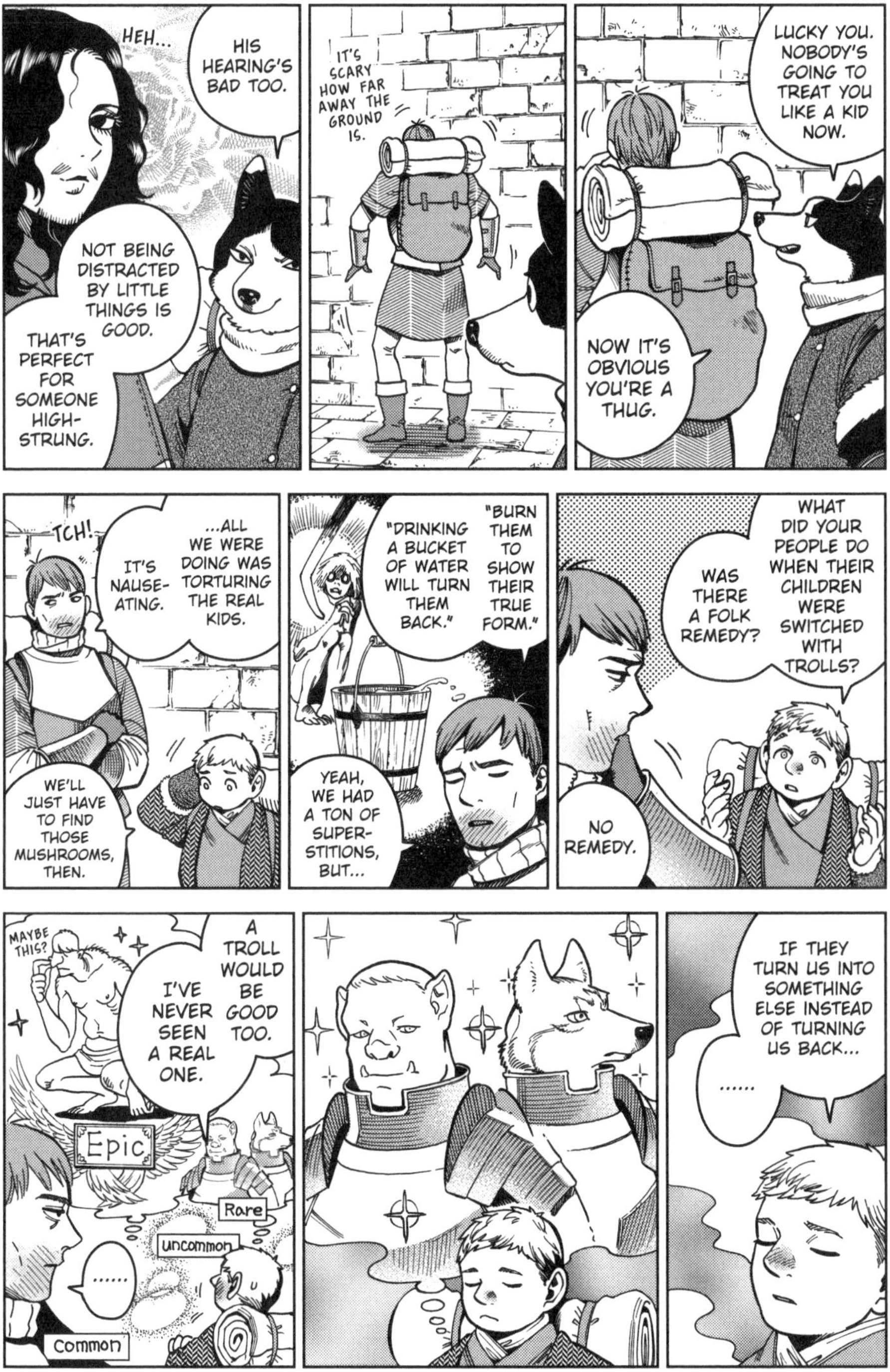
LUCKY YOU. NOBODY'S GOING TO TREAT YOU LIKE A KID NOW.
NOW IT'S OBVIOUS YOU'RE A THUG.
IT'S SCARY HOW FAR AWAY THE GROUND IS.
HIS HEARING'S BAD TOO.
HEH...
NOT BEING DISTRACTED BY LITTLE THINGS IS GOOD.
THAT'S PERFECT FOR SOMEONE HIGH-STRUNG.
WHAT DID YOUR PEOPLE DO WHEN THEIR CHILDREN WERE SWITCHED WITH TROLLS?
WAS THERE A FOLK REMEDY?
NO REMEDY.
"BURN THEM TO SHOW THEIR TRUE FORM."
"DRINKING A BUCKET OF WATER WILL TURN THEM BACK."
YEAH, WE HAD A TON OF SUPER-STITIONS, BUT...
...ALL WE WERE DOING WAS TORTURING THE REAL KIDS.
IT'S NAUSE-ATING.
TCH!
WE'LL JUST HAVE TO FIND THOSE MUSHROOMS, THEN.
IF THEY TURN US INTO SOMETHING ELSE INSTEAD OF TURNING US BACK...
......
A TROLL WOULD BE GOOD TOO.
I'VE NEVER SEEN A REAL ONE.
MAYBE THIS?
Epic
Rare
uncommon
Common
......

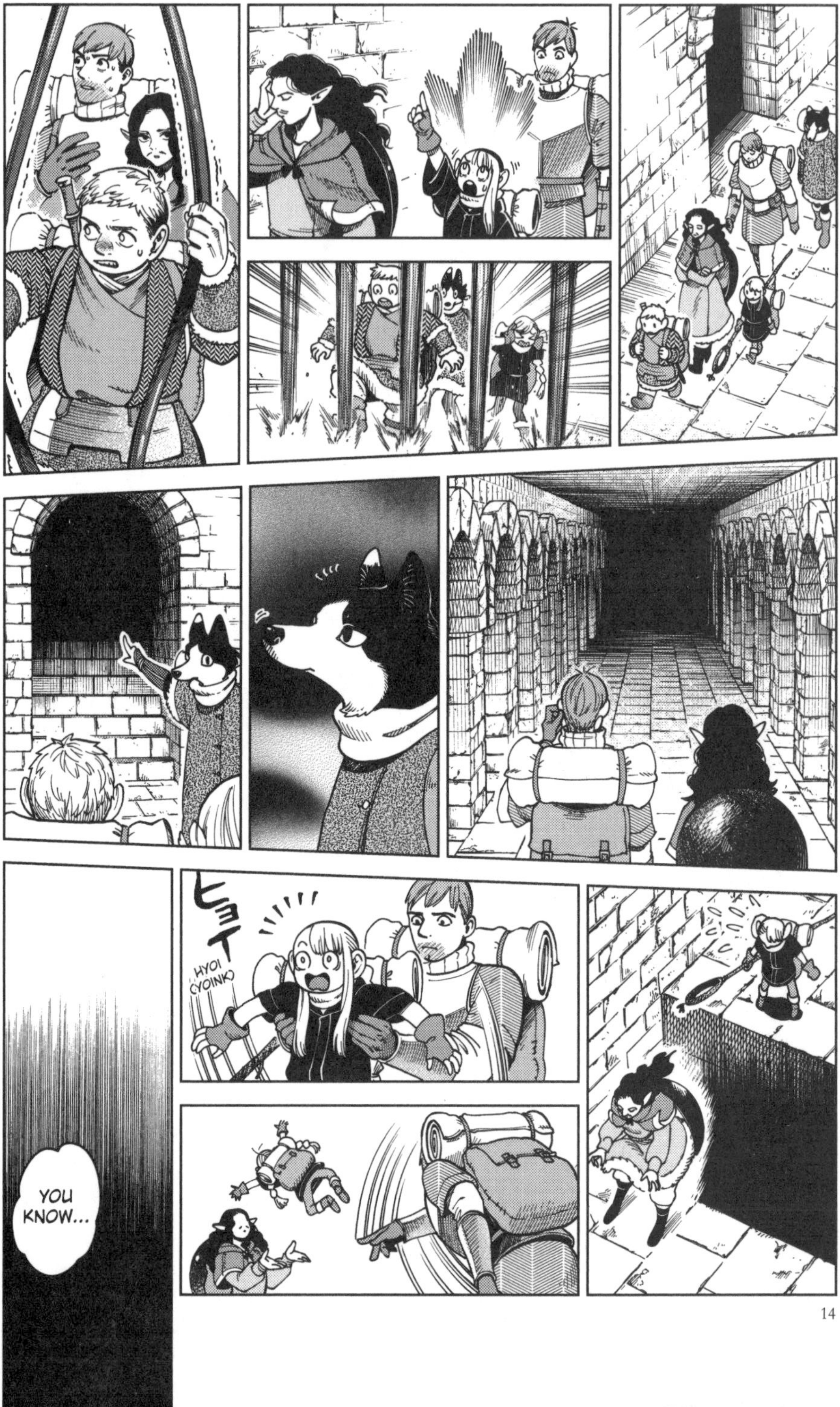
ヒョイ
HYOI
(YOINK)
YOU KNOW...

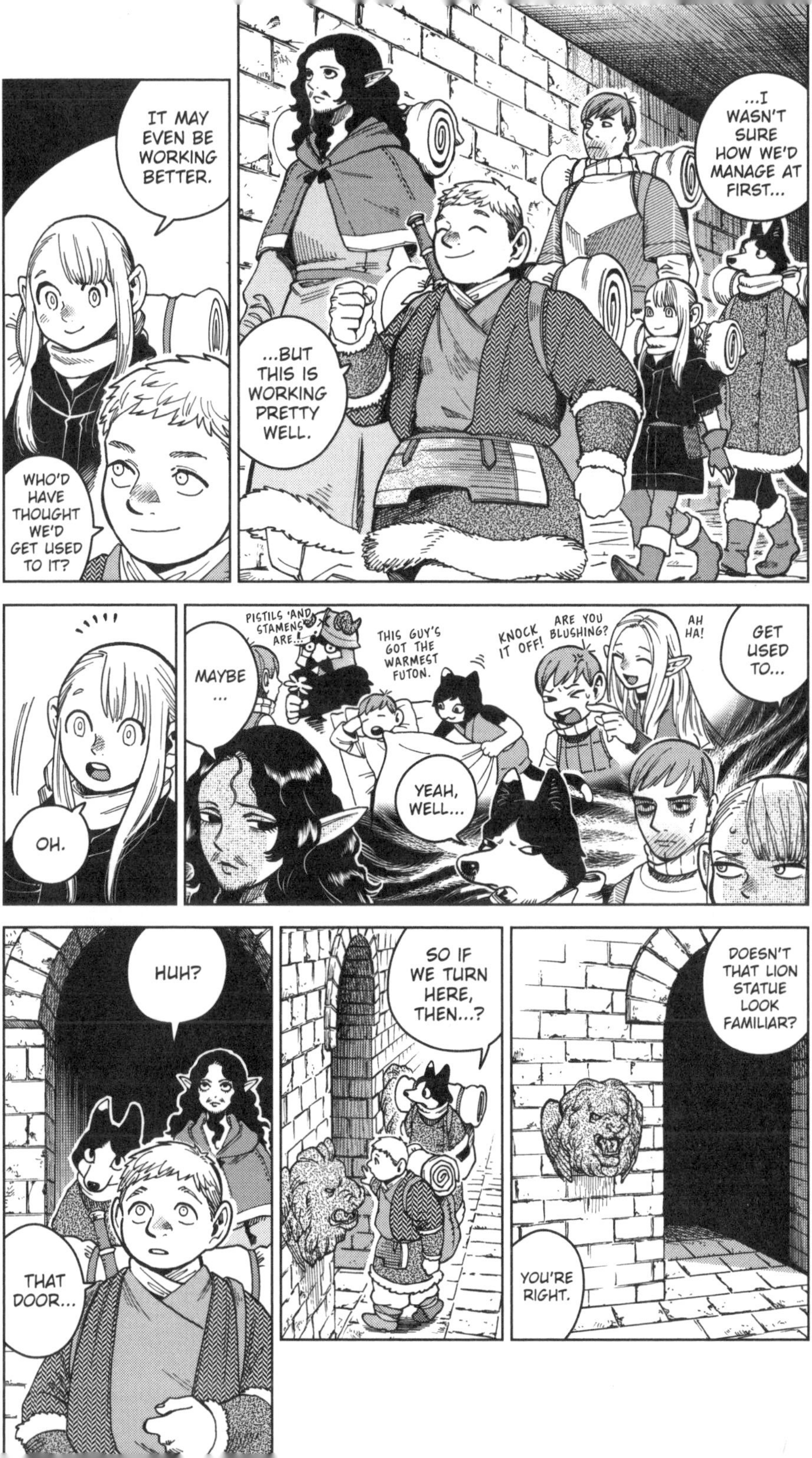
...I WASN'T SURE HOW WE'D MANAGE AT FIRST...
...BUT THIS IS WORKING PRETTY WELL.
IT MAY EVEN BE WORKING BETTER.
WHO'D HAVE THOUGHT WE'D GET USED TO IT?
GET USED TO...
AH HA!
ARE YOU BLUSHING?
KNOCK IT OFF!
THIS GUY'S GOT THE WARMEST FUTON.
PISTILS 'AND STAMENS' ARE...!
MAYBE...
YEAH, WELL...
OH.
DOESN'T THAT LION STATUE LOOK FAMILIAR?
YOU'RE RIGHT.
SO IF WE TURN HERE, THEN...?
HUH?
THAT DOOR...

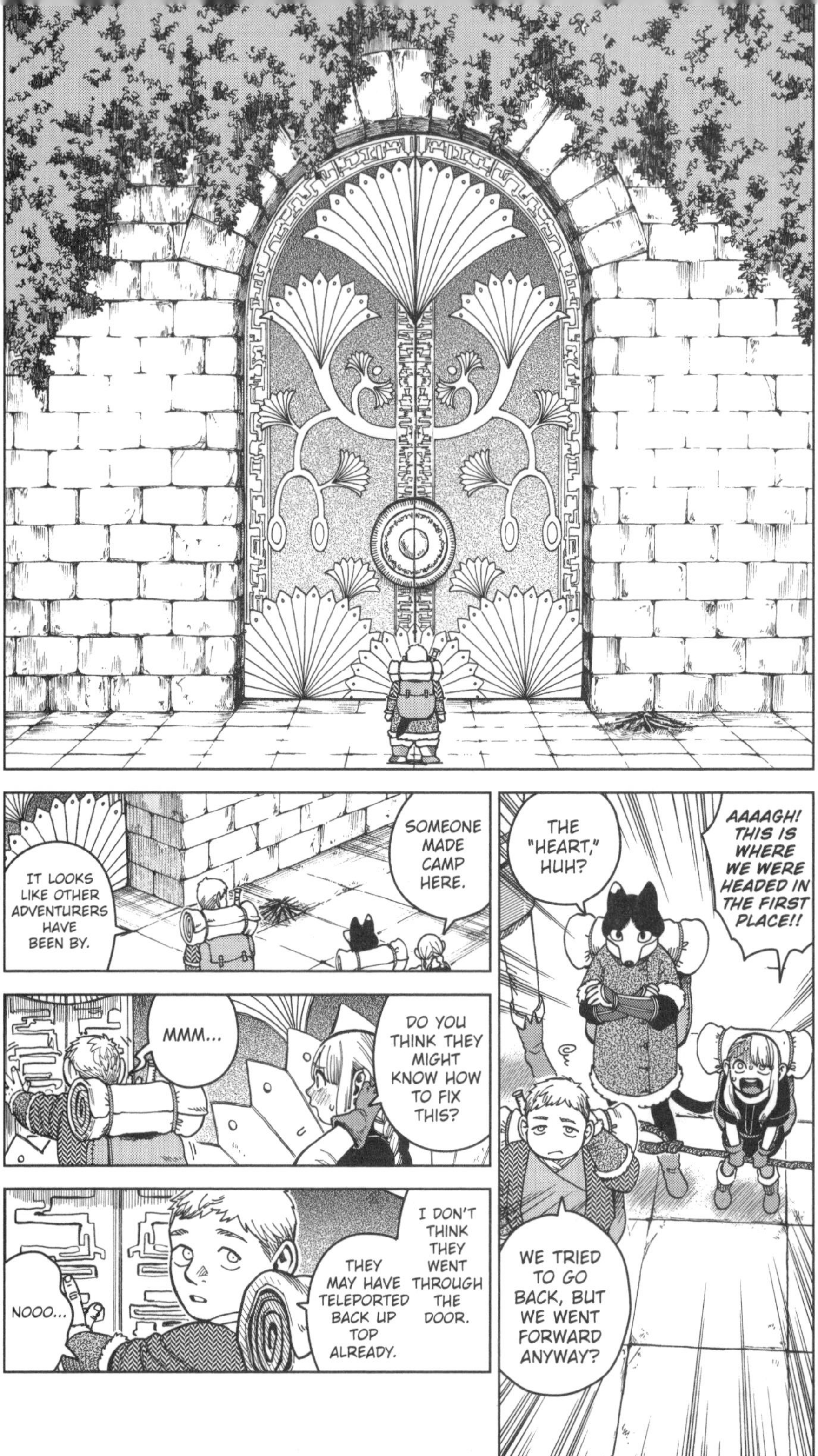
AAAAGH! THIS IS WHERE WE WERE HEADED IN THE FIRST PLACE!!
THE "HEART," HUH?
WE TRIED TO GO BACK, BUT WE WENT FORWARD ANYWAY?
SOMEONE MADE CAMP HERE.
IT LOOKS LIKE OTHER ADVENTURERS HAVE BEEN BY.
DO YOU THINK THEY MIGHT KNOW HOW TO FIX THIS?
MMM...
I DON'T THINK THEY WENT THROUGH THE DOOR.
THEY MAY HAVE TELEPORTED BACK UP TOP ALREADY.
NOOO...

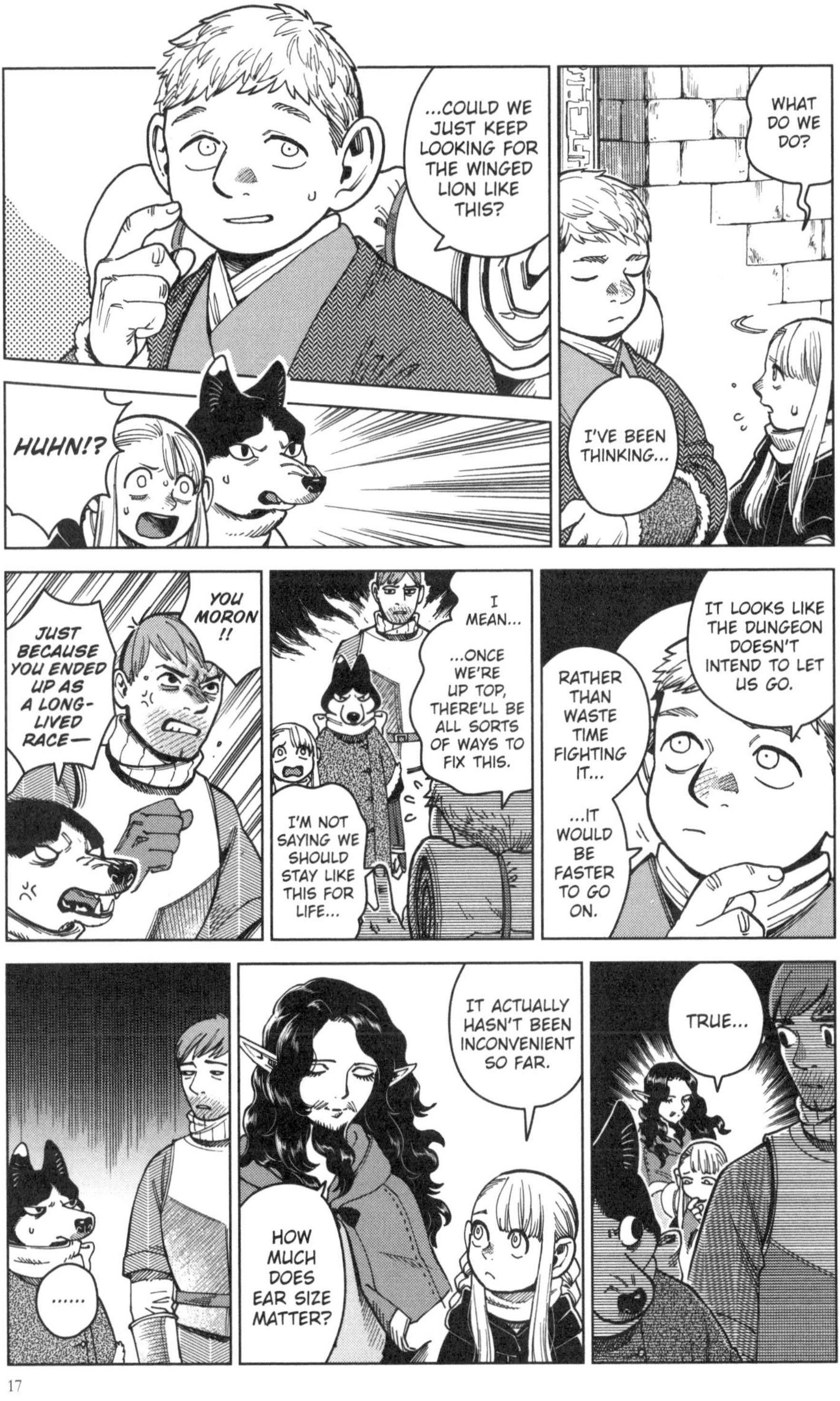
WHAT DO WE DO?
I'VE BEEN THINKING...
...COULD WE JUST KEEP LOOKING FOR THE WINGED LION LIKE THIS?
HUHN!?
IT LOOKS LIKE THE DUNGEON DOESN'T INTEND TO LET US GO.
RATHER THAN WASTE TIME FIGHTING IT...
...IT WOULD BE FASTER TO GO ON.
I MEAN...
...ONCE WE'RE UP TOP, THERE'LL BE ALL SORTS OF WAYS TO FIX THIS.
I'M NOT SAYING WE SHOULD STAY LIKE THIS FOR LIFE...
YOU MORON!!
JUST BECAUSE YOU ENDED UP AS A LONG-LIVED RACE—
TRUE...
IT ACTUALLY HASN'T BEEN INCONVENIENT SO FAR.
HOW MUCH DOES EAR SIZE MATTER?
......

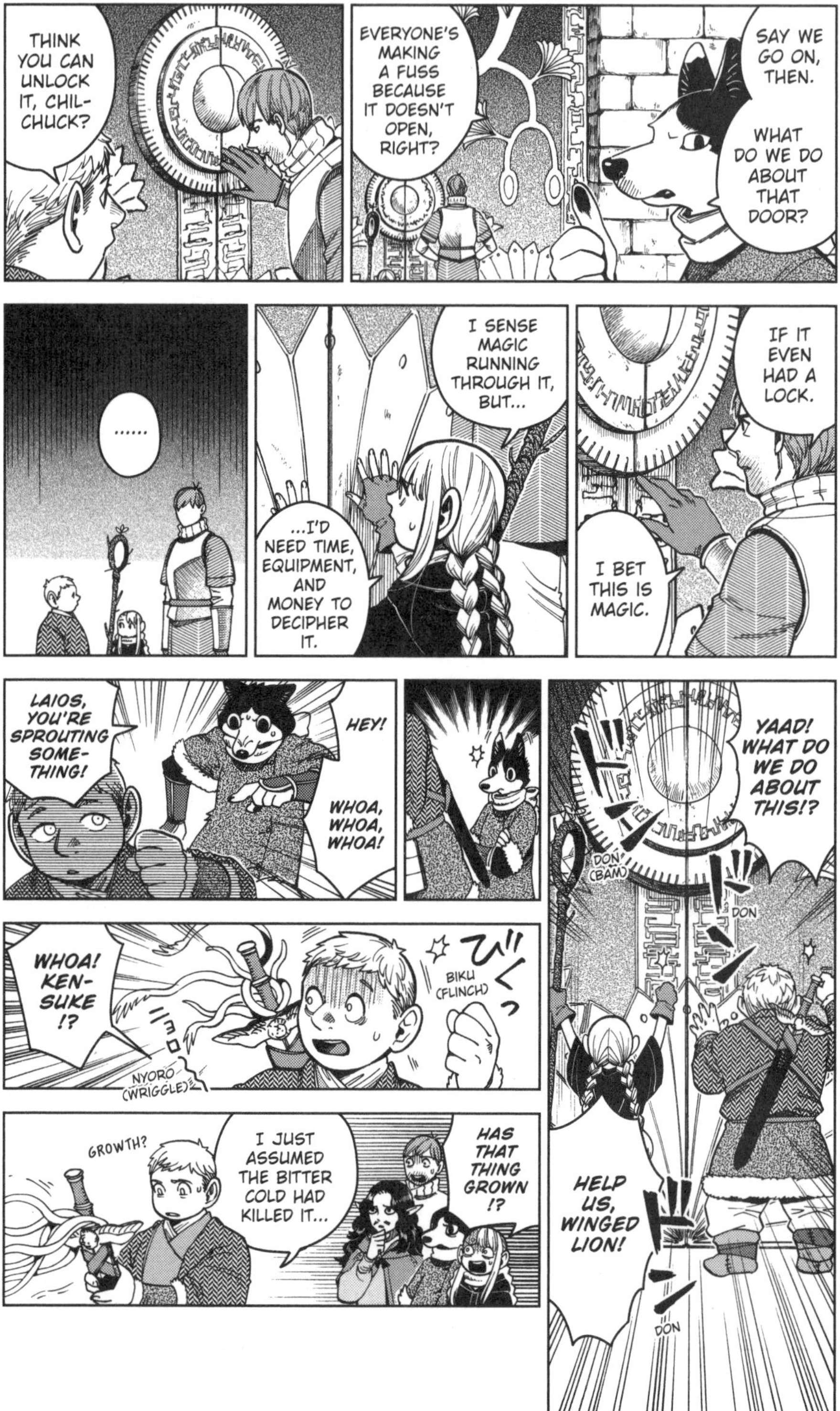
SAY WE GO ON, THEN.
WHAT DO WE DO ABOUT THAT DOOR?
EVERYONE'S MAKING A FUSS BECAUSE IT DOESN'T OPEN, RIGHT?
THINK YOU CAN UNLOCK IT, CHIL-CHUCK?
IF IT EVEN HAD A LOCK.
I BET THIS IS MAGIC.
I SENSE MAGIC RUNNING THROUGH IT, BUT...
...I'D NEED TIME, EQUIPMENT, AND MONEY TO DECIPHER IT.
......
YAAD! WHAT DO WE DO ABOUT THIS!?
DON (BAM)
DON
HELP US, WINGED LION!
DON
HEY!
WHOA, WHOA, WHOA!
LAIOS, YOU'RE SPROUTING SOMETHING!
BIKU (FLINCH)
WHOA! KEN-SUKE !?
NYORO (WRIGGLE)
HAS THAT THING GROWN !?
I JUST ASSUMED THE BITTER COLD HAD KILLED IT...
GROWTH?

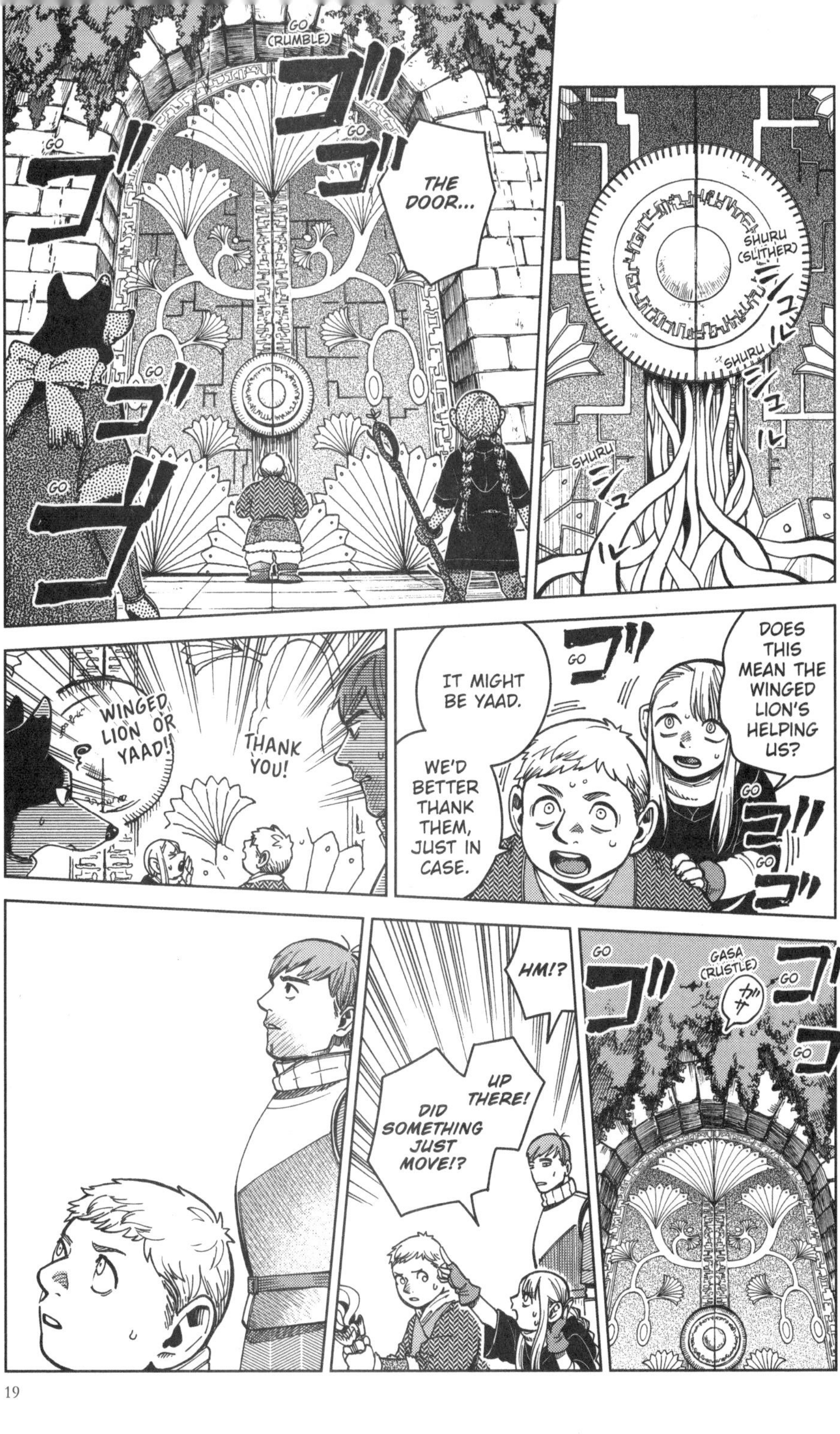
SHURU (SLITHER)
SHURU
SHURU
GO (RUMBLE)
GO
GO
GO
GO
THE DOOR...
DOES THIS MEAN THE WINGED LION'S HELPING US?
GO
IT MIGHT BE YAAD.
WE'D BETTER THANK THEM, JUST IN CASE.
GO
GO
THANK YOU!
WINGED LION OR YAAD!
GO
GASA (RUSTLE)
GO
GO
HM!?
UP THERE!
DID SOMETHING JUST MOVE!?

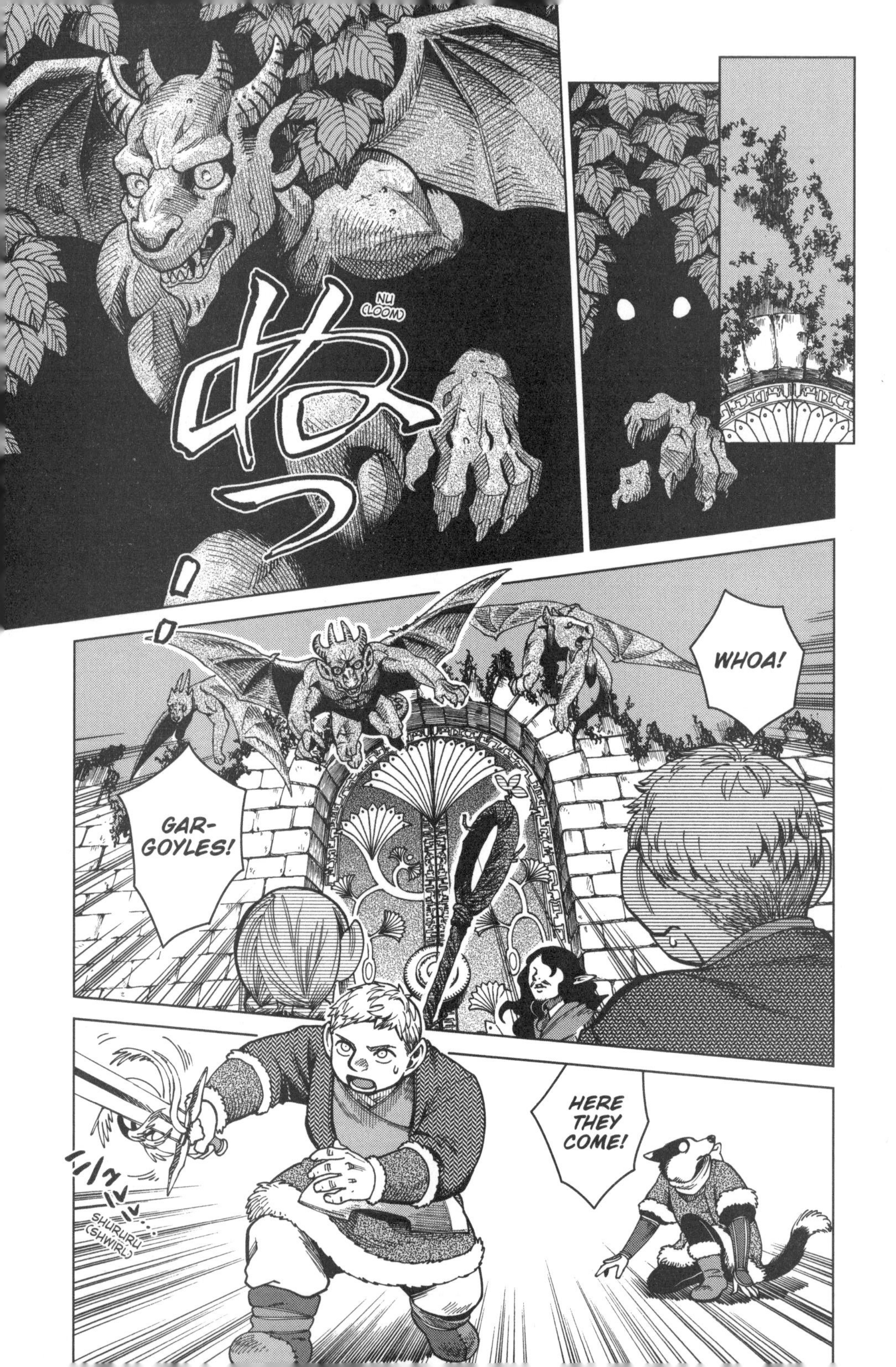
ぬっ
NU (LOOM)
WHOA!
GAR-GOYLES!
HERE THEY COME!
SHURURU (SHWIRL)

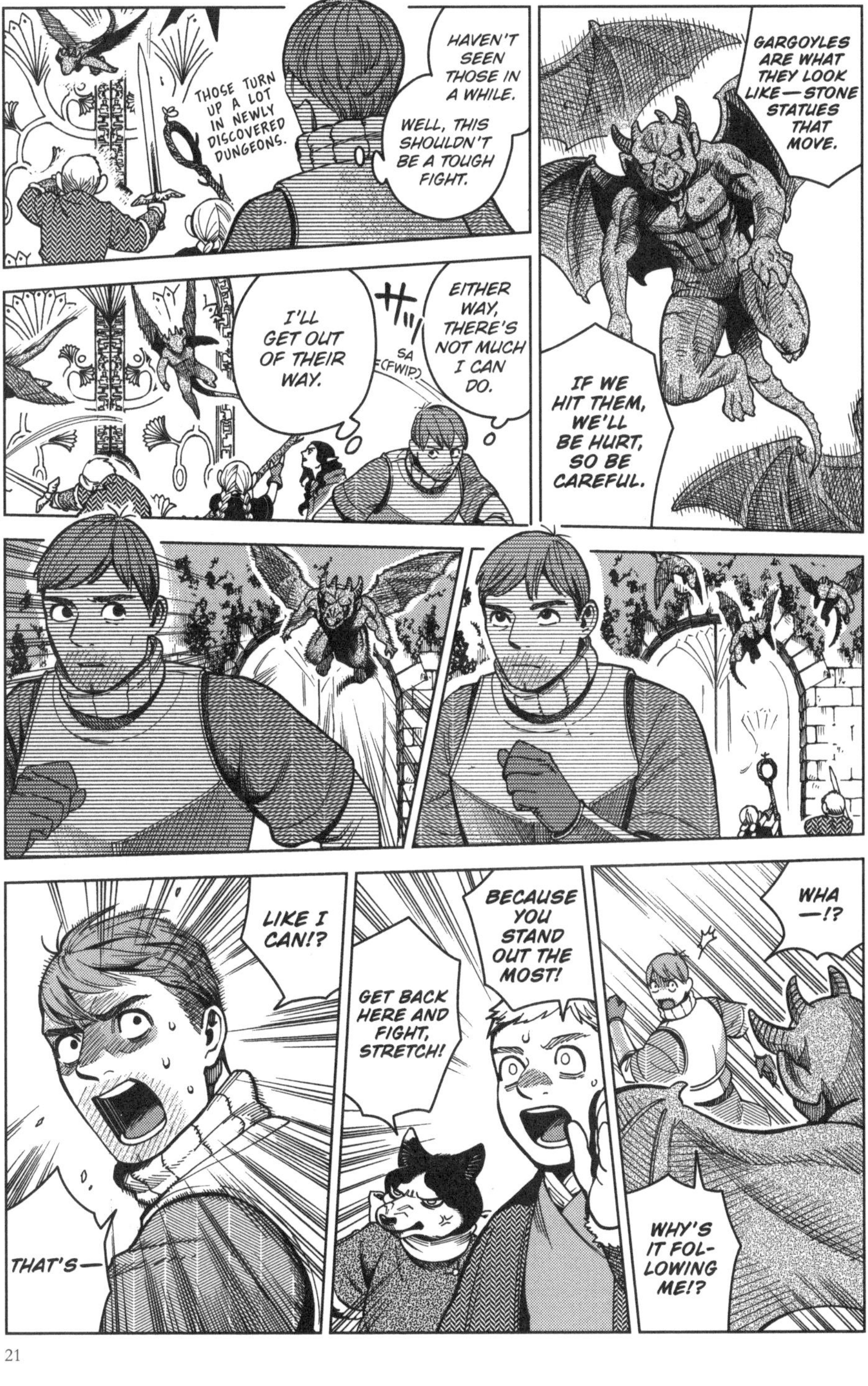
GARGOYLES ARE WHAT THEY LOOK LIKE—STONE STATUES THAT MOVE.
IF WE HIT THEM, WE'LL BE HURT, SO BE CAREFUL.
HAVEN'T SEEN THOSE IN A WHILE.
WELL, THIS SHOULDN'T BE A TOUGH FIGHT.
THOSE TURN UP A LOT IN NEWLY DISCOVERED DUNGEONS.
EITHER WAY, THERE'S NOT MUCH I CAN DO.
SA (FWIP)
I'LL GET OUT OF THEIR WAY.
WHA—!?
WHY'S IT FOL-LOWING ME!?
BECAUSE YOU STAND OUT THE MOST!
GET BACK HERE AND FIGHT, STRETCH!
LIKE I CAN!?
THAT'S—

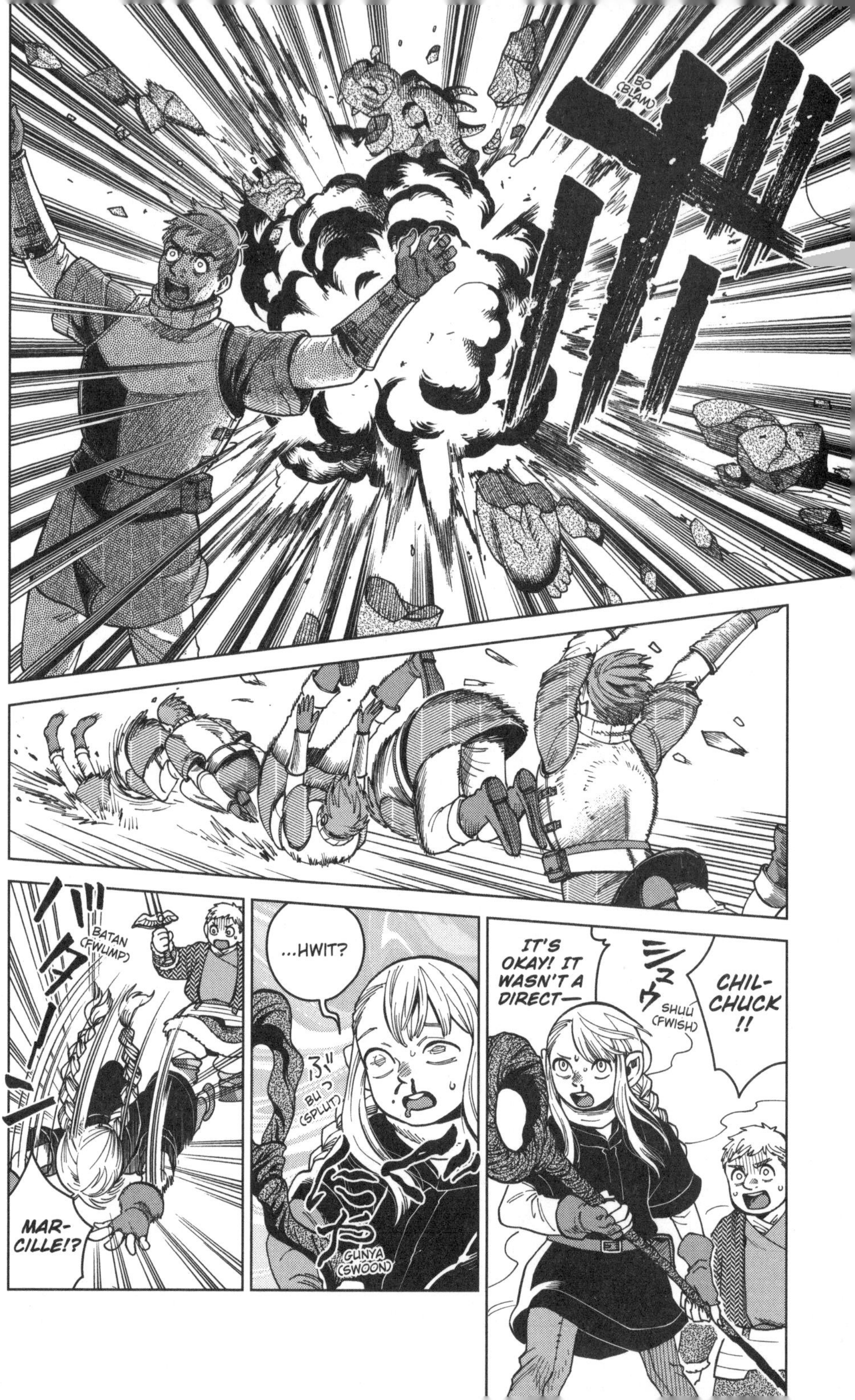

BO (BLAM)
CHIL-CHUCK!!
SHUU (FWISH)
IT'S OKAY! IT WASN'T A DIRECT—
...HWIT?
BU (SPLUT)
GUNYA (SWOON)
BATAN (FWUMP)
MAR-CILLE!?

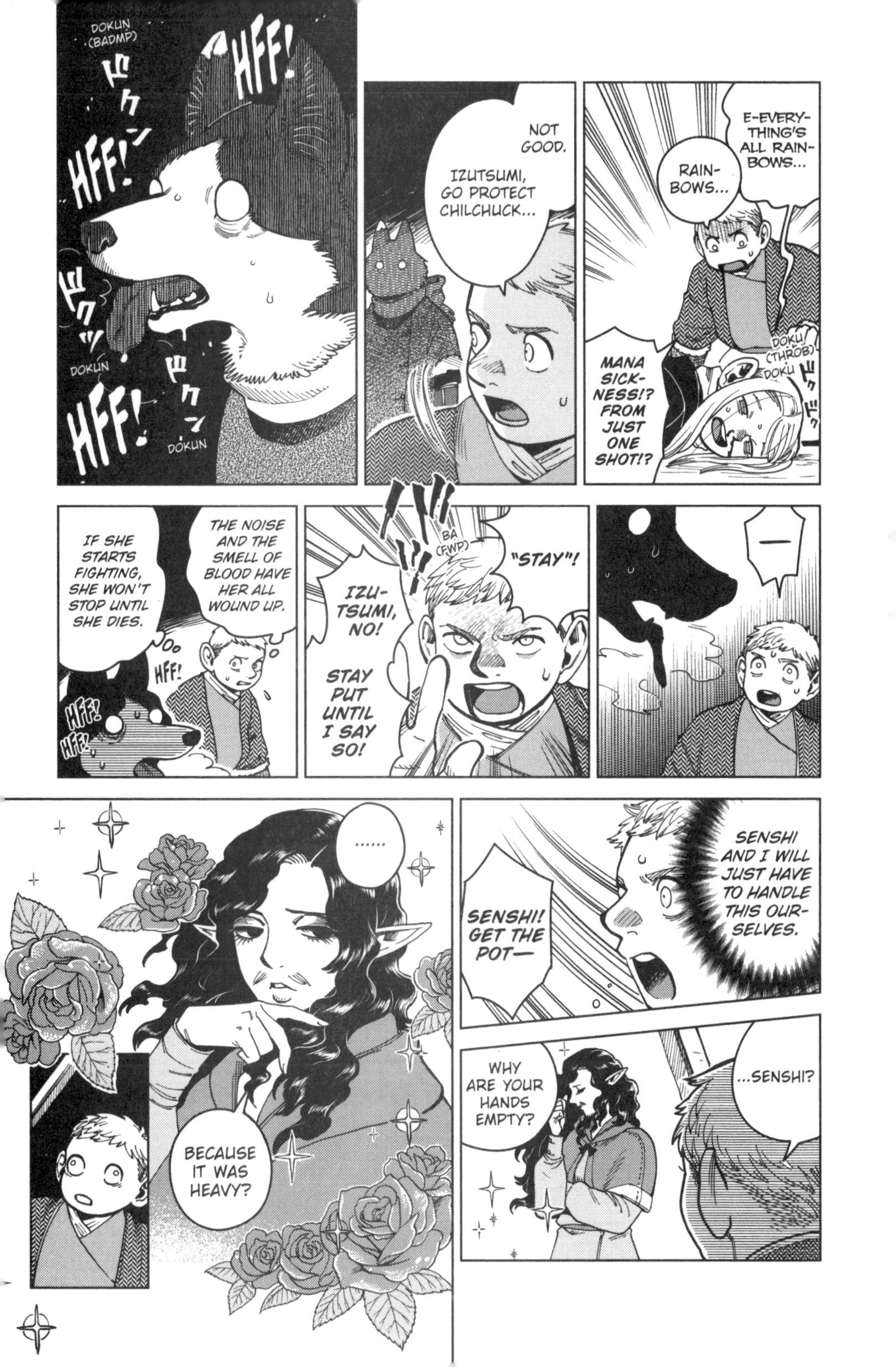

E-EVERY-THING'S ALL RAIN-BOWS...
RAIN-BOWS...
DOKU (THROB) DOKU
MANA SICK-NESS!? FROM JUST ONE SHOT!?
NOT GOOD.
IZUTSUMI, GO PROTECT CHILCHUCK...
DOKUN (BADMP)
ドクン
HFF!
HFF!
DOKUN
HFF!
DOKUN
—
BA (FWP)
"STAY"!
IZU-TSUMI, NO!
STAY PUT UNTIL I SAY SO!
THE NOISE AND THE SMELL OF BLOOD HAVE HER ALL WOUND UP.
IF SHE STARTS FIGHTING, SHE WON'T STOP UNTIL SHE DIES.
HFF!
HFF! HFF!
SENSHI AND I WILL JUST HAVE TO HANDLE THIS OUR-SELVES.
SENSHI! GET THE POT—
...SENSHI?
WHY ARE YOUR HANDS EMPTY?
......
BECAUSE IT WAS HEAVY?

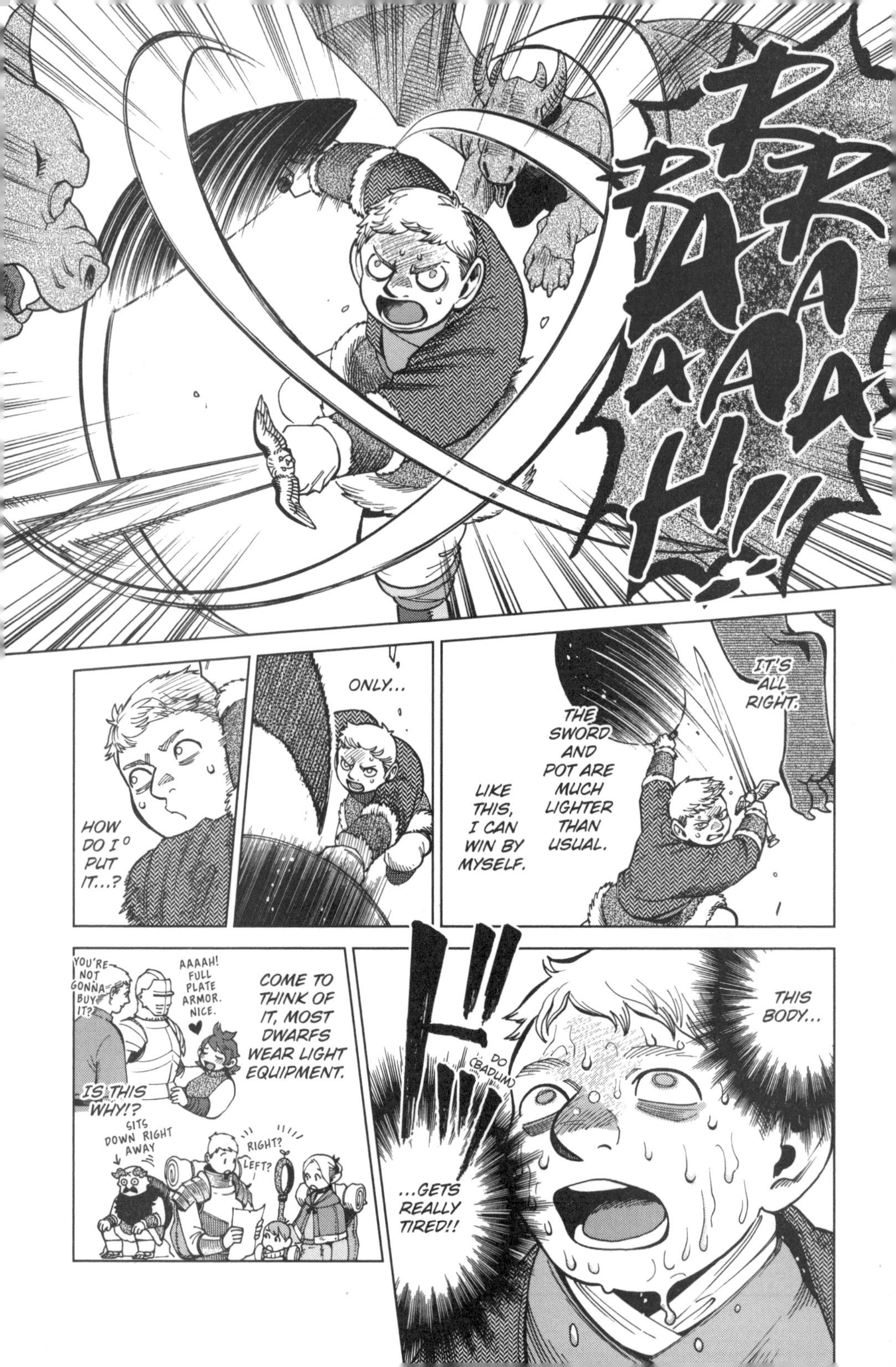
RRAAAAAH!!
IT'S ALL RIGHT.
THE SWORD AND POT ARE MUCH LIGHTER THAN USUAL.
LIKE THIS, I CAN WIN BY MYSELF.
ONLY...
HOW DO I PUT IT...?
THIS BODY...
DO (BADUM)
...GETS REALLY TIRED!!
COME TO THINK OF IT, MOST DWARFS WEAR LIGHT EQUIPMENT.
AAAAH! FULL PLATE ARMOR. NICE.
YOU'RE NOT GONNA BUY IT?
IS THIS WHY!?
RIGHT?
LEFT?
SITS DOWN RIGHT AWAY

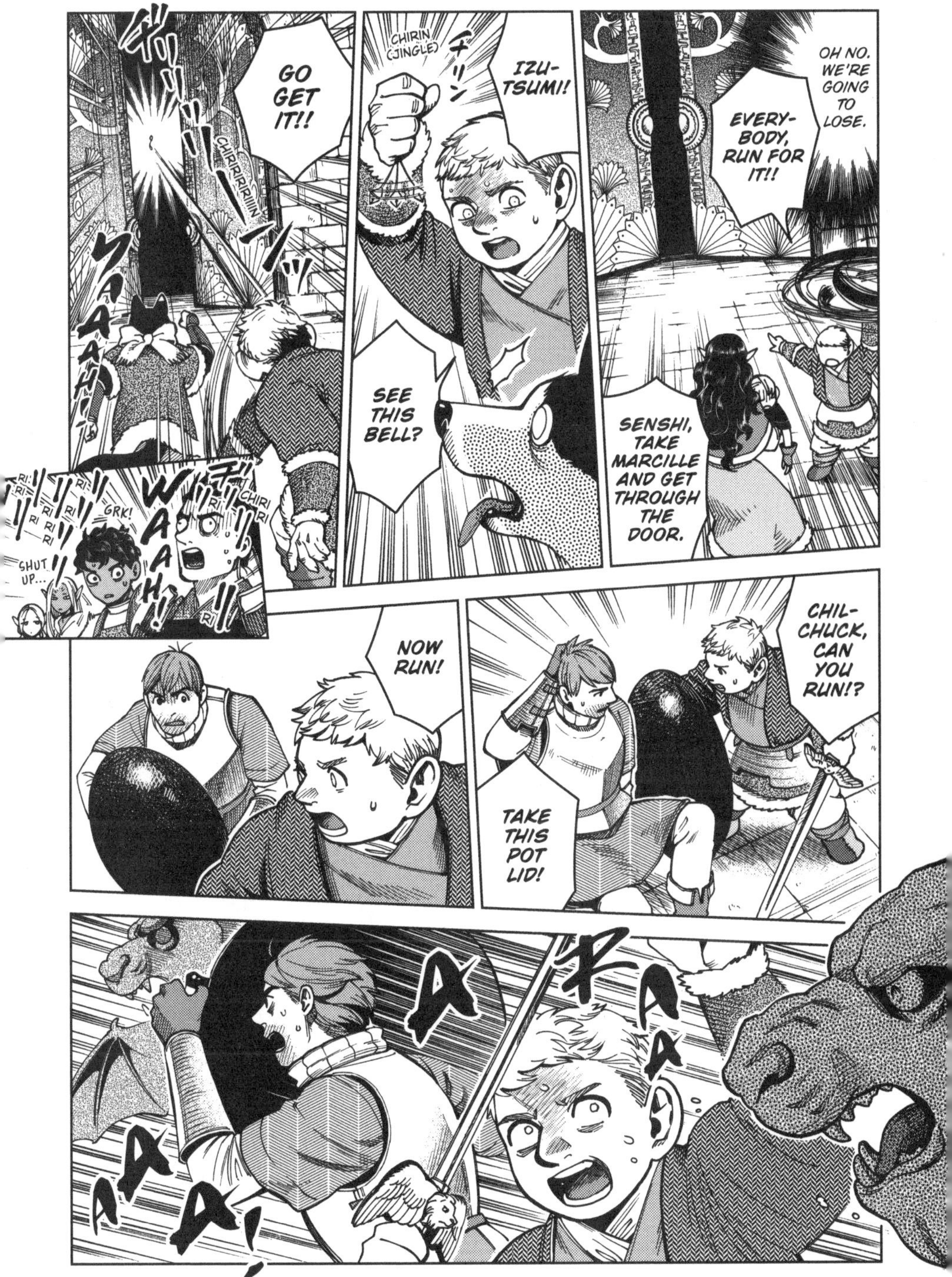
OH NO. WE'RE GOING TO LOSE.
EVERY-BODY, RUN FOR IT!!
SENSHI, TAKE MARCILLE AND GET THROUGH THE DOOR.
CHIRIN (JINGLE)
IZU-TSUMI!
SEE THIS BELL?
GO GET IT!!
CHIRIRIRIRIIN
AAAAH...
WAAAH!!
CHIRI RI
GRK!
SHUT UP...
CHIL-CHUCK, CAN YOU RUN!?
TAKE THIS POT LID!
NOW RUN!

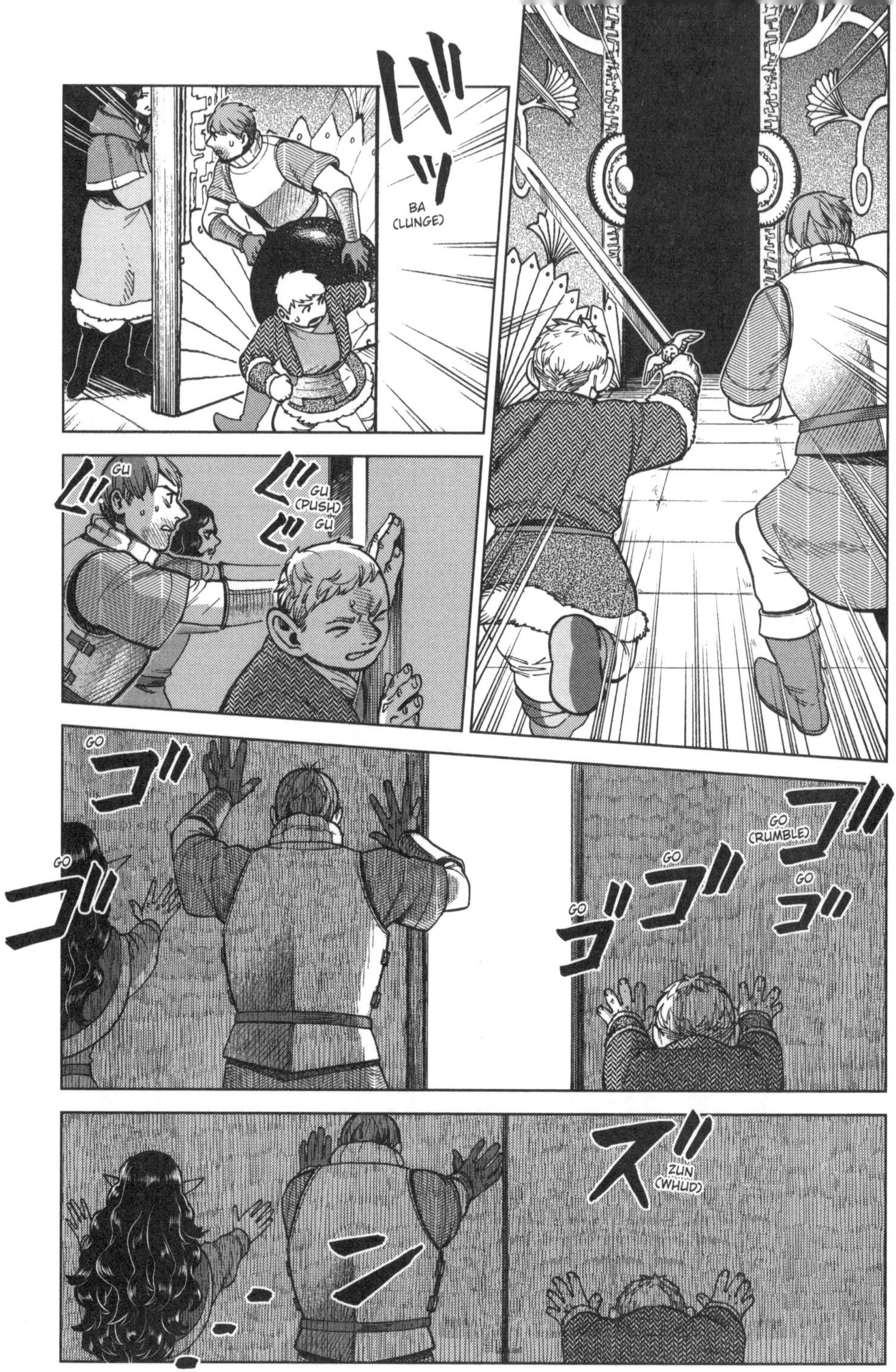
BA
(LUNGE)
GU
GU
(PUSH)
GU
GO
(RUMBLE)
GO
GO
GO
GO
GO
ZUN
(WHUD)

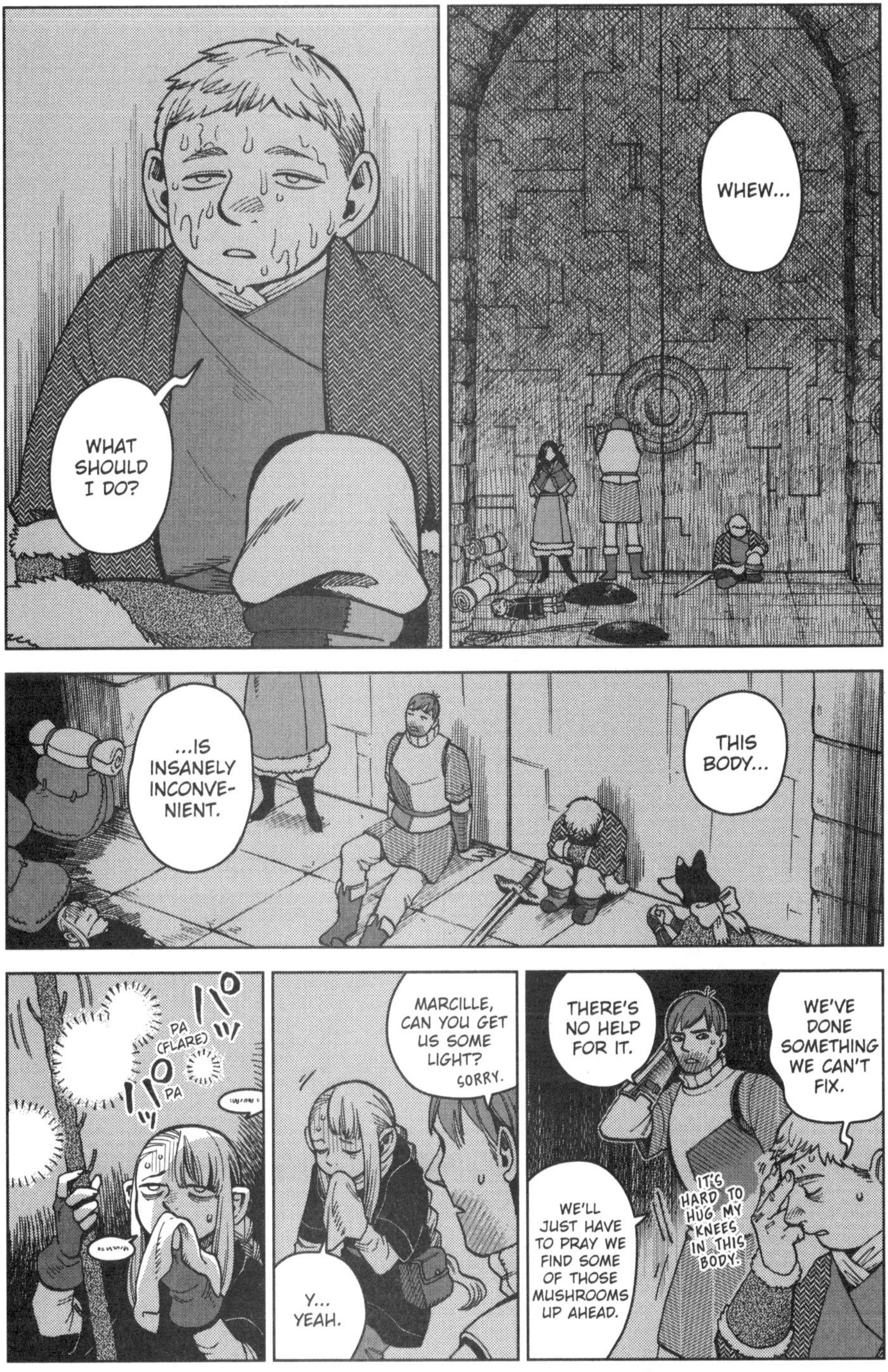

WHEW...
WHAT SHOULD I DO?
THIS BODY...
...IS INSANELY INCONVENIENT.
WE'VE DONE SOMETHING WE CAN'T FIX.
THERE'S NO HELP FOR IT.
IT'S HARD TO HUG MY KNEES IN THIS BODY.
WE'LL JUST HAVE TO PRAY WE FIND SOME OF THOSE MUSHROOMS UP AHEAD.
MARCILLE, CAN YOU GET US SOME LIGHT?
SORRY.
Y... YEAH.
PA (FLARE)
PA

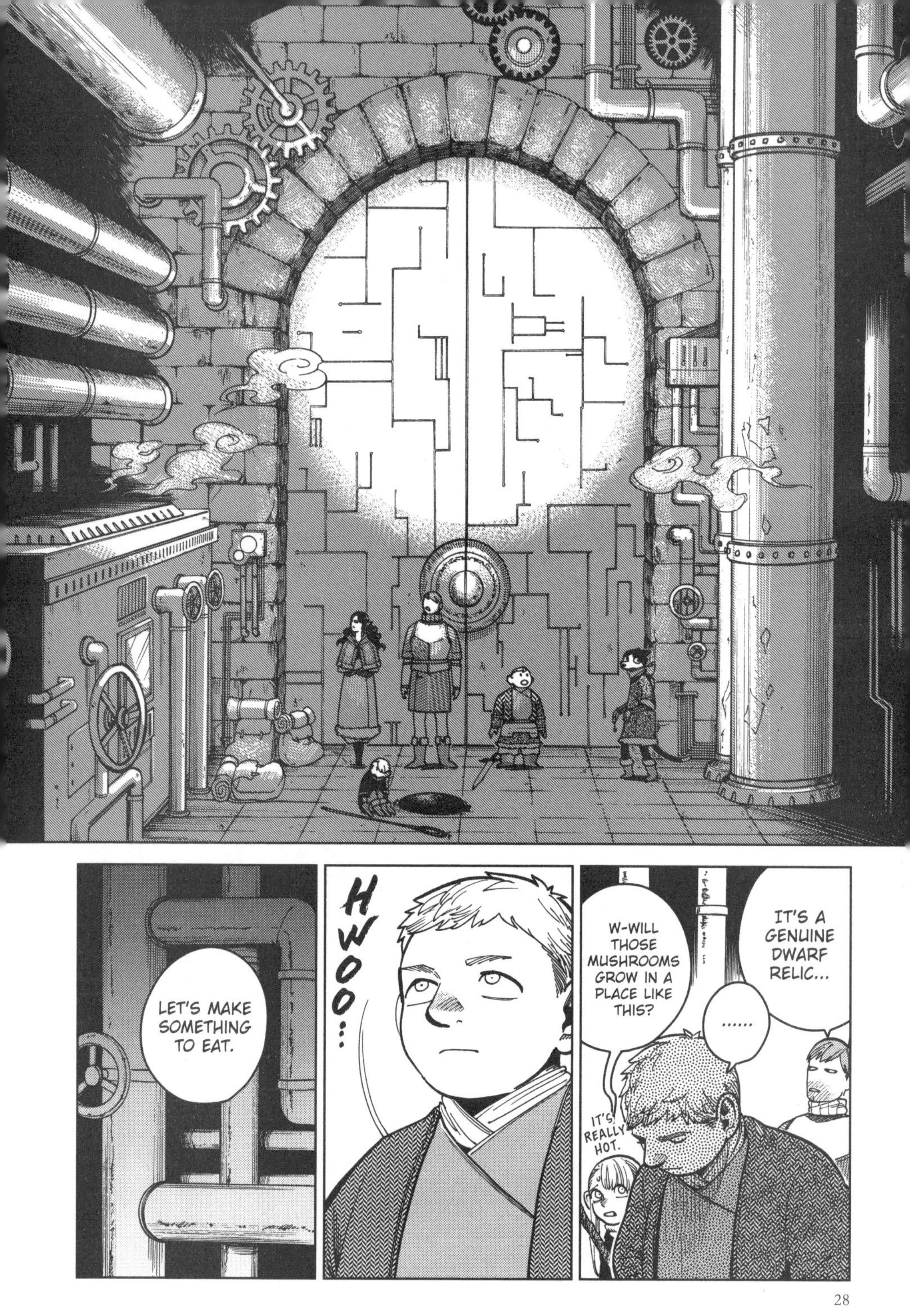

IT'S A GENUINE DWARF RELIC...
W-WILL THOSE MUSHROOMS GROW IN A PLACE LIKE THIS?
......
IT'S REALLY HOT.
HWOOO...
LET'S MAKE SOMETHING TO EAT.

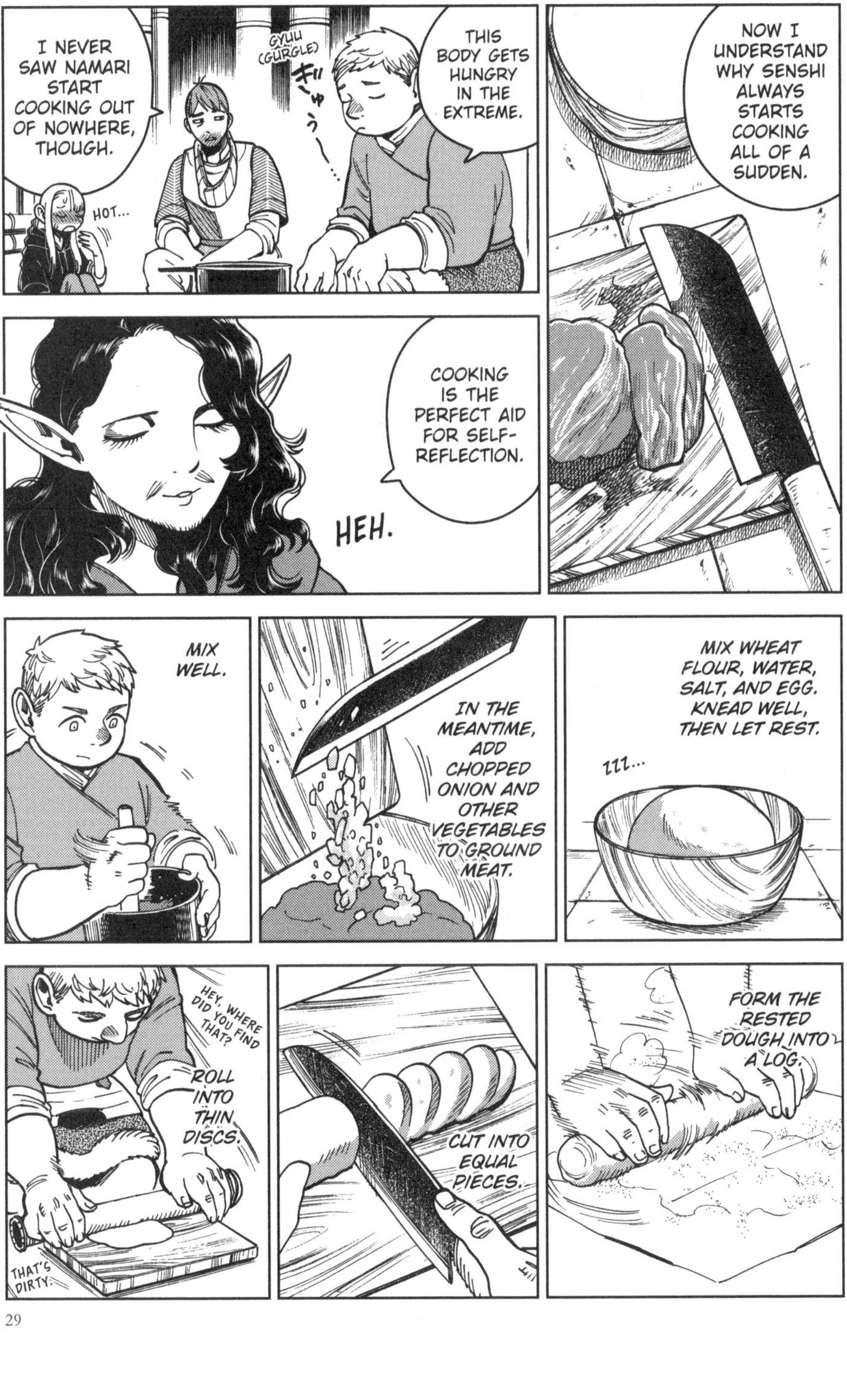
NOW I UNDERSTAND WHY SENSHI ALWAYS STARTS COOKING ALL OF A SUDDEN.
THIS BODY GETS HUNGRY IN THE EXTREME.
GYUU (GURGLE)
I NEVER SAW NAMARI START COOKING OUT OF NOWHERE, THOUGH.
HOT...
COOKING IS THE PERFECT AID FOR SELF-REFLECTION.
HEH.
MIX WHEAT FLOUR, WATER, SALT, AND EGG. KNEAD WELL, THEN LET REST.
ZZZ...
IN THE MEANTIME, ADD CHOPPED ONION AND OTHER VEGETABLES TO GROUND MEAT.
MIX WELL.
FORM THE RESTED DOUGH INTO A LOG.
CUT INTO EQUAL PIECES.
HEY, WHERE DID YOU FIND THAT?
ROLL INTO THIN DISCS.
THAT'S DIRTY.

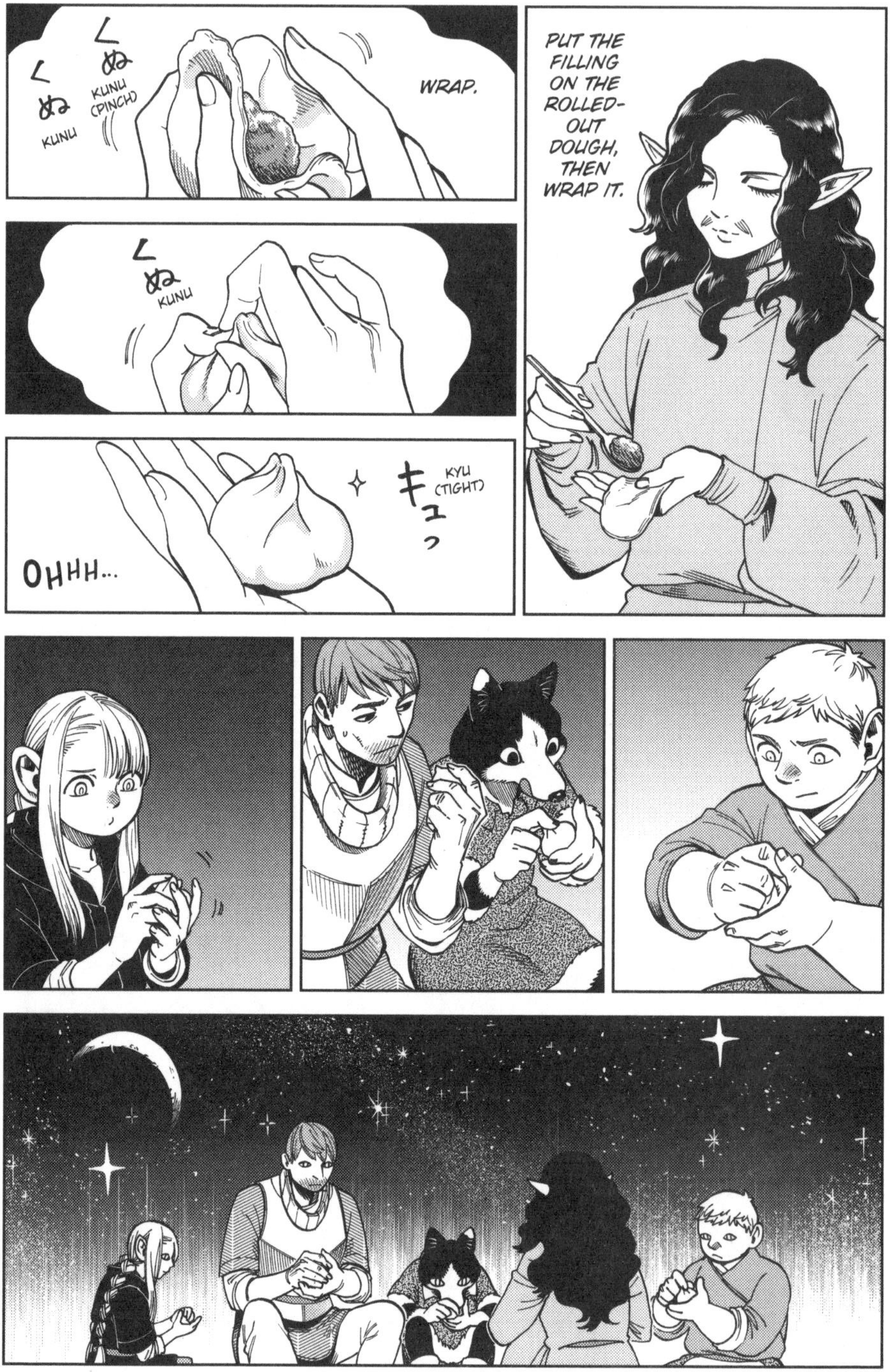
PUT THE FILLING ON THE ROLLED-OUT DOUGH, THEN WRAP IT.
WRAP.
くぬ
KUNU (PINCH)
くぬ
KUNU
くぬ
KUNU
キュッ
KYU (TIGHT)
OHHH...

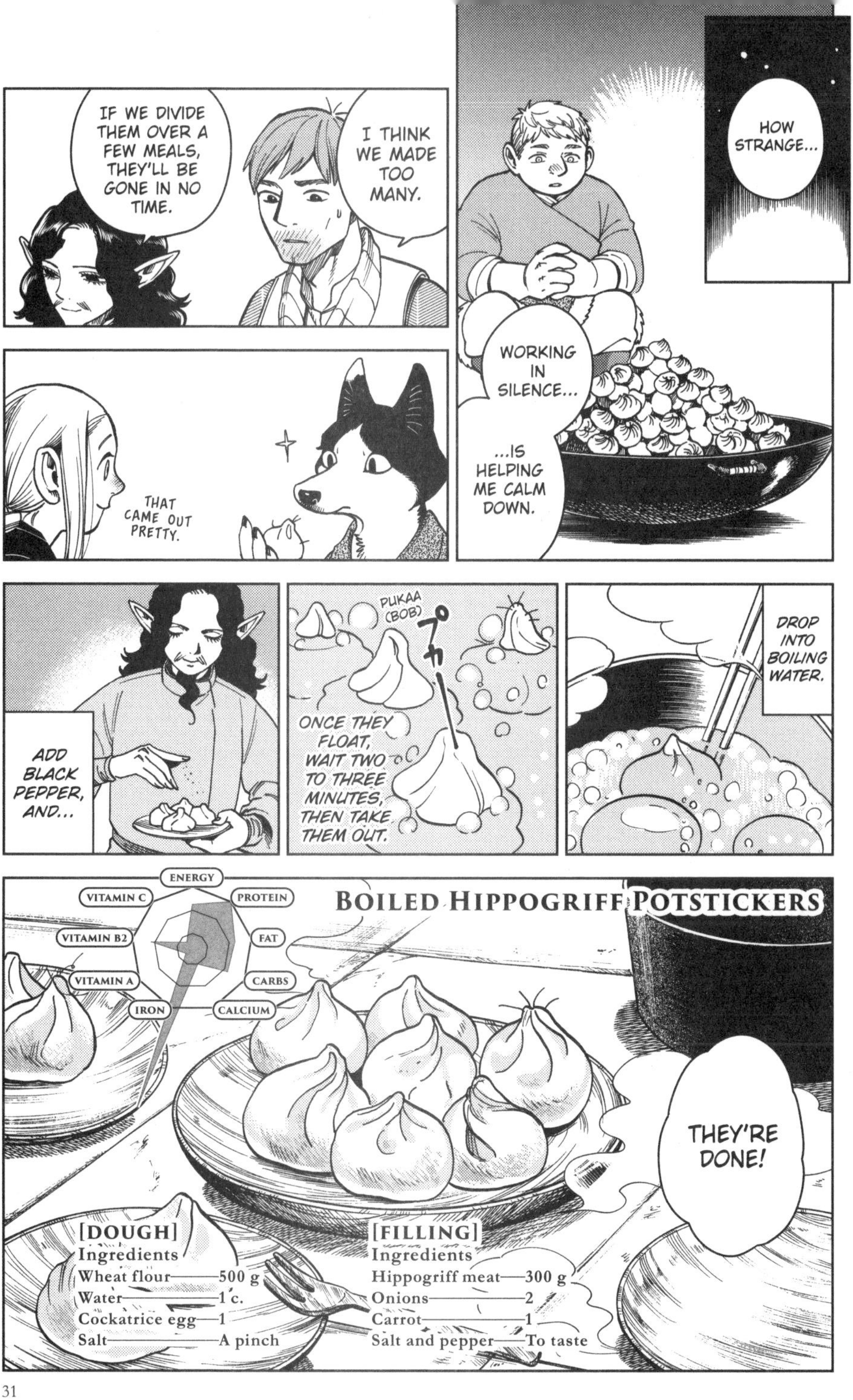
HOW STRANGE...
WORKING IN SILENCE...
...IS HELPING ME CALM DOWN.
I THINK WE MADE TOO MANY.
IF WE DIVIDE THEM OVER A FEW MEALS, THEY'LL BE GONE IN NO TIME.
THAT CAME OUT PRETTY.
DROP INTO BOILING WATER.
PUKAA (BOB)
プカー
ONCE THEY FLOAT, WAIT TWO TO THREE MINUTES, THEN TAKE THEM OUT.
ADD BLACK PEPPER, AND...
THEY'RE DONE!
BOILED HIPPOGRIFF POTSTICKERS
ENERGY
PROTEIN
FAT
CARBS
CALCIUM
IRON
VITAMIN A
VITAMIN B2
VITAMIN C
[DOUGH]
Ingredients
Wheat flour——500 g
Water——1 c.
Cockatrice egg——1
Salt——A pinch
[FILLING]
Ingredients
Hippogriff meat——300 g
Onions——2
Carrot——1
Salt and pepper——To taste

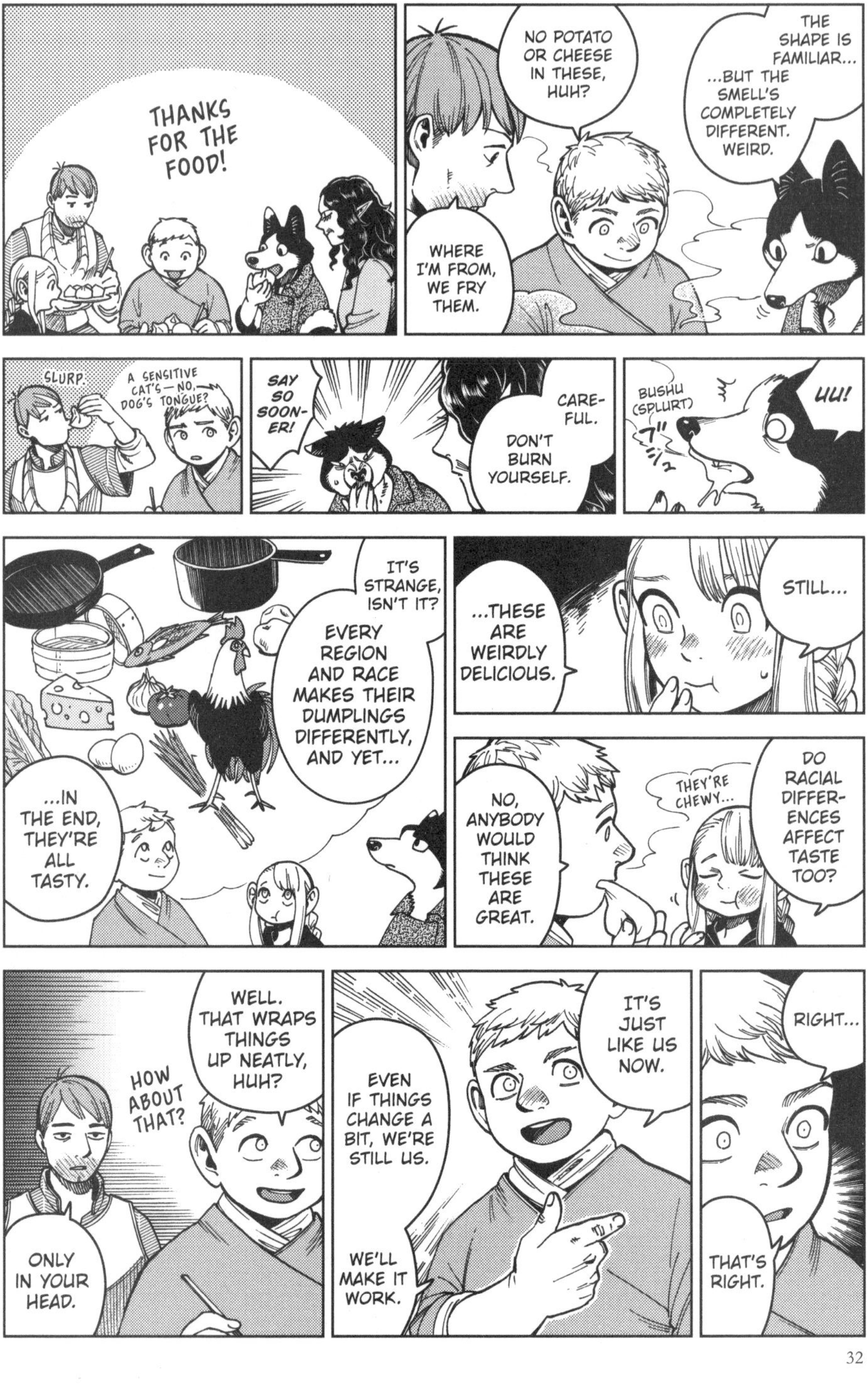
THE SHAPE IS FAMILIAR... ...BUT THE SMELL'S COMPLETELY DIFFERENT. WEIRD.
NO POTATO OR CHEESE IN THESE, HUH?
WHERE I'M FROM, WE FRY THEM.
THANKS FOR THE FOOD!
UU!
BUSHU (SPLURT)
CARE-FUL.
DON'T BURN YOURSELF.
SAY SO SOON-ER!
A SENSITIVE CAT'S—NO, DOG'S TONGUE?
SLURP.
STILL...
...THESE ARE WEIRDLY DELICIOUS.
DO RACIAL DIFFER-ENCES AFFECT TASTE TOO?
THEY'RE CHEWY...
NO, ANYBODY WOULD THINK THESE ARE GREAT.
IT'S STRANGE, ISN'T IT?
EVERY REGION AND RACE MAKES THEIR DUMPLINGS DIFFERENTLY, AND YET...
...IN THE END, THEY'RE ALL TASTY.
RIGHT...
THAT'S RIGHT.
IT'S JUST LIKE US NOW.
EVEN IF THINGS CHANGE A BIT, WE'RE STILL US.
WE'LL MAKE IT WORK.
WELL. THAT WRAPS THINGS UP NEATLY, HUH?
HOW ABOUT THAT?
ONLY IN YOUR HEAD.

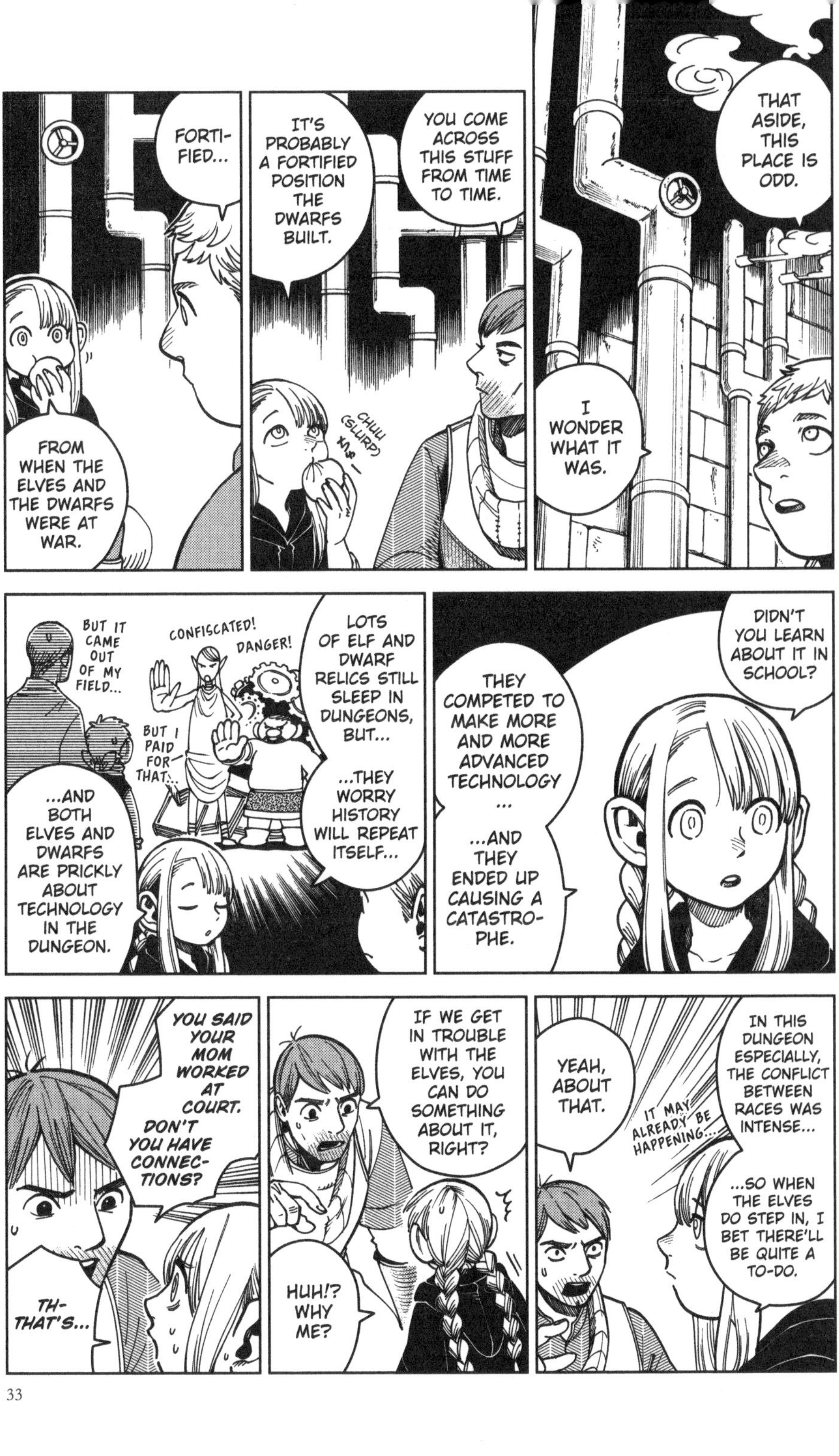
THAT ASIDE, THIS PLACE IS ODD.
I WONDER WHAT IT WAS.
YOU COME ACROSS THIS STUFF FROM TIME TO TIME.
IT'S PROBABLY A FORTIFIED POSITION THE DWARFS BUILT.
CHUU (SLLIRP)
FORTI-FIED...
FROM WHEN THE ELVES AND THE DWARFS WERE AT WAR.
DIDN'T YOU LEARN ABOUT IT IN SCHOOL?
THEY COMPETED TO MAKE MORE AND MORE ADVANCED TECHNOLOGY...
...AND THEY ENDED UP CAUSING A CATASTROPHE.
LOTS OF ELF AND DWARF RELICS STILL SLEEP IN DUNGEONS, BUT...
...THEY WORRY HISTORY WILL REPEAT ITSELF...
DANGER!
CONFISCATED!
BUT IT CAME OUT OF MY FIELD...
BUT I PAID FOR THAT...
...AND BOTH ELVES AND DWARFS ARE PRICKLY ABOUT TECHNOLOGY IN THE DUNGEON.
IN THIS DUNGEON ESPECIALLY, THE CONFLICT BETWEEN RACES WAS INTENSE...
...SO WHEN THE ELVES DO STEP IN, I BET THERE'LL BE QUITE A TO-DO.
YEAH, ABOUT THAT.
IT MAY ALREADY BE HAPPENING...
IF WE GET IN TROUBLE WITH THE ELVES, YOU CAN DO SOMETHING ABOUT IT, RIGHT?
HUH!? WHY ME?
YOU SAID YOUR MOM WORKED AT COURT. DON'T YOU HAVE CONNECTIONS?
TH-THAT'S...

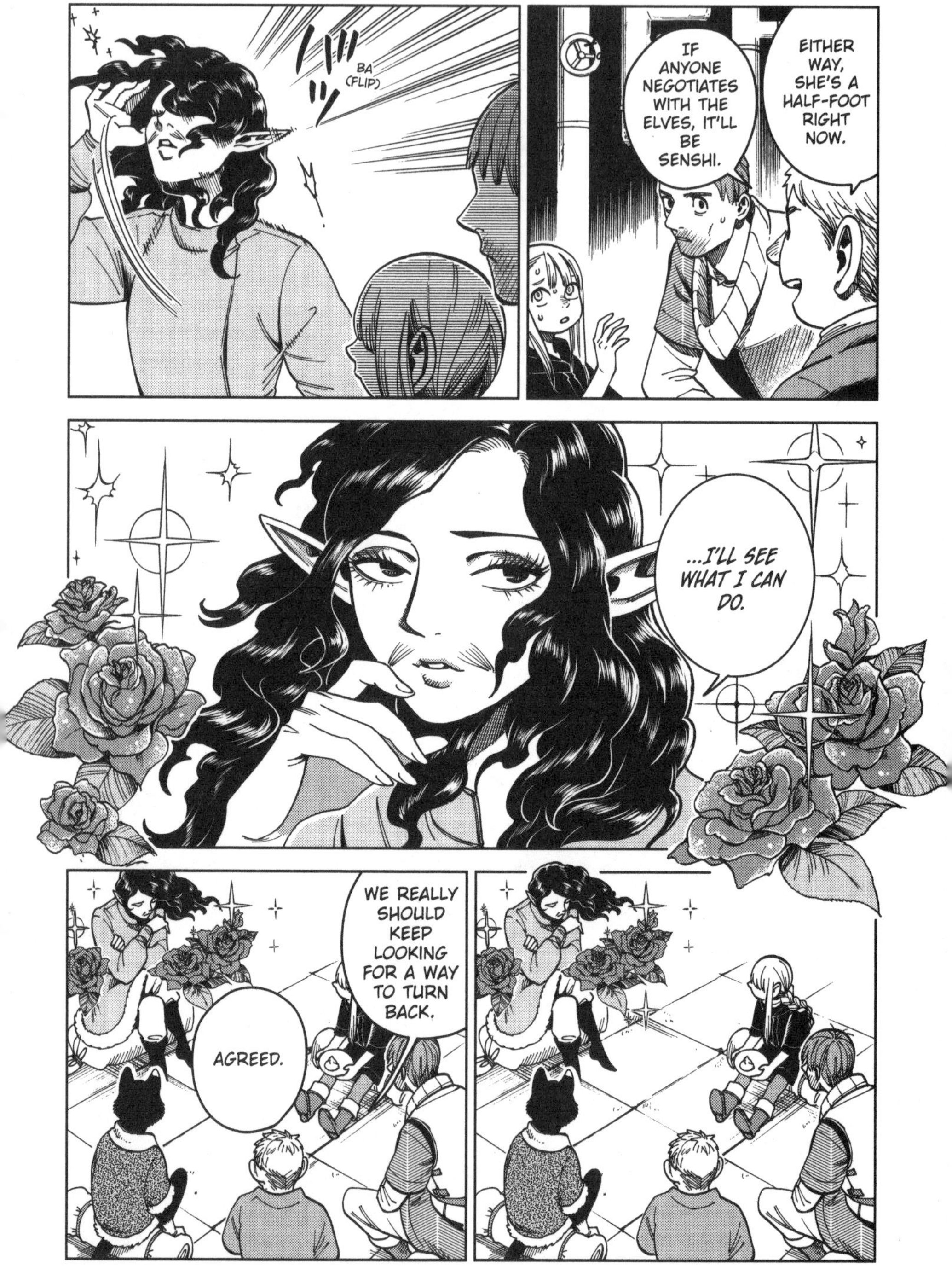
EITHER WAY, SHE'S A HALF-FOOT RIGHT NOW.
IF ANYONE NEGOTIATES WITH THE ELVES, IT'LL BE SENSHI.
BA (FLIP)
...I'LL SEE WHAT I CAN DO.
WE REALLY SHOULD KEEP LOOKING FOR A WAY TO TURN BACK.
AGREED.

CHAPTER 51: THE END

	TALL-MAN	ELF	HALF-FOOT	DWARF	GNOME
LAIOS					
MARCILLE					
CHILCHUCK					
SENSHI					
IZUTSUMI					

51. DUMPLINGS -2-

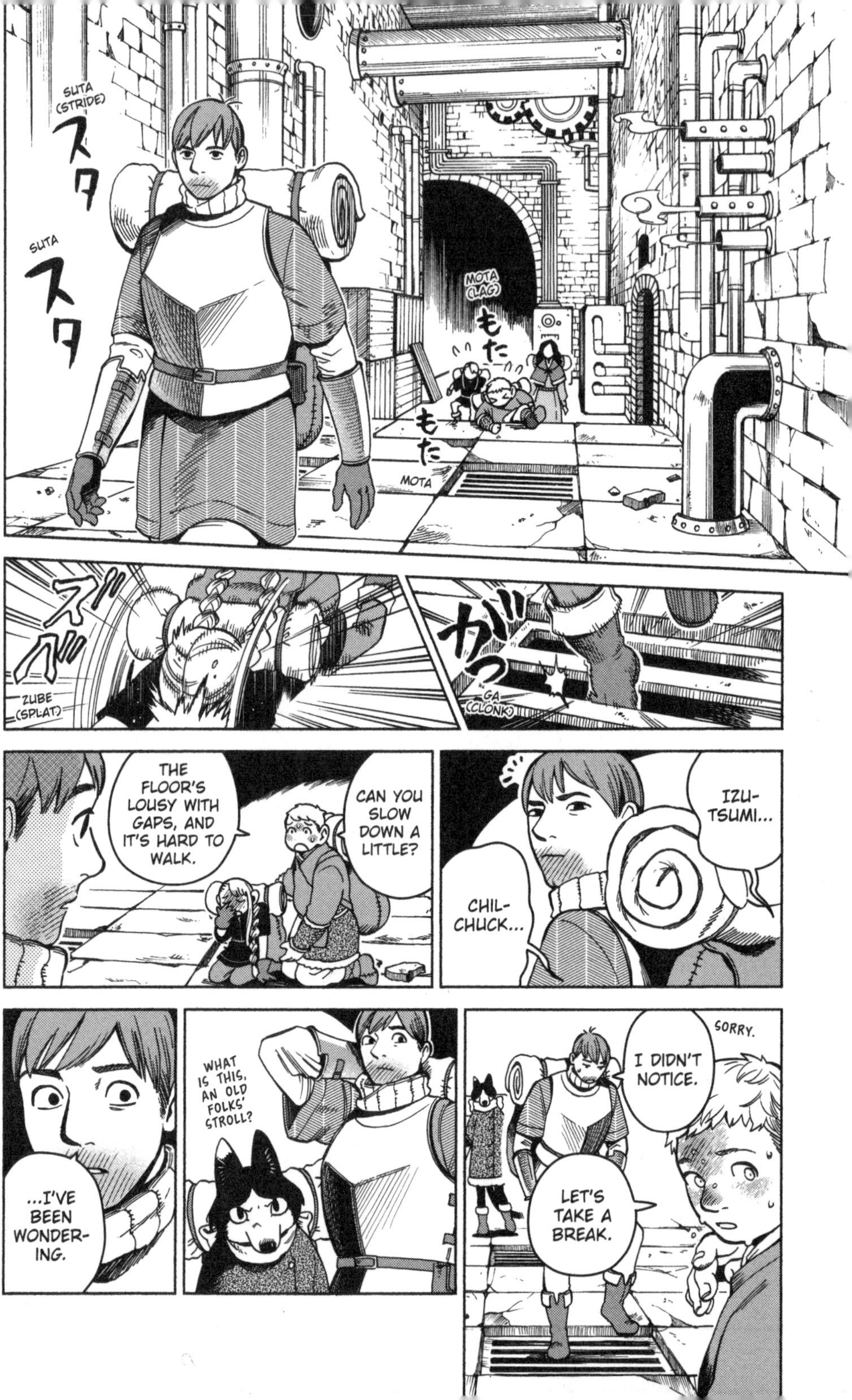
SUTA (STRIDE)
スタ
SUTA
スタ
MOTA (LAG)
もた
もた
MOTA
がっ
GA (CLONK)
ズベ
ZUBE (SPLAT)
IZU-TSUMI...
CHIL-CHUCK...
CAN YOU SLOW DOWN A LITTLE?
THE FLOOR'S LOUSY WITH GAPS, AND IT'S HARD TO WALK.
SORRY.
I DIDN'T NOTICE.
LET'S TAKE A BREAK.
WHAT IS THIS, AN OLD FOLKS' STROLL?
...I'VE BEEN WONDERING.

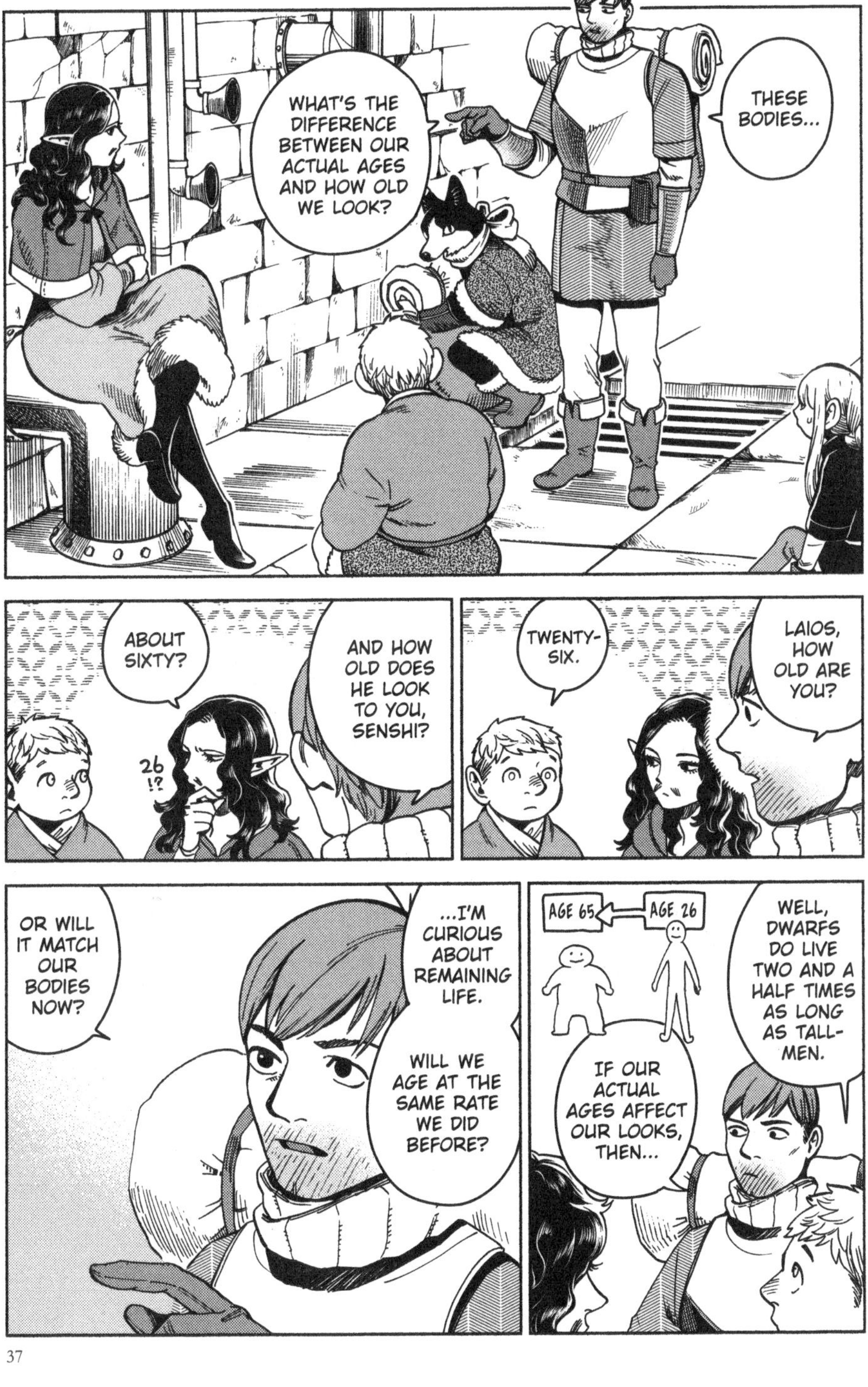
THESE BODIES...
WHAT'S THE DIFFERENCE BETWEEN OUR ACTUAL AGES AND HOW OLD WE LOOK?
LAIOS, HOW OLD ARE YOU?
TWENTY-SIX.
AND HOW OLD DOES HE LOOK TO YOU, SENSHI?
ABOUT SIXTY?
26 !?
WELL, DWARFS DO LIVE TWO AND A HALF TIMES AS LONG AS TALL-MEN.
AGE 26
AGE 65
IF OUR ACTUAL AGES AFFECT OUR LOOKS, THEN...
...I'M CURIOUS ABOUT REMAINING LIFE.
WILL WE AGE AT THE SAME RATE WE DID BEFORE?
OR WILL IT MATCH OUR BODIES NOW?

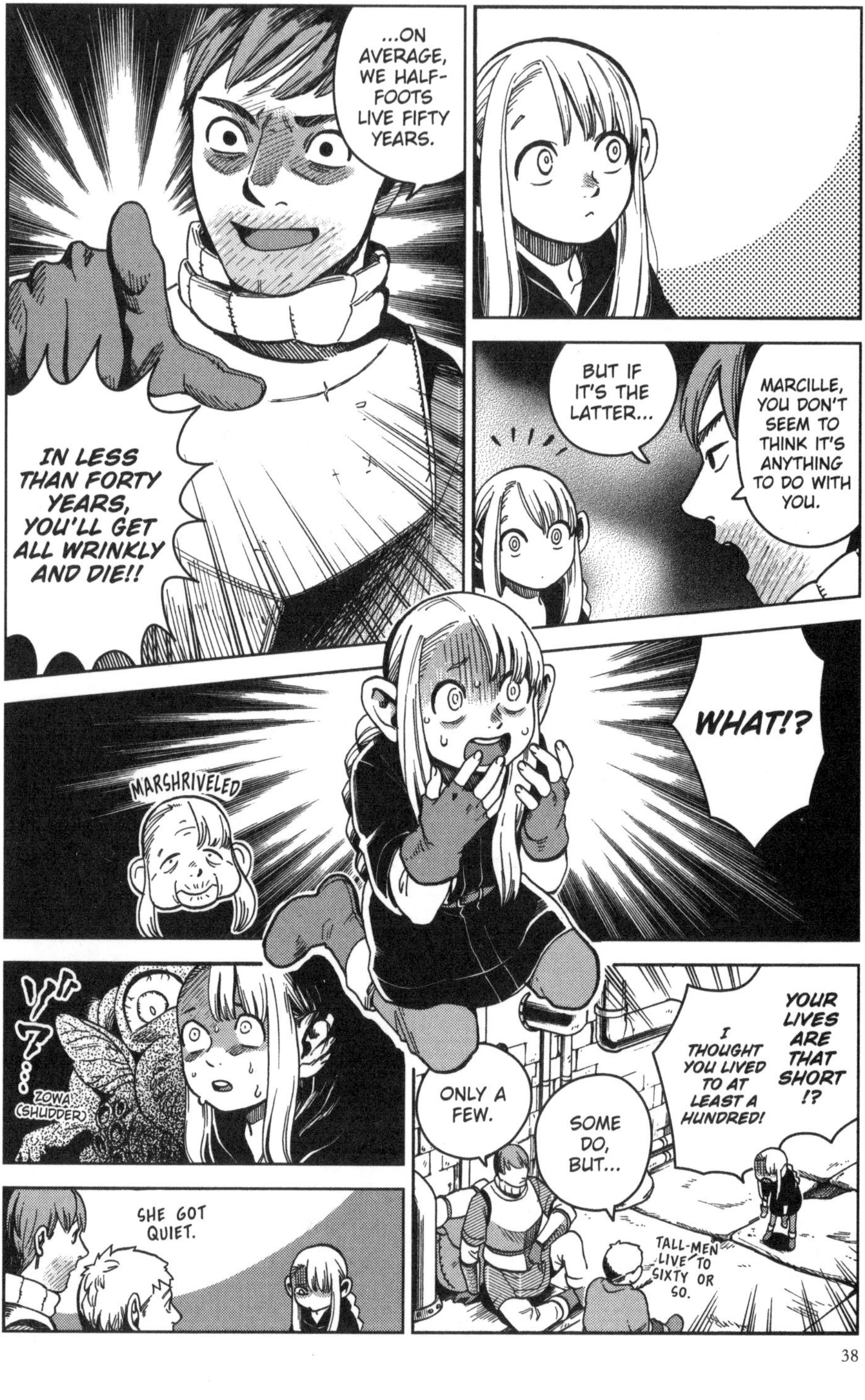
MARCILLE, YOU DON'T SEEM TO THINK IT'S ANYTHING TO DO WITH YOU.
BUT IF IT'S THE LATTER...
...ON AVERAGE, WE HALF-FOOTS LIVE FIFTY YEARS.
IN LESS THAN FORTY YEARS, YOU'LL GET ALL WRINKLY AND DIE!!
WHAT!?
MARSHRIVELED
YOUR LIVES ARE THAT SHORT!?
I THOUGHT YOU LIVED TO AT LEAST A HUNDRED!
SOME DO, BUT...
ONLY A FEW.
TALL-MEN LIVE TO SIXTY OR SO.
ZOWA (SHUDDER)
SHE GOT QUIET.

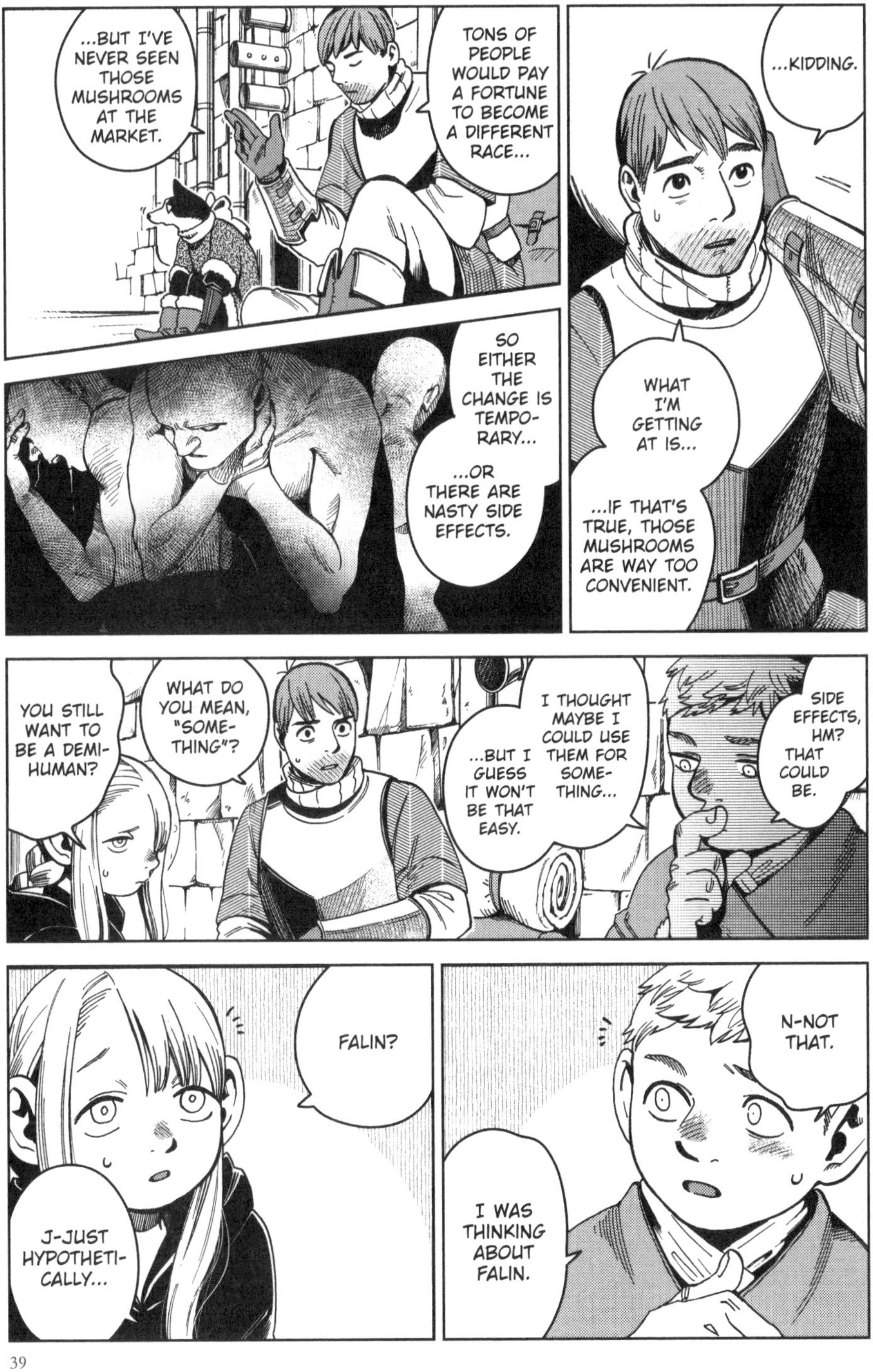
...KIDDING.
WHAT I'M GETTING AT IS...
...IF THAT'S TRUE, THOSE MUSHROOMS ARE WAY TOO CONVENIENT.
TONS OF PEOPLE WOULD PAY A FORTUNE TO BECOME A DIFFERENT RACE...
...BUT I'VE NEVER SEEN THOSE MUSHROOMS AT THE MARKET.
SO EITHER THE CHANGE IS TEMPO-RARY...
...OR THERE ARE NASTY SIDE EFFECTS.
SIDE EFFECTS, HM? THAT COULD BE.
I THOUGHT MAYBE I COULD USE THEM FOR SOME-THING...
...BUT I GUESS IT WON'T BE THAT EASY.
WHAT DO YOU MEAN, "SOME-THING"?
YOU STILL WANT TO BE A DEMI-HUMAN?
N-NOT THAT.
I WAS THINKING ABOUT FALIN.
FALIN?
J-JUST HYPOTHETI-CALLY...

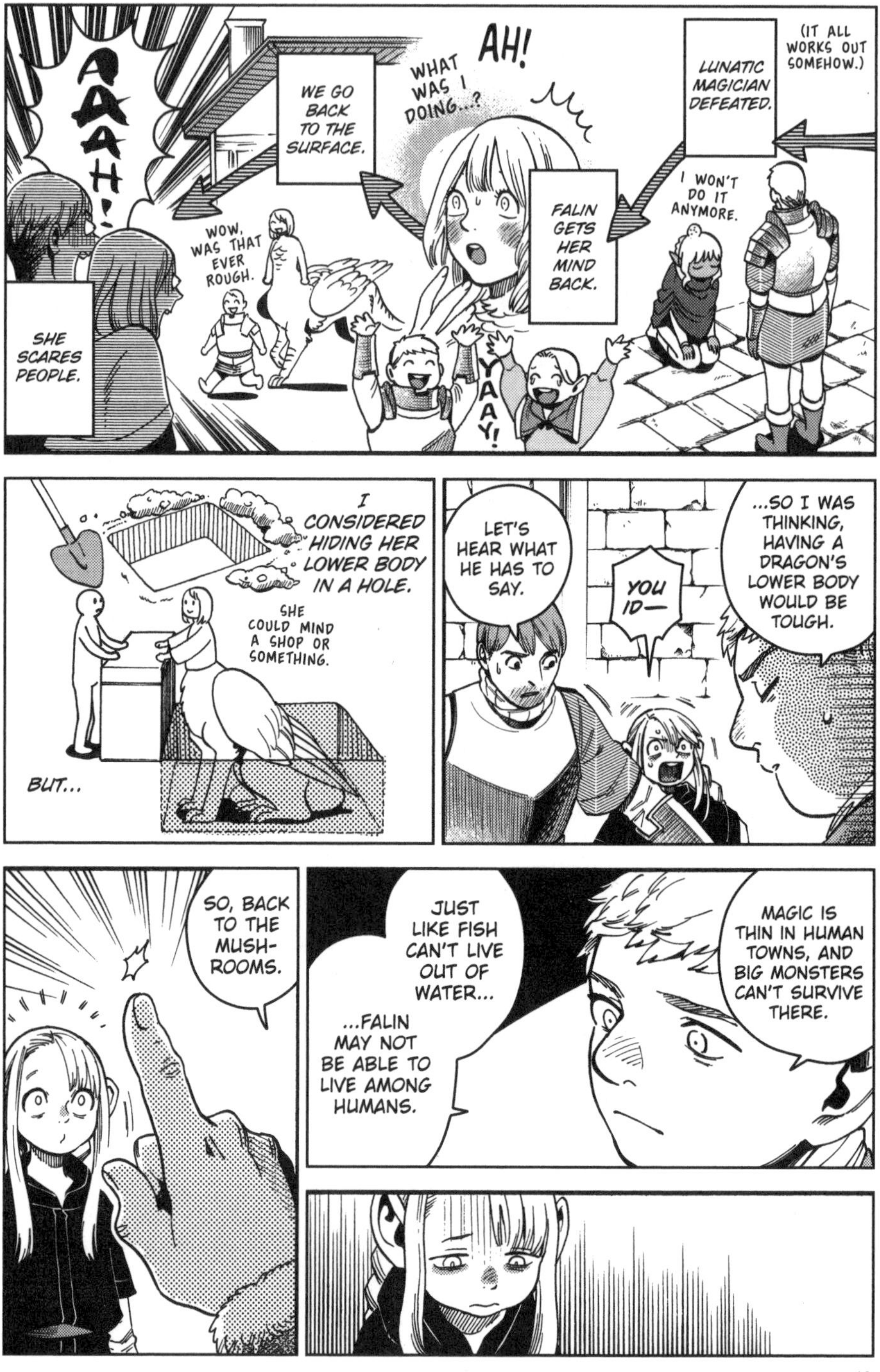
(IT ALL WORKS OUT SOMEHOW.)
LUNATIC MAGICIAN DEFEATED.
AH!
WHAT WAS I DOING...?
WE GO BACK TO THE SURFACE.
AAAH!
I WON'T DO IT ANYMORE.
FALIN GETS HER MIND BACK.
WOW, WAS THAT EVER ROUGH.
YAAAY!
SHE SCARES PEOPLE.
...SO I WAS THINKING, HAVING A DRAGON'S LOWER BODY WOULD BE TOUGH.
YOU ID—
LET'S HEAR WHAT HE HAS TO SAY.
I CONSIDERED HIDING HER LOWER BODY IN A HOLE.
SHE COULD MIND A SHOP OR SOMETHING.
BUT...
MAGIC IS THIN IN HUMAN TOWNS, AND BIG MONSTERS CAN'T SURVIVE THERE.
JUST LIKE FISH CAN'T LIVE OUT OF WATER...
...FALIN MAY NOT BE ABLE TO LIVE AMONG HUMANS.
SO, BACK TO THE MUSH-ROOMS.

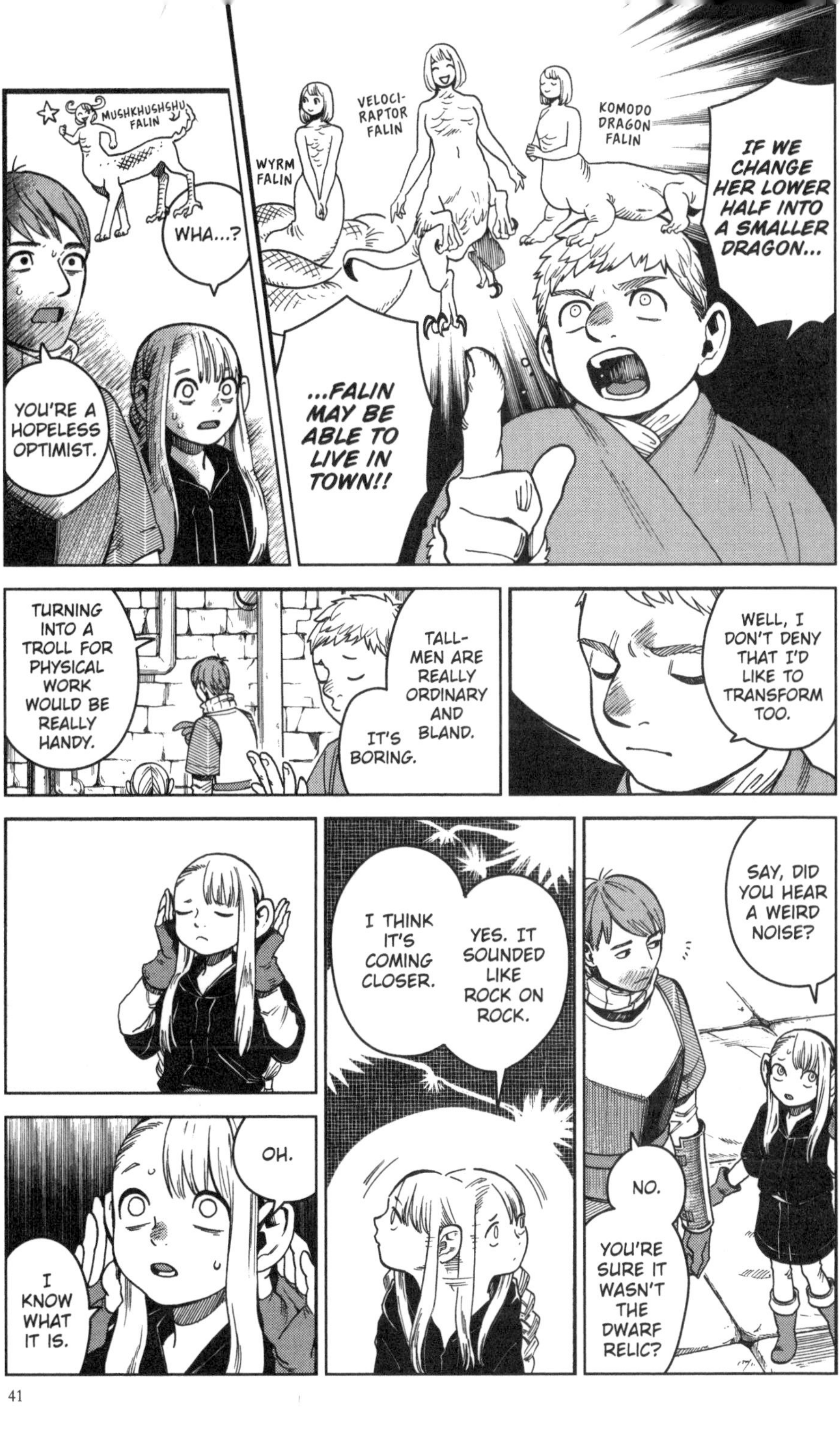
IF WE CHANGE HER LOWER HALF INTO A SMALLER DRAGON...
KOMODO DRAGON FALIN
VELOCI-RAPTOR FALIN
WYRM FALIN
...FALIN MAY BE ABLE TO LIVE IN TOWN!!
MUSHKHUSHSHU FALIN
WHA...?
YOU'RE A HOPELESS OPTIMIST.
WELL, I DON'T DENY THAT I'D LIKE TO TRANSFORM TOO.
TALL-MEN ARE REALLY ORDINARY AND BLAND.
IT'S BORING.
TURNING INTO A TROLL FOR PHYSICAL WORK WOULD BE REALLY HANDY.
SAY, DID YOU HEAR A WEIRD NOISE?
NO.
YOU'RE SURE IT WASN'T THE DWARF RELIC?
YES. IT SOUNDED LIKE ROCK ON ROCK.
I THINK IT'S COMING CLOSER.
OH.
I KNOW WHAT IT IS.

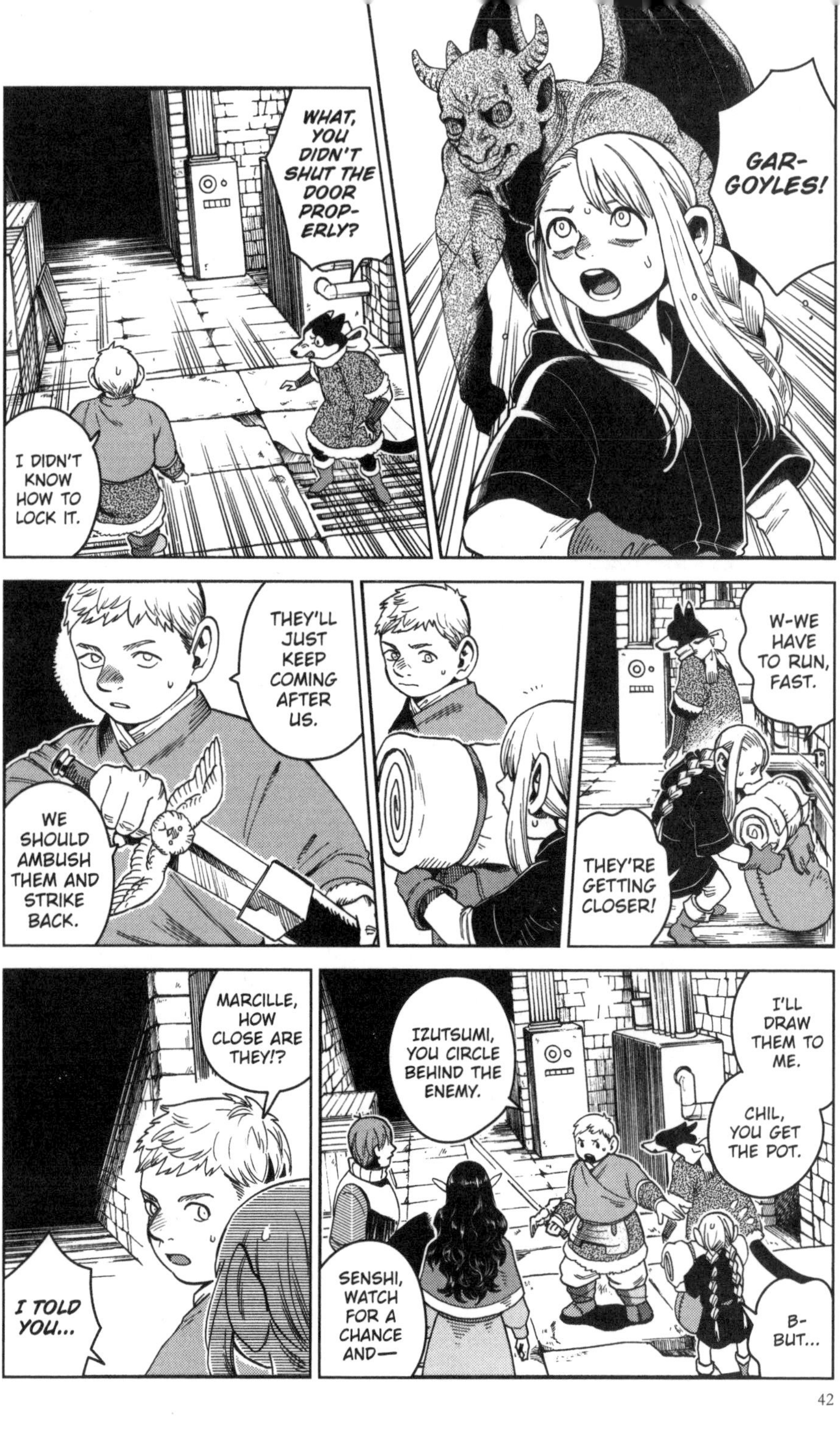
GAR-GOYLES!
WHAT, YOU DIDN'T SHUT THE DOOR PROPER-ERLY?
I DIDN'T KNOW HOW TO LOCK IT.
W-WE HAVE TO RUN, FAST.
THEY'RE GETTING CLOSER!
THEY'LL JUST KEEP COMING AFTER US.
WE SHOULD AMBUSH THEM AND STRIKE BACK.
I'LL DRAW THEM TO ME.
CHIL, YOU GET THE POT.
IZUTSUMI, YOU CIRCLE BEHIND THE ENEMY.
SENSHI, WATCH FOR A CHANCE AND—
B-BUT...
MARCILLE, HOW CLOSE ARE THEY!?
I TOLD YOU...

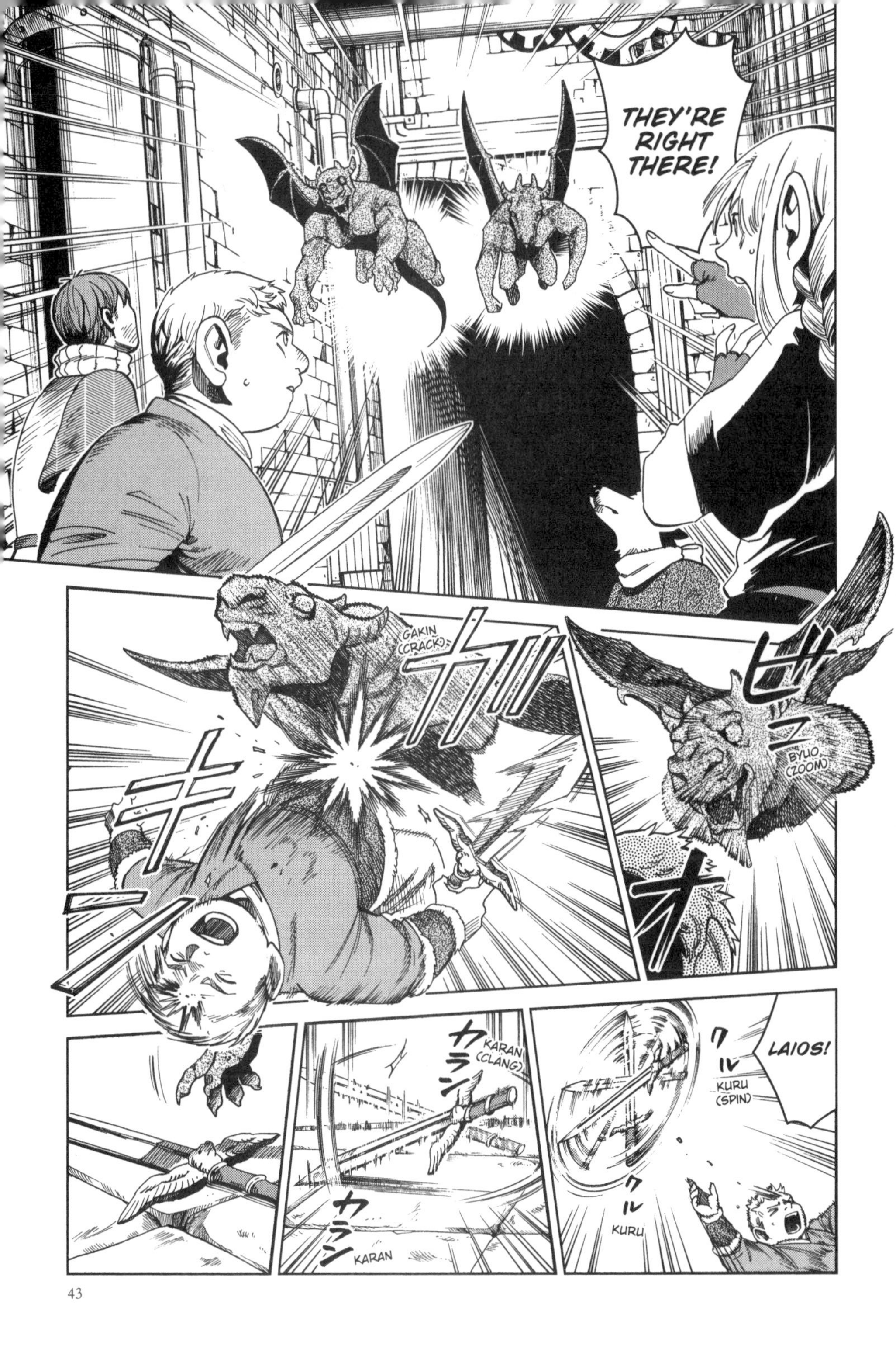

THEY'RE RIGHT THERE!
BYUO (ZOOM)
GAKIN (CRACK)
クル
KURU (SPIN)
LAIOS!
クル
KURU
カラン
KARAN (CLANG)
カラン
KARAN

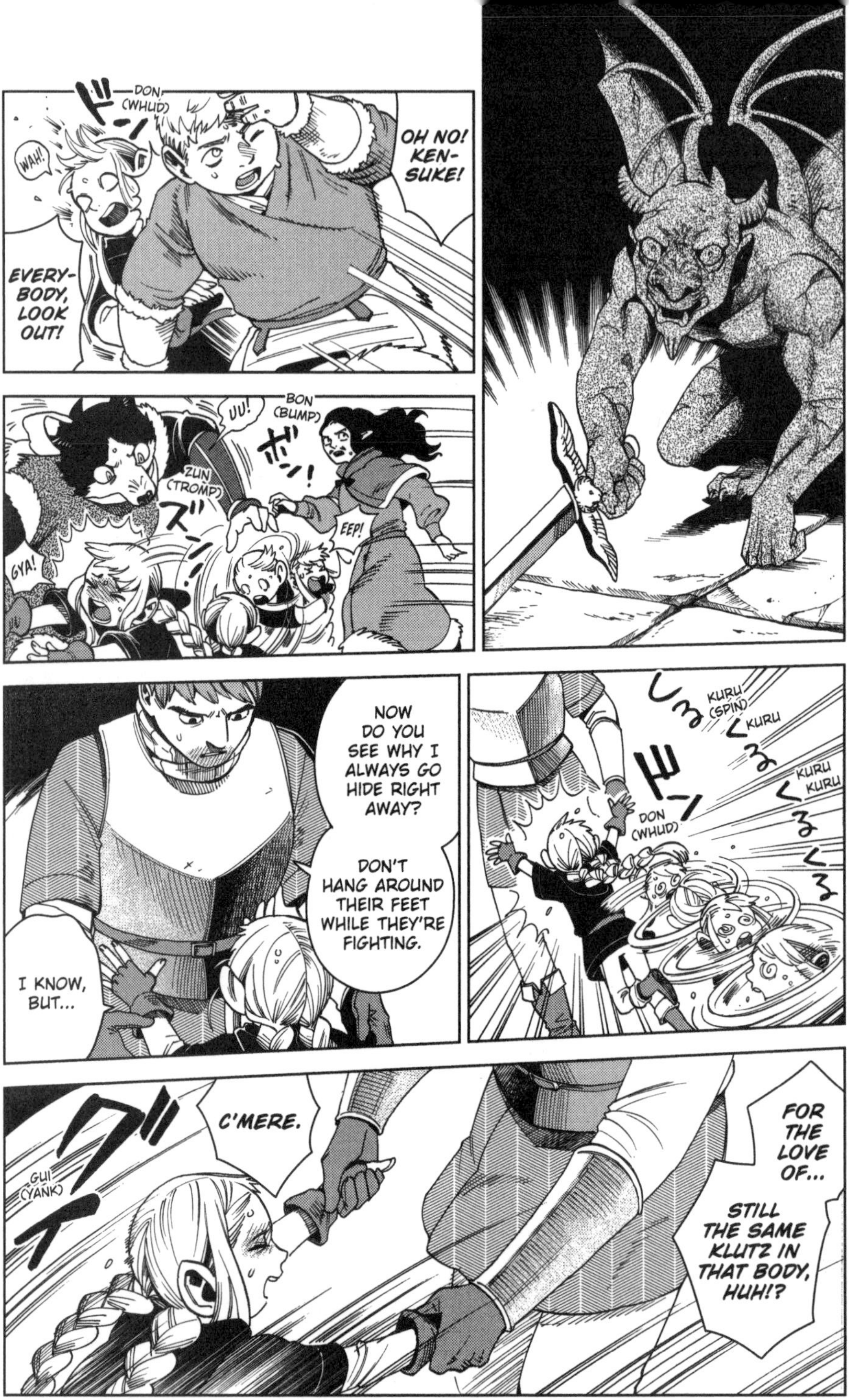
OH NO! KEN-SUKE!
DON (WHUD)
WAH!
EVERY-BODY, LOOK OUT!
BON (BUMP)
UU!
ZUN (TROMP)
EEP!
GYA!
KURU (SPIN) KURU
KURU KURU
DON (WHUD)
NOW DO YOU SEE WHY I ALWAYS GO HIDE RIGHT AWAY?
DON'T HANG AROUND THEIR FEET WHILE THEY'RE FIGHTING.
I KNOW, BUT...
FOR THE LOVE OF...
STILL THE SAME KLUTZ IN THAT BODY, HUH!?
C'MERE.
GUI (YANK)

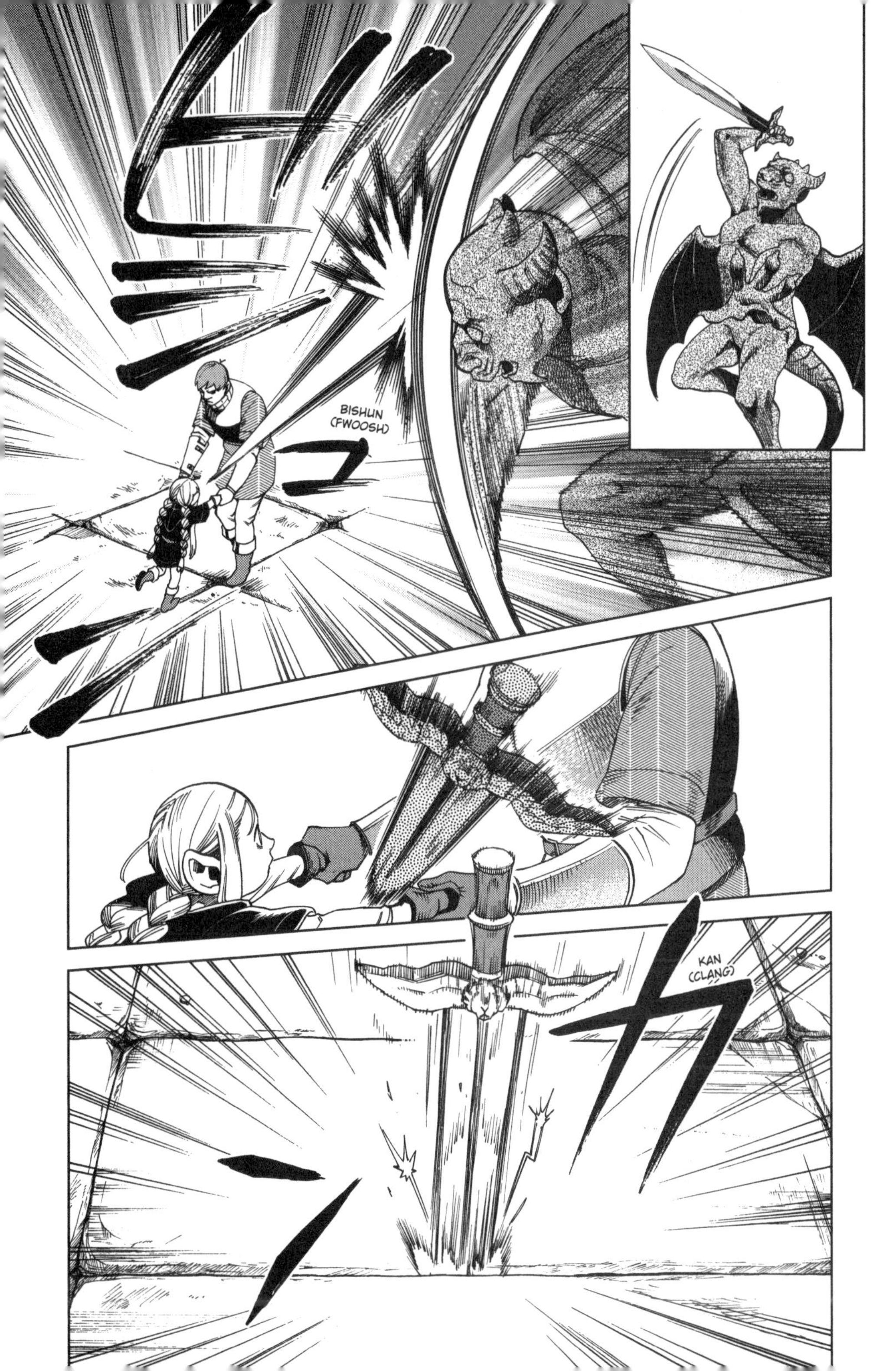
BISHUN (FWOOSH)
KAN (CLANG)

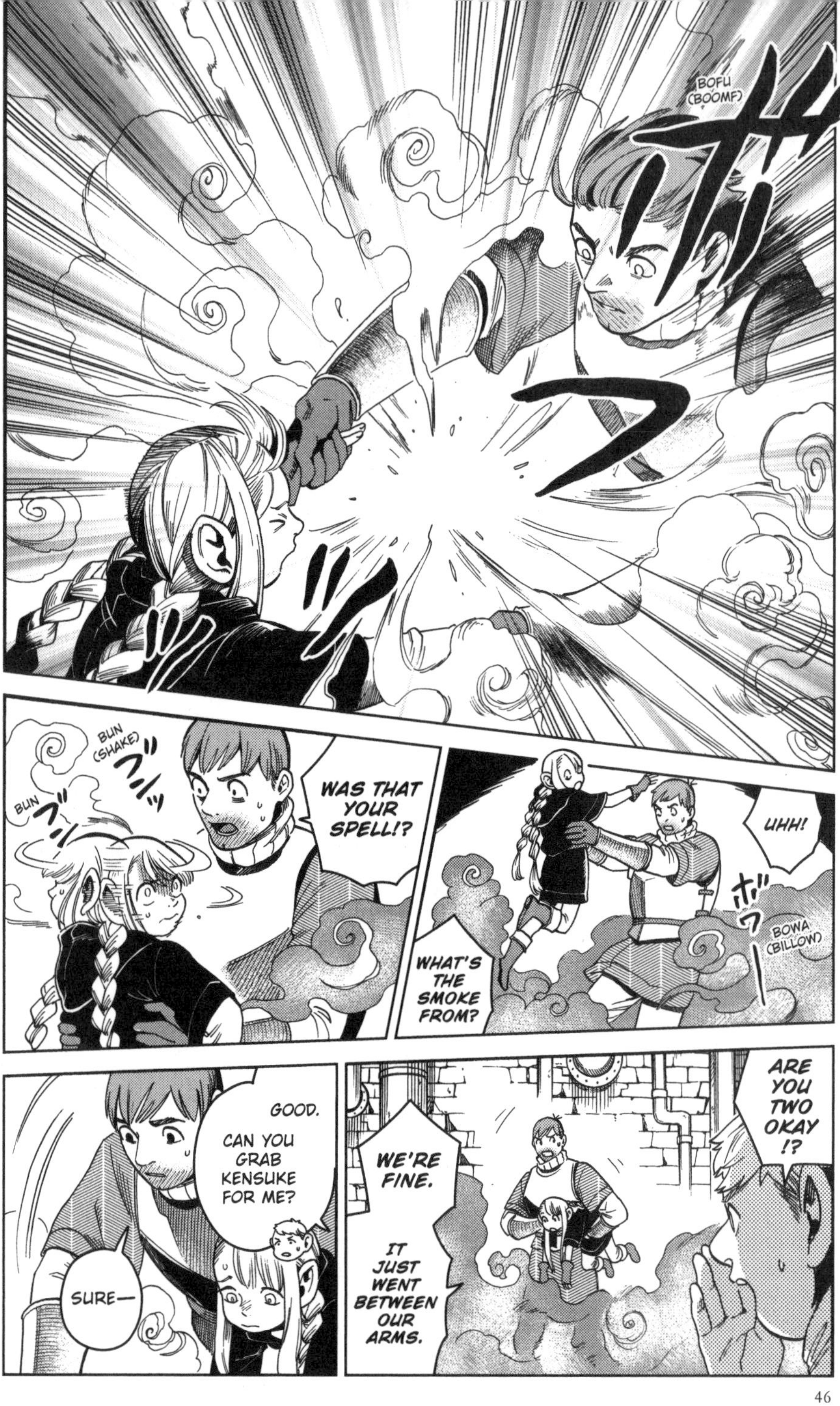
BOFU (BOOMF)
UHH!
BOWA (BILLOW)
WHAT'S THE SMOKE FROM?
WAS THAT YOUR SPELL!?
BUN (SHAKE)
BUN
ARE YOU TWO OKAY!?
WE'RE FINE.
IT JUST WENT BETWEEN OUR ARMS.
GOOD.
CAN YOU GRAB KENSUKE FOR ME?
SURE—

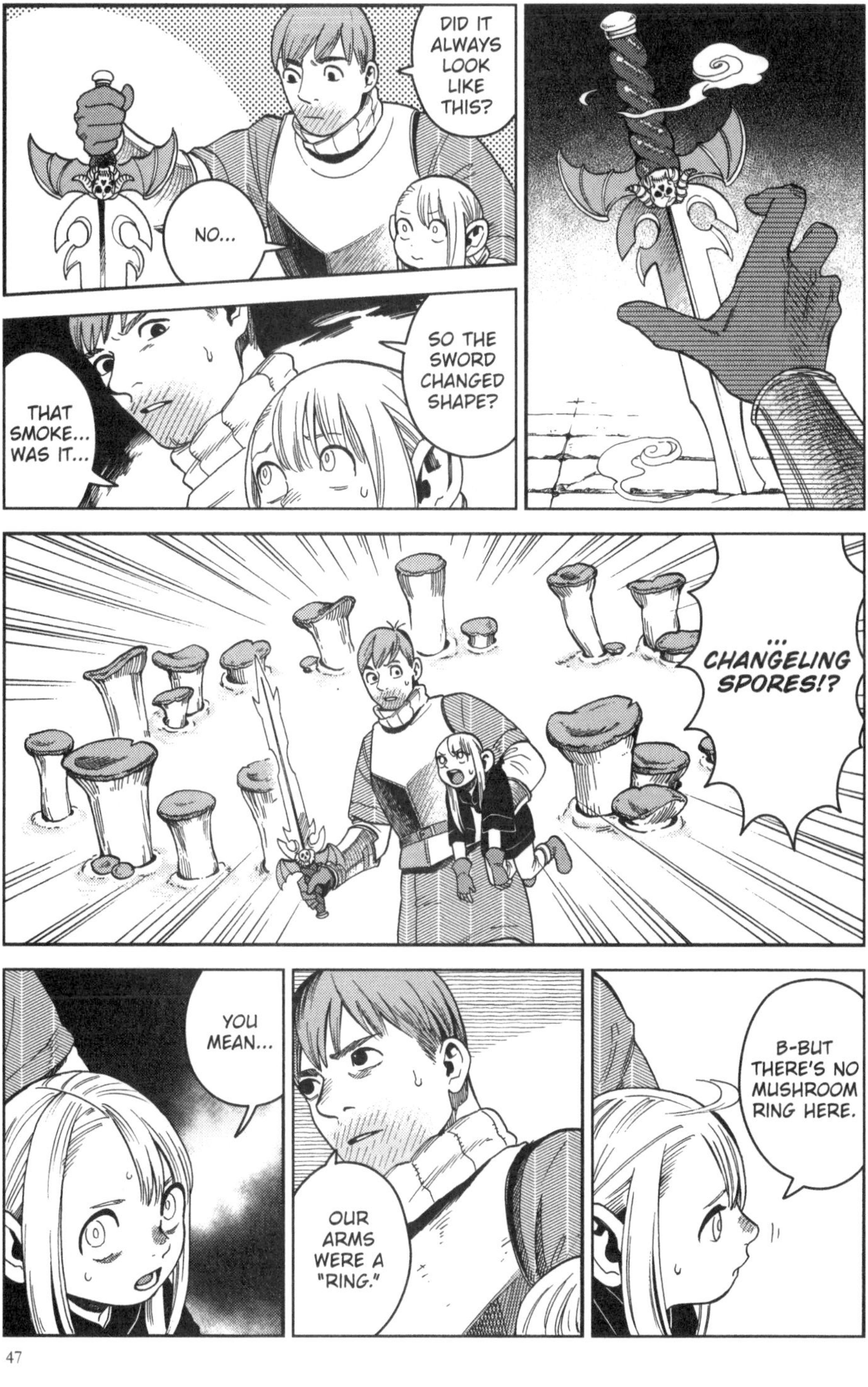
DID IT ALWAYS LOOK LIKE THIS?
NO...
SO THE SWORD CHANGED SHAPE?
THAT SMOKE... WAS IT...
...CHANGELING SPORES!?
B-BUT THERE'S NO MUSHROOM RING HERE.
OUR ARMS WERE A "RING."
YOU MEAN...

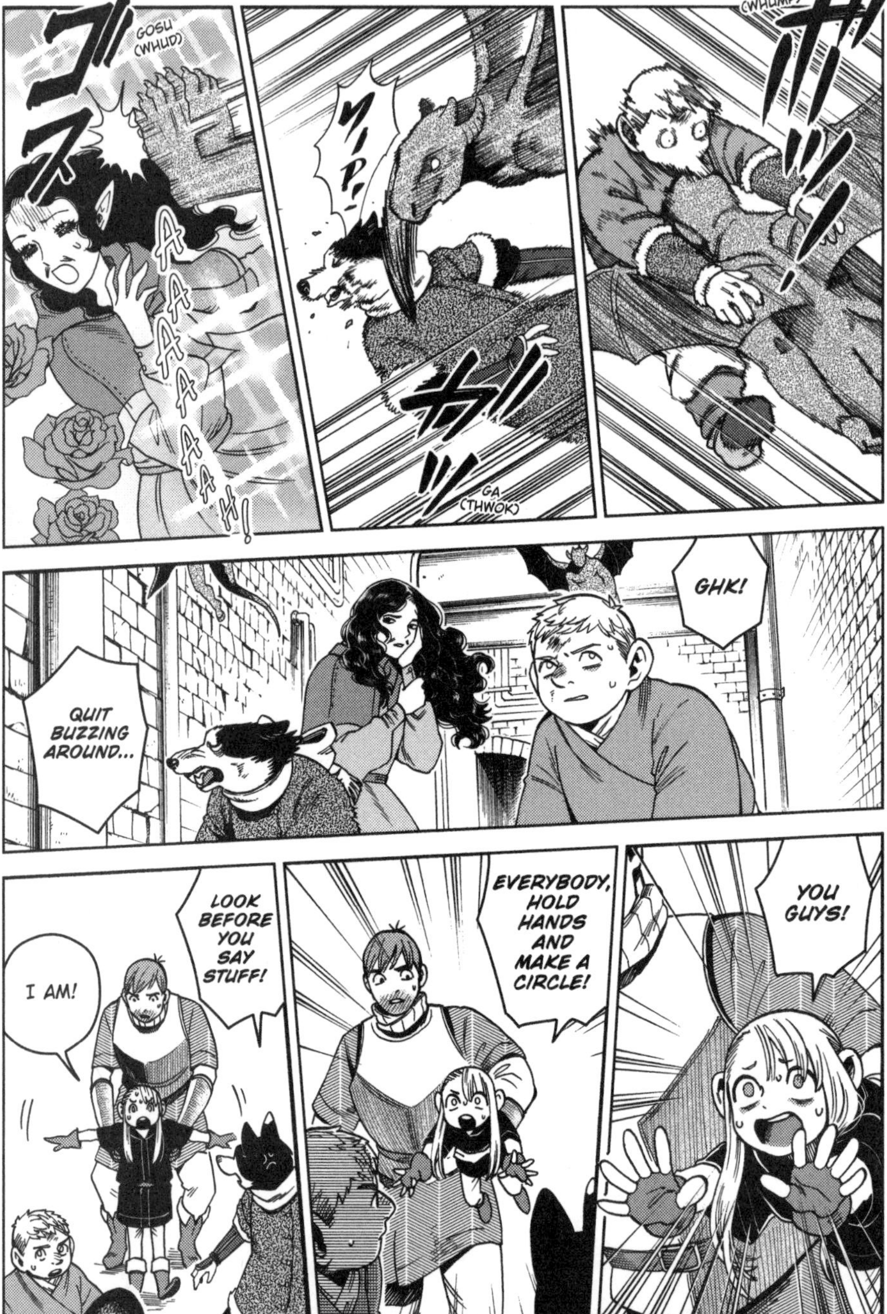
BO
(WHUMP)
YIP!
GA
(THWOK)
GOSU
(WHUD)
AAAAAAAAH!
GHK!
QUIT BUZZING AROUND...
YOU GUYS!
EVERYBODY, HOLD HANDS AND MAKE A CIRCLE!
LOOK BEFORE YOU SAY STUFF!
I AM!

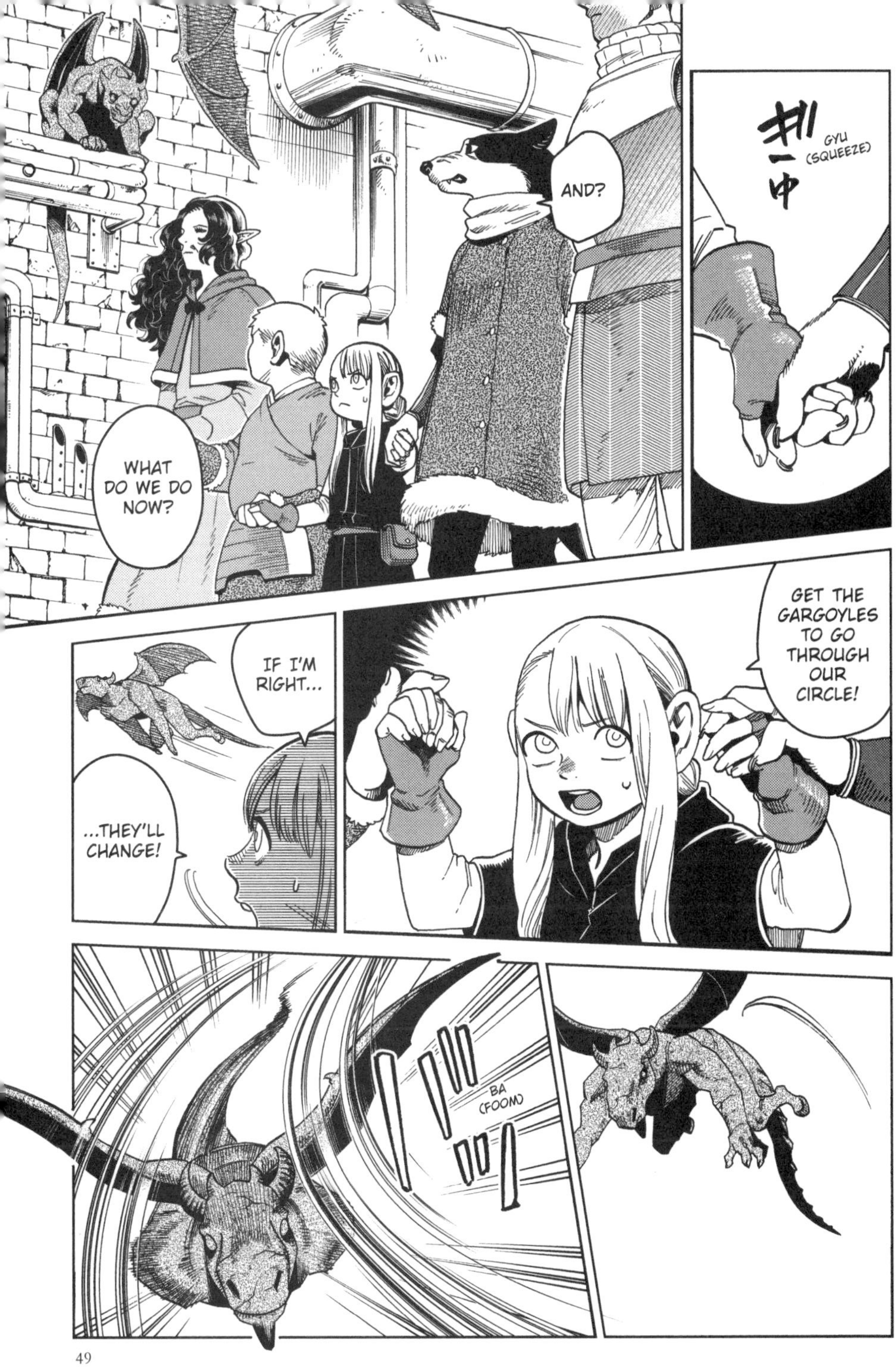
GYU (SQUEEZE)
AND?
WHAT DO WE DO NOW?
GET THE GARGOYLES TO GO THROUGH OUR CIRCLE!
IF I'M RIGHT...
...THEY'LL CHANGE!
BA (FOOM)

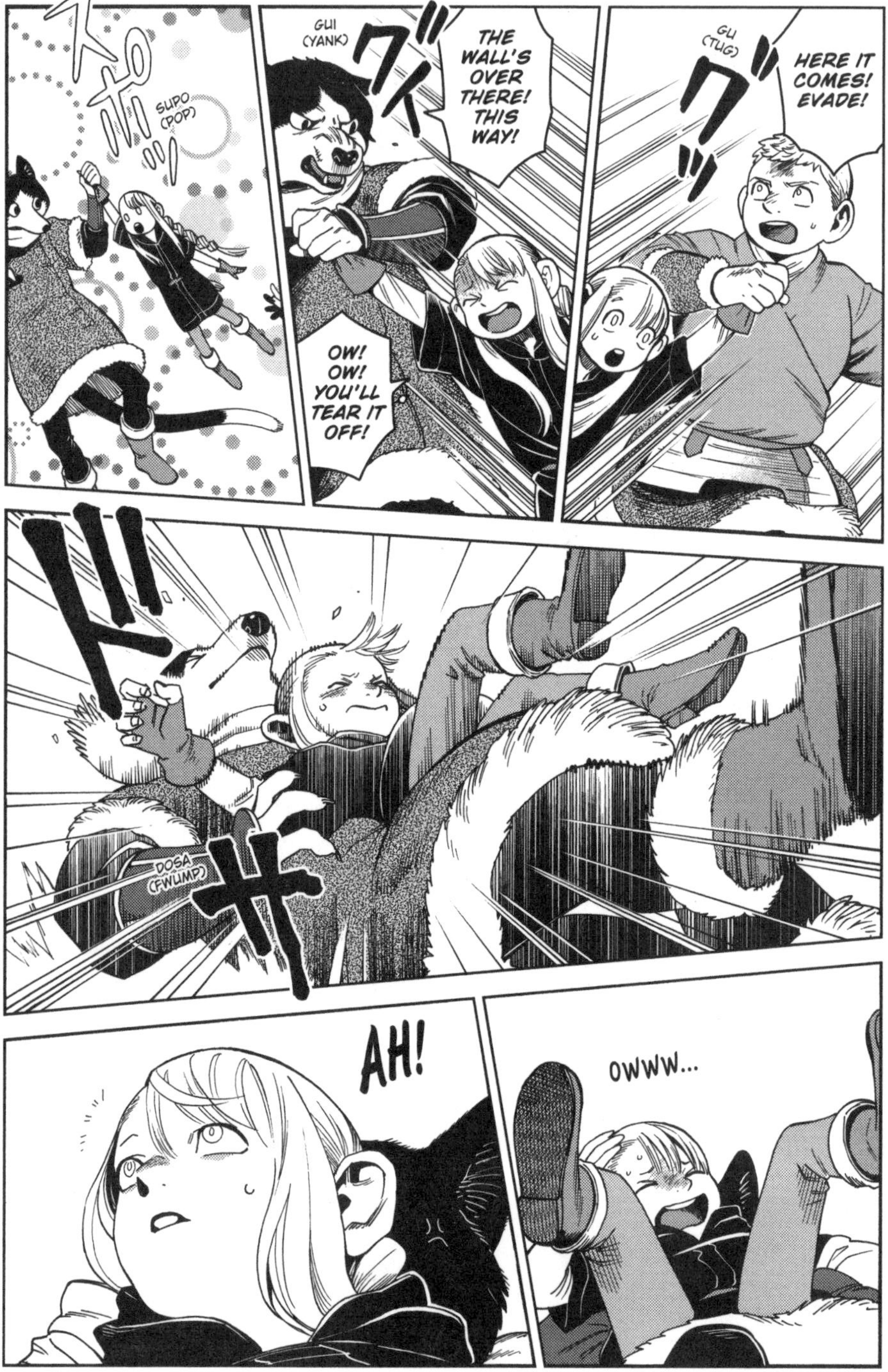
HERE IT COMES! EVADE!
GU (TUG)
THE WALL'S OVER THERE! THIS WAY!
GUI (YANK)
OW! OW! YOU'LL TEAR IT OFF!
SUPO (POP)
DOSA (FWUMP)
OWWW...
AH!

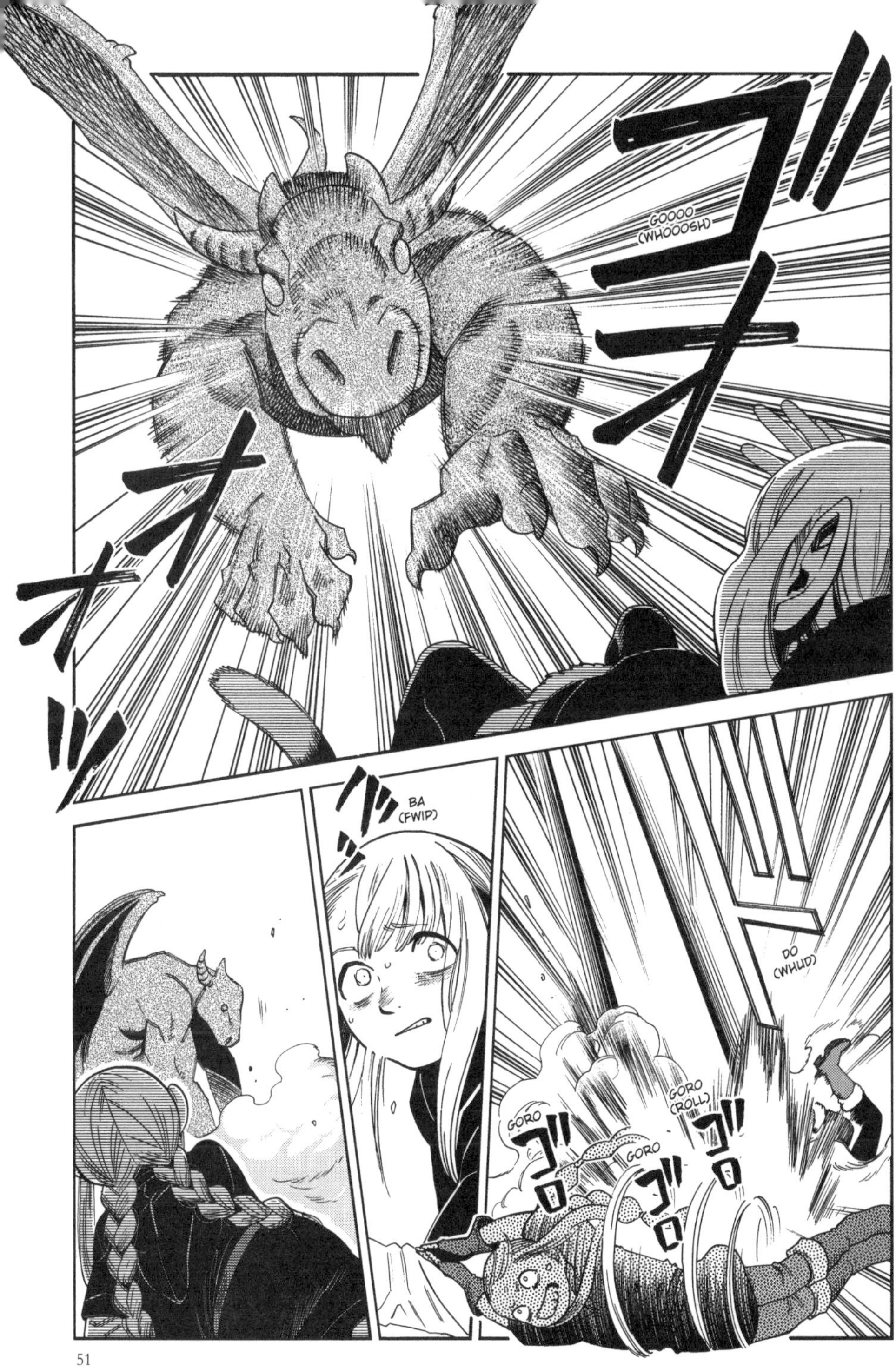
GOOOO
(WHOOOSH)
DO
(WHUD)
GORO
(ROLL)
GORO
GORO
BA
(FWIP)

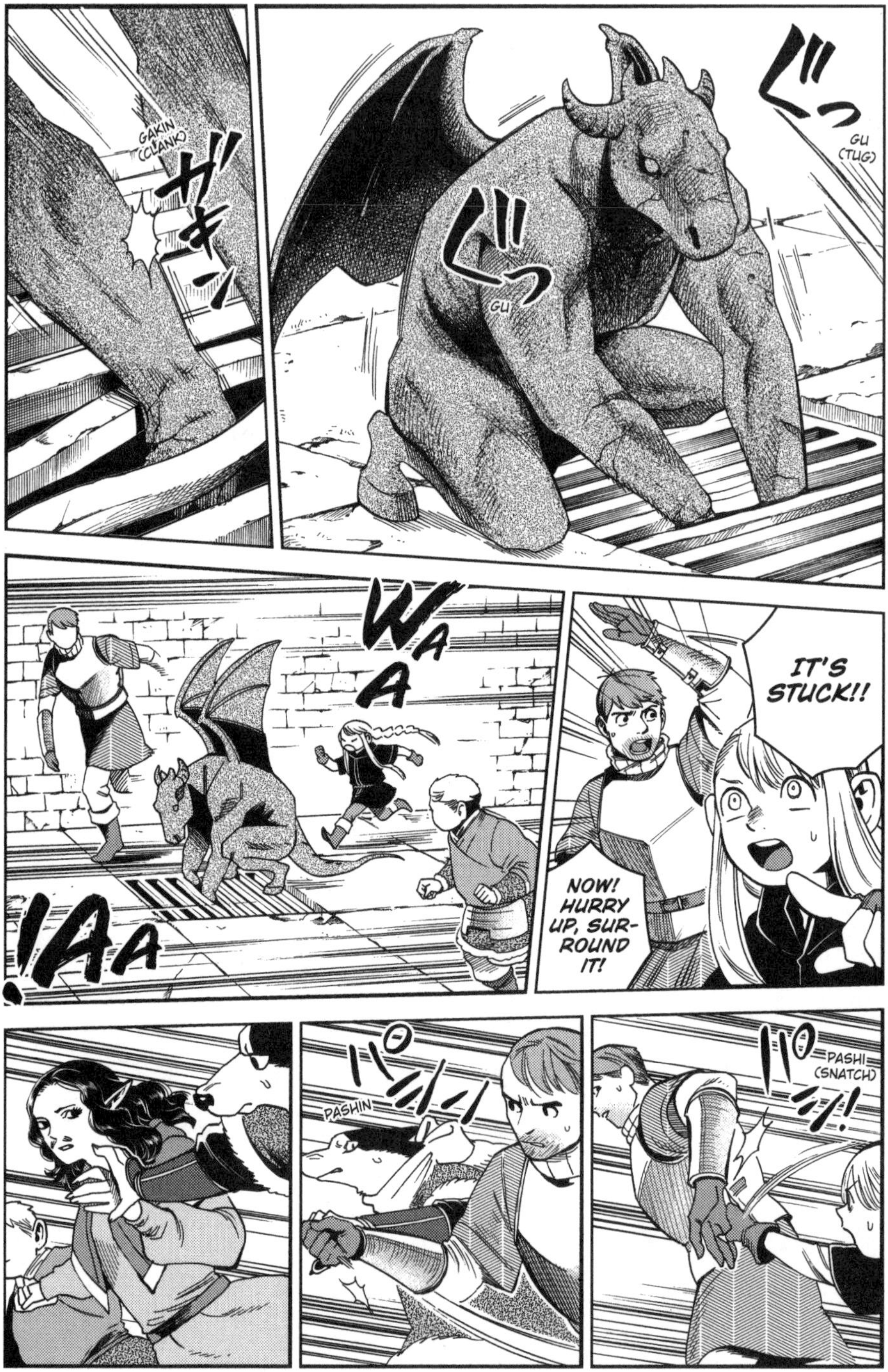
ぐっ
GU (TUG)
ぐっ
GU
ガキン
GAKIN (CLANK)
IT'S STUCK!!
NOW! HURRY UP, SUR-ROUND IT!
WAA
AA!
パシッ
PASHI (SNATCH)
パシン
PASHIN

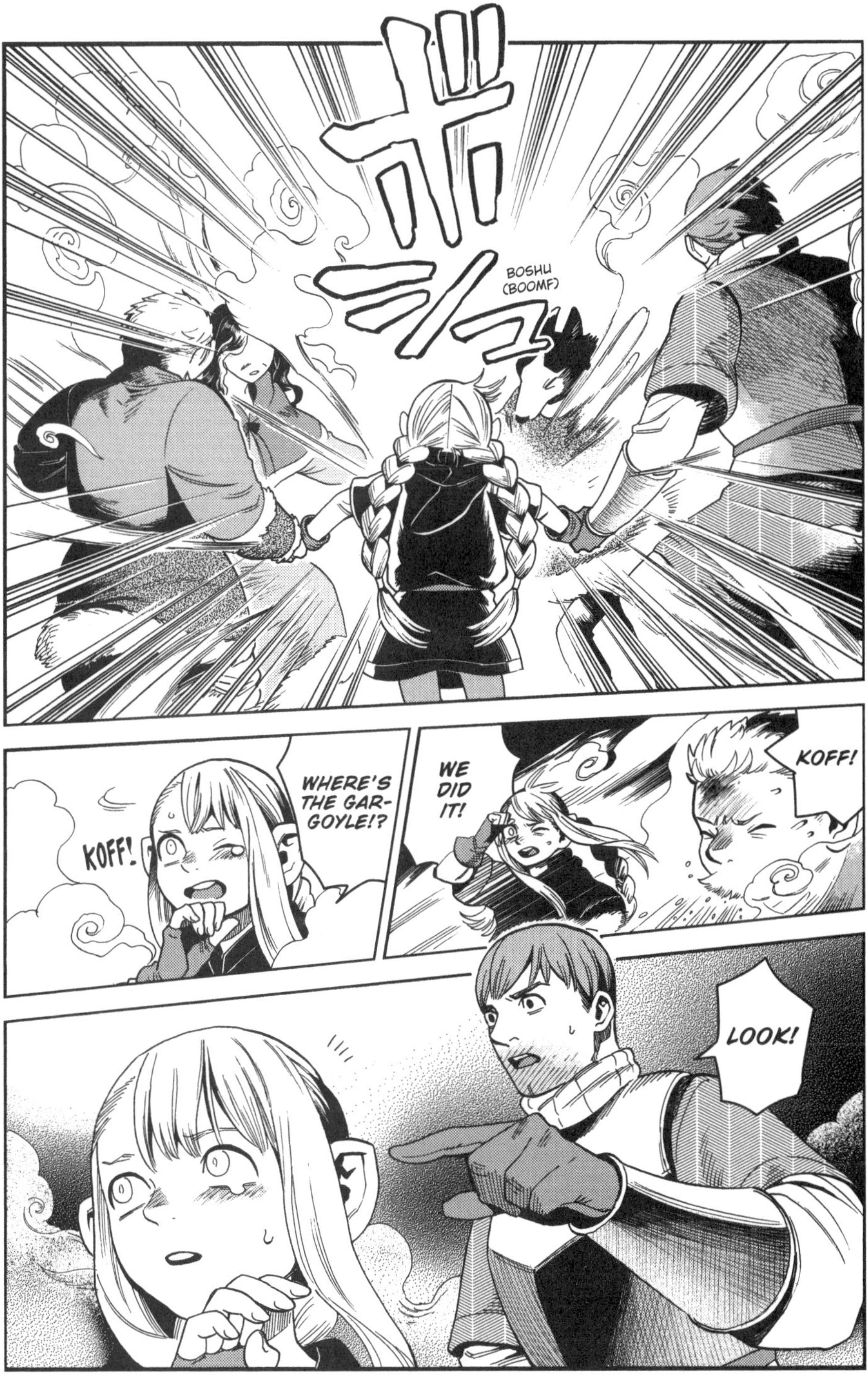
BOSHU
(BOOMF)
KOFF!
WE DID IT!
WHERE'S THE GAR-GOYLE!?
KOFF!
LOOK!

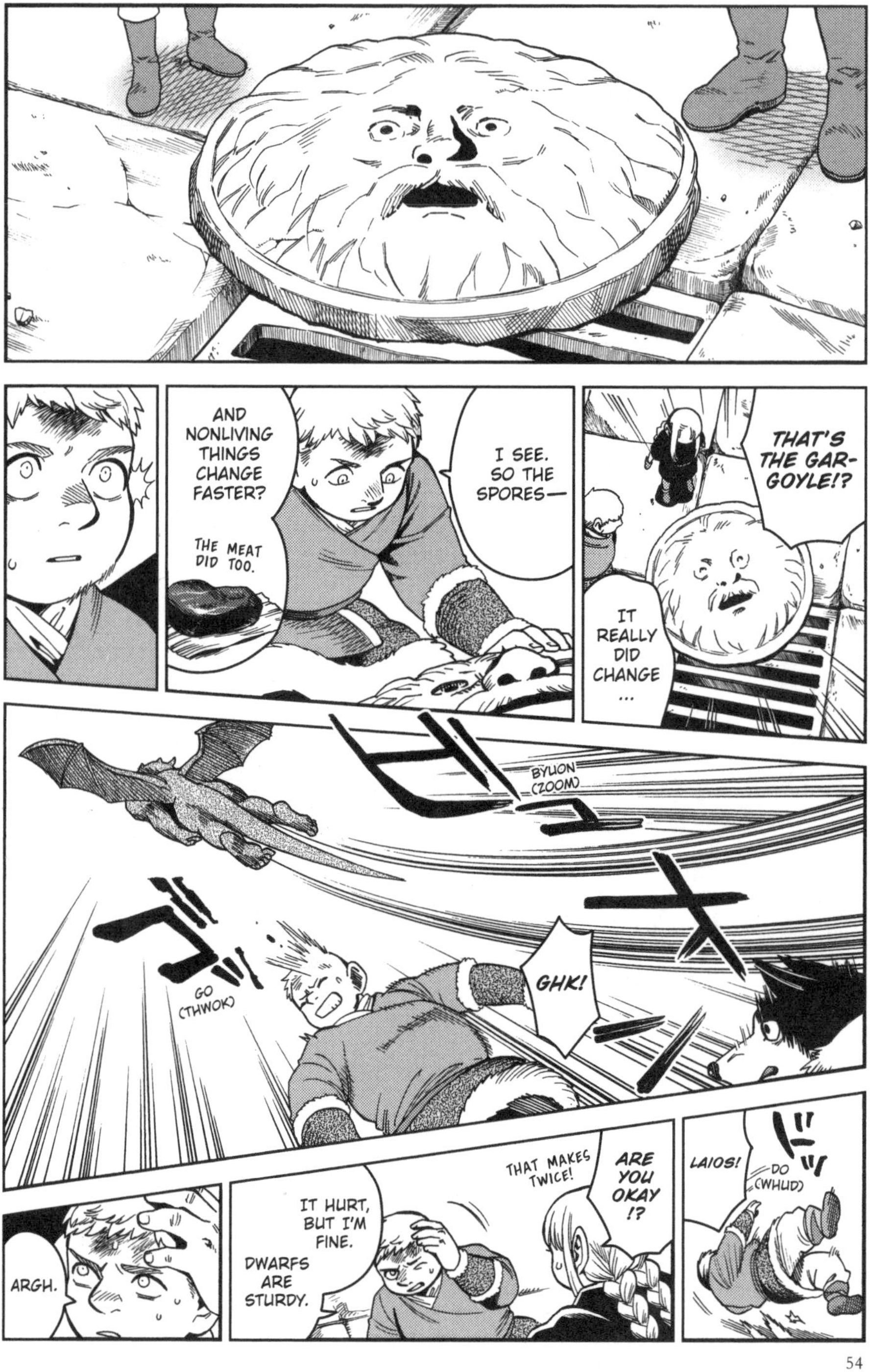
THAT'S THE GAR-GOYLE!?
IT REALLY DID CHANGE ...
I SEE. SO THE SPORES—
AND NONLIVING THINGS CHANGE FASTER?
THE MEAT DID TOO.
BYUON (ZOOM)
GHK!
GO (THWOK)
LAIOS!
DO (WHUD)
ARE YOU OKAY!?
THAT MAKES TWICE!
IT HURT, BUT I'M FINE.
DWARFS ARE STURDY.
ARGH.

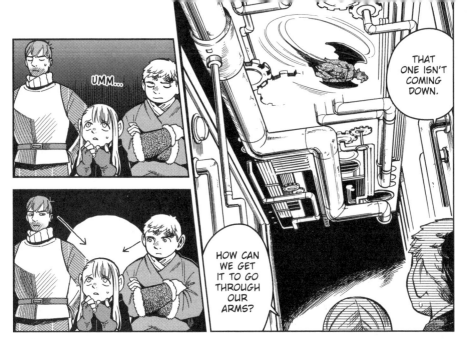

UMM...

THAT ONE ISN'T COMING DOWN.

HOW CAN WE GET IT TO GO THROUGH OUR ARMS?

HUH?

GYU (SQUEEZE)

ギゅっ

MARCILLE, COME HERE A SECOND.

IT SHOULD WORK.

LET'S GO.

UM...

ぐっ GU

ぐっ GU (HEFT?)

ぐっ GU...

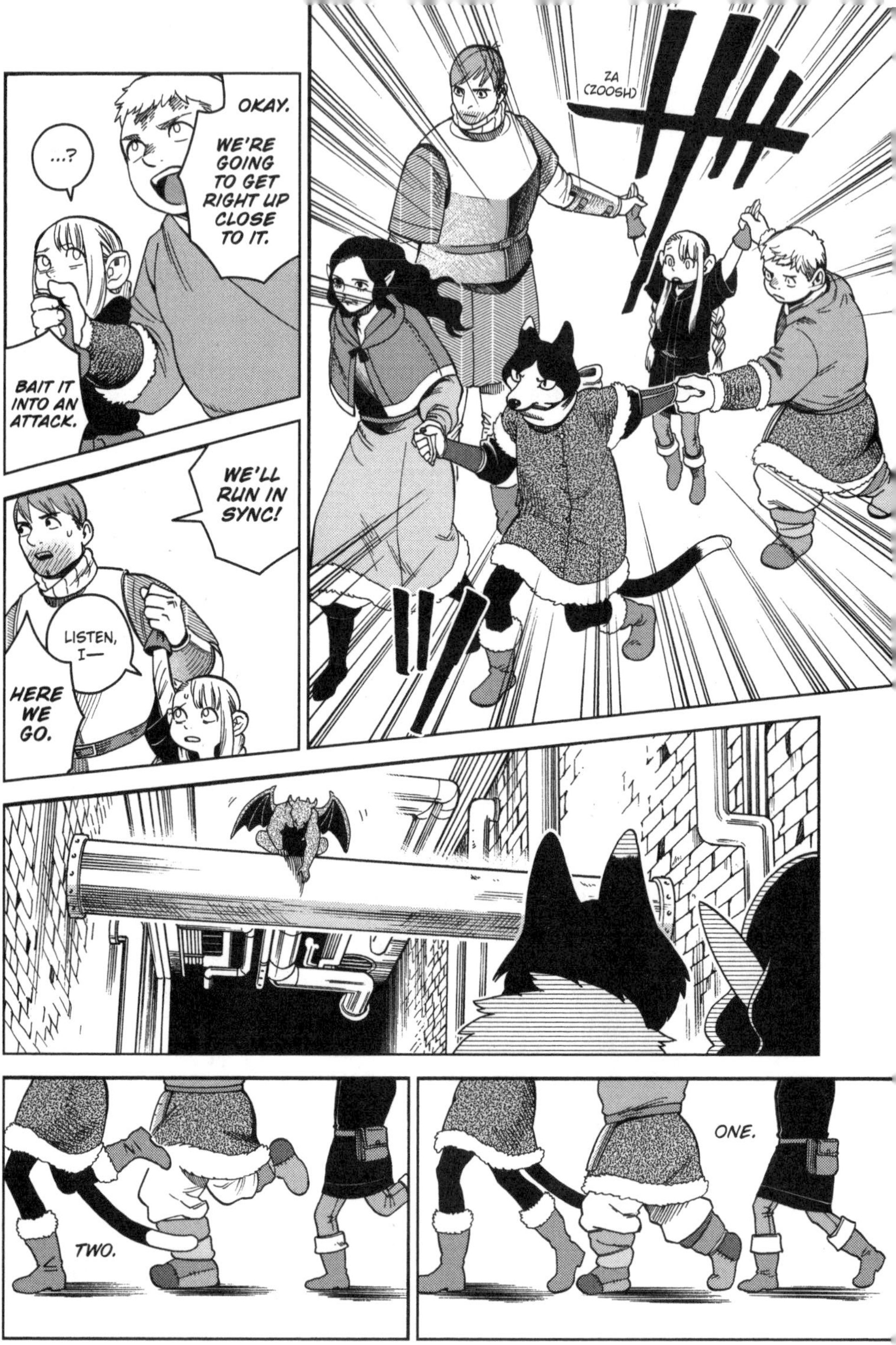
ZA (ZOOSH)
OKAY.
WE'RE GOING TO GET RIGHT UP CLOSE TO IT.
...?
BAIT IT INTO AN ATTACK.
WE'LL RUN IN SYNC!
LISTEN, I—
HERE WE GO.
ONE.
TWO.

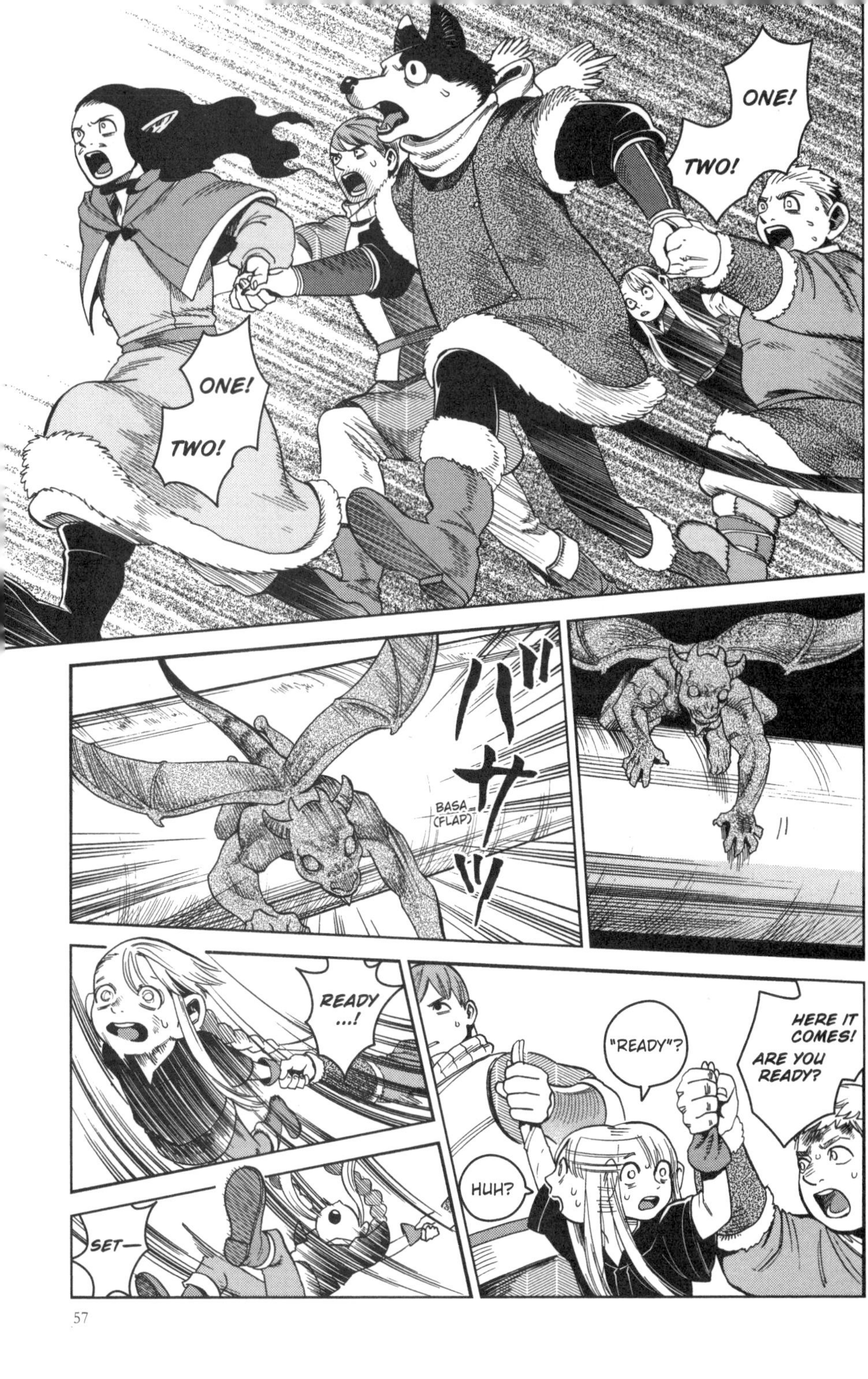
ONE! TWO!
ONE! TWO!
バサッ
BASA (FLAP)
HERE IT COMES! ARE YOU READY?
"READY"?
HUH?
READY ...!
SET—

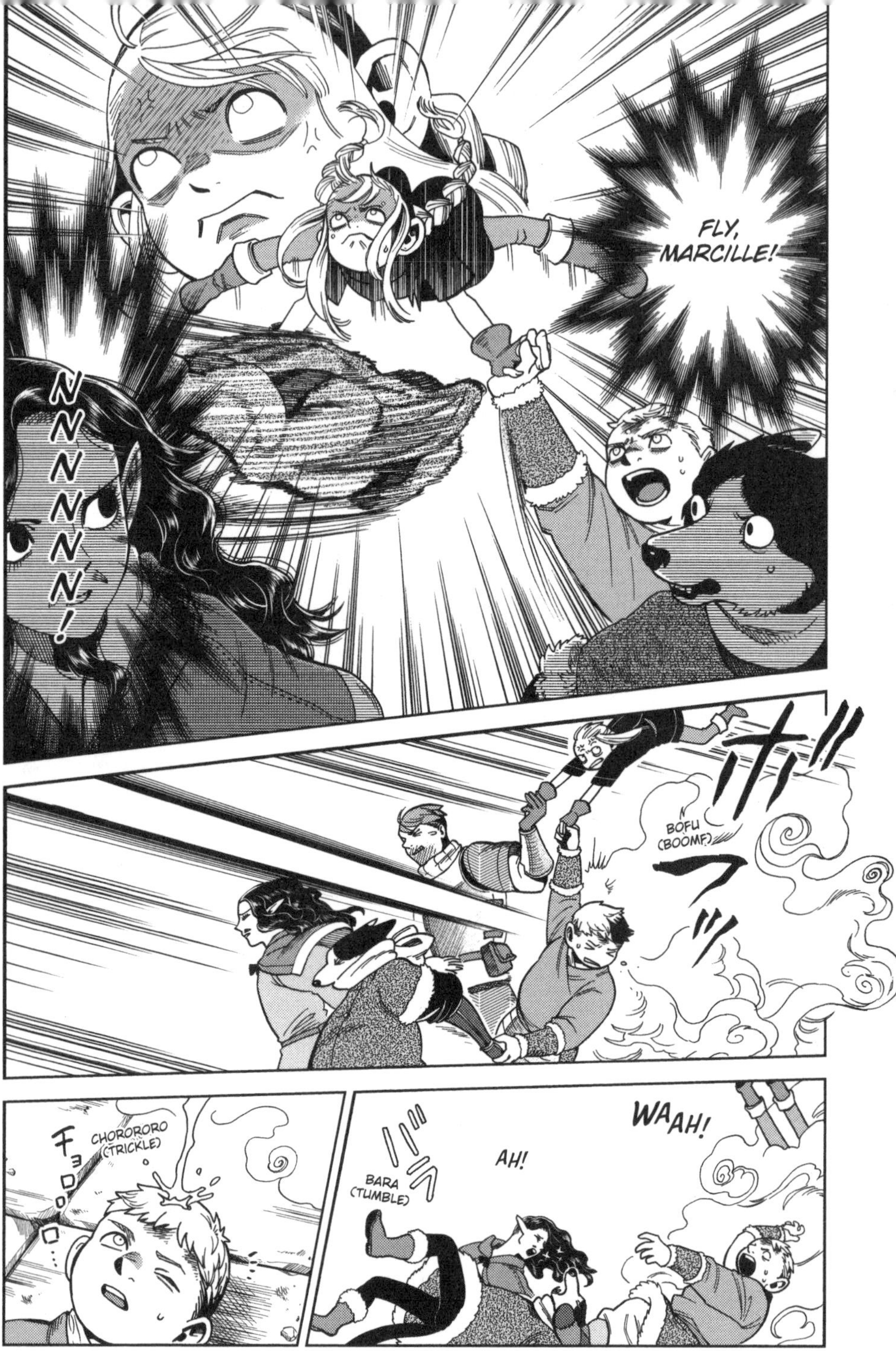

FLY, MARCILLE!
NNNNNNN!
ボフッ
BOFU (BOOMF)
WAAH!
AH!
バラ
BARA (TUMBLE)
チョロロ…
CHOROROR0 (TRICKLE)

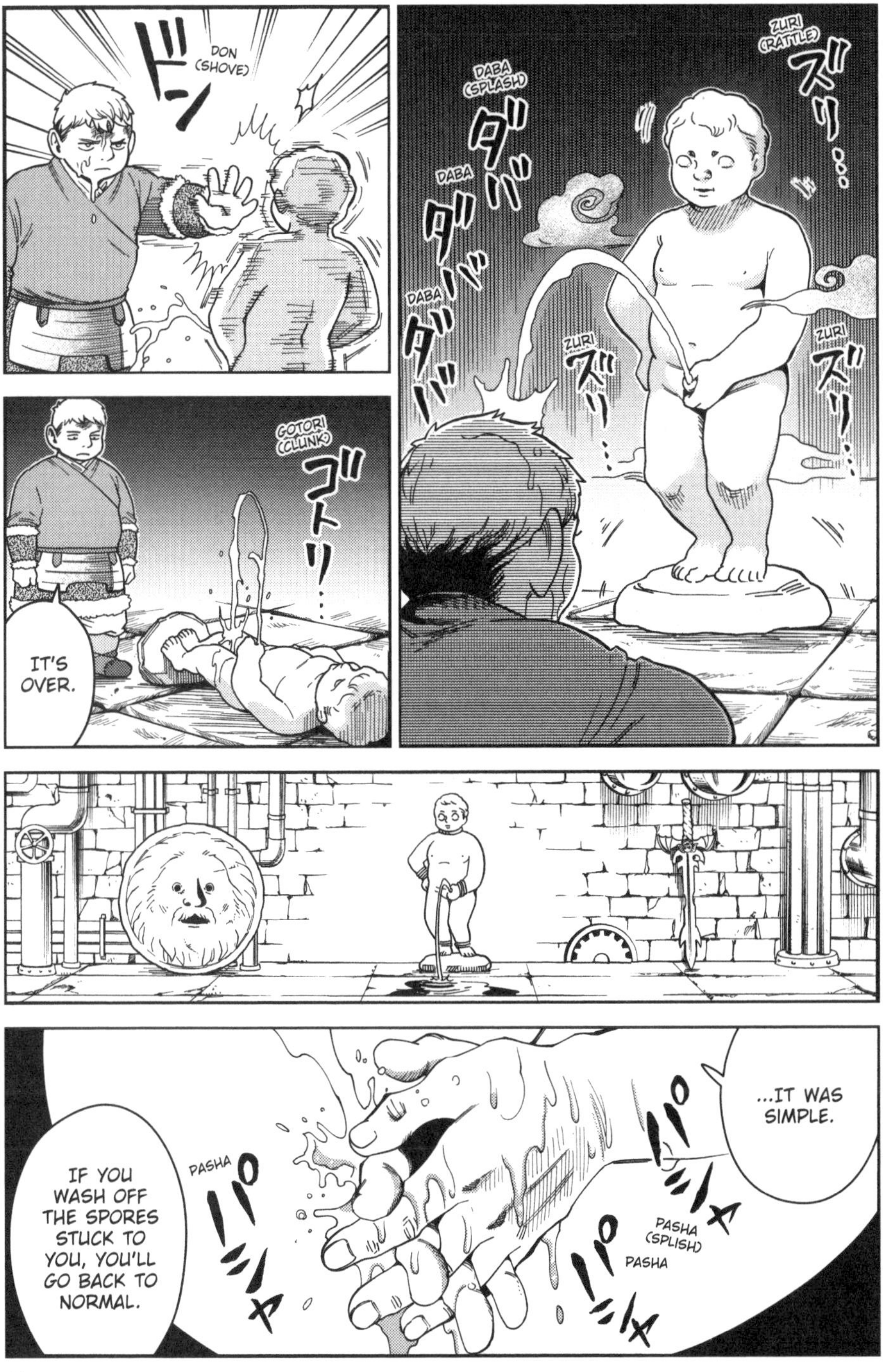

ZURI (RATTLE)
ズリ…
DABA (SPLASH)
ダバ
DABA
ダバ
DABA
ダバ
ZURI
ズリ…
ZURI
ズリ…
DON (SHOVE)
ドン
GOTORI (CLUNK)
ゴトリ…
IT'S OVER.
...IT WAS SIMPLE.
PASHA (SPLISH)
パシャ
PASHA
パシャ
PASHA
パシャ
IF YOU WASH OFF THE SPORES STUCK TO YOU, YOU'LL GO BACK TO NORMAL.

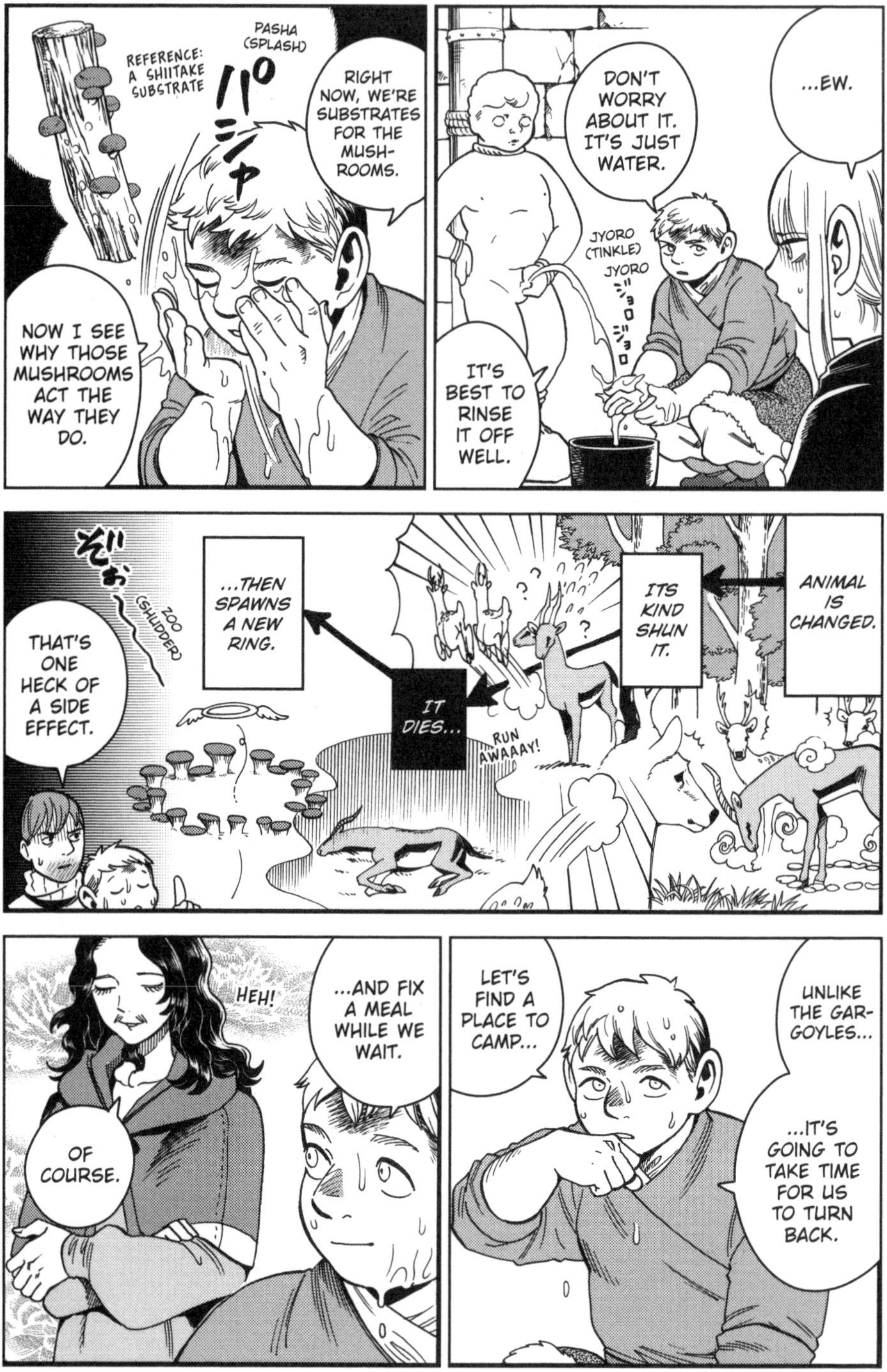
...EW.
DON'T WORRY ABOUT IT. IT'S JUST WATER.
JYORO (TINKLE) JYORO
ジョロジョロ
IT'S BEST TO RINSE IT OFF WELL.
RIGHT NOW, WE'RE SUBSTRATES FOR THE MUSH-ROOMS.
PASHA (SPLASH)
パシャ
REFERENCE: A SHIITAKE SUBSTRATE
NOW I SEE WHY THOSE MUSHROOMS ACT THE WAY THEY DO.
ANIMAL IS CHANGED.
ITS KIND SHUN IT.
IT DIES...
RUN AWAAAY!
...THEN SPAWNS A NEW RING.
ZOO (SHUDDER)
ぞぉ〜
THAT'S ONE HECK OF A SIDE EFFECT.
UNLIKE THE GAR-GOYLES...
...IT'S GOING TO TAKE TIME FOR US TO TURN BACK.
LET'S FIND A PLACE TO CAMP...
...AND FIX A MEAL WHILE WE WAIT.
HEH!
OF COURSE.

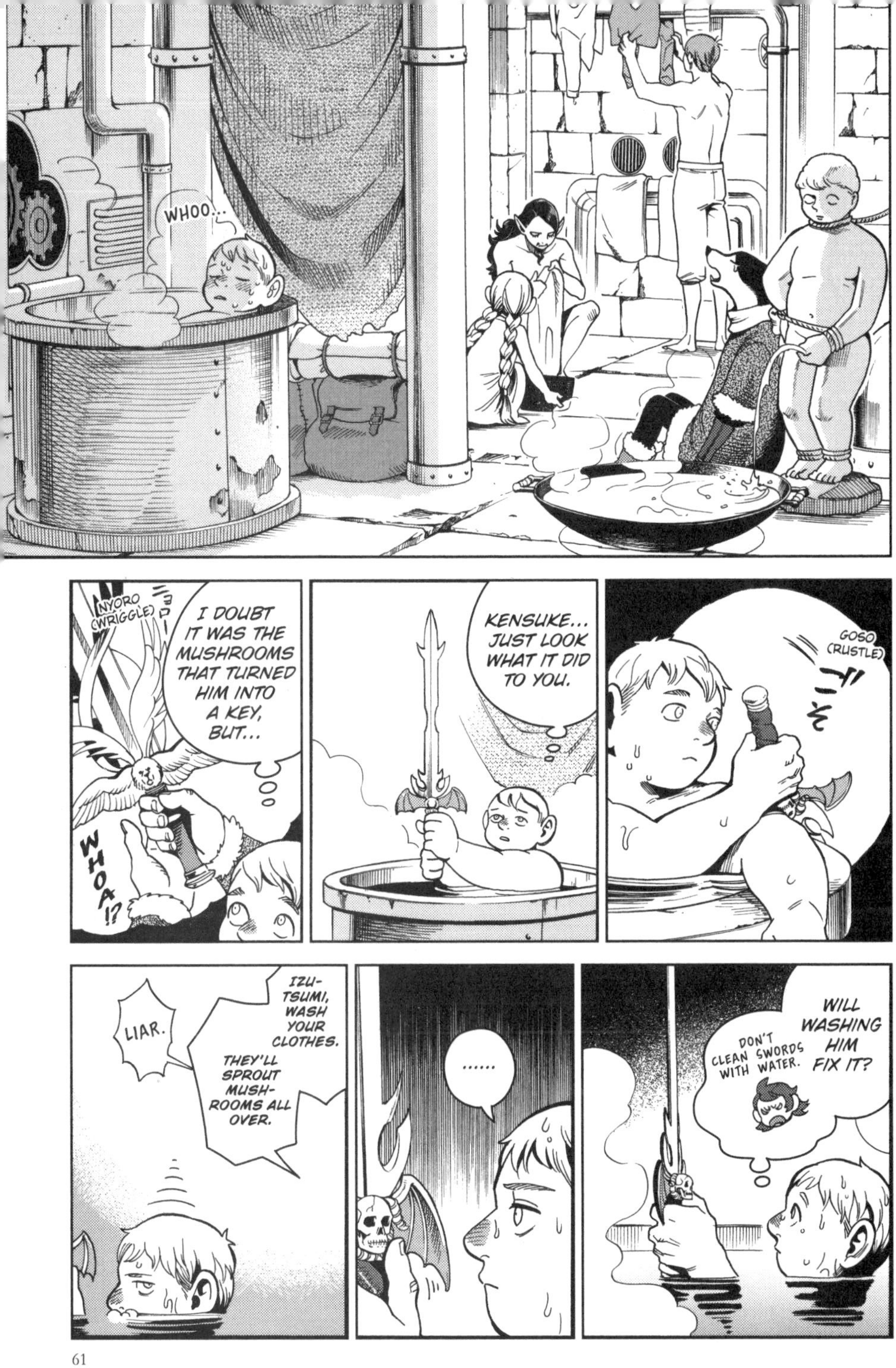
WHOO...
GOSO (RUSTLE)
KENSUKE... JUST LOOK WHAT IT DID TO YOU.
I DOUBT IT WAS THE MUSHROOMS THAT TURNED HIM INTO A KEY, BUT...
NYORO (WRIGGLE)
WHOA!?
WILL WASHING HIM FIX IT?
DON'T CLEAN SWORDS WITH WATER.
......
IZUTSUMI, WASH YOUR CLOTHES.
THEY'LL SPROUT MUSHROOMS ALL OVER.
LIAR.

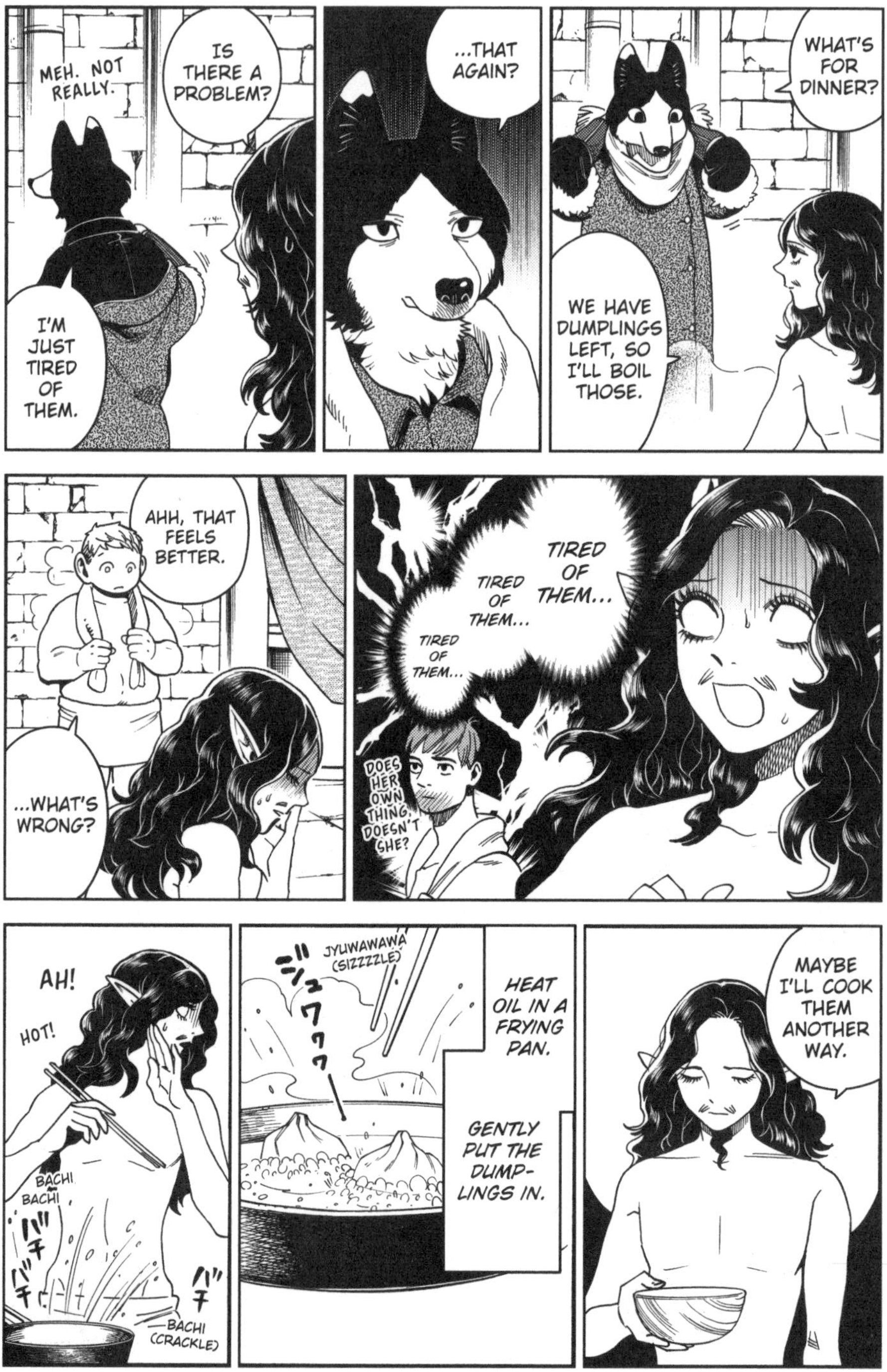
WHAT'S FOR DINNER?
WE HAVE DUMPLINGS LEFT, SO I'LL BOIL THOSE.
...THAT AGAIN?
IS THERE A PROBLEM?
MEH. NOT REALLY.
I'M JUST TIRED OF THEM.
TIRED OF THEM...
TIRED OF THEM...
TIRED OF THEM...
DOES HER OWN THING, DOESN'T SHE?
AHH, THAT FEELS BETTER.
...WHAT'S WRONG?
MAYBE I'LL COOK THEM ANOTHER WAY.
HEAT OIL IN A FRYING PAN.
GENTLY PUT THE DUMPLINGS IN.
JYUWAWAWA (SIZZZZLE)
AH!
HOT!
BACHI BACHI
バチバチ
バチ
BACHI (CRACKLE)

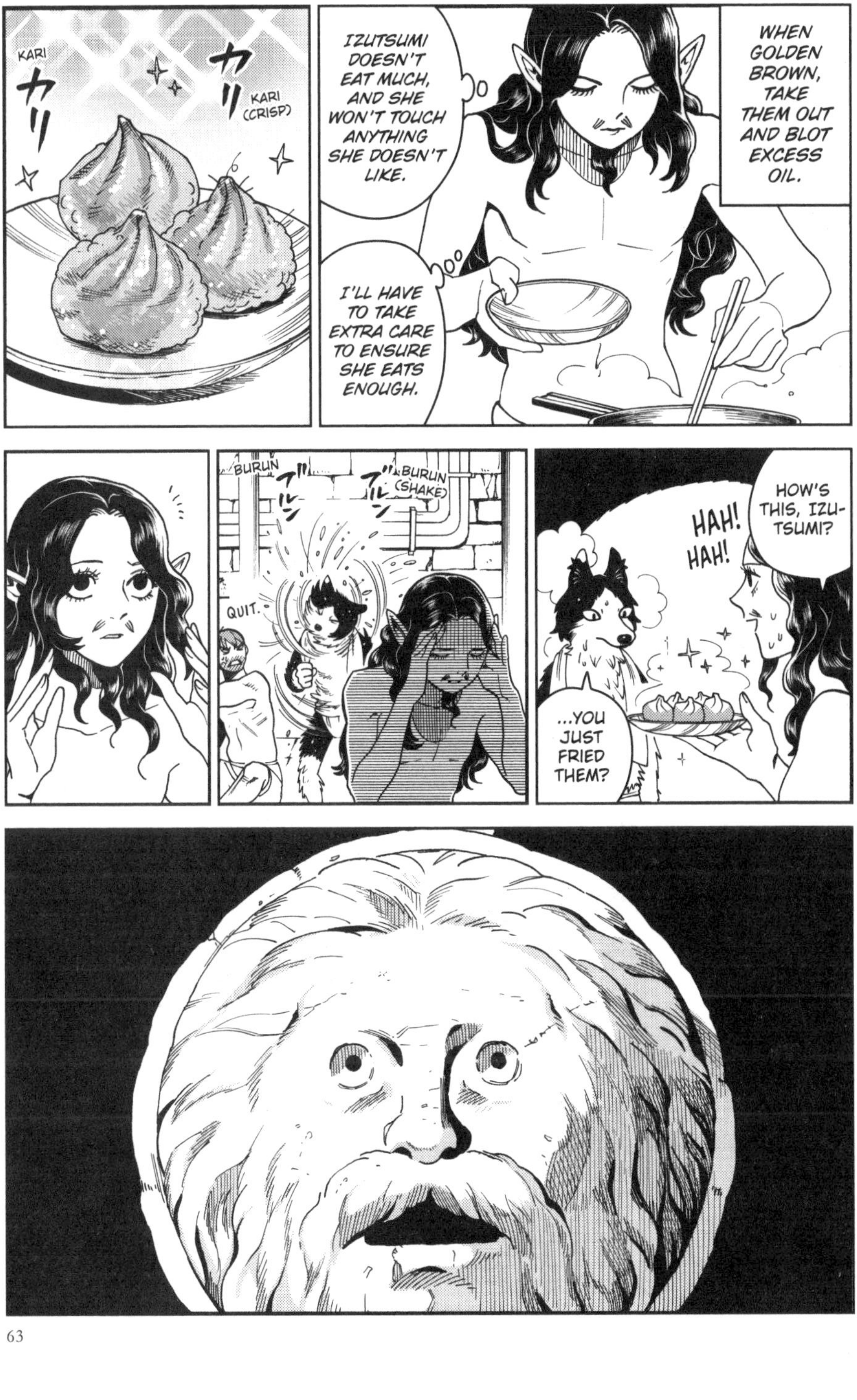
WHEN GOLDEN BROWN, TAKE THEM OUT AND BLOT EXCESS OIL.
IZUTSUMI DOESN'T EAT MUCH, AND SHE WON'T TOUCH ANYTHING SHE DOESN'T LIKE.
I'LL HAVE TO TAKE EXTRA CARE TO ENSURE SHE EATS ENOUGH.
KARI (CRISP)
KARI
HOW'S THIS, IZUTSUMI?
HAH! HAH!
...YOU JUST FRIED THEM?
BURUN (SHAKE)
BURUN
QUIT.

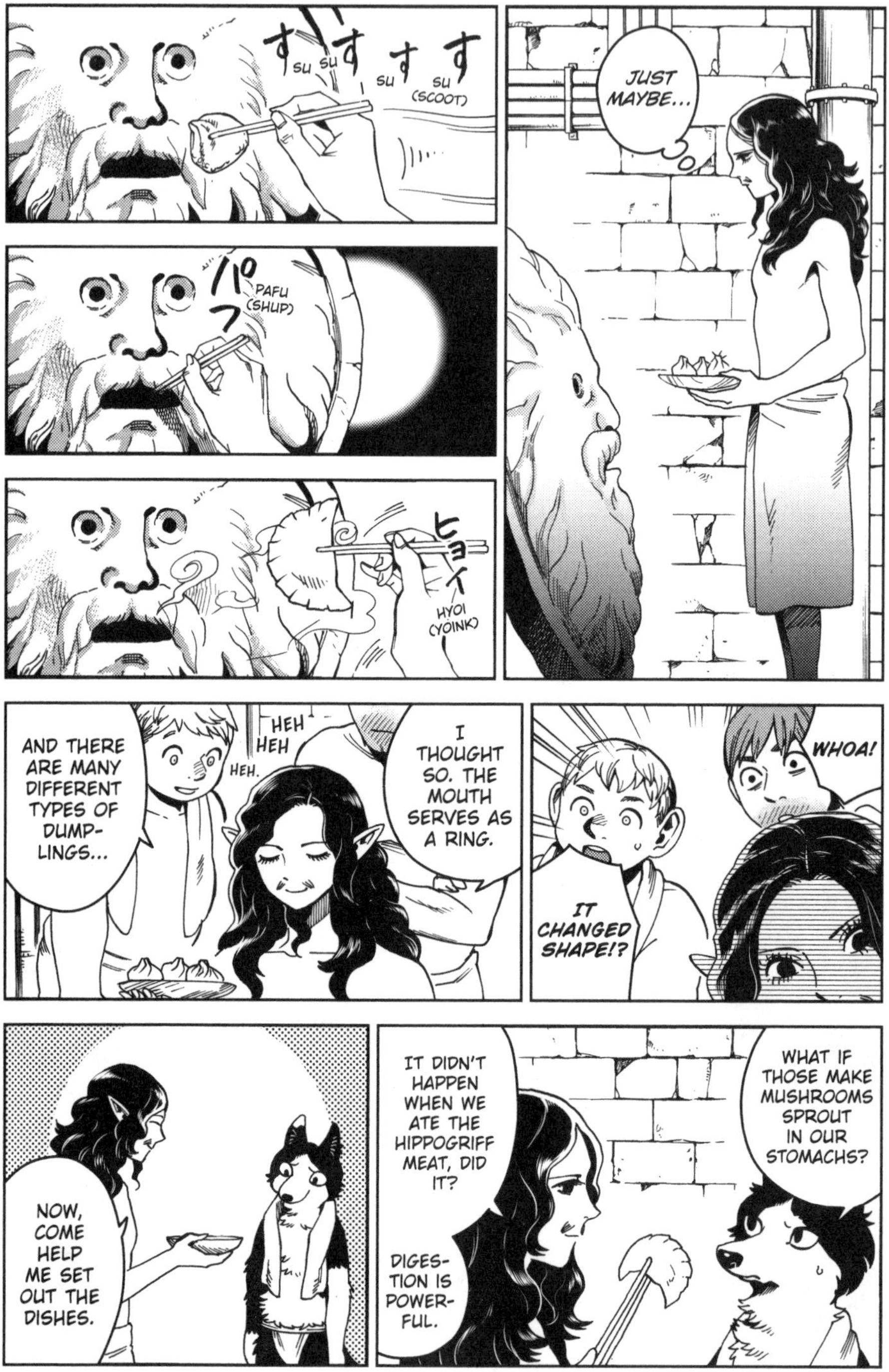
JUST MAYBE...
すすすす
SU SU SU SU (SCOOT)
パフ
PAFU (SHUP)
ヒョイ
HYOI (YOINK)
WHOA!
IT CHANGED SHAPE!?
I THOUGHT SO. THE MOUTH SERVES AS A RING.
HEH HEH HEH.
AND THERE ARE MANY DIFFERENT TYPES OF DUMPLINGS...
WHAT IF THOSE MAKE MUSHROOMS SPROUT IN OUR STOMACHS?
IT DIDN'T HAPPEN WHEN WE ATE THE HIPPOGRIFF MEAT, DID IT?
DIGESTION IS POWERFUL.
NOW, COME HELP ME SET OUT THE DISHES.

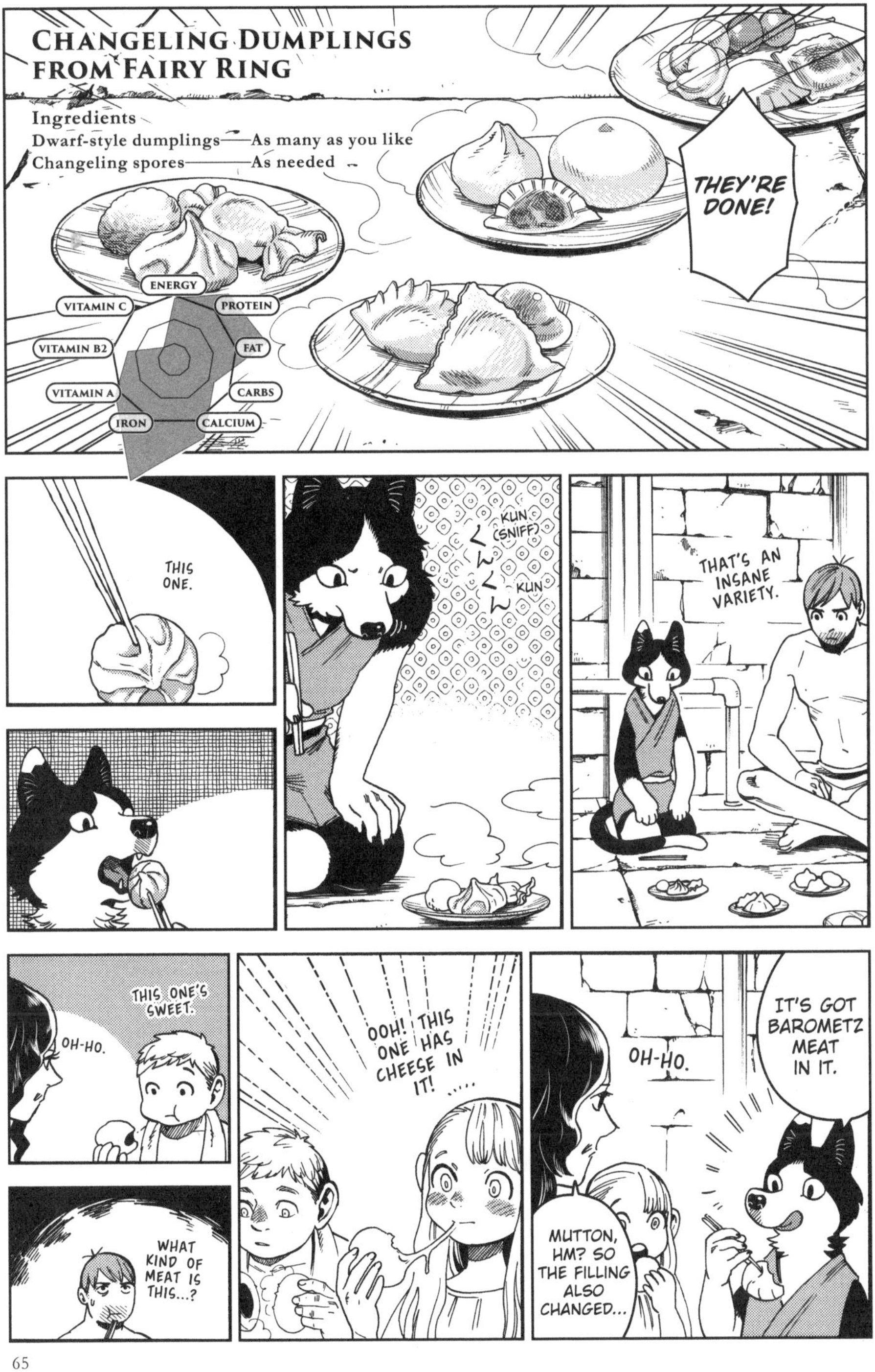
Changeling Dumplings from Fairy Ring
Ingredients
Dwarf-style dumplings——As many as you like
Changeling spores———As needed
ENERGY
PROTEIN
FAT
CARBS
CALCIUM
IRON
VITAMIN A
VITAMIN B2
VITAMIN C
THEY'RE DONE!
THAT'S AN INSANE VARIETY.
KUN (SNIFF)
くんくん
KUN
THIS ONE.
IT'S GOT BAROMETZ MEAT IN IT.
OH-HO.
MUTTON, HM? SO THE FILLING ALSO CHANGED...
OOH! THIS ONE HAS CHEESE IN IT!
THIS ONE'S SWEET.
OH-HO.
WHAT KIND OF MEAT IS THIS...?

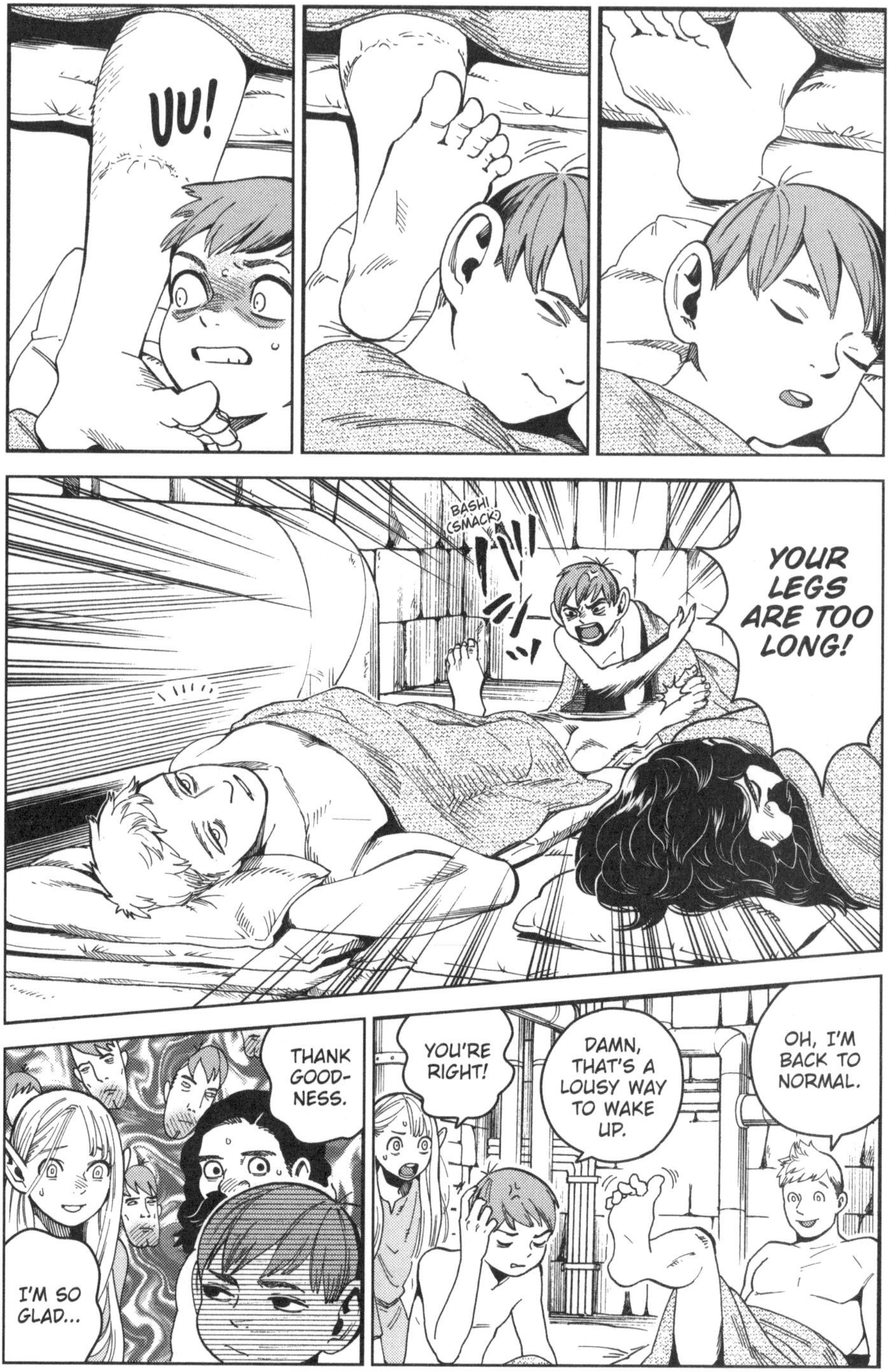
UU!
BASHI (SMACK)
YOUR LEGS ARE TOO LONG!
OH, I'M BACK TO NORMAL.
DAMN, THAT'S A LOUSY WAY TO WAKE UP.
YOU'RE RIGHT!
THANK GOODNESS.
I'M SO GLAD...

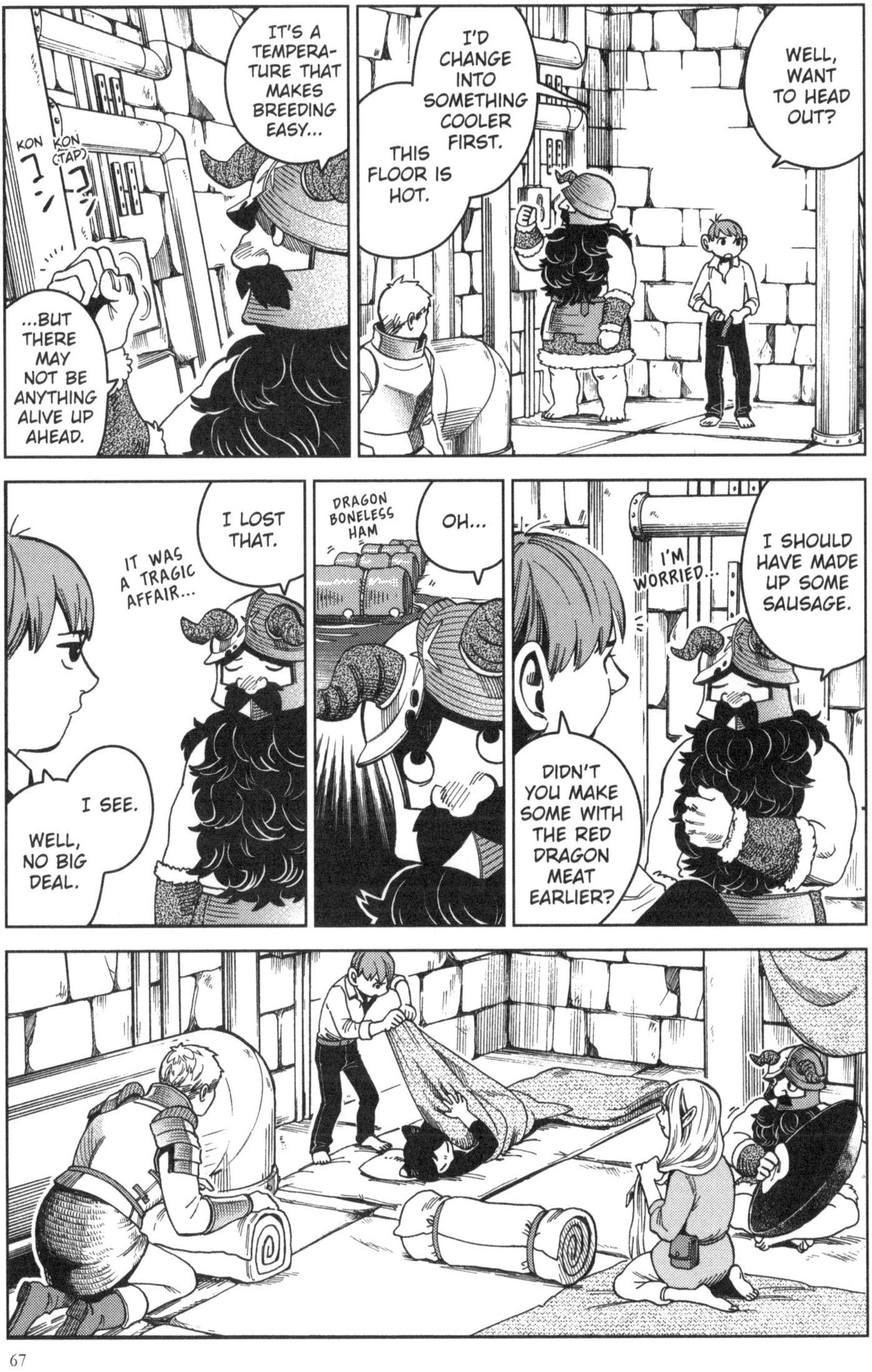
WELL, WANT TO HEAD OUT?
I'D CHANGE INTO SOMETHING COOLER FIRST.
THIS FLOOR IS HOT.
IT'S A TEMPERATURE THAT MAKES BREEDING EASY...
KON KON (TAP)
...BUT THERE MAY NOT BE ANYTHING ALIVE UP AHEAD.
I SHOULD HAVE MADE UP SOME SAUSAGE.
I'M WORRIED...
DIDN'T YOU MAKE SOME WITH THE RED DRAGON MEAT EARLIER?
OH...
DRAGON BONELESS HAM
I LOST THAT.
IT WAS A TRAGIC AFFAIR...
I SEE.
WELL, NO BIG DEAL.

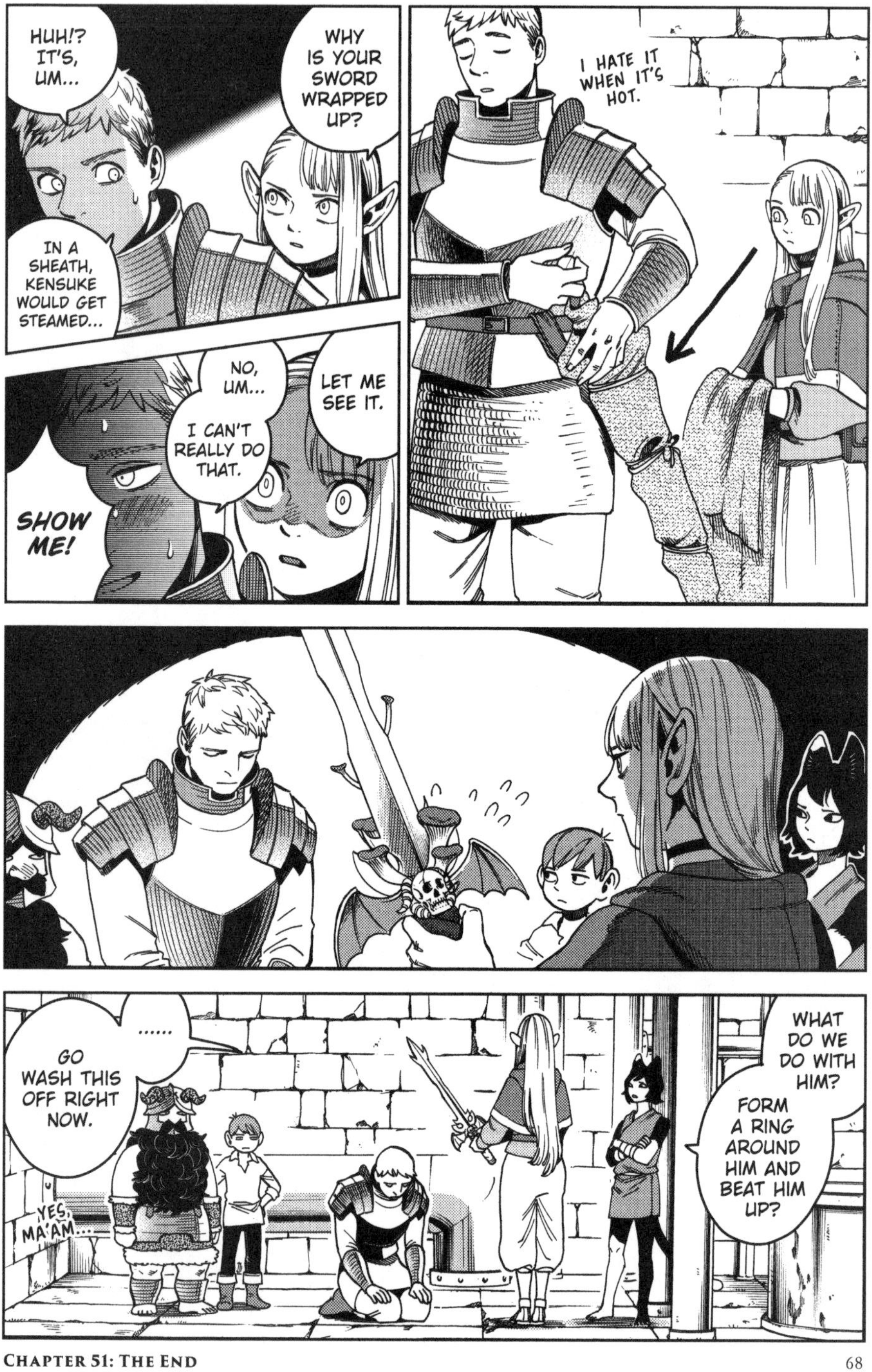
I HATE IT WHEN IT'S HOT.
WHY IS YOUR SWORD WRAPPED UP?
HUH!? IT'S, UM...
IN A SHEATH, KENSUKE WOULD GET STEAMED...
LET ME SEE IT.
NO, UM...
I CAN'T REALLY DO THAT.
SHOW ME!
WHAT DO WE DO WITH HIM?
FORM A RING AROUND HIM AND BEAT HIM UP?
......
GO WASH THIS OFF RIGHT NOW.
YES, MA'AM...

52. Bacon and Eggs

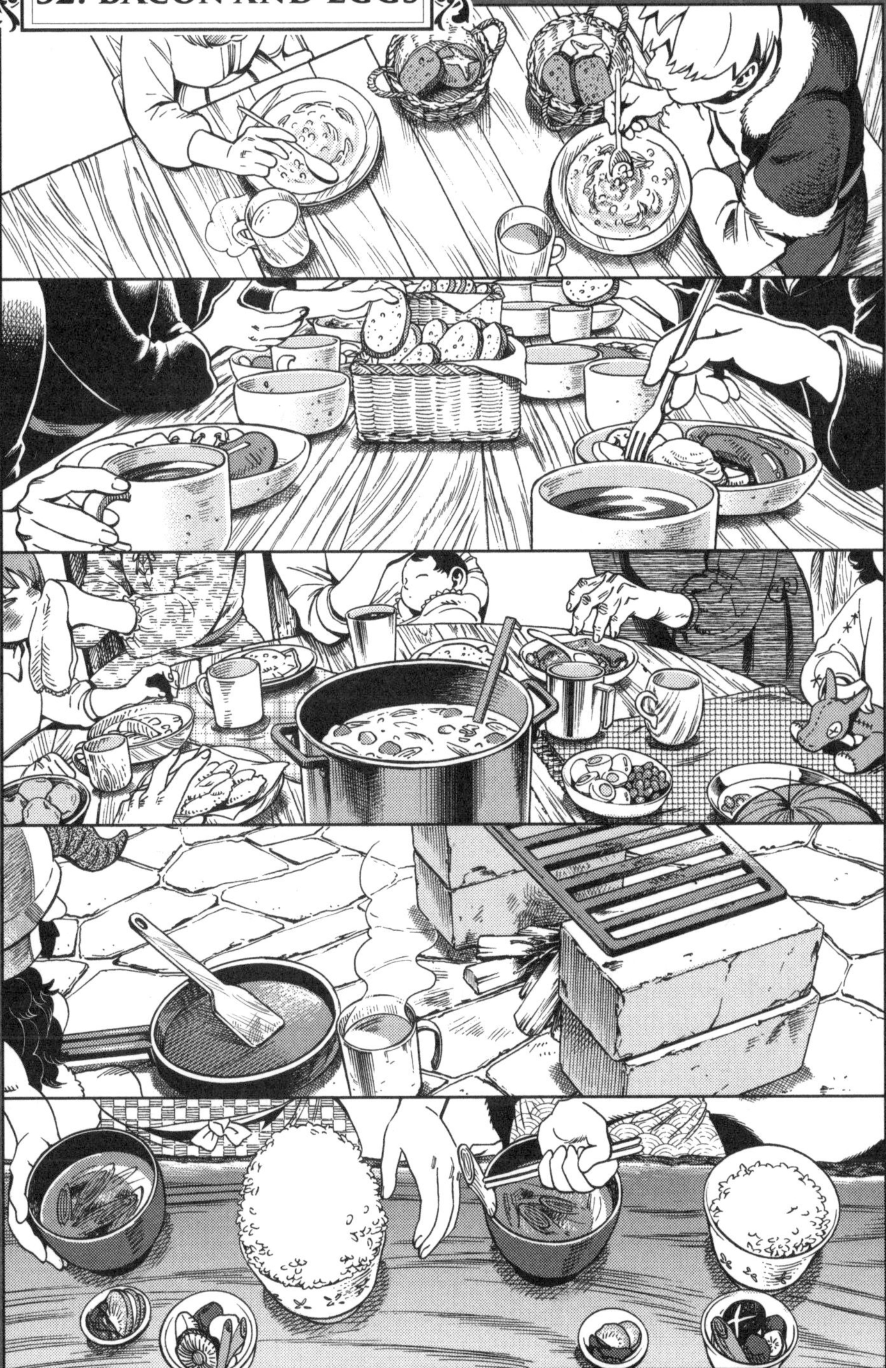

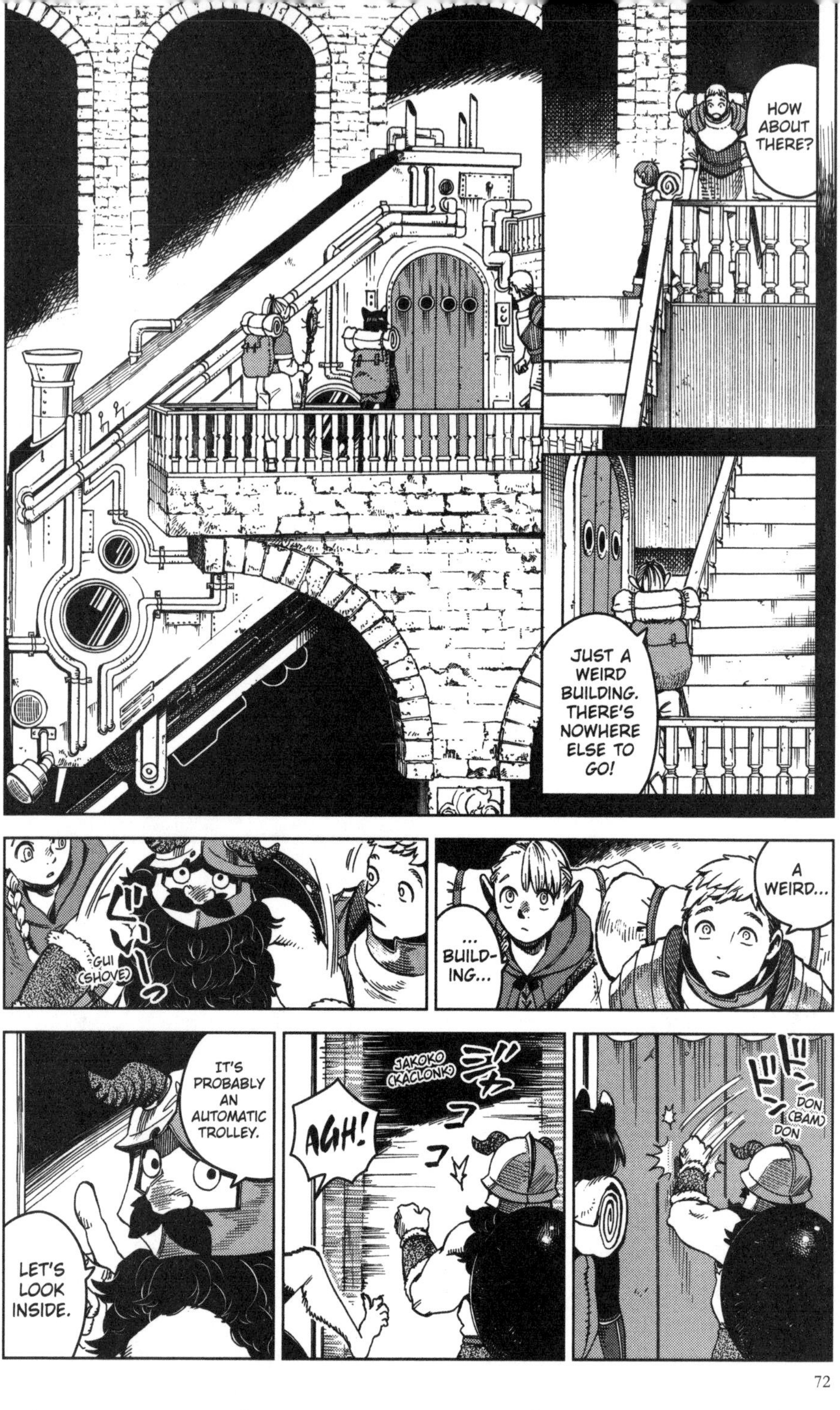
HOW ABOUT THERE?
JUST A WEIRD BUILDING. THERE'S NOWHERE ELSE TO GO!
A WEIRD...
...BUILDING...
GUI (SHOVE)
DON (BAM) DON
JAKOKO (KACLONK)
AGH!
IT'S PROBABLY AN AUTOMATIC TROLLEY.
LET'S LOOK INSIDE.

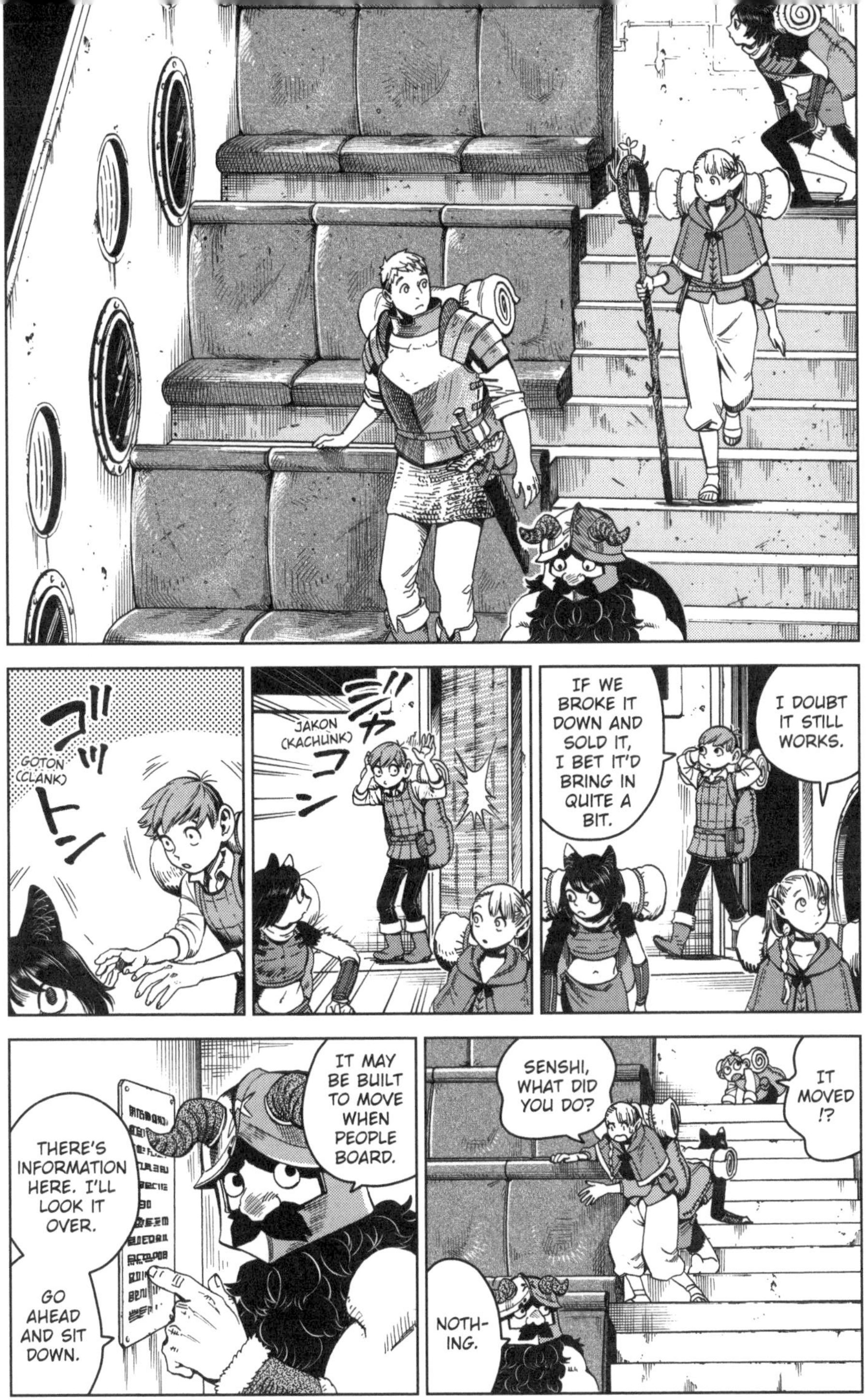
I DOUBT IT STILL WORKS.
IF WE BROKE IT DOWN AND SOLD IT, I BET IT'D BRING IN QUITE A BIT.
JAKON (KACHUNK)
GOTON (CLANK)
IT MOVED !?
SENSHI, WHAT DID YOU DO?
NOTHING.
IT MAY BE BUILT TO MOVE WHEN PEOPLE BOARD.
THERE'S INFORMATION HERE. I'LL LOOK IT OVER.
GO AHEAD AND SIT DOWN.

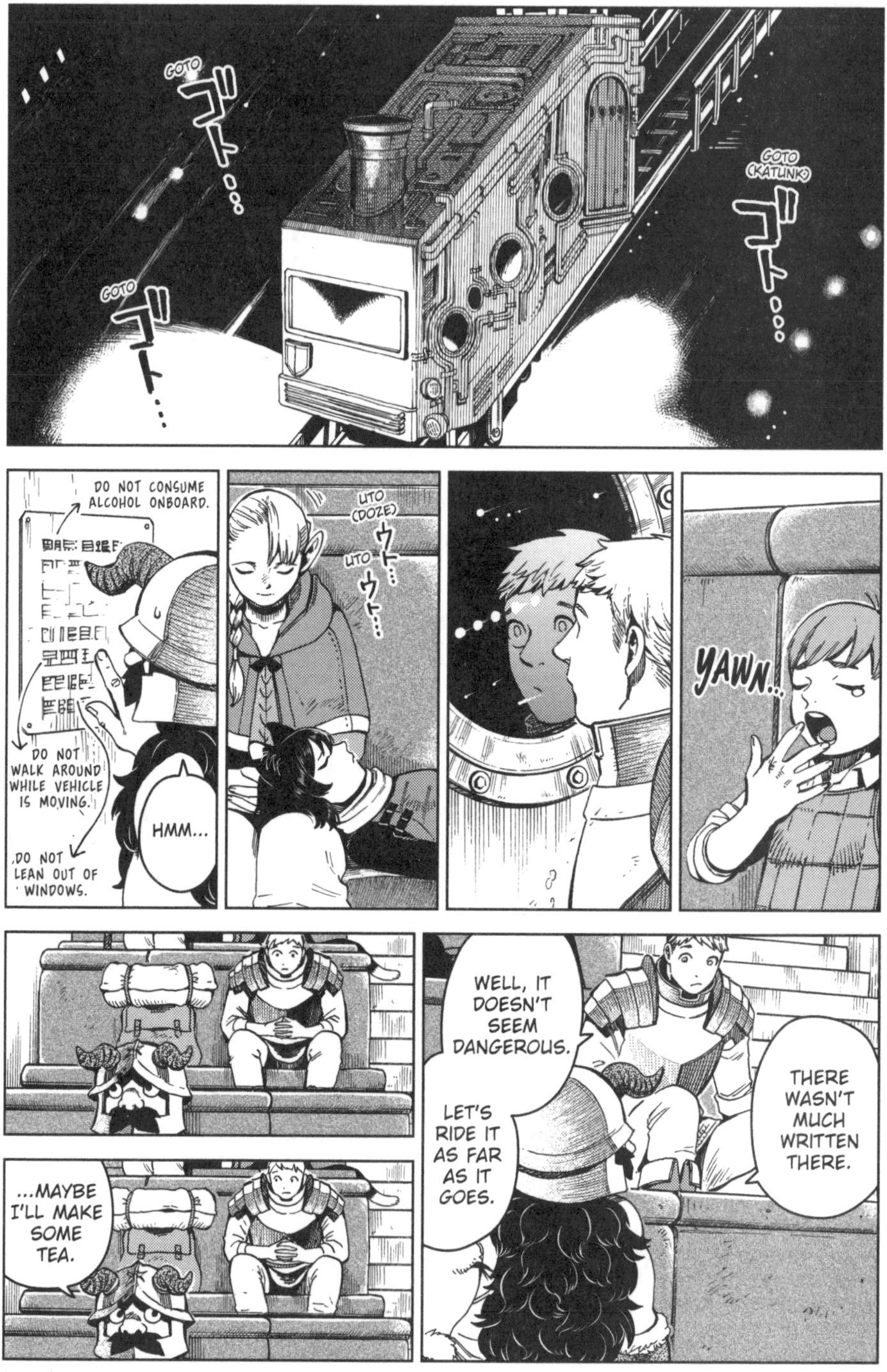
GOTO (KATUNK)
ゴト…
GOTO
ゴト…
GOTO
ゴト…
YAWN...
UTO (DOZE)
ウト…
UTO
ウト…
DO NOT CONSUME ALCOHOL ONBOARD.
DO NOT WALK AROUND WHILE VEHICLE IS MOVING.
DO NOT LEAN OUT OF WINDOWS.
HMM...
THERE WASN'T MUCH WRITTEN THERE.
WELL, IT DOESN'T SEEM DANGEROUS.
LET'S RIDE IT AS FAR AS IT GOES.
...MAYBE I'LL MAKE SOME TEA.

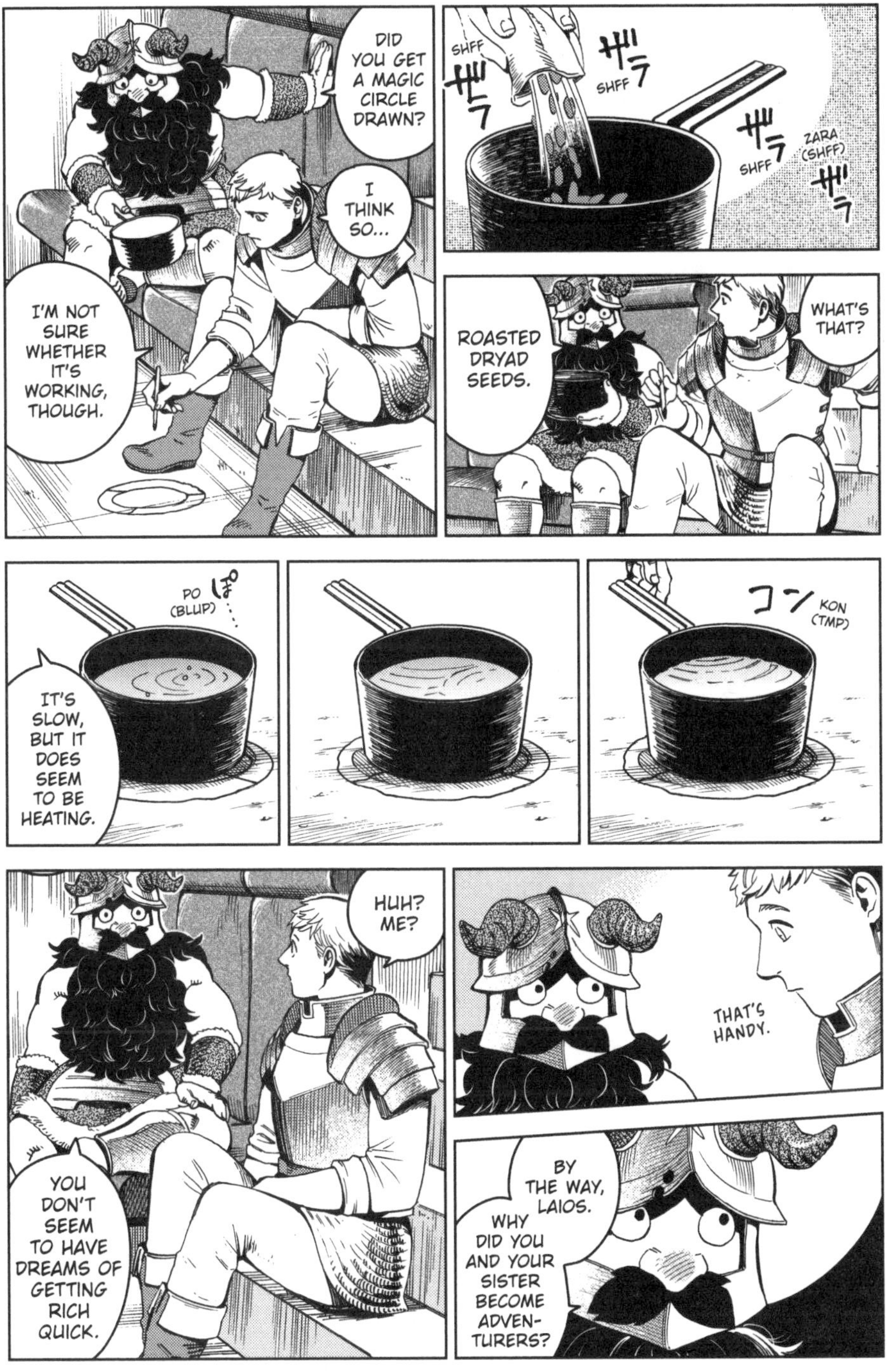
ザラ
ZARA (SHFF)
ザラ
SHFF
ザラ
SHFF
ザラ
SHFF
WHAT'S THAT?
ROASTED DRYAD SEEDS.
DID YOU GET A MAGIC CIRCLE DRAWN?
I THINK SO...
I'M NOT SURE WHETHER IT'S WORKING, THOUGH.
コン
KON (TMP)
ぽ
PO (BLUP)
IT'S SLOW, BUT IT DOES SEEM TO BE HEATING.
THAT'S HANDY.
BY THE WAY, LAIOS.
WHY DID YOU AND YOUR SISTER BECOME ADVEN-TURERS?
HUH? ME?
YOU DON'T SEEM TO HAVE DREAMS OF GETTING RICH QUICK.

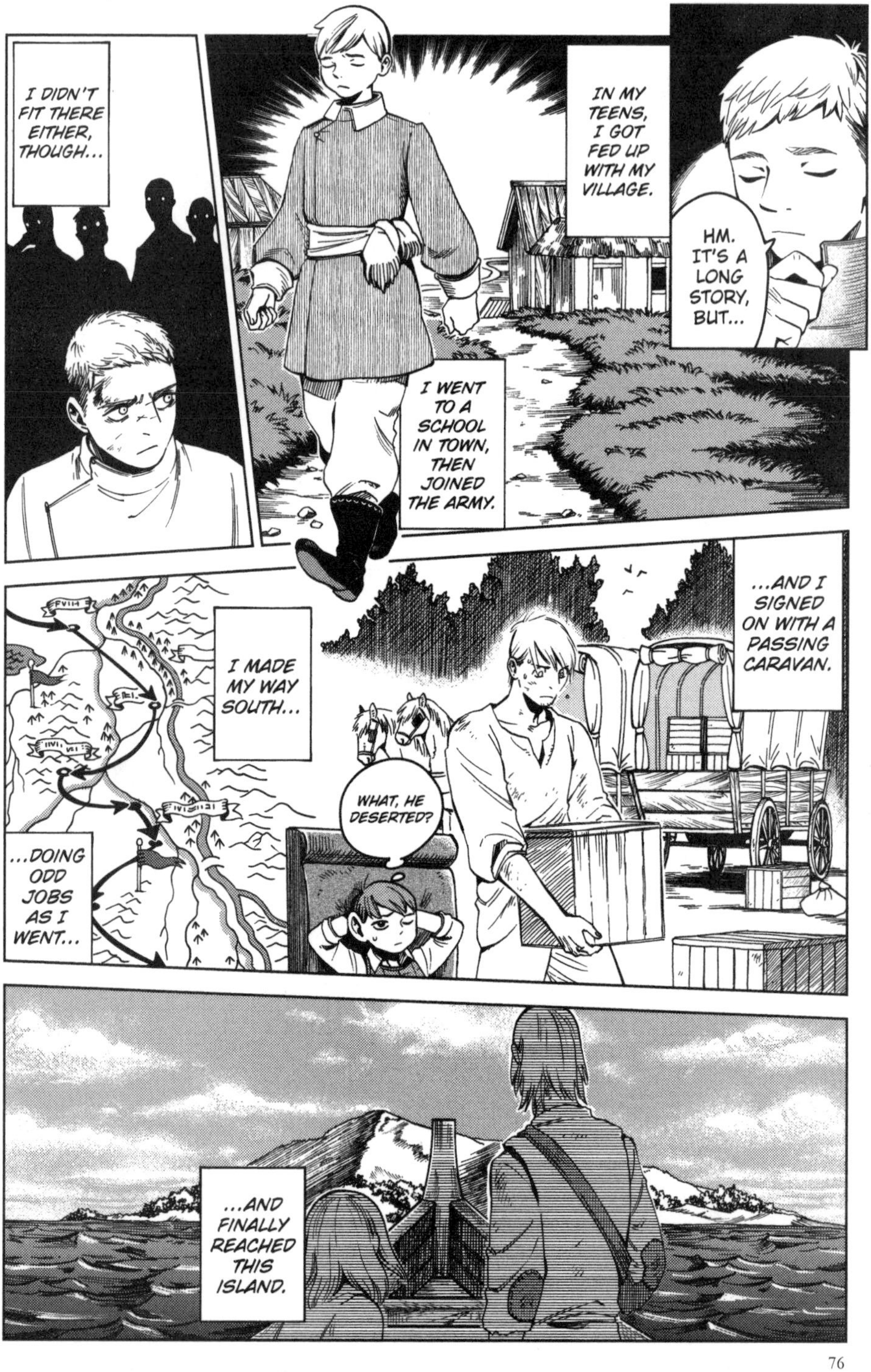
HM. IT'S A LONG STORY, BUT...
IN MY TEENS, I GOT FED UP WITH MY VILLAGE.
I WENT TO A SCHOOL IN TOWN, THEN JOINED THE ARMY.
I DIDN'T FIT THERE EITHER, THOUGH...
...AND I SIGNED ON WITH A PASSING CARAVAN.
WHAT, HE DESERTED?
I MADE MY WAY SOUTH...
...DOING ODD JOBS AS I WENT...
...AND FINALLY REACHED THIS ISLAND.

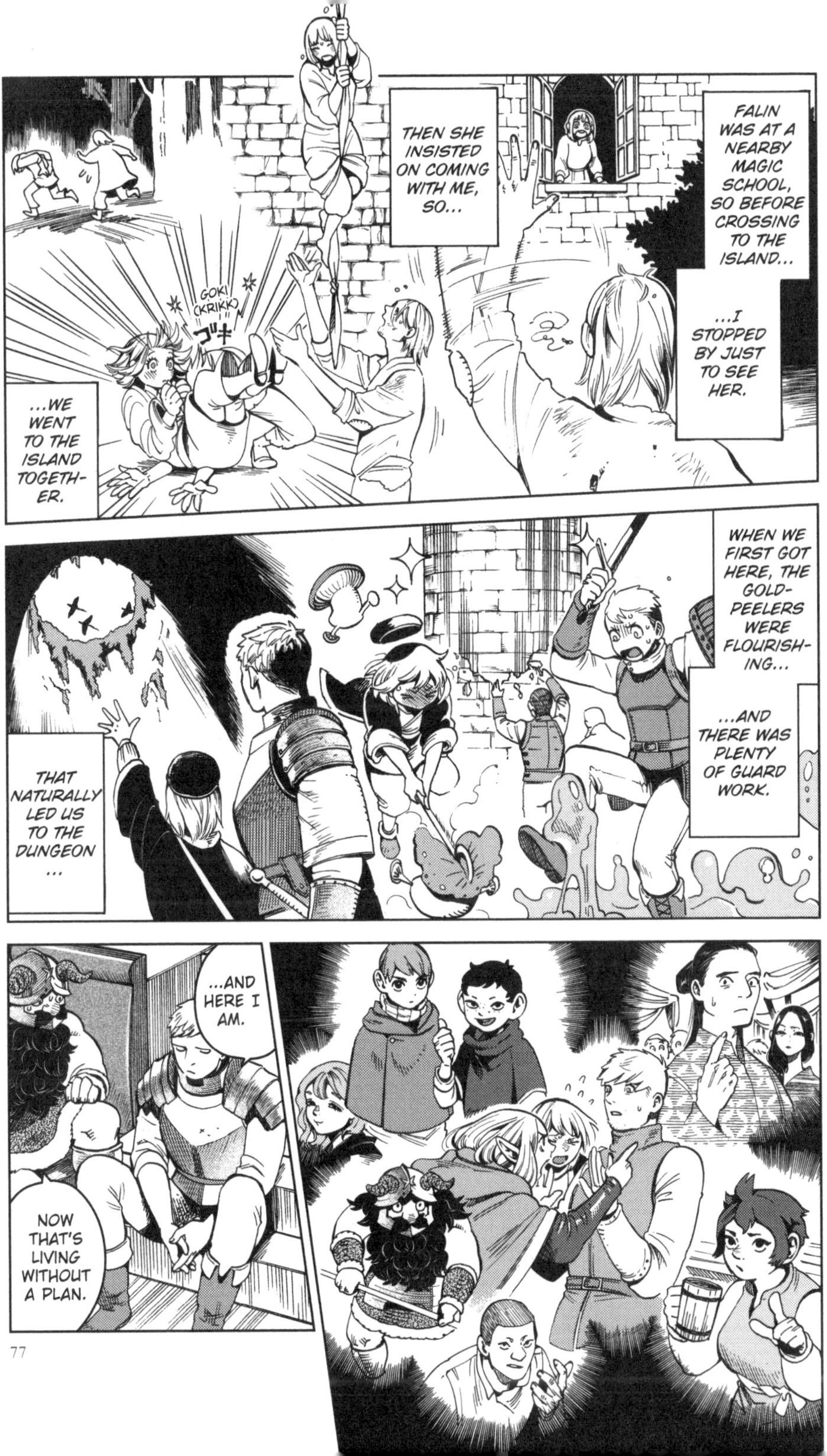
FALIN WAS AT A NEARBY MAGIC SCHOOL, SO BEFORE CROSSING TO THE ISLAND...
...I STOPPED BY JUST TO SEE HER.
THEN SHE INSISTED ON COMING WITH ME, SO...
GOKI (KRIKK)
ゴキ
...WE WENT TO THE ISLAND TOGETHER.
WHEN WE FIRST GOT HERE, THE GOLD-PEELERS WERE FLOURISHING...
...AND THERE WAS PLENTY OF GUARD WORK.
THAT NATURALLY LED US TO THE DUNGEON...
...AND HERE I AM.
NOW THAT'S LIVING WITHOUT A PLAN.

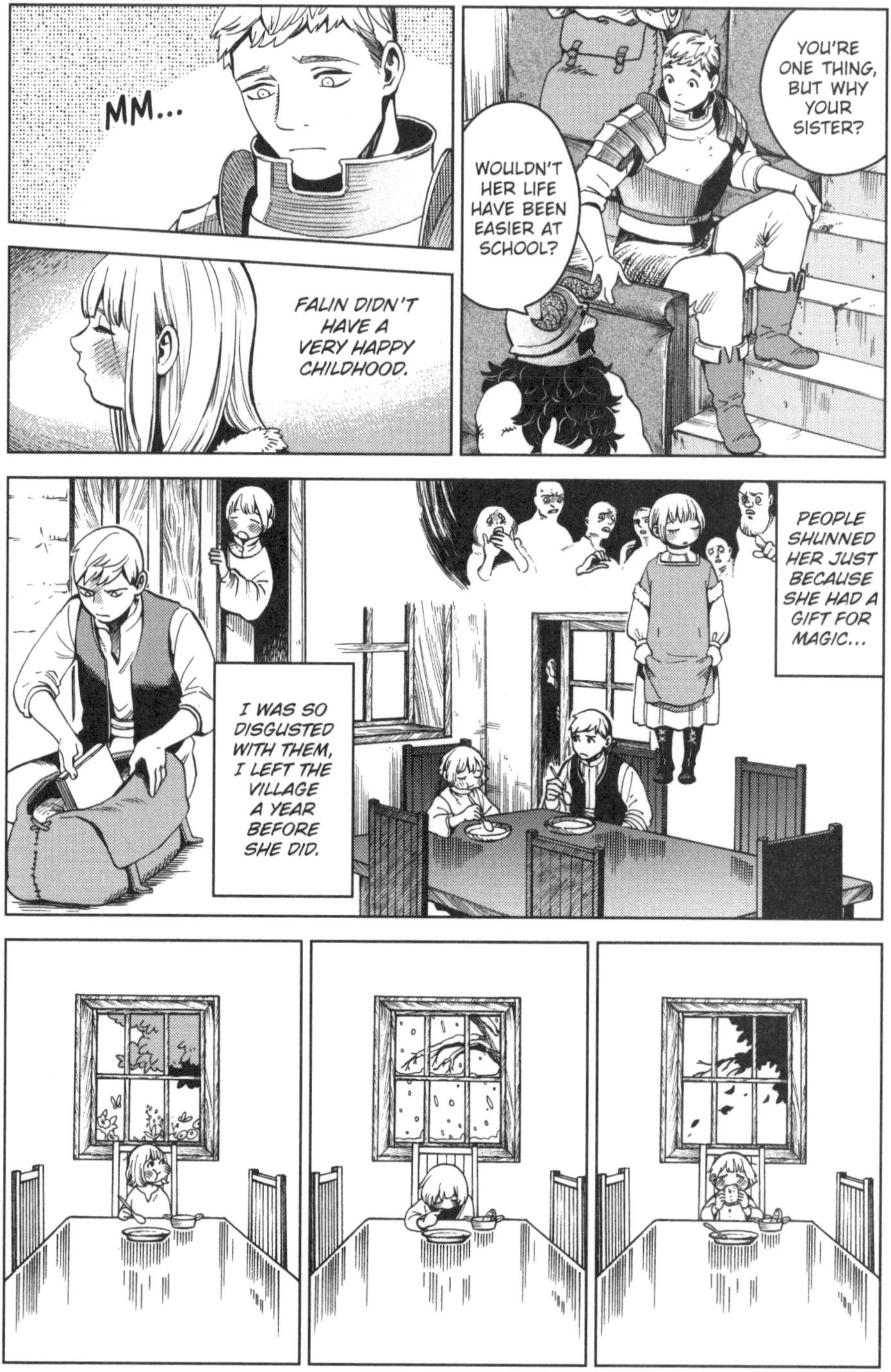
YOU'RE ONE THING, BUT WHY YOUR SISTER?
WOULDN'T HER LIFE HAVE BEEN EASIER AT SCHOOL?
MM...
FALIN DIDN'T HAVE A VERY HAPPY CHILDHOOD.
PEOPLE SHUNNED HER JUST BECAUSE SHE HAD A GIFT FOR MAGIC...
I WAS SO DISGUSTED WITH THEM, I LEFT THE VILLAGE A YEAR BEFORE SHE DID.

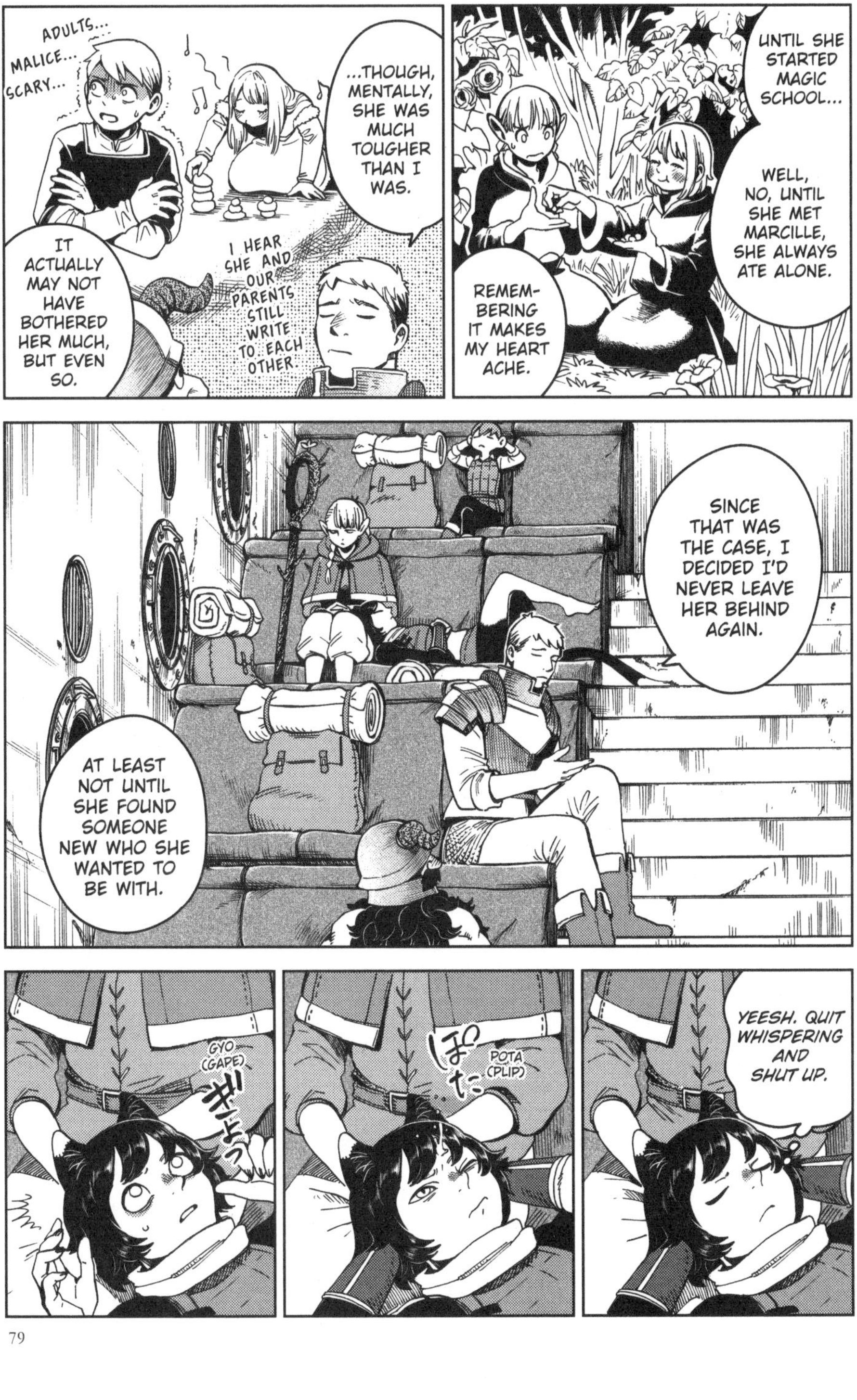
UNTIL SHE STARTED MAGIC SCHOOL...
WELL, NO, UNTIL SHE MET MARCILLE, SHE ALWAYS ATE ALONE.
REMEM-BERING IT MAKES MY HEART ACHE.
...THOUGH, MENTALLY, SHE WAS MUCH TOUGHER THAN I WAS.
ADULTS... MALICE... SCARY...
I HEAR SHE AND OUR PARENTS STILL WRITE TO EACH OTHER.
IT ACTUALLY MAY NOT HAVE BOTHERED HER MUCH, BUT EVEN SO.
SINCE THAT WAS THE CASE, I DECIDED I'D NEVER LEAVE HER BEHIND AGAIN.
AT LEAST NOT UNTIL SHE FOUND SOMEONE NEW WHO SHE WANTED TO BE WITH.
YEESH. QUIT WHISPERING AND SHUT UP.
POTA (PLIP)
GYO (GAPE)

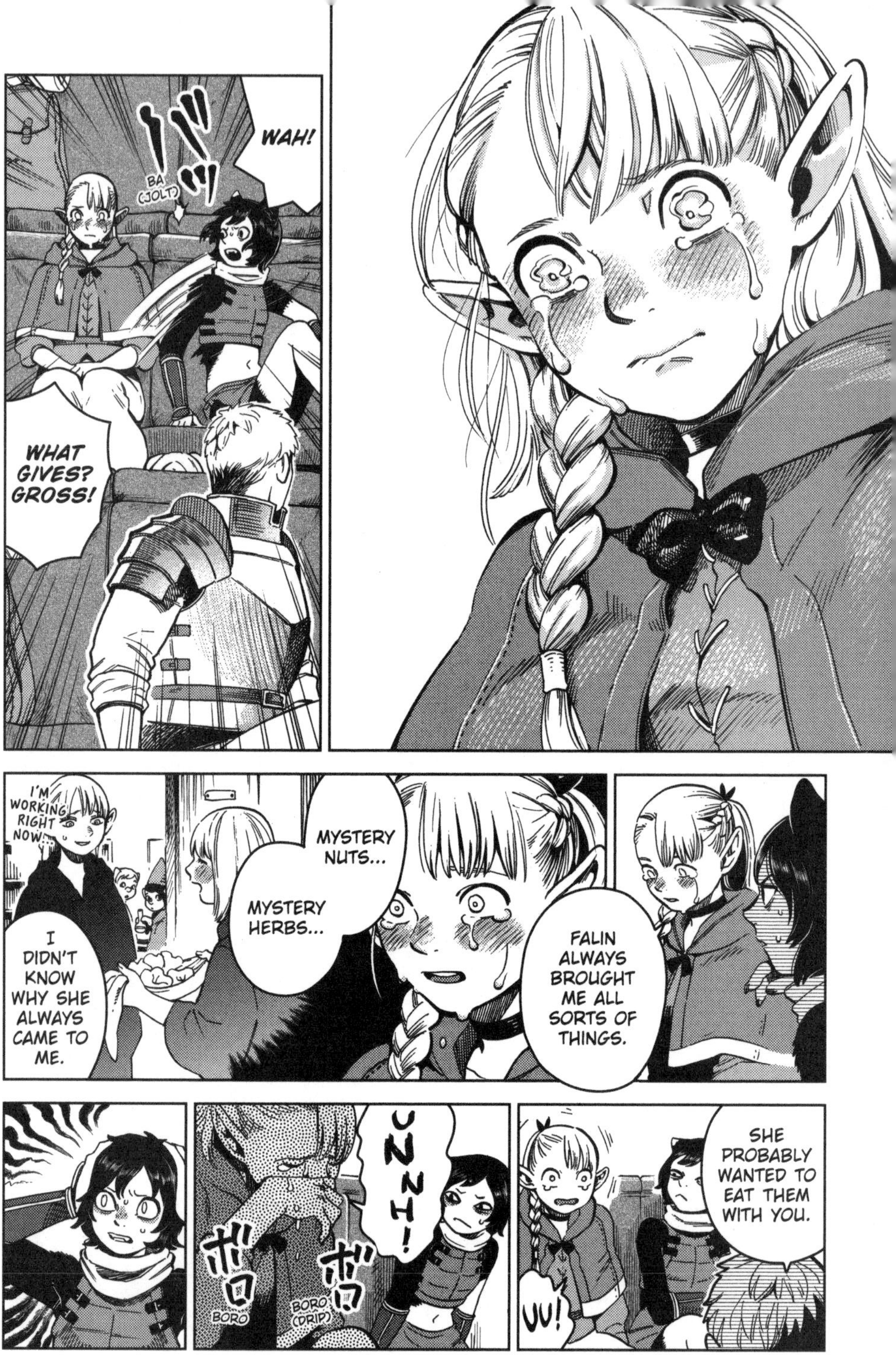
WAH!
BA (JOLT)
WHAT GIVES? GROSS!
FALIN ALWAYS BROUGHT ME ALL SORTS OF THINGS.
MYSTERY NUTS...
MYSTERY HERBS...
I'M WORKING RIGHT NOW...
I DIDN'T KNOW WHY SHE ALWAYS CAME TO ME.
SHE PROBABLY WANTED TO EAT THEM WITH YOU.
UU!
UNNH!
BORO (DRIP)
BORO

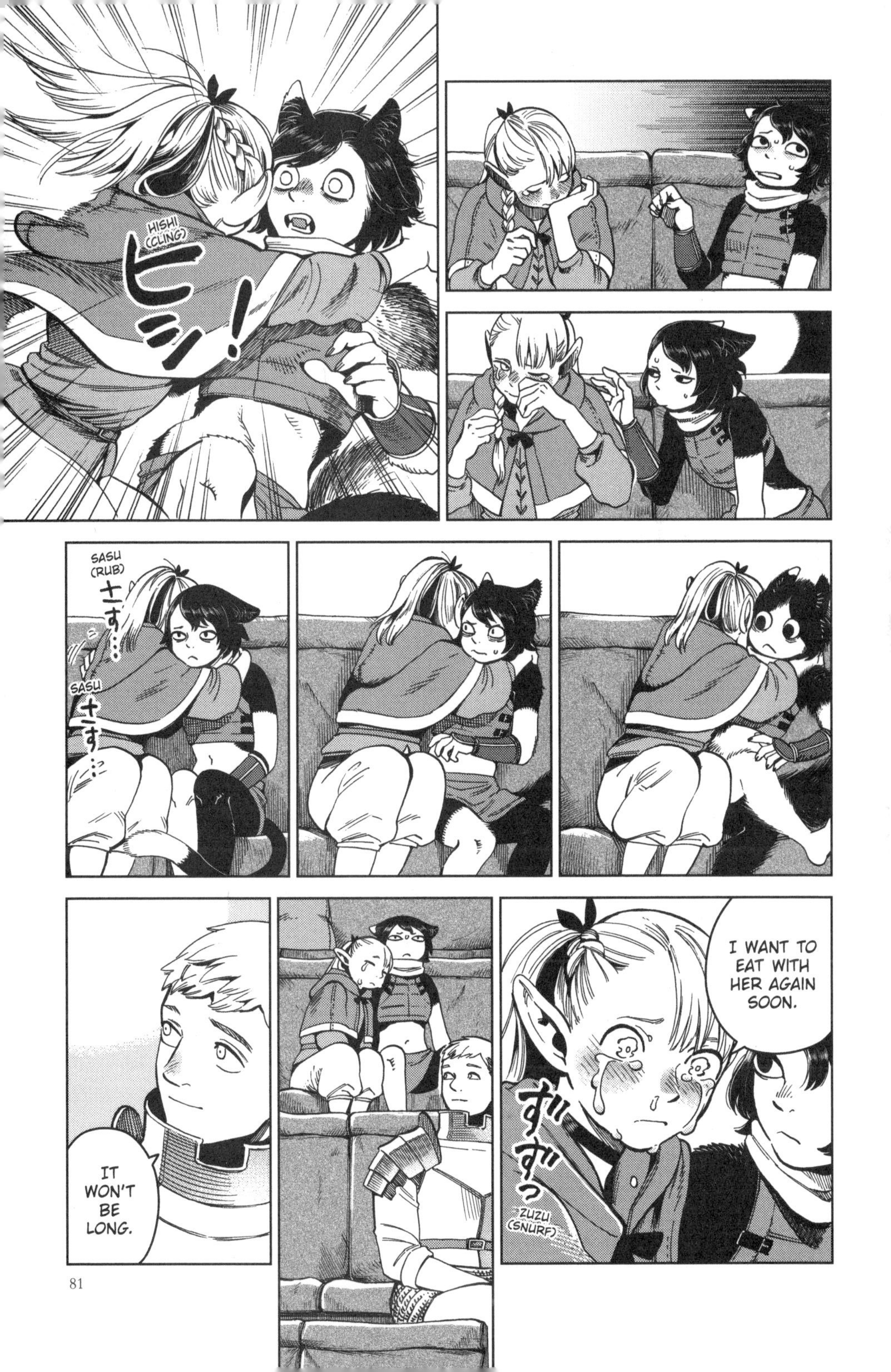
HISHI (CLING)
ヒシ！
SASU (RUB)
さす…
SASU
さす…
I WANT TO EAT WITH HER AGAIN SOON.
ずずっ
ZUZU (SNURF)
IT WON'T BE LONG.

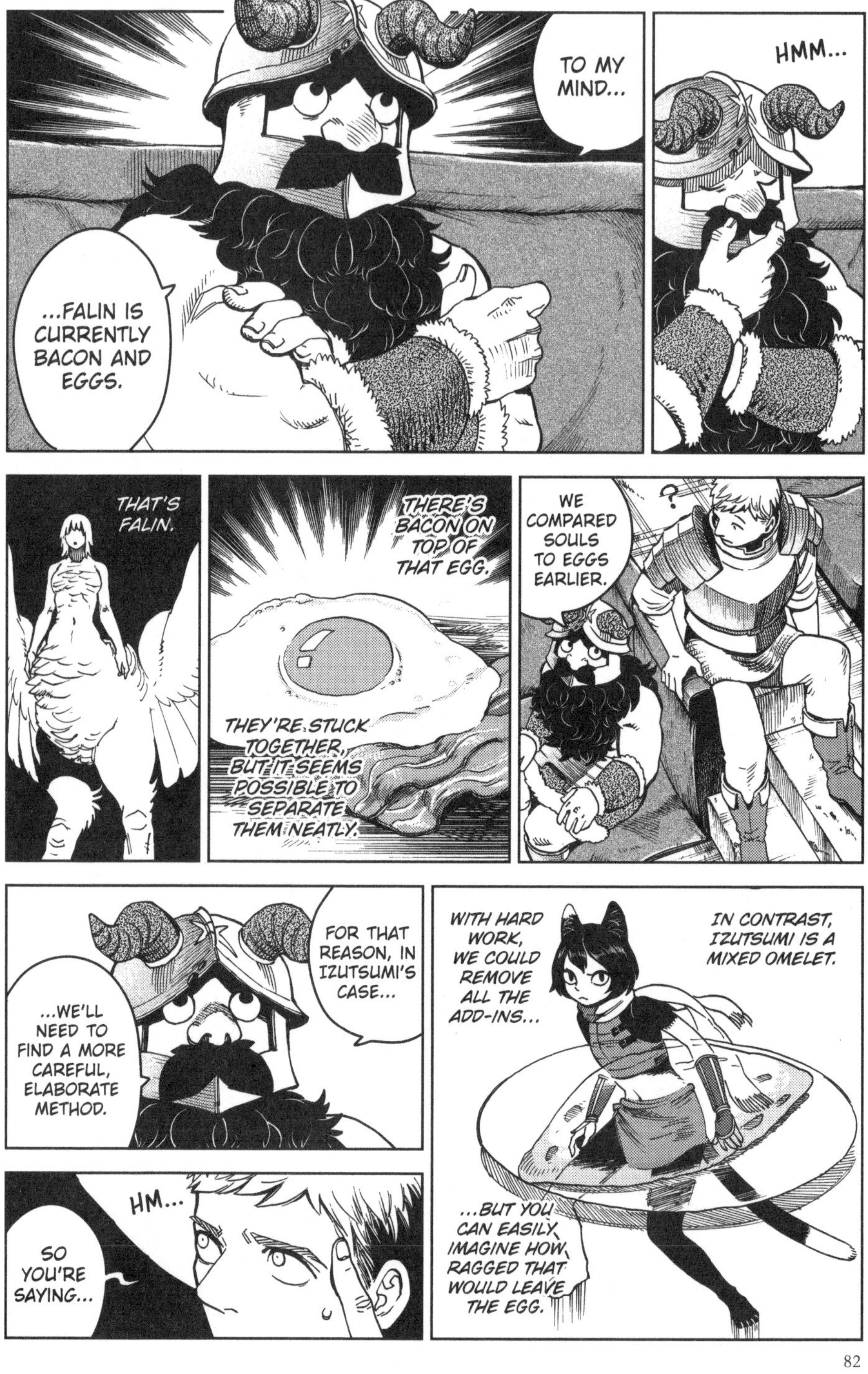
HMM...
TO MY MIND...
...FALIN IS CURRENTLY BACON AND EGGS.
WE COMPARED SOULS TO EGGS EARLIER.
?
THERE'S BACON ON TOP OF THAT EGG.
THEY'RE STUCK TOGETHER, BUT IT SEEMS POSSIBLE TO SEPARATE THEM NEATLY.
THAT'S FALIN.
IN CONTRAST, IZUTSUMI IS A MIXED OMELET.
WITH HARD WORK, WE COULD REMOVE ALL THE ADD-INS...
...BUT YOU CAN EASILY IMAGINE HOW RAGGED THAT WOULD LEAVE THE EGG.
FOR THAT REASON, IN IZUTSUMI'S CASE...
...WE'LL NEED TO FIND A MORE CAREFUL, ELABORATE METHOD.
HM...
SO YOU'RE SAYING...

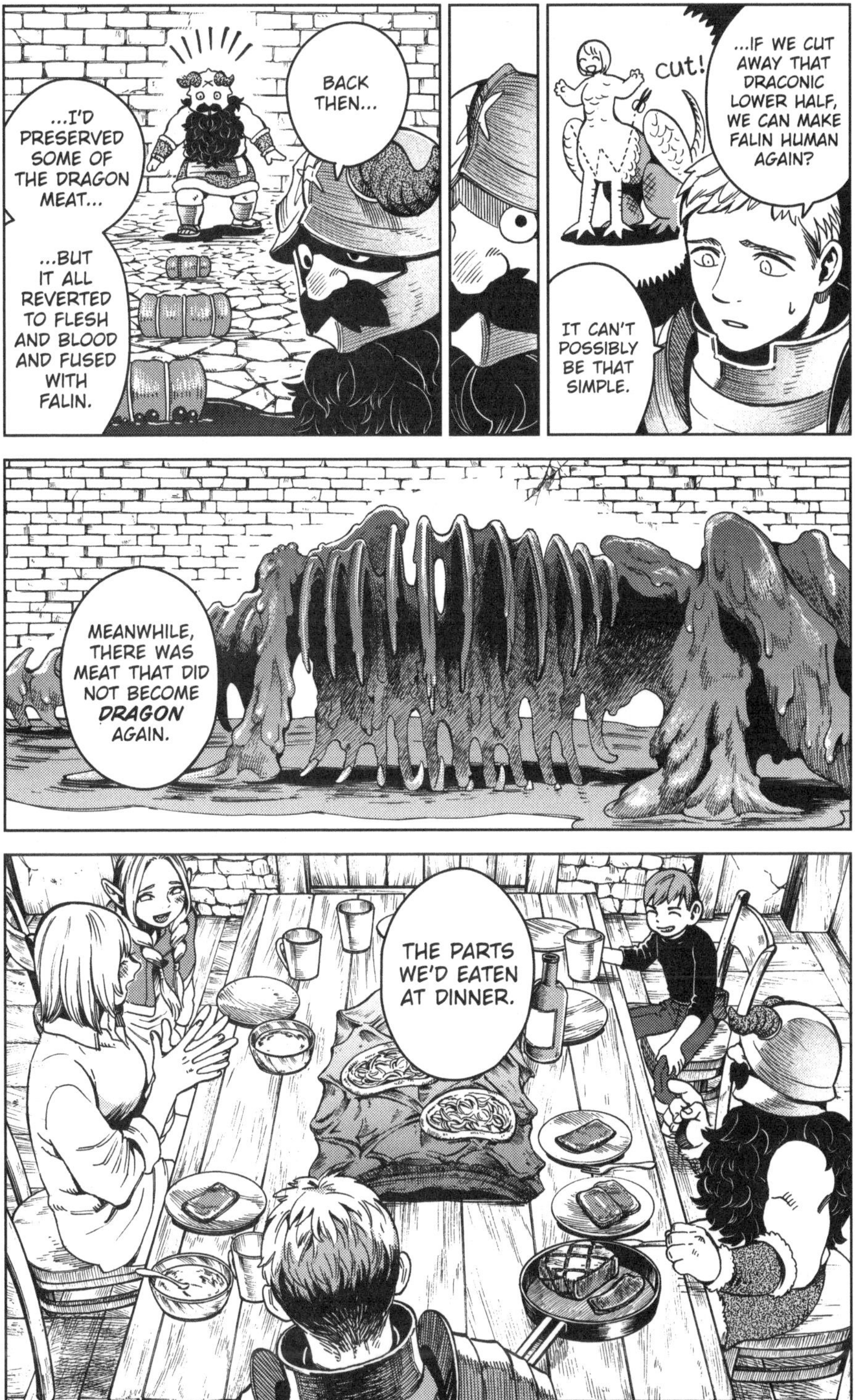
...IF WE CUT AWAY THAT DRACONIC LOWER HALF, WE CAN MAKE FALIN HUMAN AGAIN?
cut!
IT CAN'T POSSIBLY BE THAT SIMPLE.
BACK THEN...
...I'D PRESERVED SOME OF THE DRAGON MEAT...
...BUT IT ALL REVERTED TO FLESH AND BLOOD AND FUSED WITH FALIN.
MEANWHILE, THERE WAS MEAT THAT DID NOT BECOME *DRAGON* AGAIN.
THE PARTS WE'D EATEN AT DINNER.

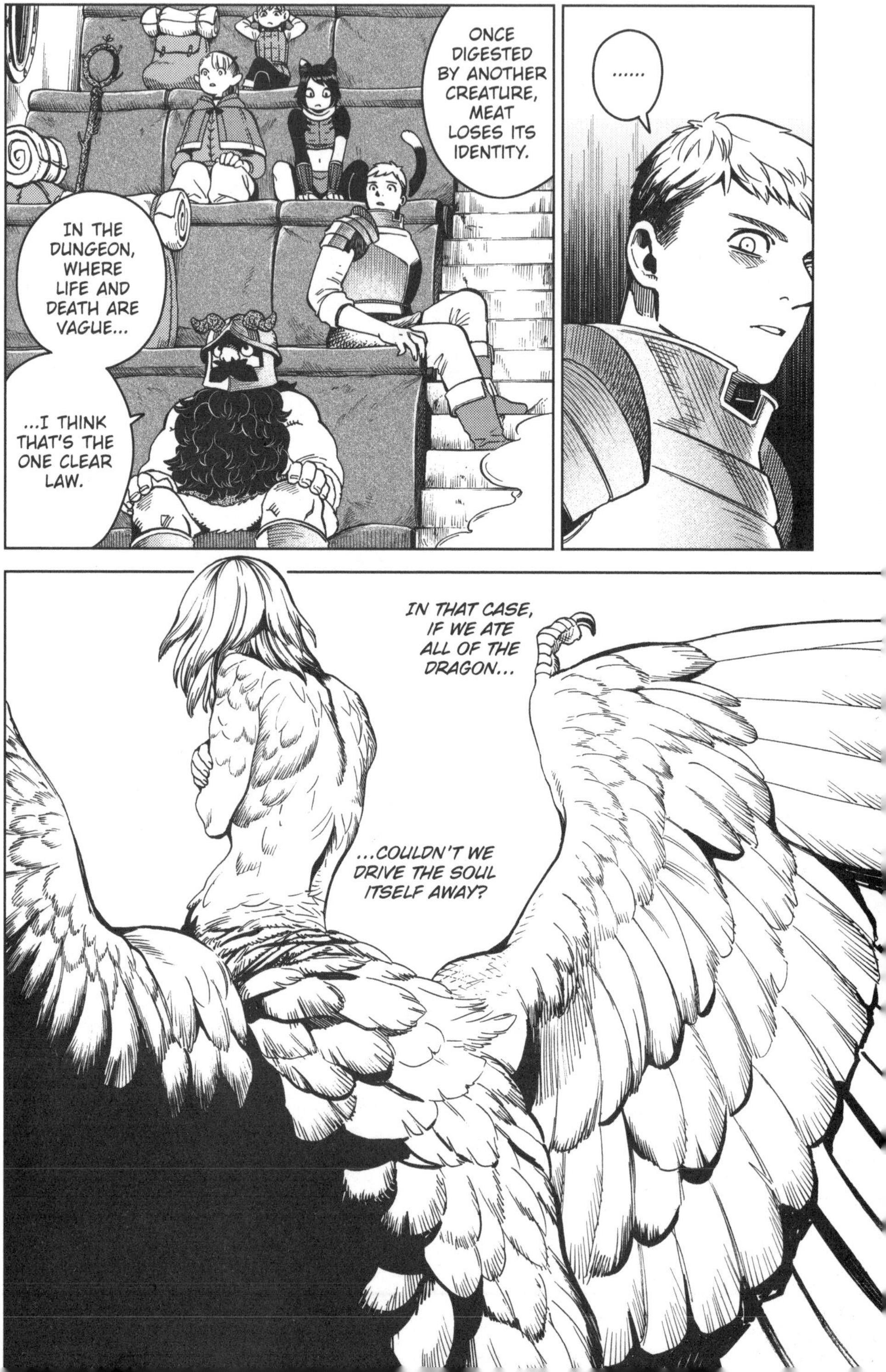
......
ONCE DIGESTED BY ANOTHER CREATURE, MEAT LOSES ITS IDENTITY.
IN THE DUNGEON, WHERE LIFE AND DEATH ARE VAGUE...
...I THINK THAT'S THE ONE CLEAR LAW.
IN THAT CASE, IF WE ATE ALL OF THE DRAGON...
...COULDN'T WE DRIVE THE SOUL ITSELF AWAY?

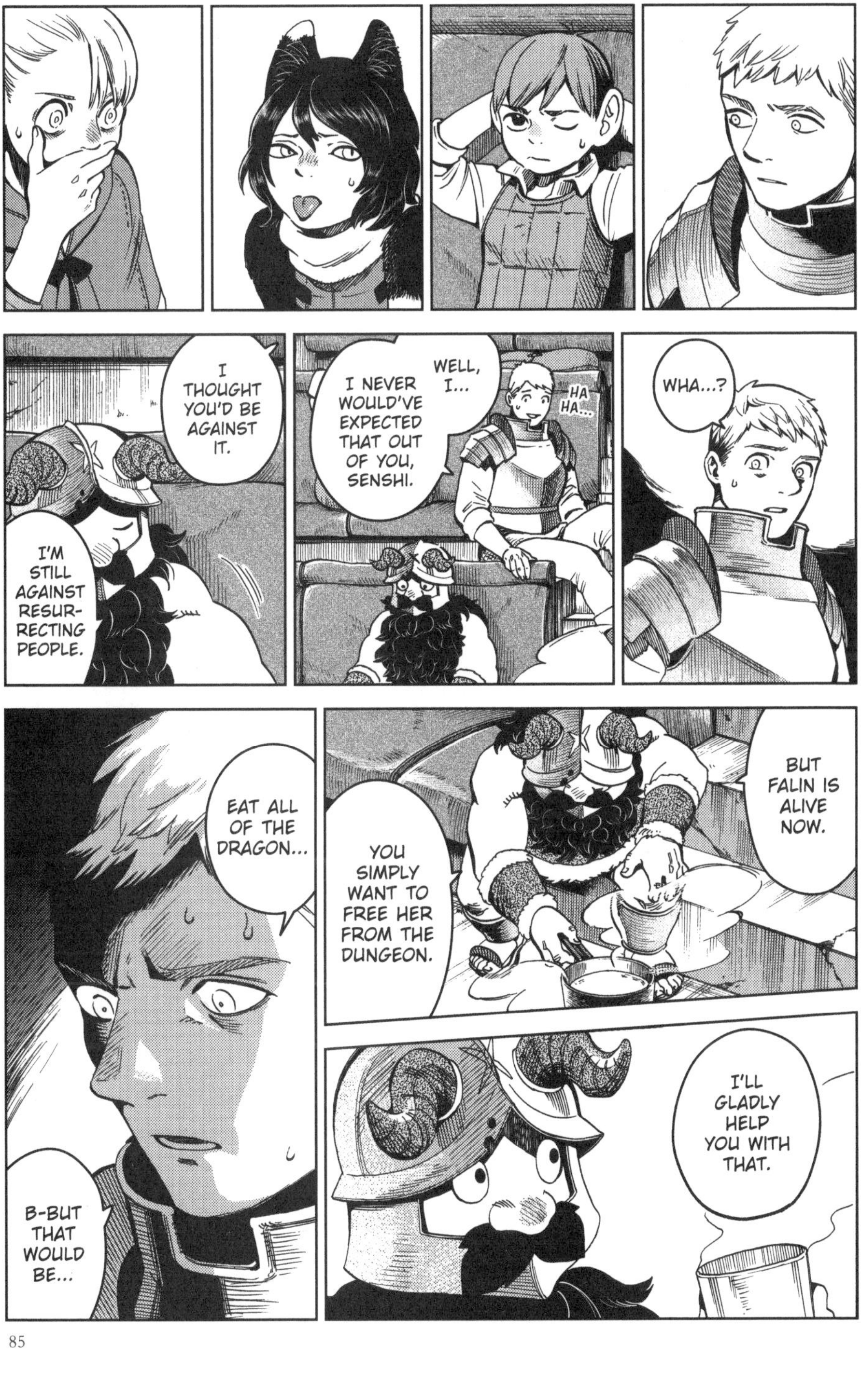
WHA...?
WELL, I...
HA HA...
I NEVER WOULD'VE EXPECTED THAT OUT OF YOU, SENSHI.
I THOUGHT YOU'D BE AGAINST IT.
I'M STILL AGAINST RESUR-RECTING PEOPLE.
BUT FALIN IS ALIVE NOW.
YOU SIMPLY WANT TO FREE HER FROM THE DUNGEON.
I'LL GLADLY HELP YOU WITH THAT.
EAT ALL OF THE DRAGON...
B-BUT THAT WOULD BE...

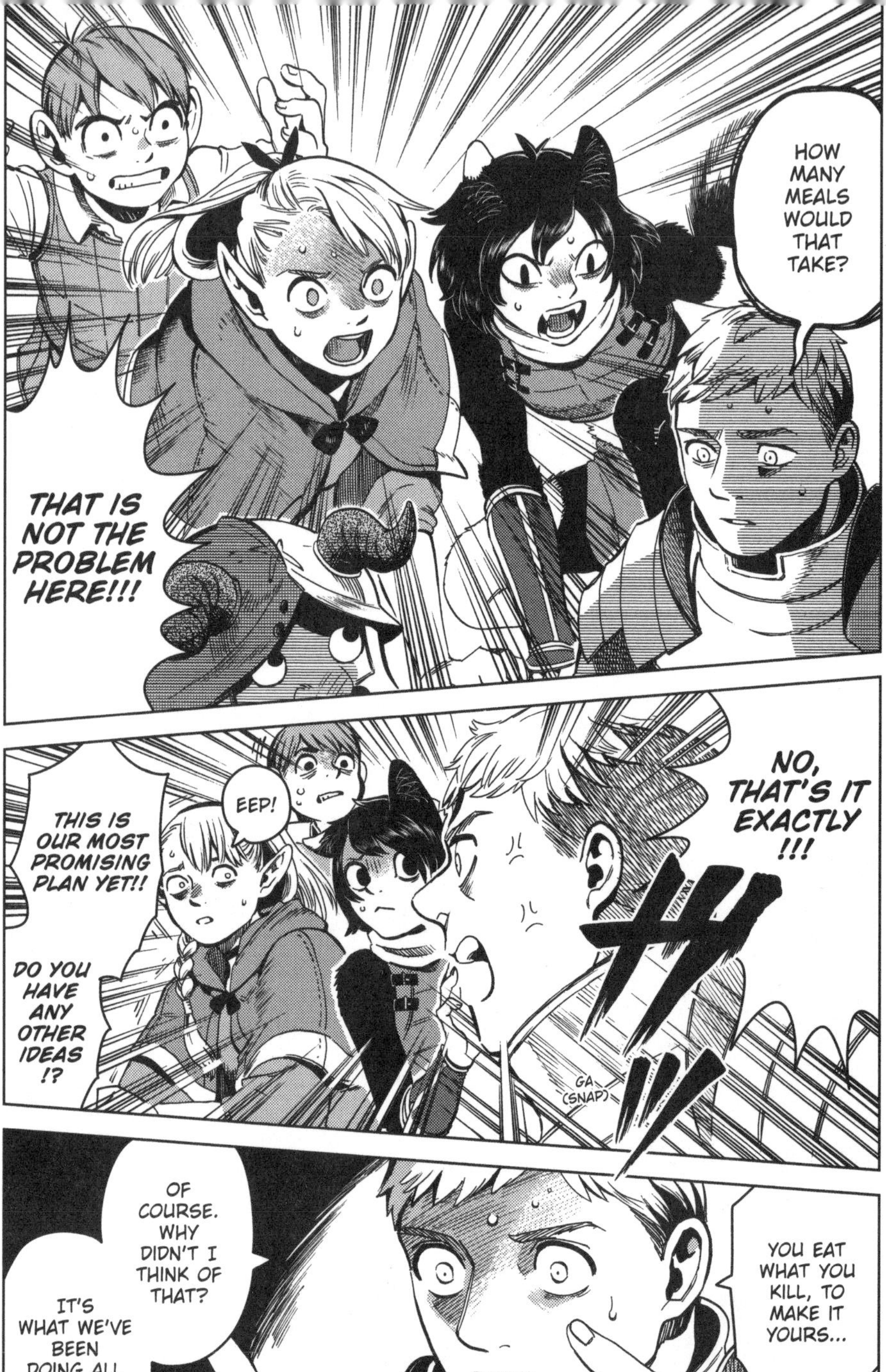
HOW MANY MEALS WOULD THAT TAKE?
THAT IS NOT THE PROBLEM HERE!!!
NO, THAT'S IT EXACTLY !!!
EEP!
THIS IS OUR MOST PROMISING PLAN YET!!
DO YOU HAVE ANY OTHER IDEAS !?
GA (SNAP)
YOU EAT WHAT YOU KILL, TO MAKE IT YOURS...
OF COURSE. WHY DIDN'T I THINK OF THAT?
IT'S WHAT WE'VE BEEN DOING ALL ALONG!

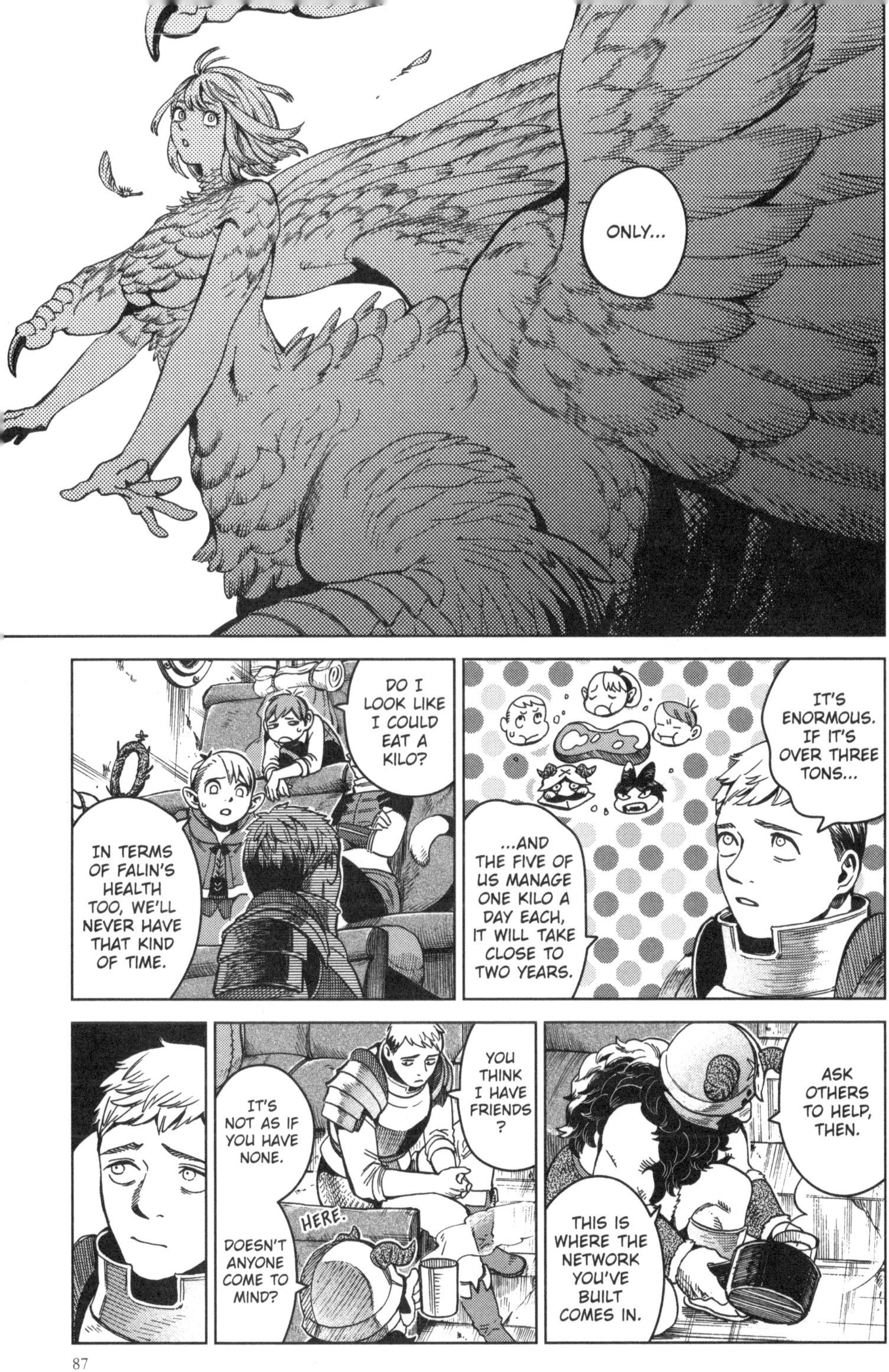
ONLY...
IT'S ENORMOUS. IF IT'S OVER THREE TONS...
...AND THE FIVE OF US MANAGE ONE KILO A DAY EACH, IT WILL TAKE CLOSE TO TWO YEARS.
DO I LOOK LIKE I COULD EAT A KILO?
IN TERMS OF FALIN'S HEALTH TOO, WE'LL NEVER HAVE THAT KIND OF TIME.
ASK OTHERS TO HELP, THEN.
THIS IS WHERE THE NETWORK YOU'VE BUILT COMES IN.
YOU THINK I HAVE FRIENDS?
IT'S NOT AS IF YOU HAVE NONE.
HERE.
DOESN'T ANYONE COME TO MIND?

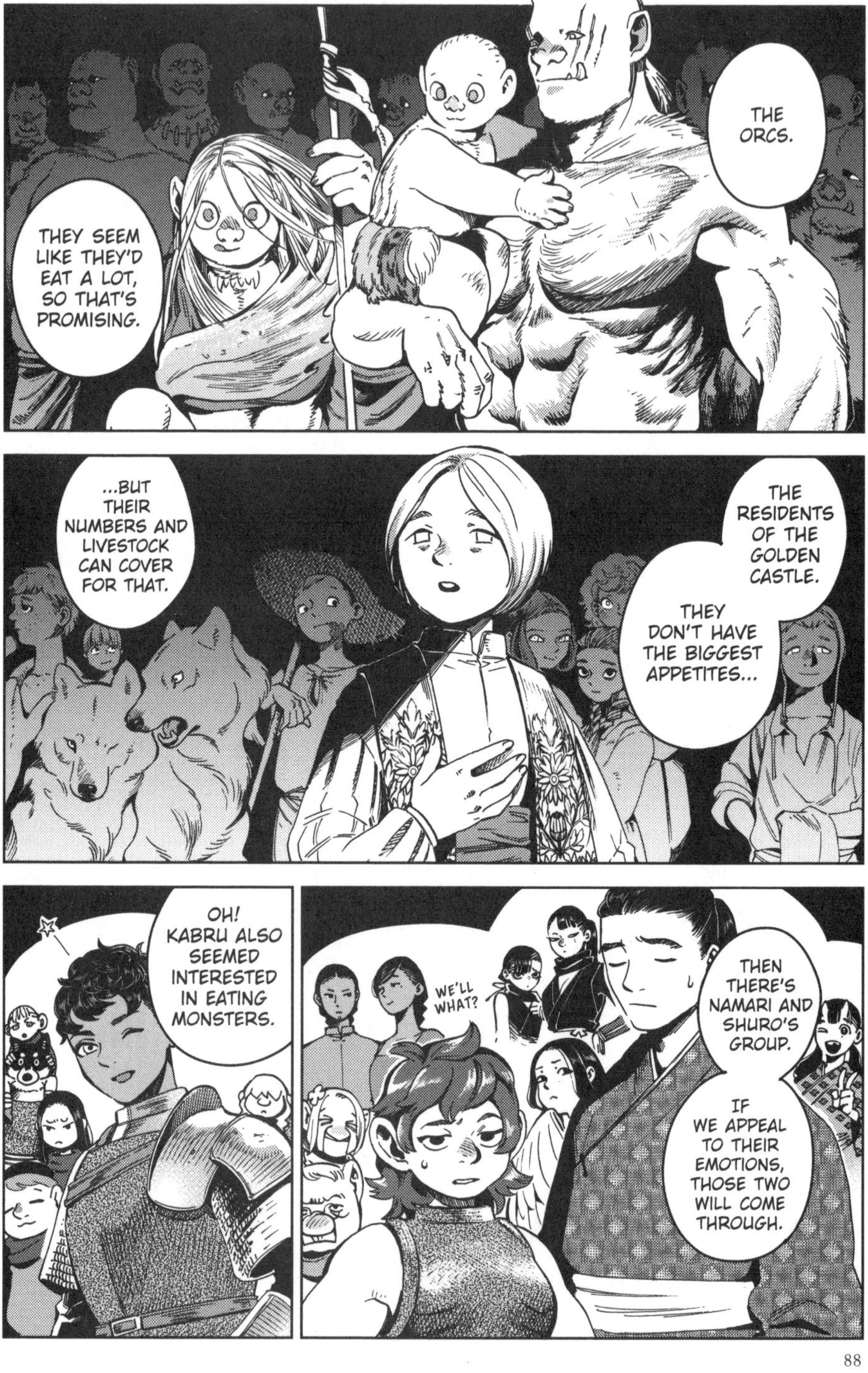
THE ORCS.
THEY SEEM LIKE THEY'D EAT A LOT, SO THAT'S PROMISING.
THE RESIDENTS OF THE GOLDEN CASTLE.
THEY DON'T HAVE THE BIGGEST APPETITES...
...BUT THEIR NUMBERS AND LIVESTOCK CAN COVER FOR THAT.
THEN THERE'S NAMARI AND SHURO'S GROUP.
IF WE APPEAL TO THEIR EMOTIONS, THOSE TWO WILL COME THROUGH.
WE'LL WHAT?
OH! KABRU ALSO SEEMED INTERESTED IN EATING MONSTERS.

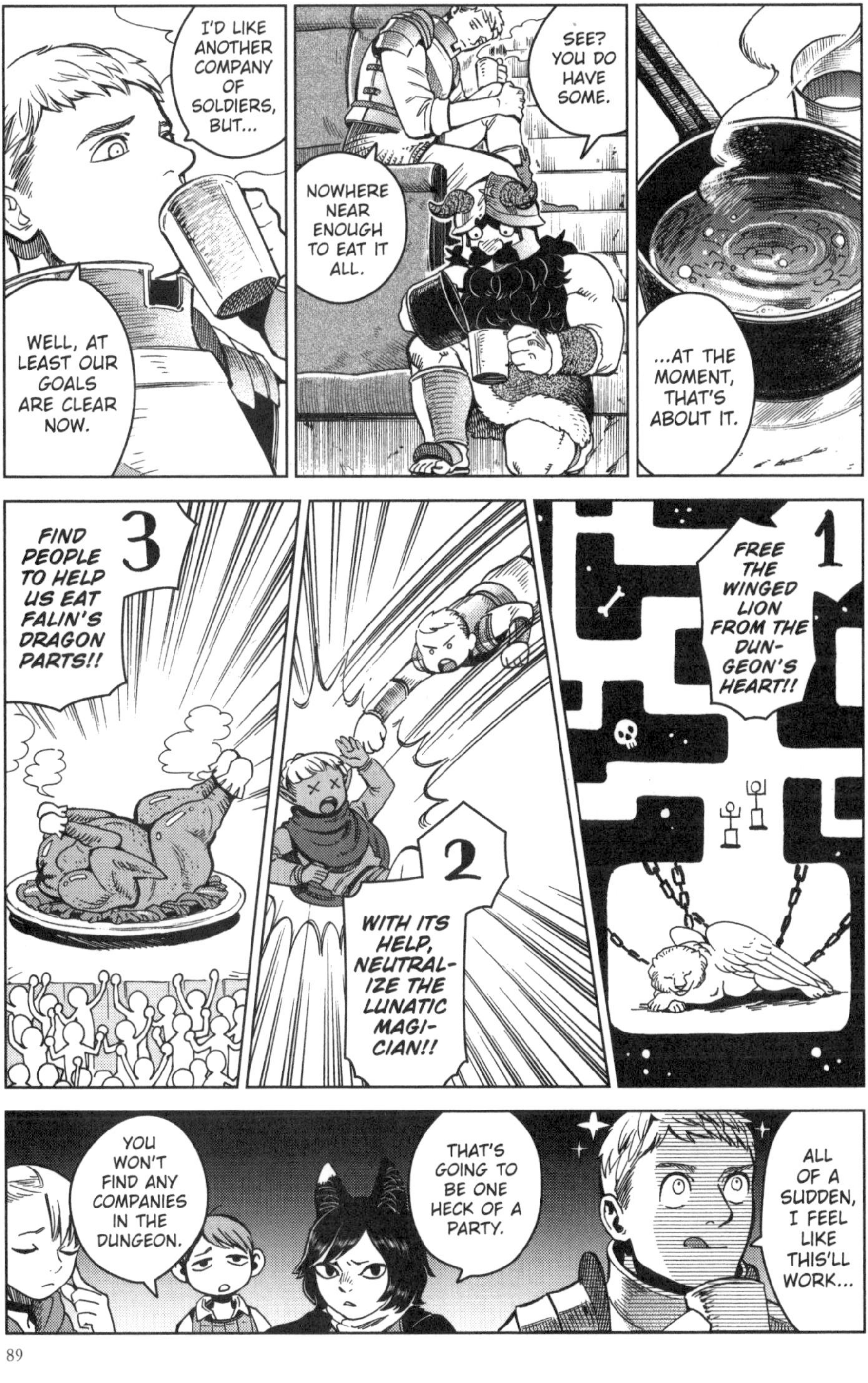
...AT THE MOMENT, THAT'S ABOUT IT.
SEE? YOU DO HAVE SOME.
NOWHERE NEAR ENOUGH TO EAT IT ALL.
I'D LIKE ANOTHER COMPANY OF SOLDIERS, BUT...
WELL, AT LEAST OUR GOALS ARE CLEAR NOW.
1
FREE THE WINGED LION FROM THE DUNGEON'S HEART!!
2
WITH ITS HELP, NEUTRALIZE THE LUNATIC MAGICIAN!!
3
FIND PEOPLE TO HELP US EAT FALIN'S DRAGON PARTS!!
ALL OF A SUDDEN, I FEEL LIKE THIS'LL WORK...
THAT'S GOING TO BE ONE HECK OF A PARTY.
YOU WON'T FIND ANY COMPANIES IN THE DUNGEON.

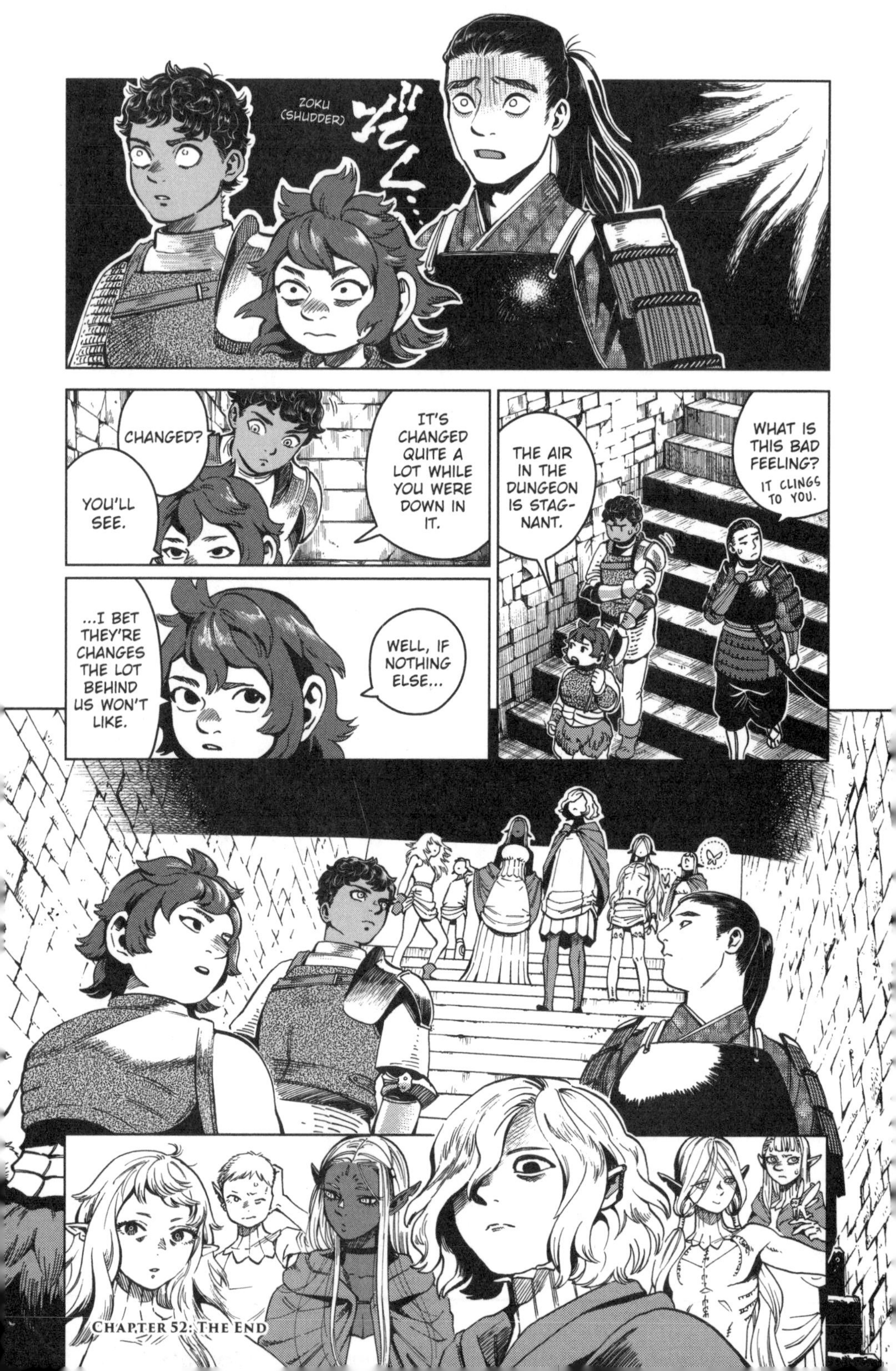
ZOKU (SHUDDER)
WHAT IS THIS BAD FEELING? IT CLINGS TO YOU.
THE AIR IN THE DUNGEON IS STAGNANT.
IT'S CHANGED QUITE A LOT WHILE YOU WERE DOWN IN IT.
CHANGED?
YOU'LL SEE.
WELL, IF NOTHING ELSE...
...I BET THEY'RE CHANGES THE LOT BEHIND US WON'T LIKE.
Chapter 52: The End

53. On Floor One -1-

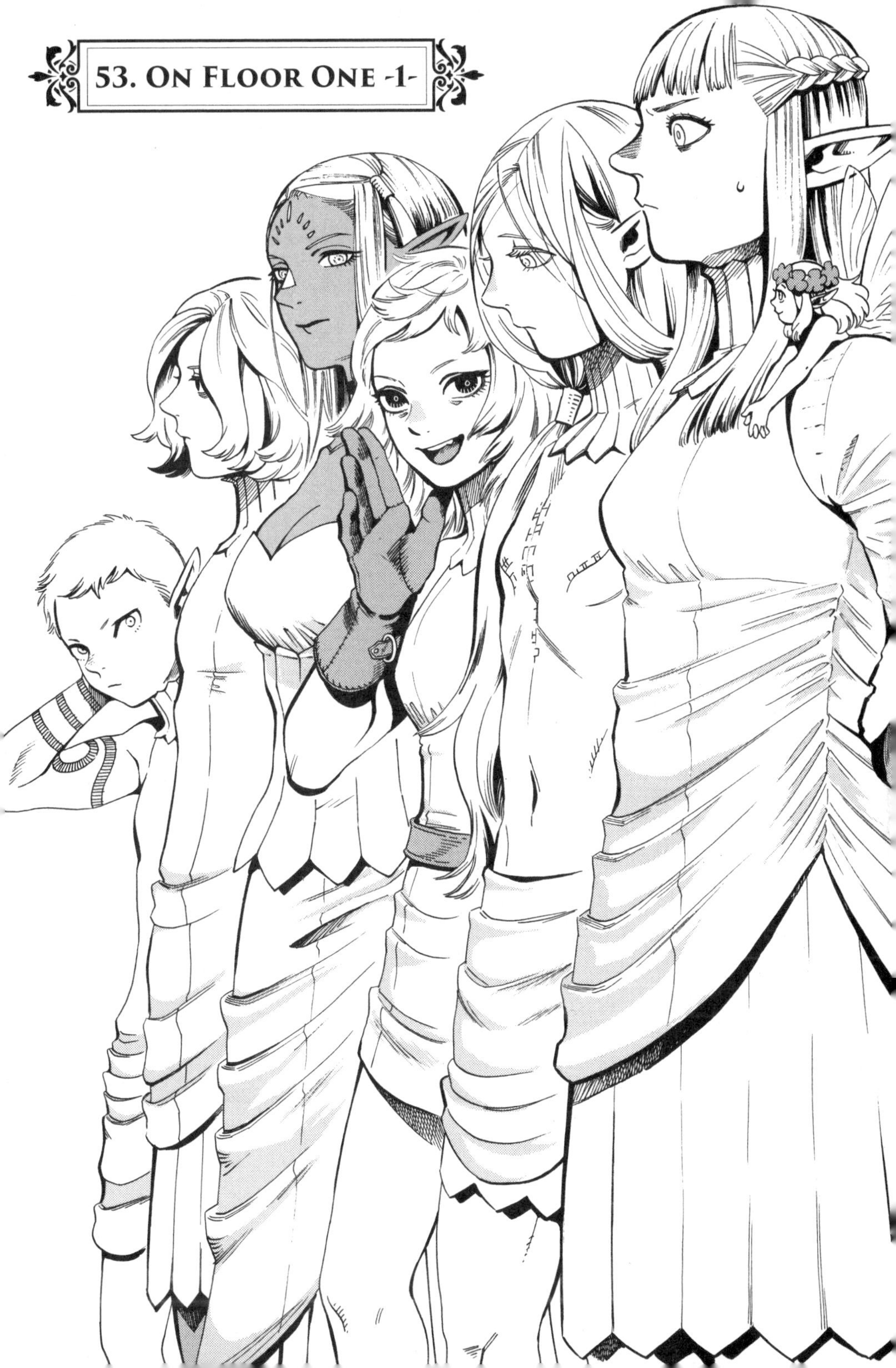

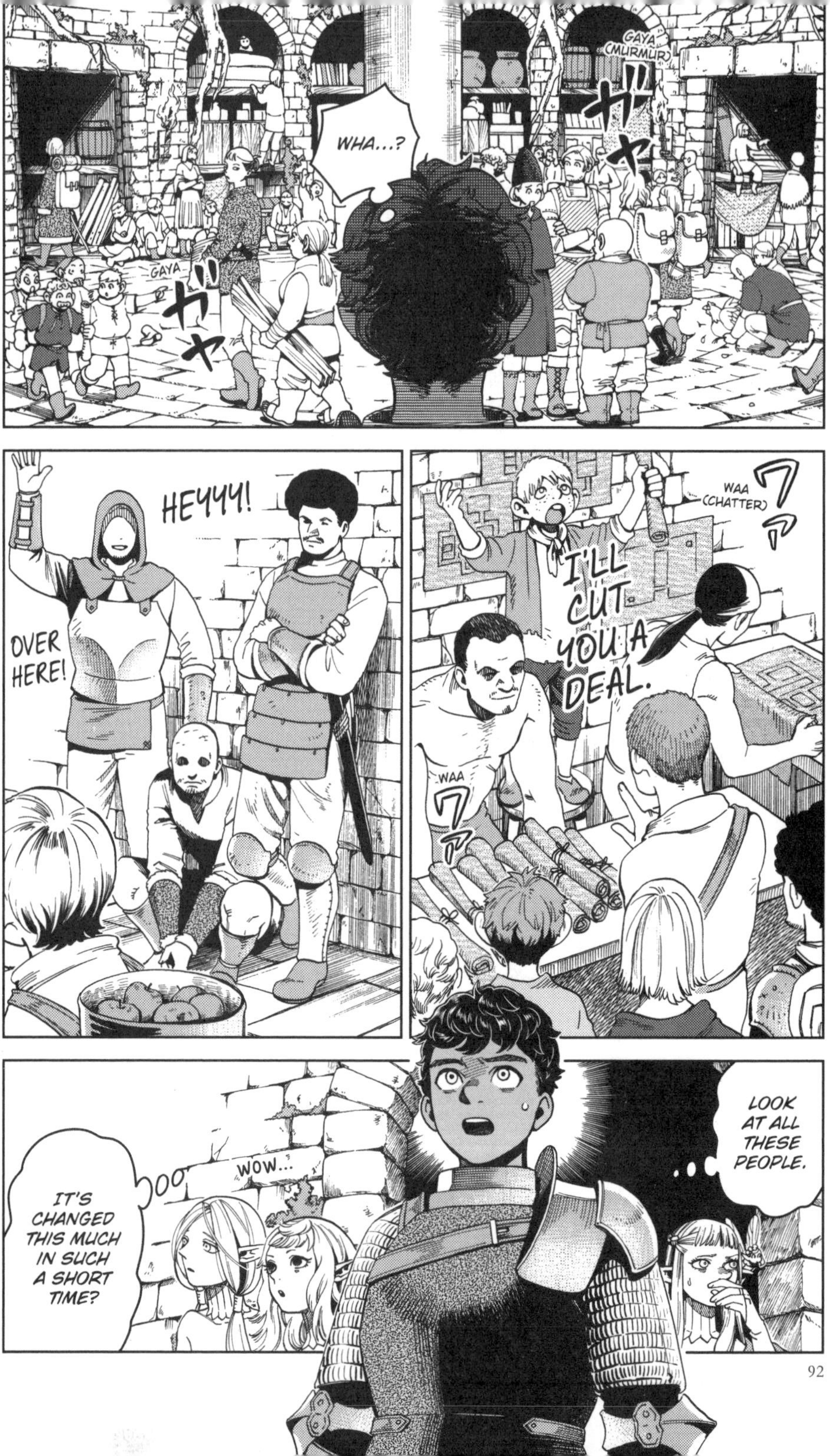

GAYA (MURMUR)
ガヤ
WHA...?
GAYA
ガヤ
WAA (CHATTER)
ワァ
I'LL CUT YOU A DEAL.
WAA
ワァ
HEYYY!
OVER HERE!
LOOK AT ALL THESE PEOPLE.
WOW...
IT'S CHANGED THIS MUCH IN SUCH A SHORT TIME?

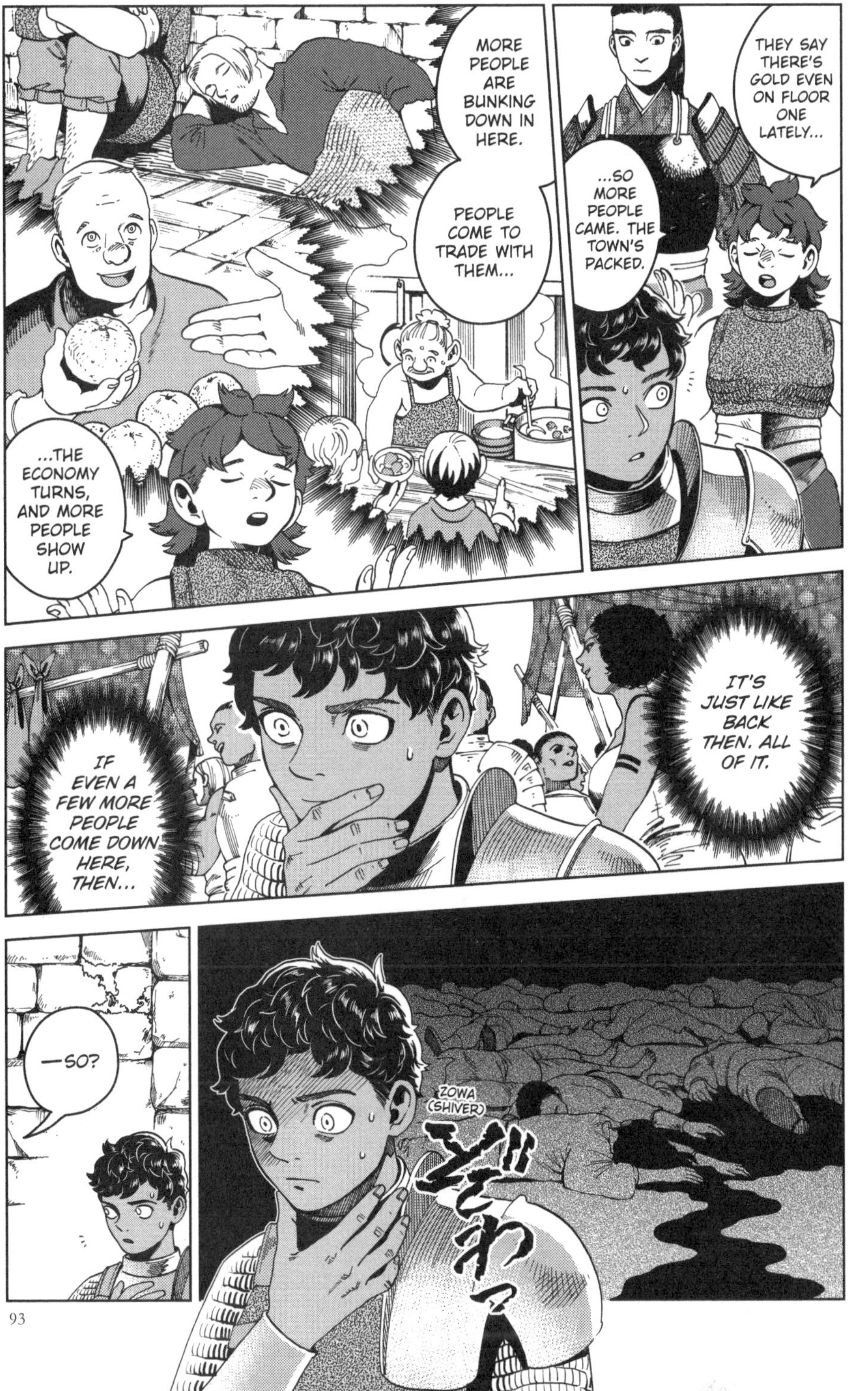
THEY SAY THERE'S GOLD EVEN ON FLOOR ONE LATELY...
...SO MORE PEOPLE CAME. THE TOWN'S PACKED.
MORE PEOPLE ARE BUNKING DOWN IN HERE.
PEOPLE COME TO TRADE WITH THEM...
...THE ECONOMY TURNS, AND MORE PEOPLE SHOW UP.
IT'S JUST LIKE BACK THEN. ALL OF IT.
IF EVEN A FEW MORE PEOPLE COME DOWN HERE, THEN...
ZOWA (SHIVER)
ゾわァ
—SO?

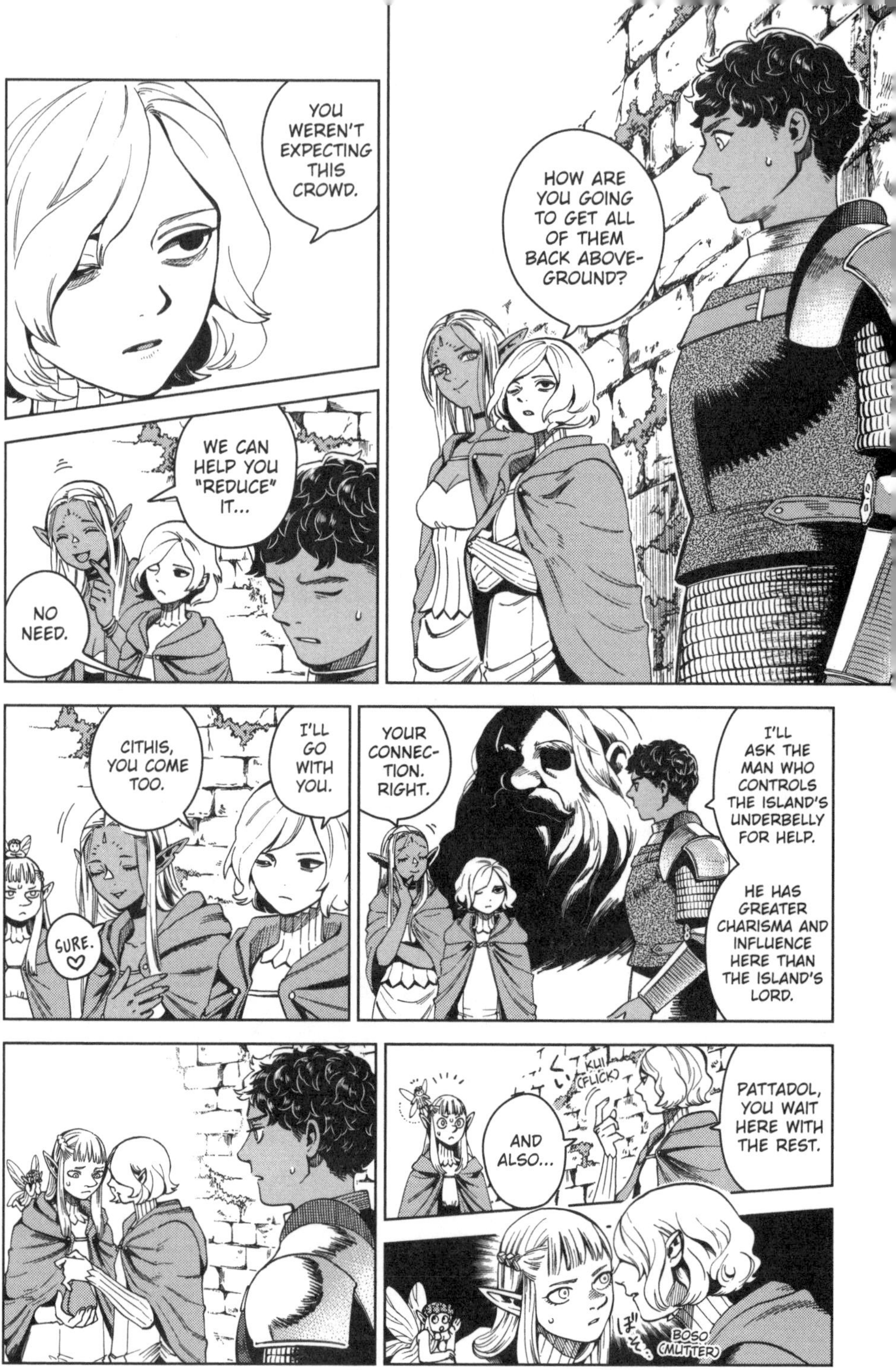
HOW ARE YOU GOING TO GET ALL OF THEM BACK ABOVE-GROUND?
YOU WEREN'T EXPECTING THIS CROWD.
WE CAN HELP YOU "REDUCE" IT...
NO NEED.
I'LL ASK THE MAN WHO CONTROLS THE ISLAND'S UNDERBELLY FOR HELP.
HE HAS GREATER CHARISMA AND INFLUENCE HERE THAN THE ISLAND'S LORD.
YOUR CONNECTION. RIGHT.
I'LL GO WITH YOU.
CITHIS, YOU COME TOO.
SURE. ♡
PATTADOL, YOU WAIT HERE WITH THE REST.
KUI (FLICK)
AND ALSO...
BOSO (MUTTER)

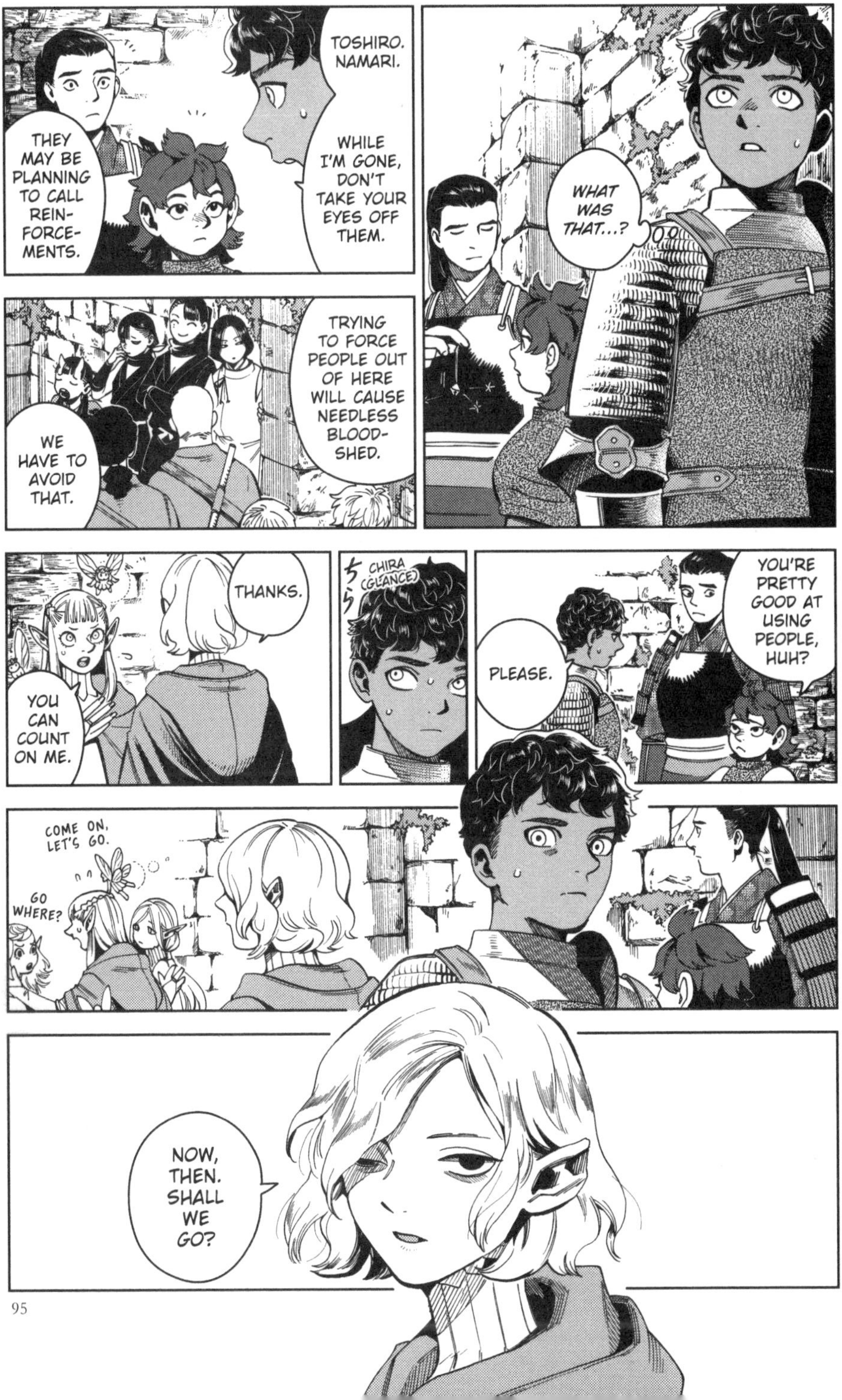

WHAT WAS THAT...?
TOSHIRO. NAMARI.
WHILE I'M GONE, DON'T TAKE YOUR EYES OFF THEM.
THEY MAY BE PLANNING TO CALL REIN-FORCEMENTS.
TRYING TO FORCE PEOPLE OUT OF HERE WILL CAUSE NEEDLESS BLOOD-SHED.
WE HAVE TO AVOID THAT.
YOU'RE PRETTY GOOD AT USING PEOPLE, HUH?
PLEASE.
ちら
CHIRA (GLANCE)
THANKS.
YOU CAN COUNT ON ME.
COME ON, LET'S GO.
GO WHERE?
NOW, THEN. SHALL WE GO?

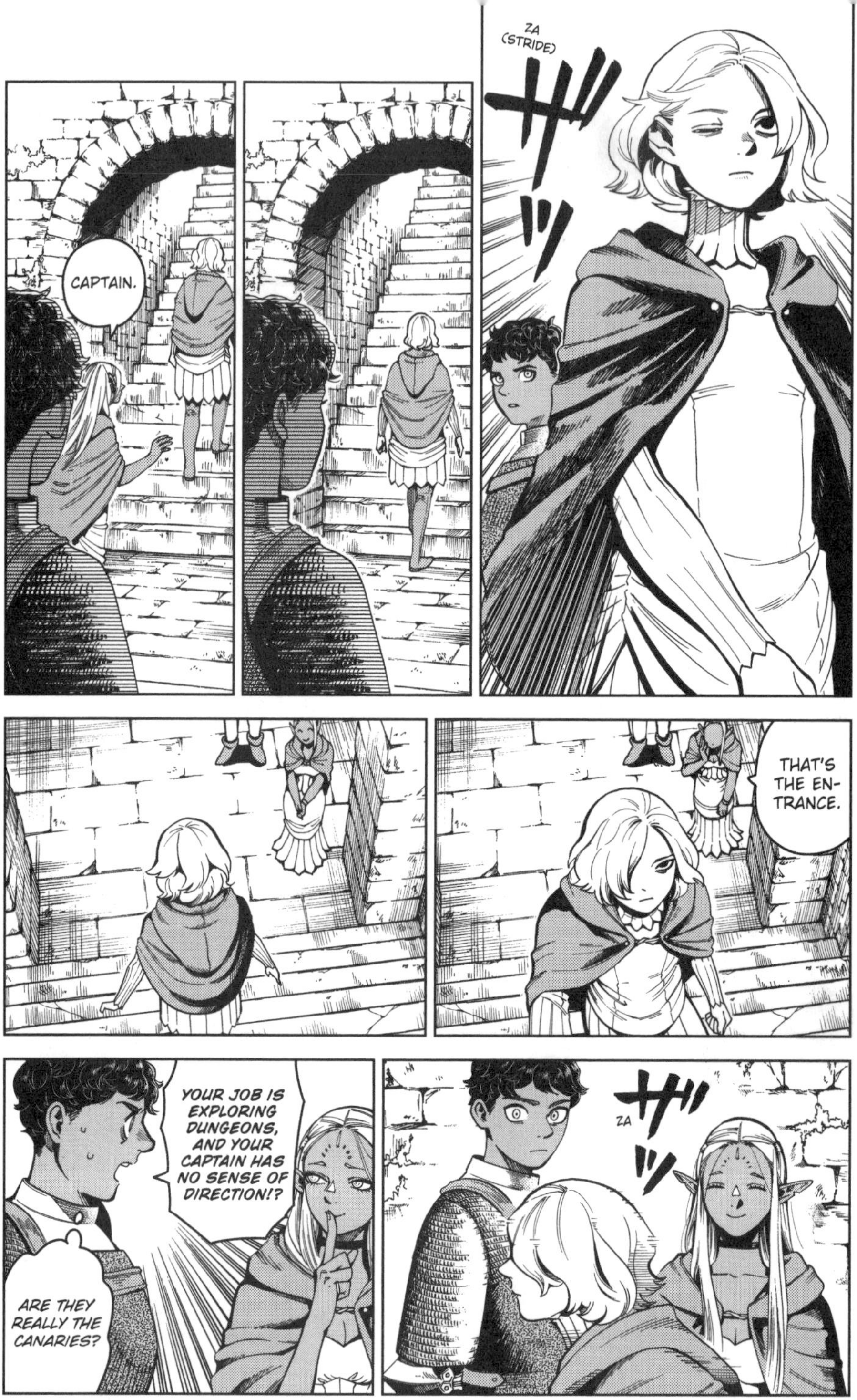
ZA (STRIDE)
ザッ
CAPTAIN.
THAT'S THE EN-TRANCE.
ZA
ザッ
YOUR JOB IS EXPLORING DUNGEONS, AND YOUR CAPTAIN HAS NO SENSE OF DIRECTION!?
ARE THEY REALLY THE CANARIES?

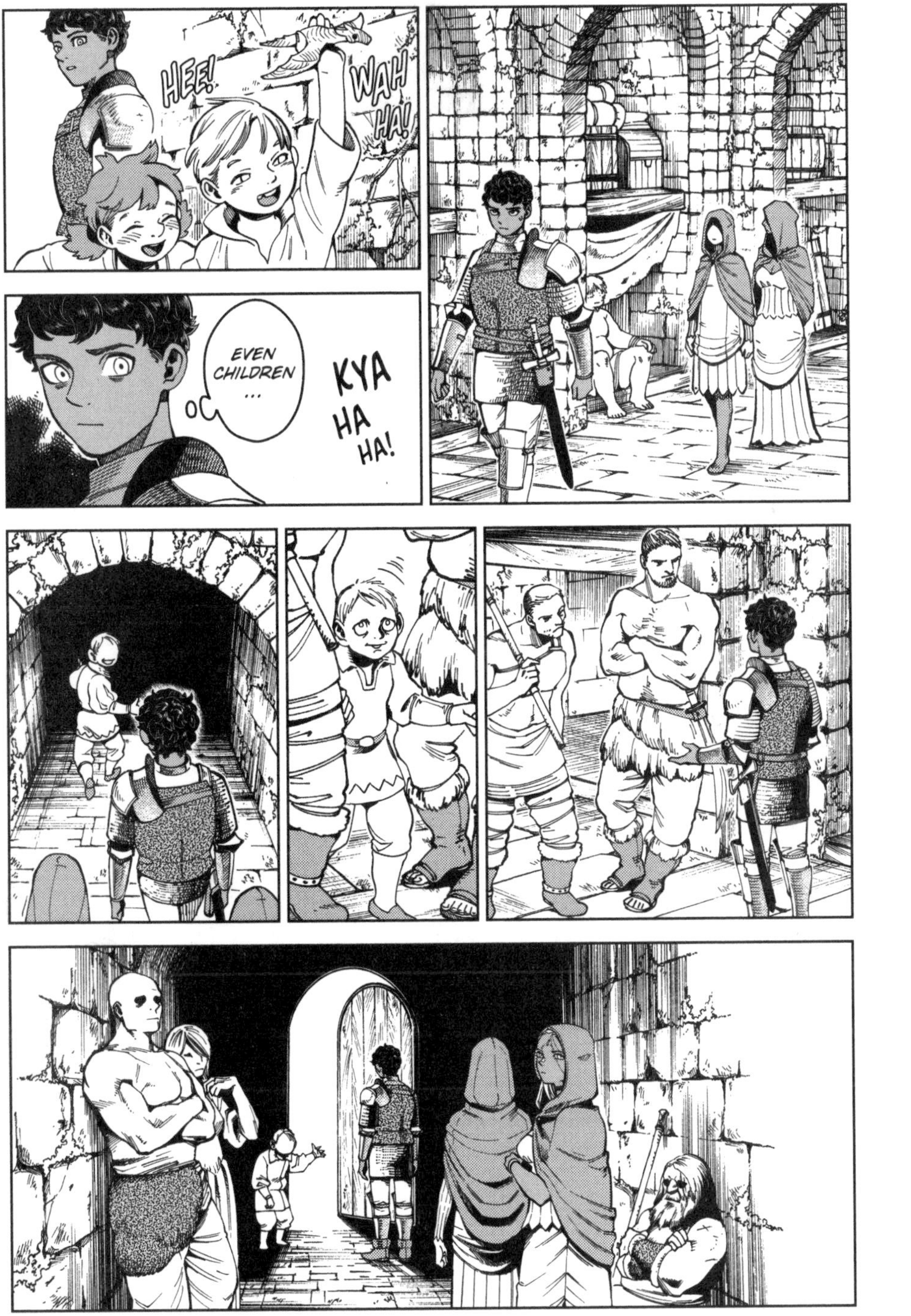
WAH HA!
HEE!
KYA HA HA!
EVEN CHILDREN ...

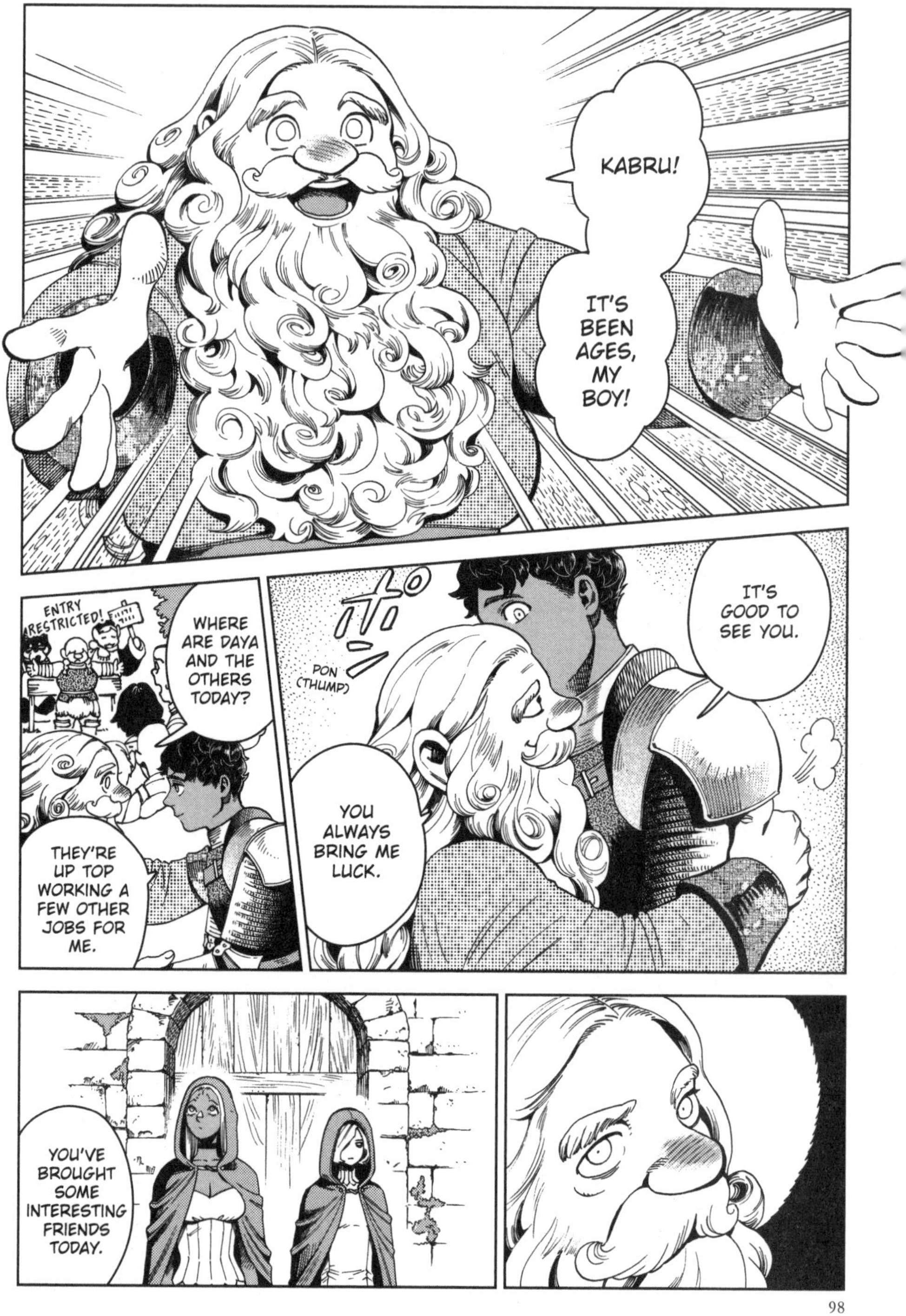
KABRU!
IT'S BEEN AGES, MY BOY!
IT'S GOOD TO SEE YOU.
PON (THUMP)
YOU ALWAYS BRING ME LUCK.
ENTRY RESTRICTED!
WHERE ARE DAYA AND THE OTHERS TODAY?
THEY'RE UP TOP WORKING A FEW OTHER JOBS FOR ME.
YOU'VE BROUGHT SOME INTERESTING FRIENDS TODAY.

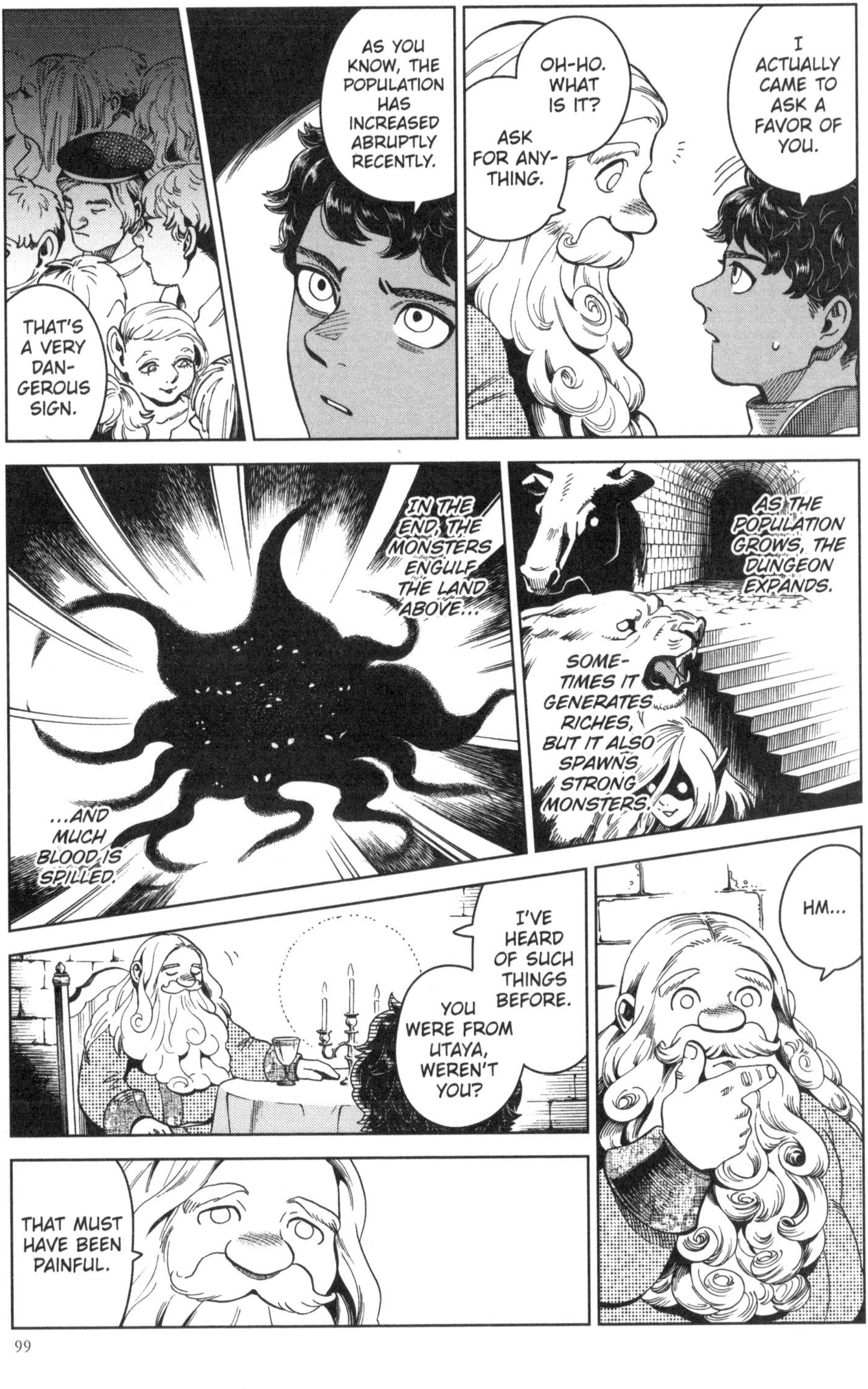
I ACTUALLY CAME TO ASK A FAVOR OF YOU.
OH-HO. WHAT IS IT?
ASK FOR ANY-THING.
AS YOU KNOW, THE POPULATION HAS INCREASED ABRUPTLY RECENTLY.
THAT'S A VERY DAN-GEROUS SIGN.
AS THE POPULATION GROWS, THE DUNGEON EXPANDS.
SOME-TIMES IT GENERATES RICHES, BUT IT ALSO SPAWNS STRONG MONSTERS.
IN THE END, THE MONSTERS ENGULF THE LAND ABOVE...
...AND MUCH BLOOD IS SPILLED.
HM...
I'VE HEARD OF SUCH THINGS BEFORE.
YOU WERE FROM UTAYA, WEREN'T YOU?
THAT MUST HAVE BEEN PAINFUL.

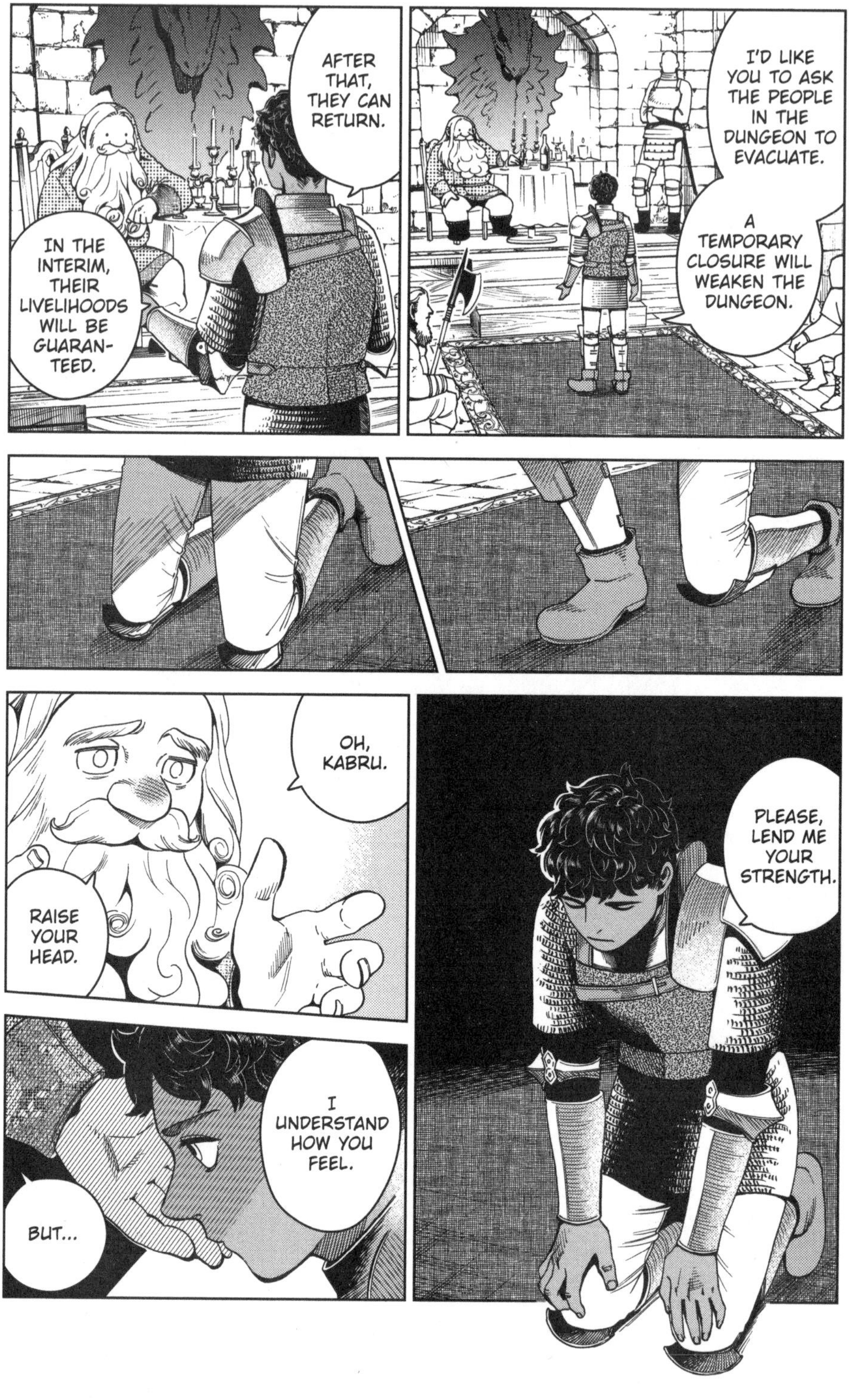
I'D LIKE YOU TO ASK THE PEOPLE IN THE DUNGEON TO EVACUATE.
A TEMPORARY CLOSURE WILL WEAKEN THE DUNGEON.
AFTER THAT, THEY CAN RETURN.
IN THE INTERIM, THEIR LIVELIHOODS WILL BE GUARAN-TEED.
PLEASE, LEND ME YOUR STRENGTH.
OH, KABRU.
RAISE YOUR HEAD.
I UNDERSTAND HOW YOU FEEL.
BUT...

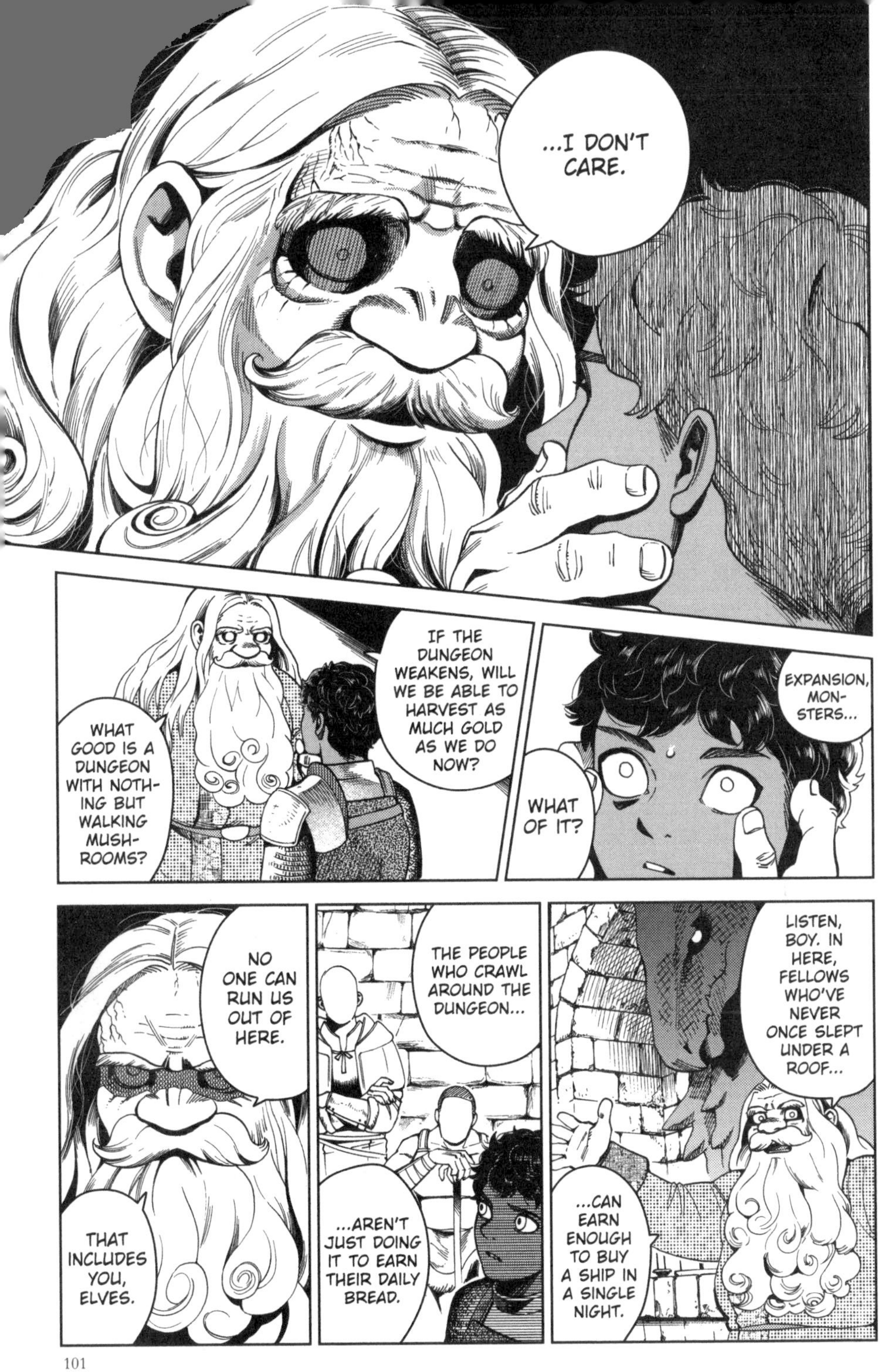
...I DON'T CARE.
EXPANSION, MONSTERS...
WHAT OF IT?
IF THE DUNGEON WEAKENS, WILL WE BE ABLE TO HARVEST AS MUCH GOLD AS WE DO NOW?
WHAT GOOD IS A DUNGEON WITH NOTHING BUT WALKING MUSHROOMS?
LISTEN, BOY. IN HERE, FELLOWS WHO'VE NEVER ONCE SLEPT UNDER A ROOF...
...CAN EARN ENOUGH TO BUY A SHIP IN A SINGLE NIGHT.
THE PEOPLE WHO CRAWL AROUND THE DUNGEON...
...AREN'T JUST DOING IT TO EARN THEIR DAILY BREAD.
NO ONE CAN RUN US OUT OF HERE.
THAT INCLUDES YOU, ELVES.

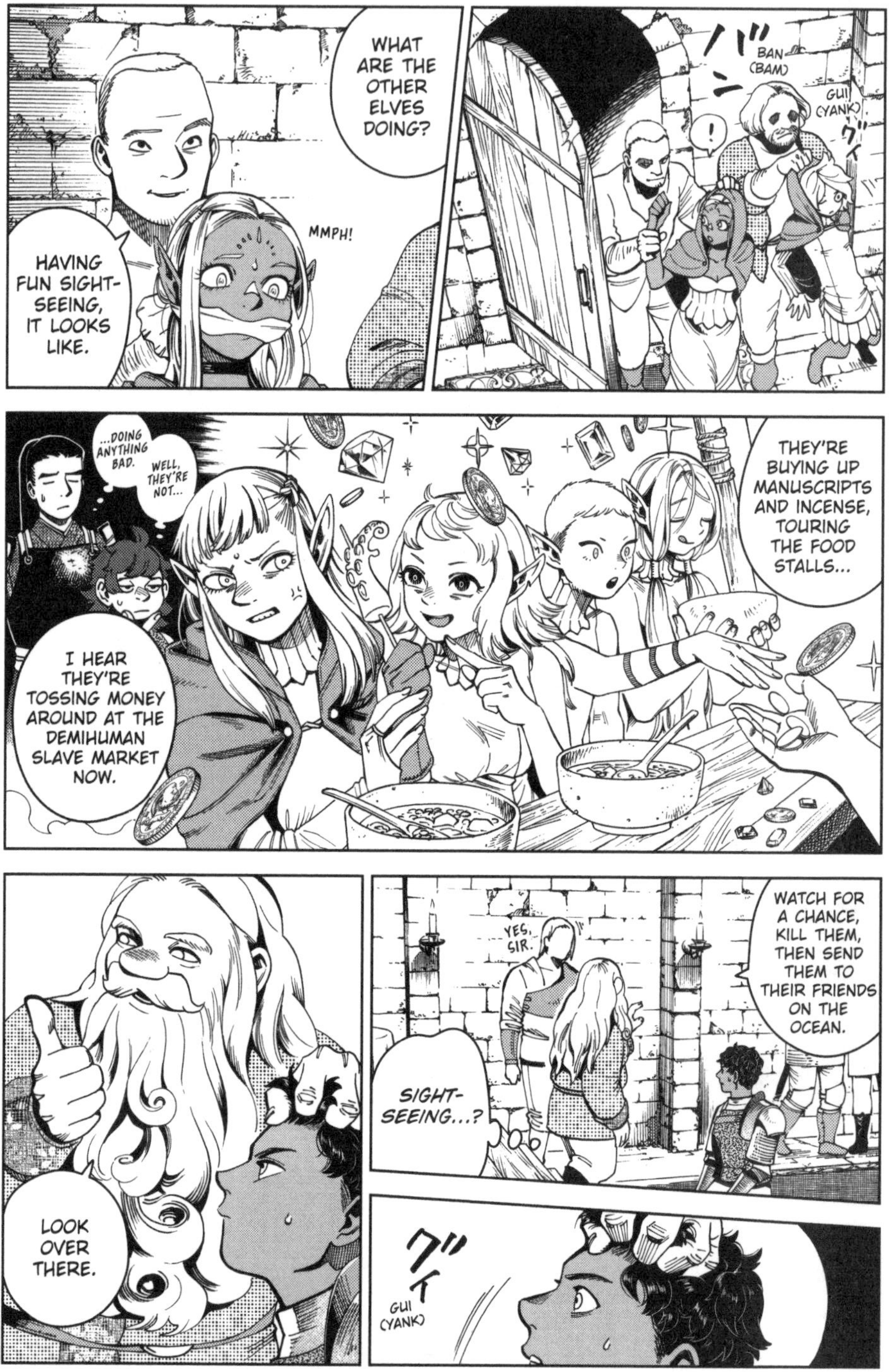
BAN (BAM)
GUI (YANK)
!
WHAT ARE THE OTHER ELVES DOING?
MMPH!
HAVING FUN SIGHT-SEEING, IT LOOKS LIKE.
THEY'RE BUYING UP MANUSCRIPTS AND INCENSE, TOURING THE FOOD STALLS...
WELL, THEY'RE NOT...
...DOING ANYTHING BAD.
I HEAR THEY'RE TOSSING MONEY AROUND AT THE DEMIHUMAN SLAVE MARKET NOW.
WATCH FOR A CHANCE, KILL THEM, THEN SEND THEM TO THEIR FRIENDS ON THE OCEAN.
YES, SIR.
SIGHT-SEEING...?
GUI (YANK)
LOOK OVER THERE.

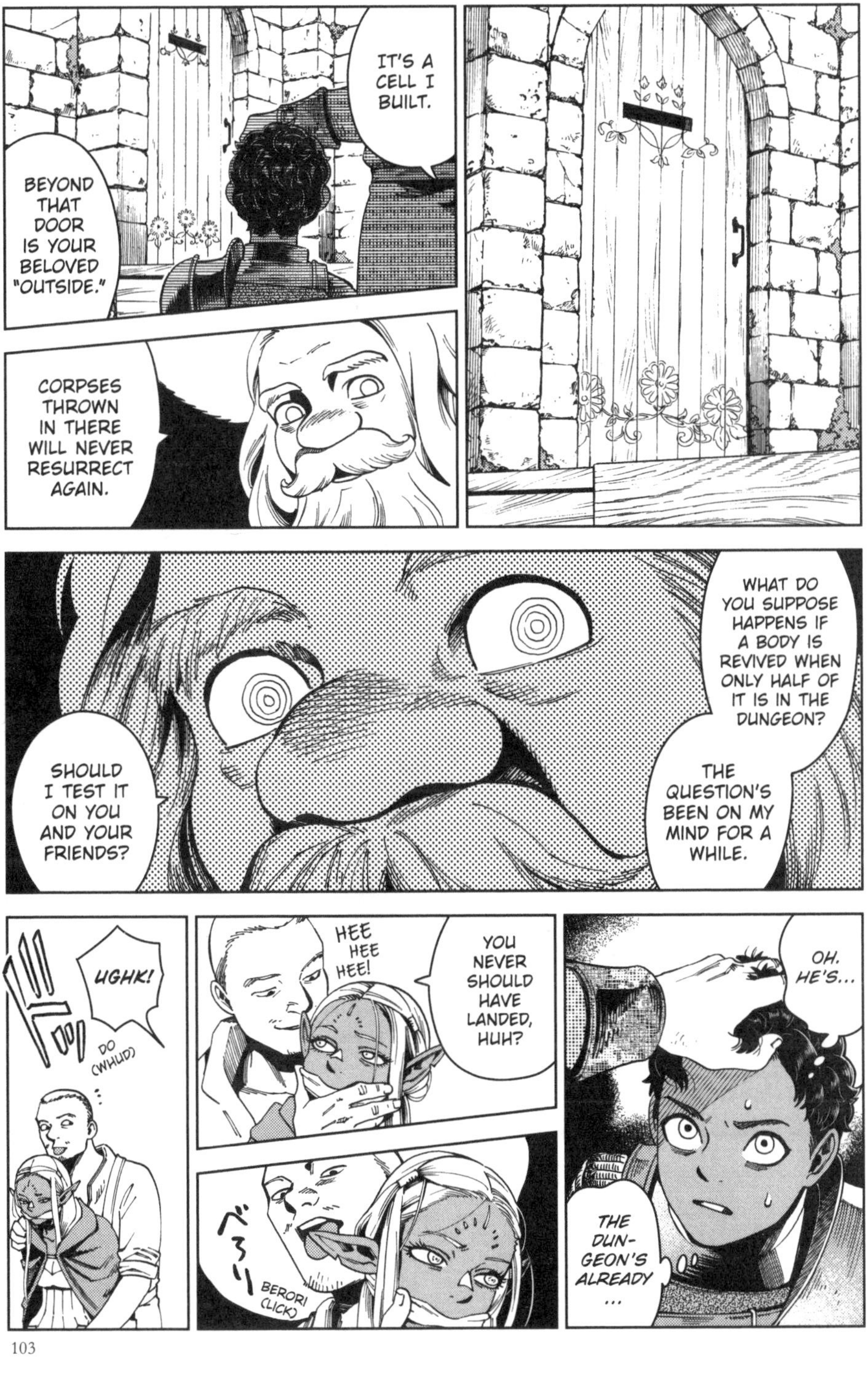
IT'S A CELL I BUILT.
BEYOND THAT DOOR IS YOUR BELOVED "OUTSIDE."
CORPSES THROWN IN THERE WILL NEVER RESURRECT AGAIN.
WHAT DO YOU SUPPOSE HAPPENS IF A BODY IS REVIVED WHEN ONLY HALF OF IT IS IN THE DUNGEON?
THE QUESTION'S BEEN ON MY MIND FOR A WHILE.
SHOULD I TEST IT ON YOU AND YOUR FRIENDS?
OH. HE'S...
THE DUN-GEON'S ALREADY ...
YOU NEVER SHOULD HAVE LANDED, HUH?
HEE HEE HEE!
べろり
BERORI (LICK)
UGHK!
DO (WHUD)
...

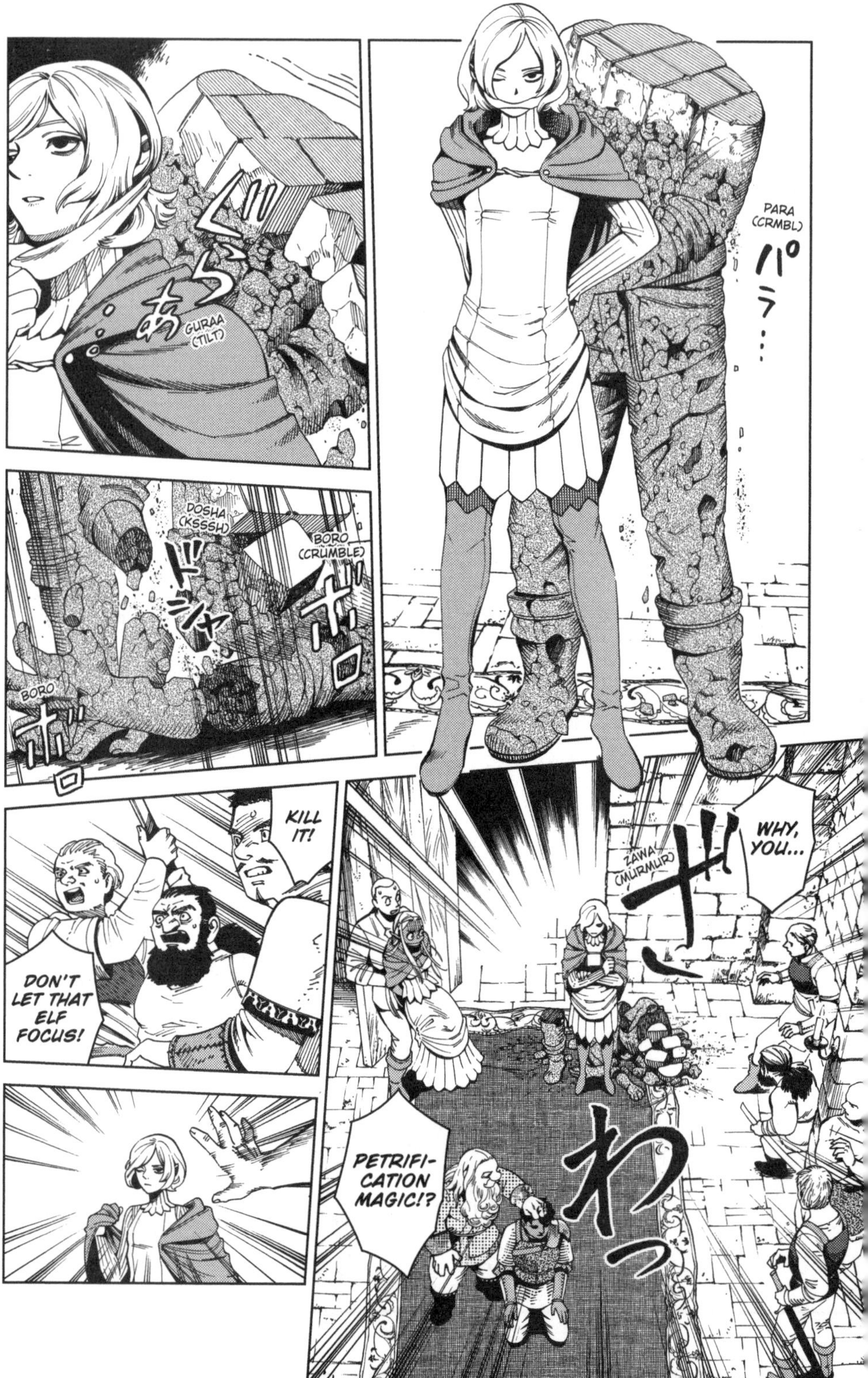
PARA (CRMBL)
パラ…
GURAA (TILT)
ぐらあ
DOSHA (KSSSH)
ドシャ
BORO (CRUMBLE)
ボロ
BORO
ボロ
WHY, YOU...
ZAWA (MURMUR)
PETRIFI-CATION MAGIC!?
わっ
KILL IT!
DON'T LET THAT ELF FOCUS!

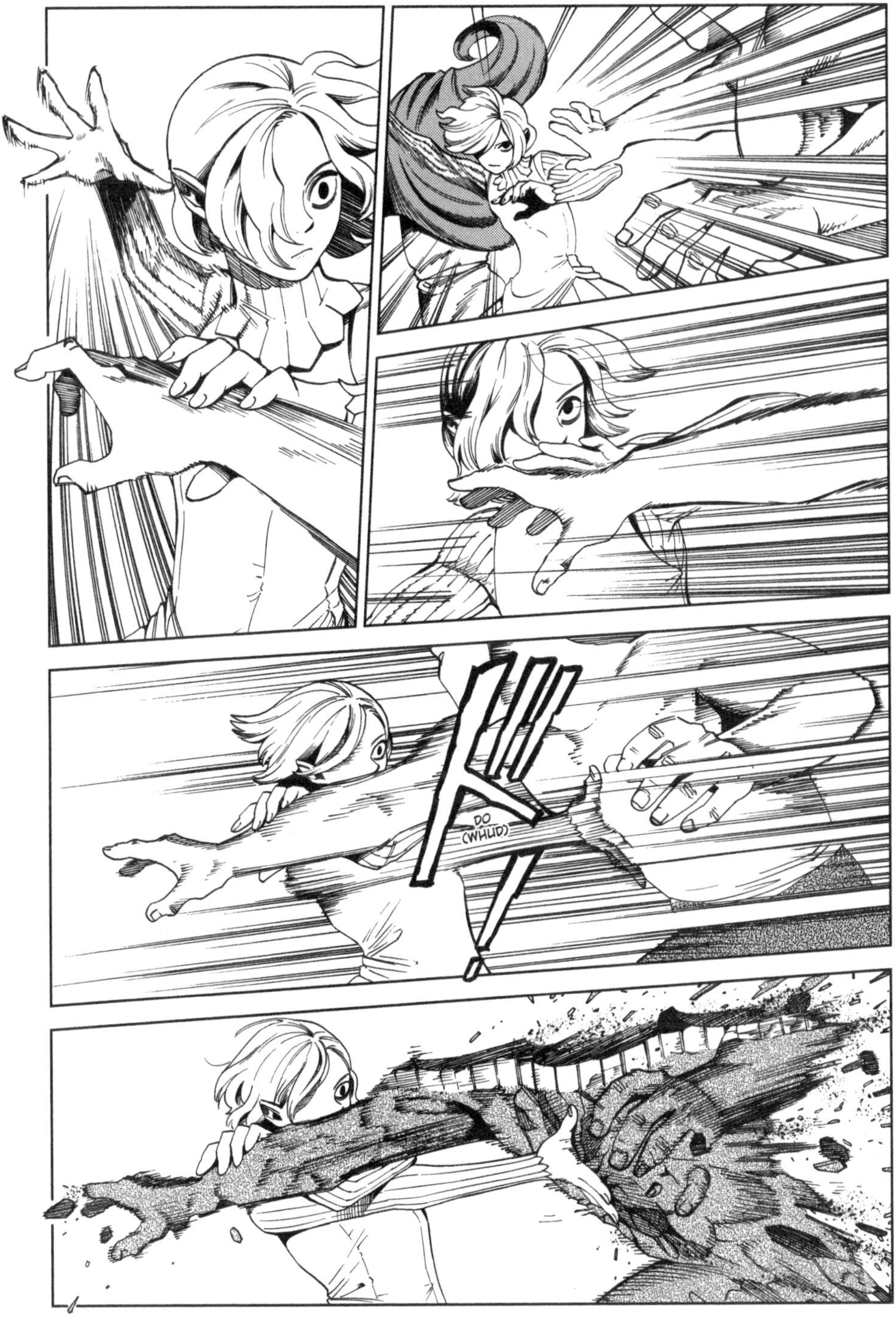
DO
(WHUD)

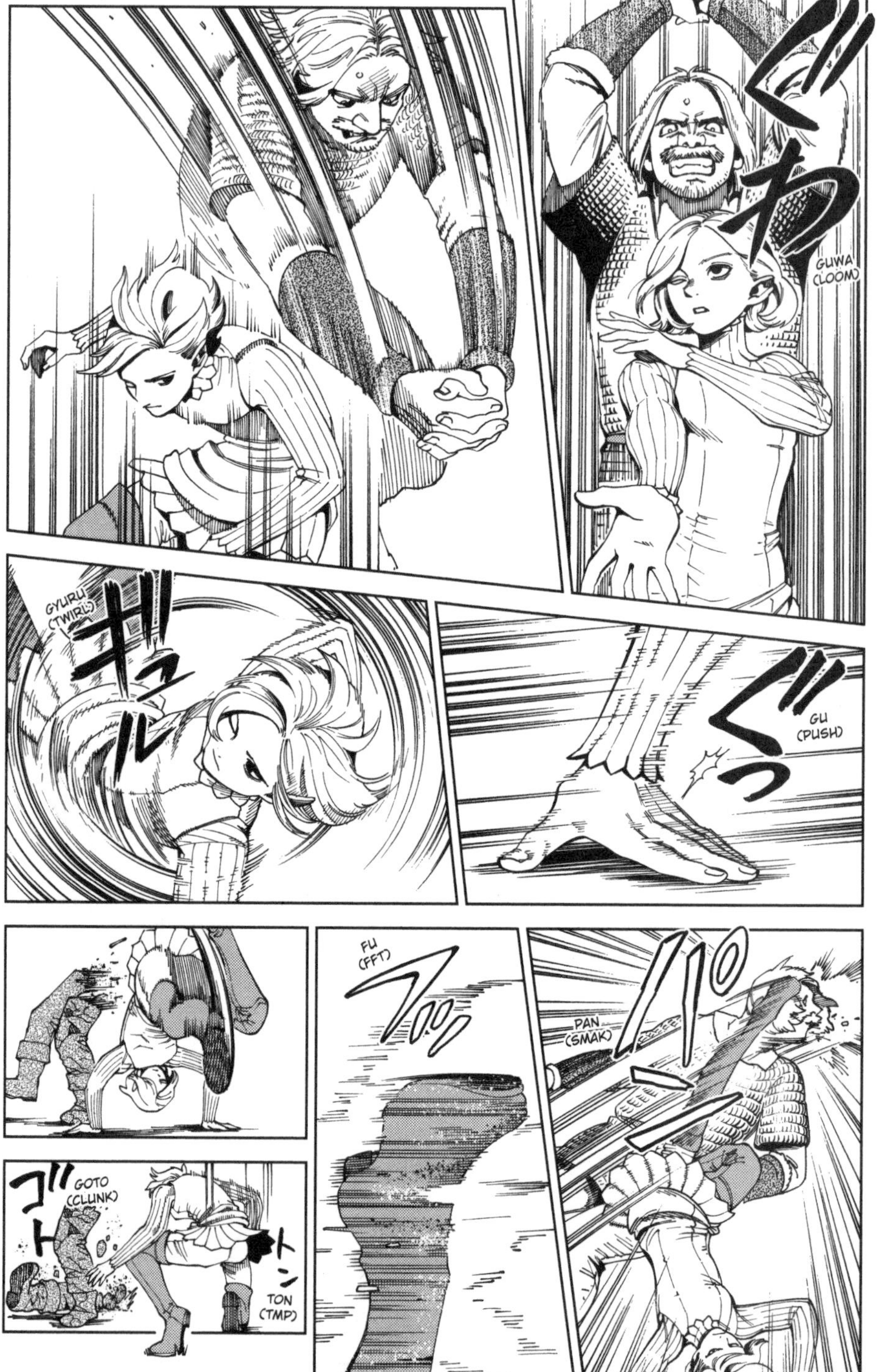
GUWA (LOOM)
GU (PUSH)
GYURU (TWIRL)
PAN (SMAK)
FU (FFT)
GOTO (CLUNK)
TON (TMP)

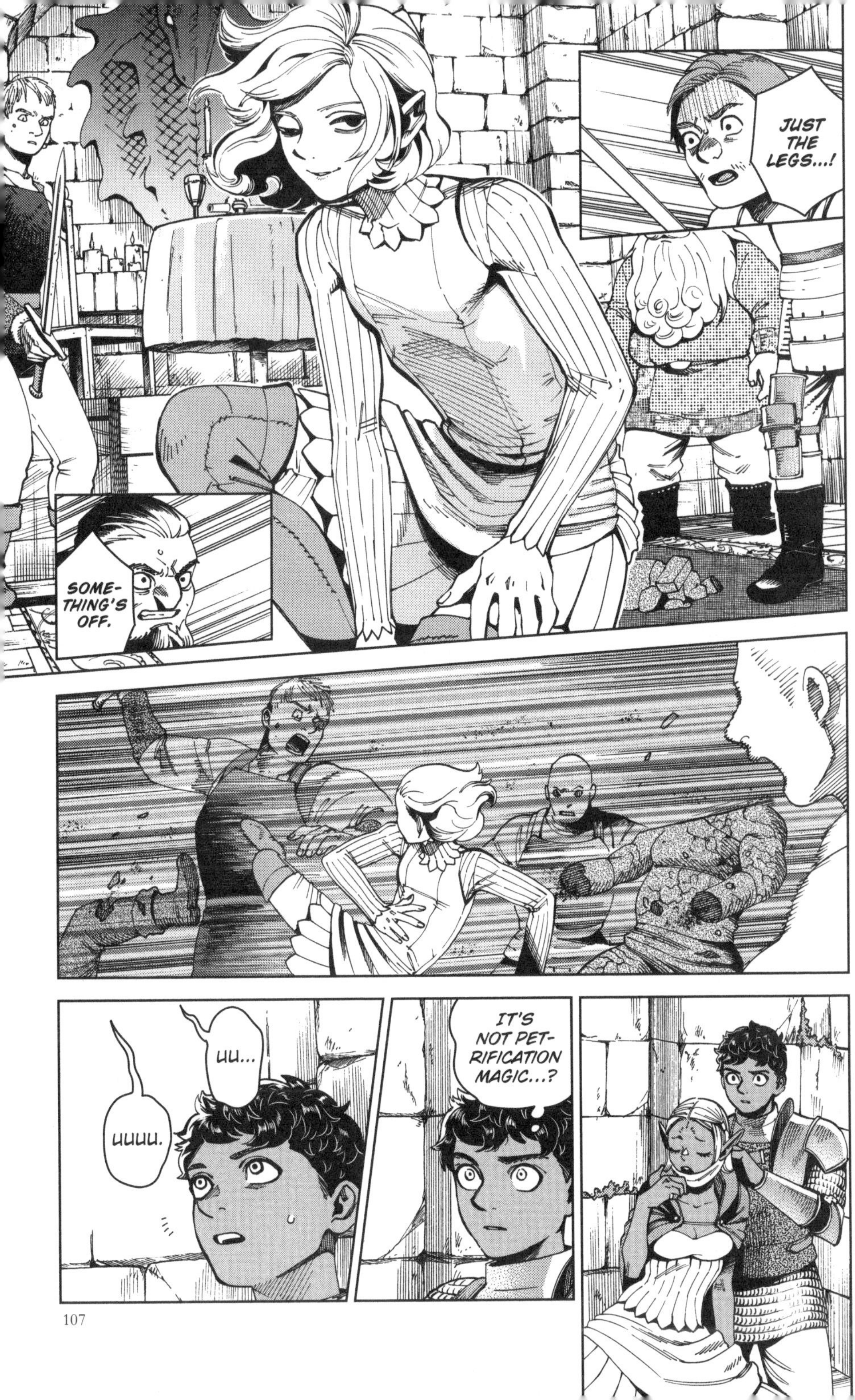
JUST THE LEGS...!
SOME-THING'S OFF.
IT'S NOT PET-RIFICATION MAGIC...?
UU...
UUUU.

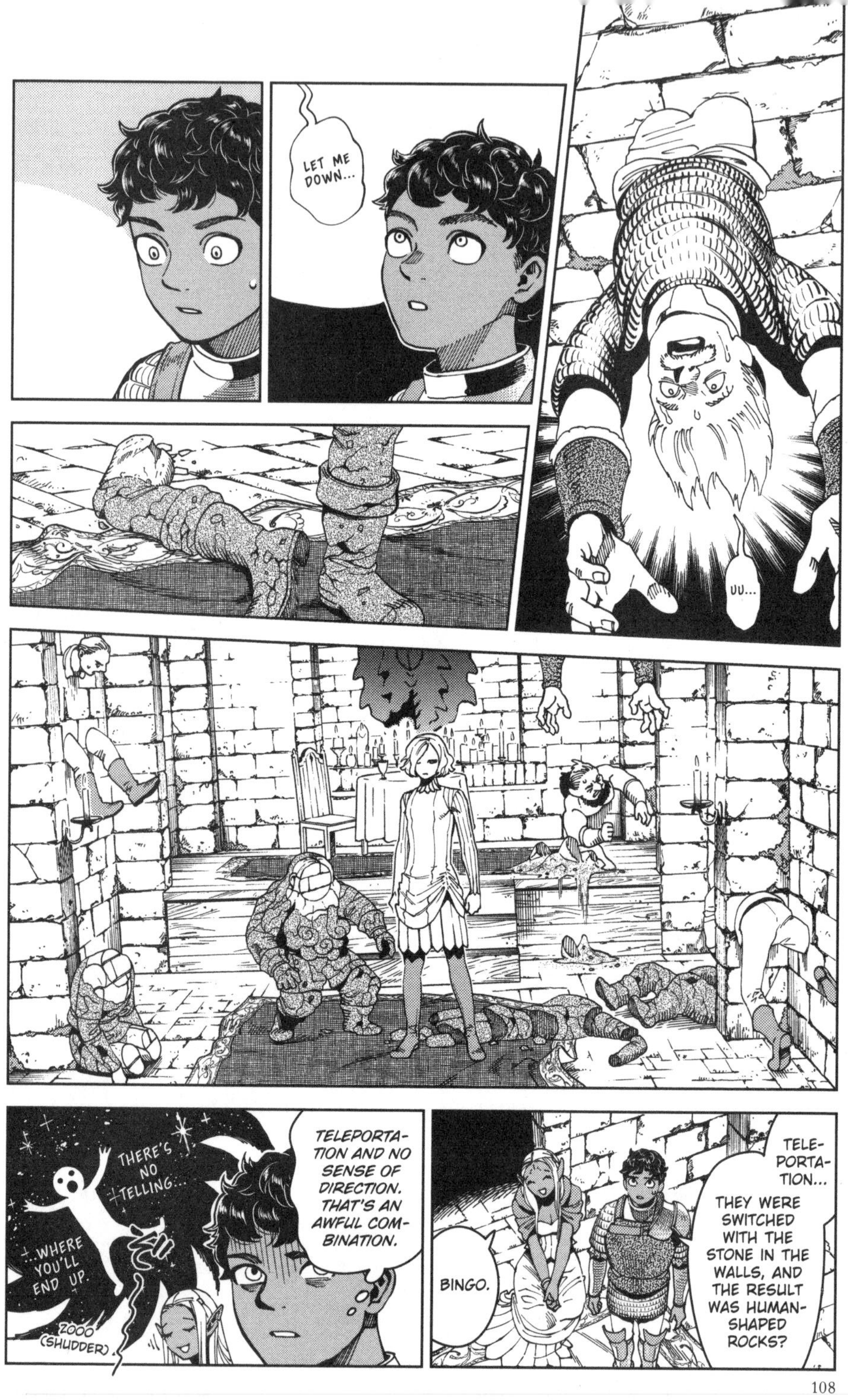
UU...
LET ME DOWN...
TELEPORTATION... THEY WERE SWITCHED WITH THE STONE IN THE WALLS, AND THE RESULT WAS HUMAN-SHAPED ROCKS?
BINGO.
TELEPORTATION AND NO SENSE OF DIRECTION. THAT'S AN AWFUL COMBINATION.
THERE'S NO TELLING...
...WHERE YOU'LL END UP.
ZOOO (SHUDDER)

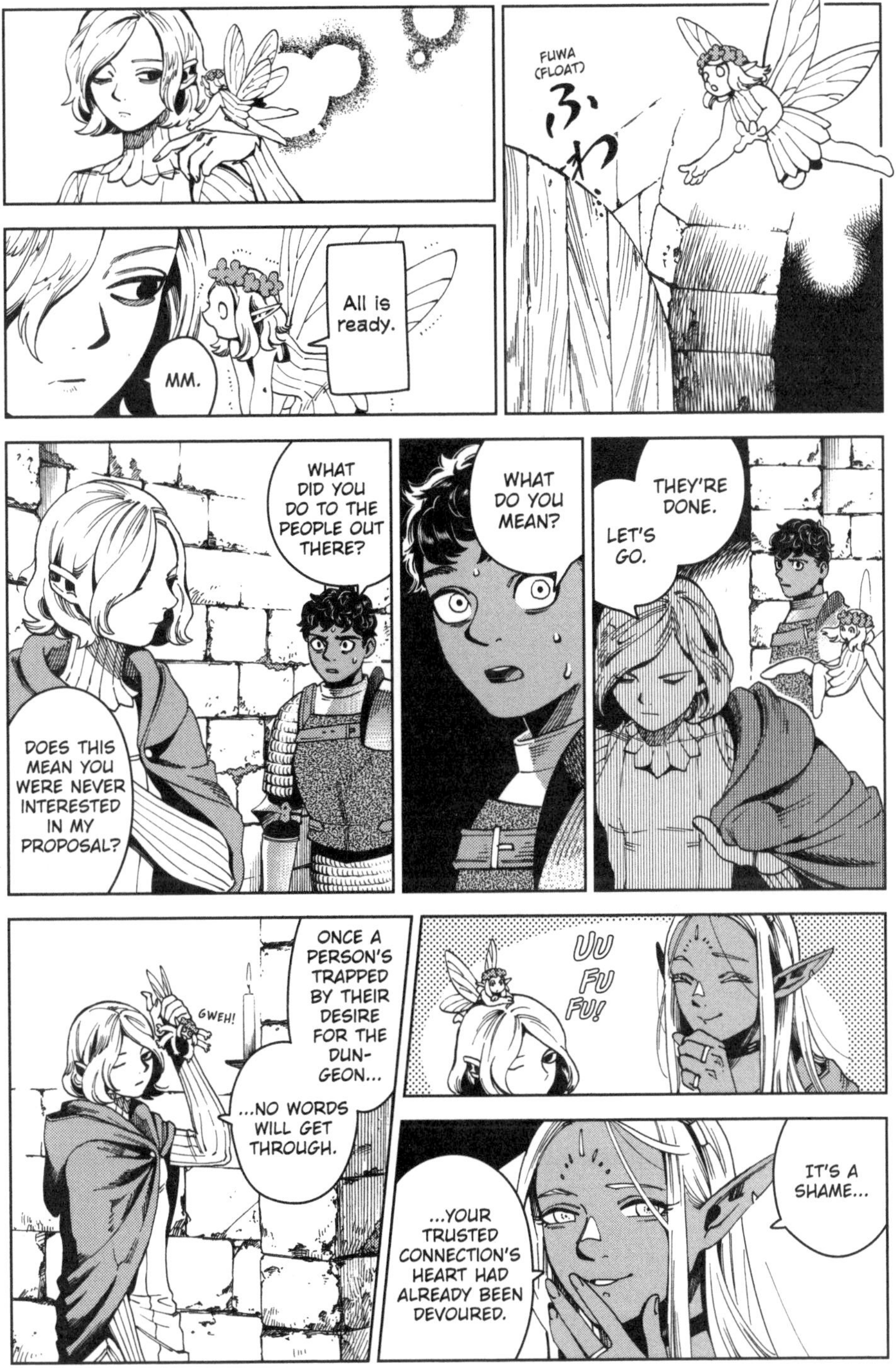

FUWA (FLOAT)
ふわ
All is ready.
MM.
THEY'RE DONE.
LET'S GO.
WHAT DO YOU MEAN?
WHAT DID YOU DO TO THE PEOPLE OUT THERE?
DOES THIS MEAN YOU WERE NEVER INTERESTED IN MY PROPOSAL?
UU FU FU!
IT'S A SHAME...
...YOUR TRUSTED CONNECTION'S HEART HAD ALREADY BEEN DEVOURED.
ONCE A PERSON'S TRAPPED BY THEIR DESIRE FOR THE DUN-GEON...
GWEH!
...NO WORDS WILL GET THROUGH.

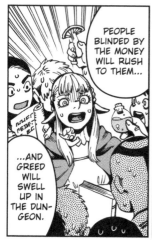

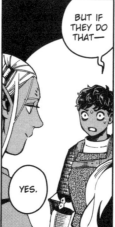

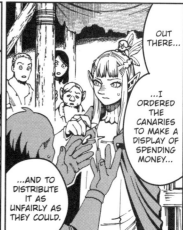

OUT THERE...
...I ORDERED THE CANARIES TO MAKE A DISPLAY OF SPENDING MONEY...
...AND TO DISTRIBUTE IT AS UNFAIRLY AS THEY COULD.
BUT IF THEY DO THAT—
YES.
PEOPLE BLINDED BY THE MONEY WILL RUSH TO THEM...
...AND GREED WILL SWELL UP IN THE DUN-GEON.
IF WORDS WON'T GET THROUGH, WE'LL JUST SHOW THEM...
...WHAT HAPPENS TO A DUNGEON THAT'S CONSUMED TOO MUCH DESIRE.
ONCE THEY'VE SEEN THAT, THEY'LL BE THRILLED TO HEAD BACK TO THE SURFACE.

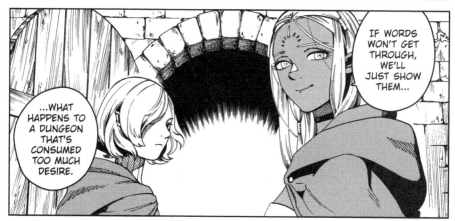

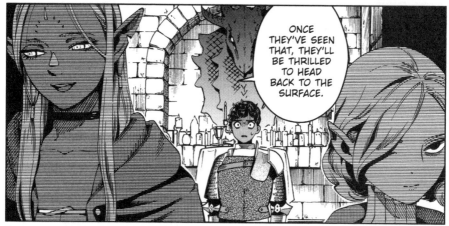

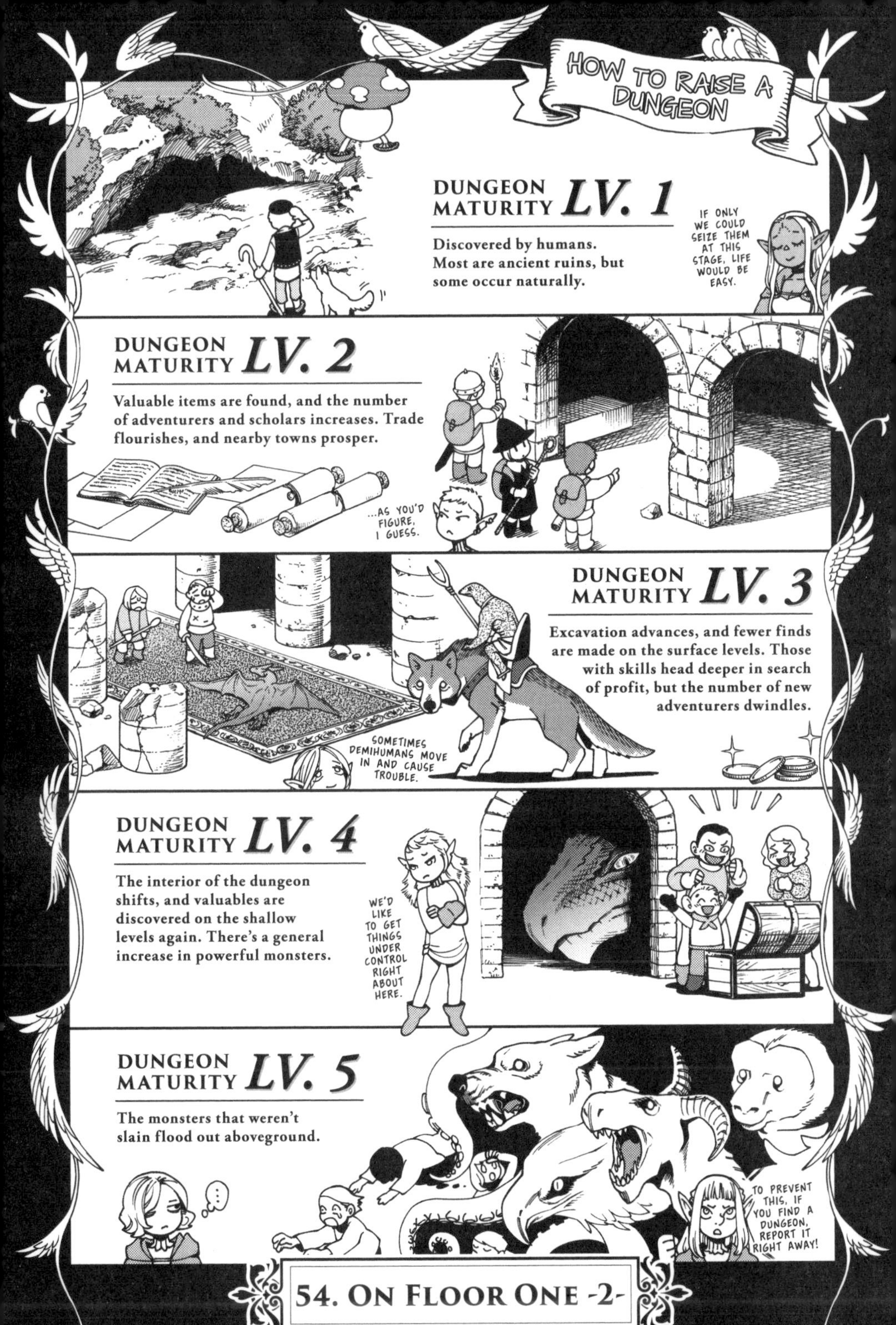
HOW TO RAISE A DUNGEON
DUNGEON MATURITY LV. 1
IF ONLY WE COULD SEIZE THEM AT THIS STAGE, LIFE WOULD BE EASY.
Discovered by humans. Most are ancient ruins, but some occur naturally.
DUNGEON MATURITY LV. 2
Valuable items are found, and the number of adventurers and scholars increases. Trade flourishes, and nearby towns prosper.
...AS YOU'D FIGURE, I GUESS.
DUNGEON MATURITY LV. 3
Excavation advances, and fewer finds are made on the surface levels. Those with skills head deeper in search of profit, but the number of new adventurers dwindles.
SOMETIMES DEMIHUMANS MOVE IN AND CAUSE TROUBLE.
DUNGEON MATURITY LV. 4
The interior of the dungeon shifts, and valuables are discovered on the shallow levels again. There's a general increase in powerful monsters.
WE'D LIKE TO GET THINGS UNDER CONTROL RIGHT ABOUT HERE.
DUNGEON MATURITY LV. 5
The monsters that weren't slain flood out aboveground.
TO PREVENT THIS, IF YOU FIND A DUNGEON, REPORT IT RIGHT AWAY!
...

54. On Floor One -2-

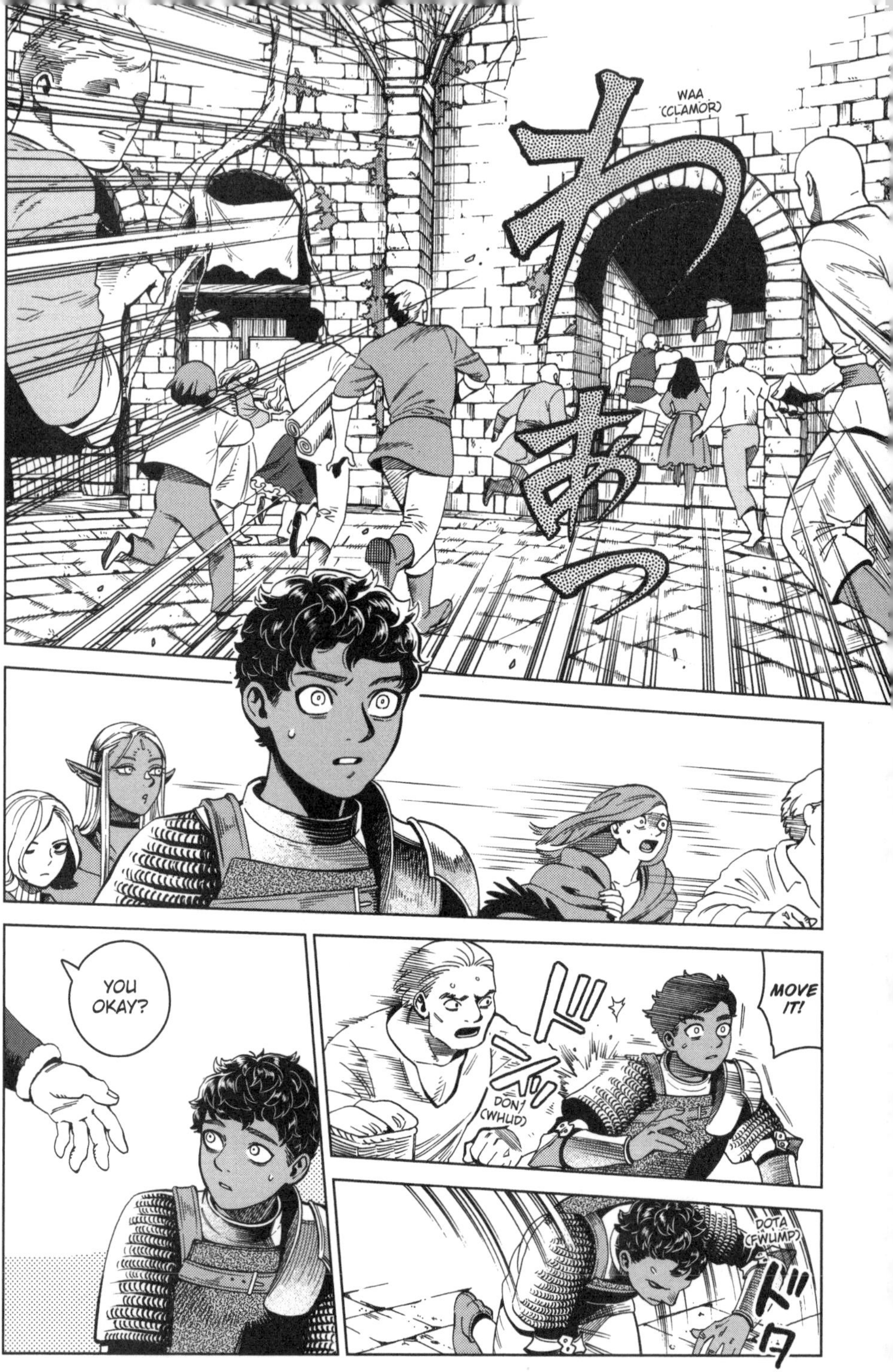

ワあっ
WAA (CLAMOR)
MOVE IT!
ドンッ
DON (WHUD)
ドタ
DOTA (FWUMP)
YOU OKAY?

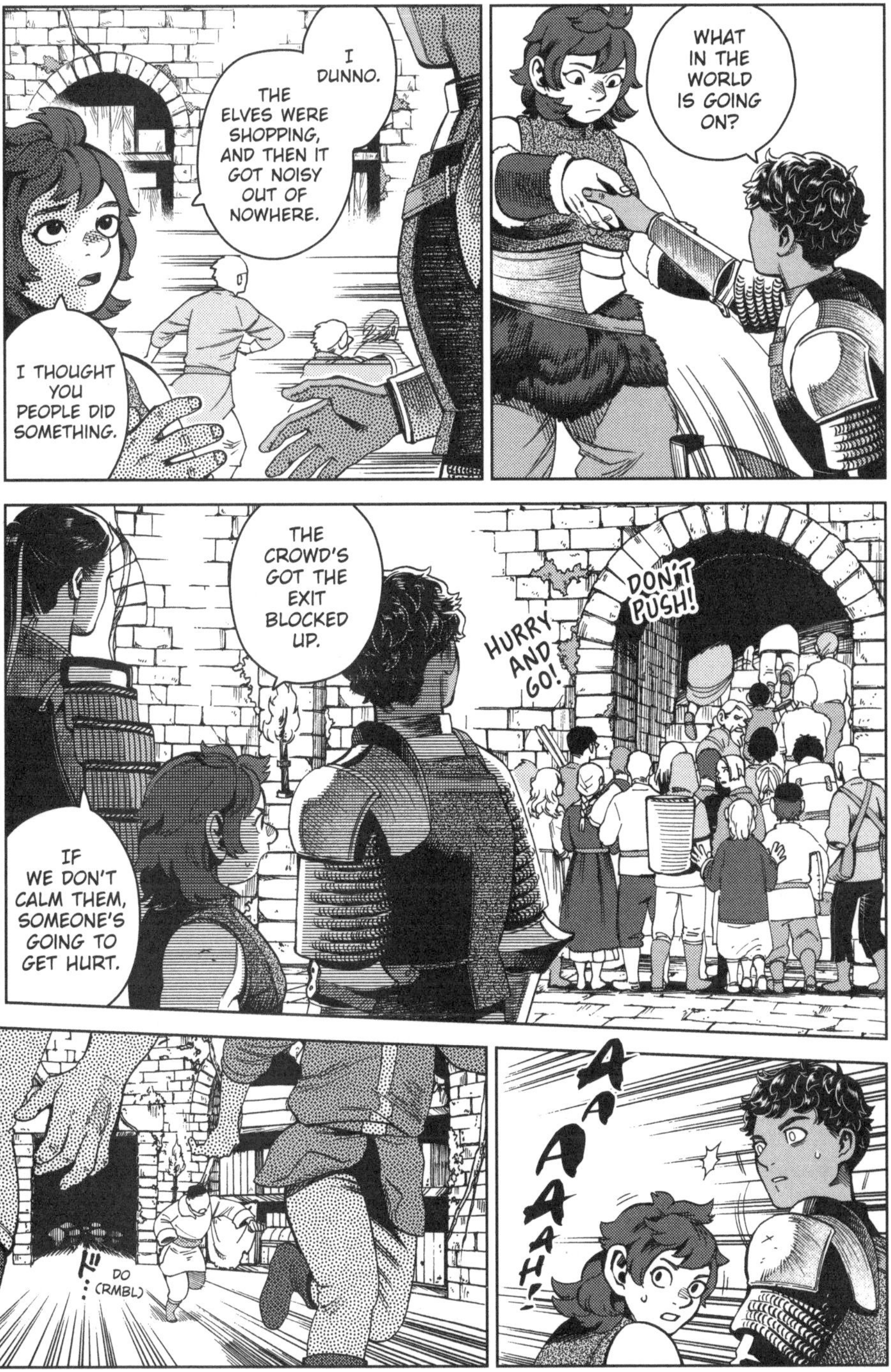
WHAT IN THE WORLD IS GOING ON?
I DUNNO. THE ELVES WERE SHOPPING, AND THEN IT GOT NOISY OUT OF NOWHERE.
I THOUGHT YOU PEOPLE DID SOMETHING.
DON'T PUSH!
HURRY AND GO!
THE CROWD'S GOT THE EXIT BLOCKED UP.
IF WE DON'T CALM THEM, SOMEONE'S GOING TO GET HURT.
AAAAAAH!
ド…
DO (RMBL)

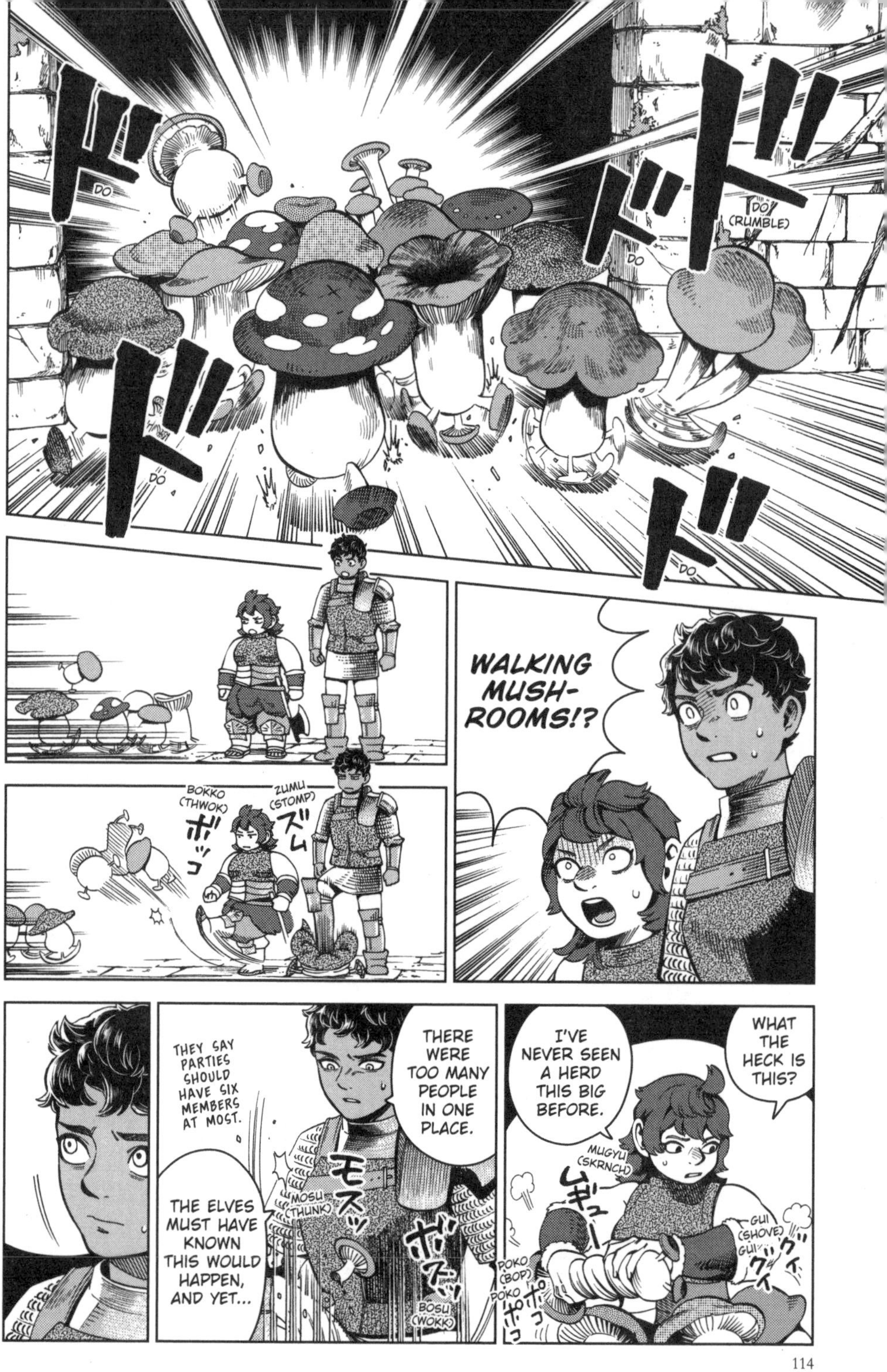
ドド
DO
DO (RUMBLE)
DO
ドド
DO
ドド
DO
WALKING MUSH-ROOMS!?
BOKKO (THWOK) ボッコ
ZUMU (STOMP) ズム
WHAT THE HECK IS THIS?
I'VE NEVER SEEN A HERD THIS BIG BEFORE.
MUGYU (SKRNCH) ムギュー
GUI (SHOVE) GUI グイグイ
POKO (BOP) POKO ポコポコ
THERE WERE TOO MANY PEOPLE IN ONE PLACE.
THEY SAY PARTIES SHOULD HAVE SIX MEMBERS AT MOST.
MOSU (THUNK) モスッ
BOSU (WOKK) ボスッ
THE ELVES MUST HAVE KNOWN THIS WOULD HAPPEN, AND YET...

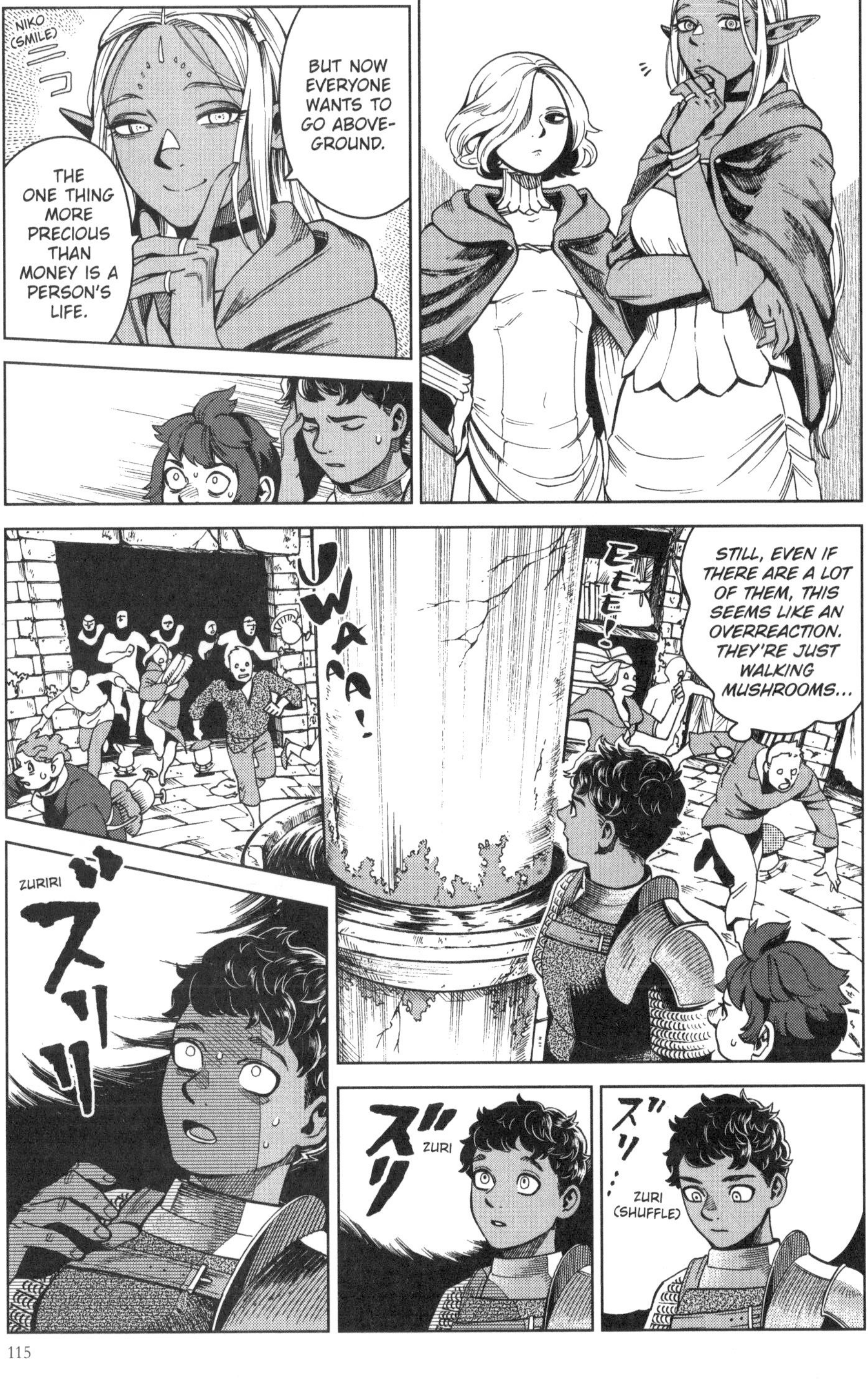
BUT NOW EVERYONE WANTS TO GO ABOVE-GROUND.
NIKO (SMILE)
ニコ
THE ONE THING MORE PRECIOUS THAN MONEY IS A PERSON'S LIFE.
STILL, EVEN IF THERE ARE A LOT OF THEM, THIS SEEMS LIKE AN OVERREACTION. THEY'RE JUST WALKING MUSHROOMS...
EEEE!
UWAAA!
ズリ…
ZURI (SHUFFLE)
ズリ
ZURI
ZURIRI
ズリリ

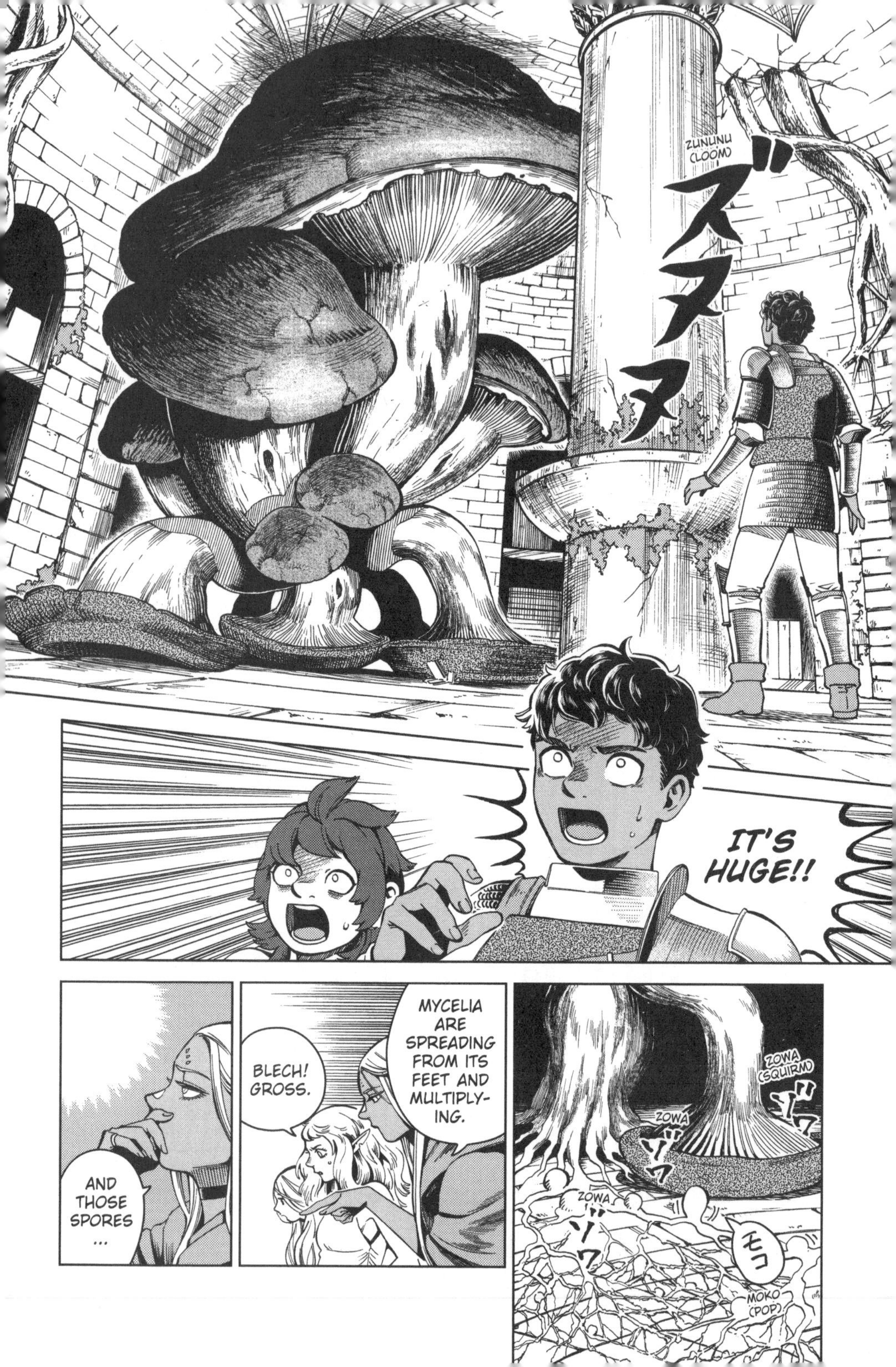
ZUNUNU (LOOM)
ズヌヌヌ
IT'S HUGE!!
ZOWA (SQUIRM)
ZOWA
ZOWA
モコ
MOKO (POP)
MYCELIA ARE SPREADING FROM ITS FEET AND MULTIPLYING.
BLECH! GROSS.
AND THOSE SPORES ...

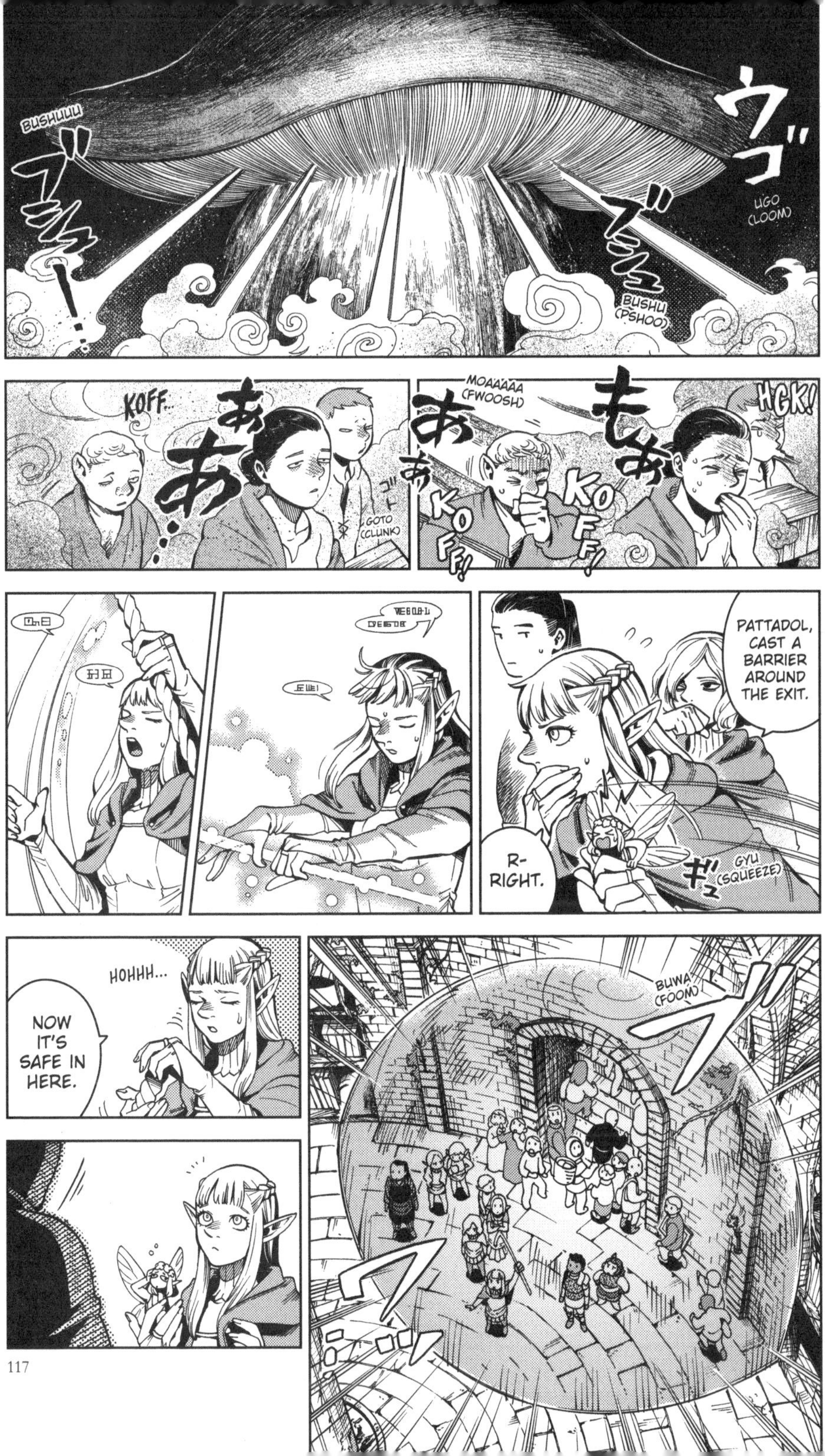

UGO (LOOM)
BUSHU (PSHOO)
BUSHUUU
HGK!
MOAAAAA (FWOOSH)
KOFF! KOFF!
GOTO (CLUNK)
KOFF...
PATTADOL, CAST A BARRIER AROUND THE EXIT.
R-RIGHT.
GYU (SQUEEZE)
BUWA (FOOM)
HOHHH...
NOW IT'S SAFE IN HERE.

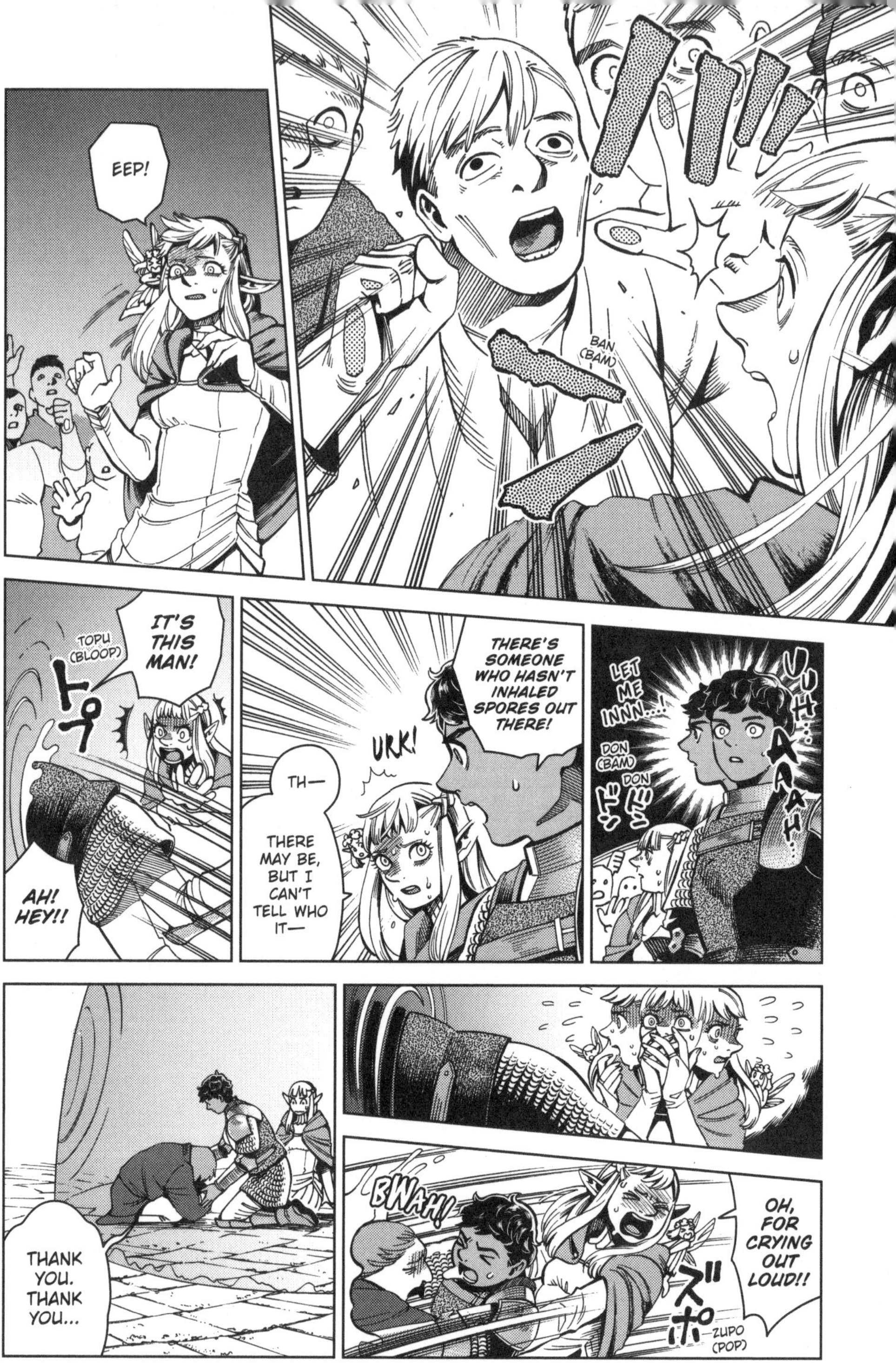
BAN (BAM)
EEP!
UUH... AAAH...
LET ME INNN...!
DON (BAM) DON
THERE'S SOMEONE WHO HASN'T INHALED SPORES OUT THERE!
URK!
TH—
THERE MAY BE, BUT I CAN'T TELL WHO IT—
IT'S THIS MAN!
TOPU (BLOOP)
AH! HEY!!
OH, FOR CRYING OUT LOUD!!
BWAH!
ZUPO (POP)
THANK YOU. THANK YOU...

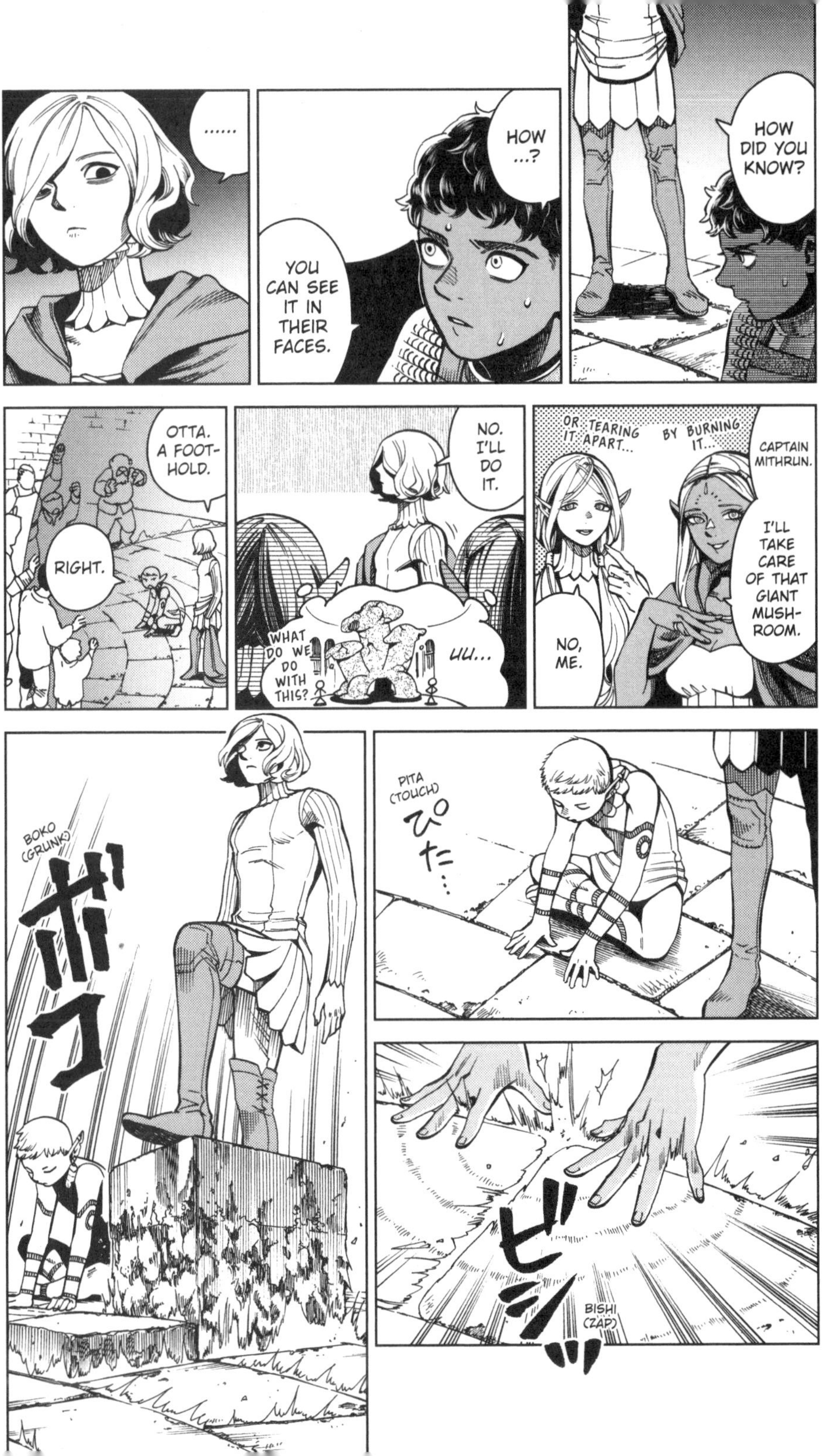
HOW DID YOU KNOW?
HOW ...?
YOU CAN SEE IT IN THEIR FACES.
......
CAPTAIN MITHRUN.
I'LL TAKE CARE OF THAT GIANT MUSH-ROOM.
BY BURNING IT...
OR TEARING IT APART...
NO, ME.
NO. I'LL DO IT.
UU...
WHAT DO WE DO WITH THIS?
OTTA. A FOOT-HOLD.
RIGHT.
PITA (TOUCH)
ぴた…
BISHI (ZAP)
ビシッ
BOKO (GRUNK)
ボコ

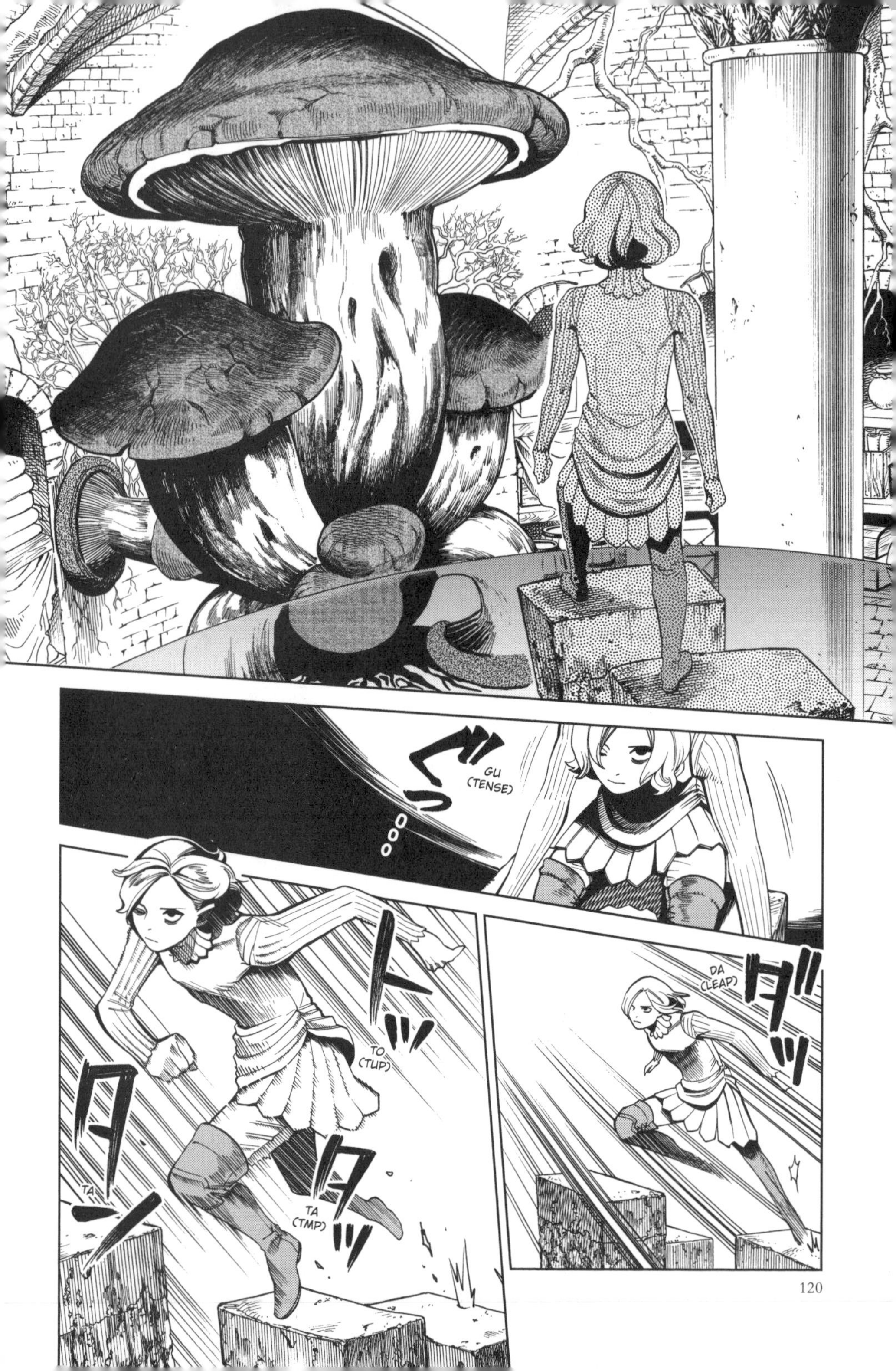
GU (TENSE)
DA (LEAP)
TO (TUP)
TA (TMP)
TA

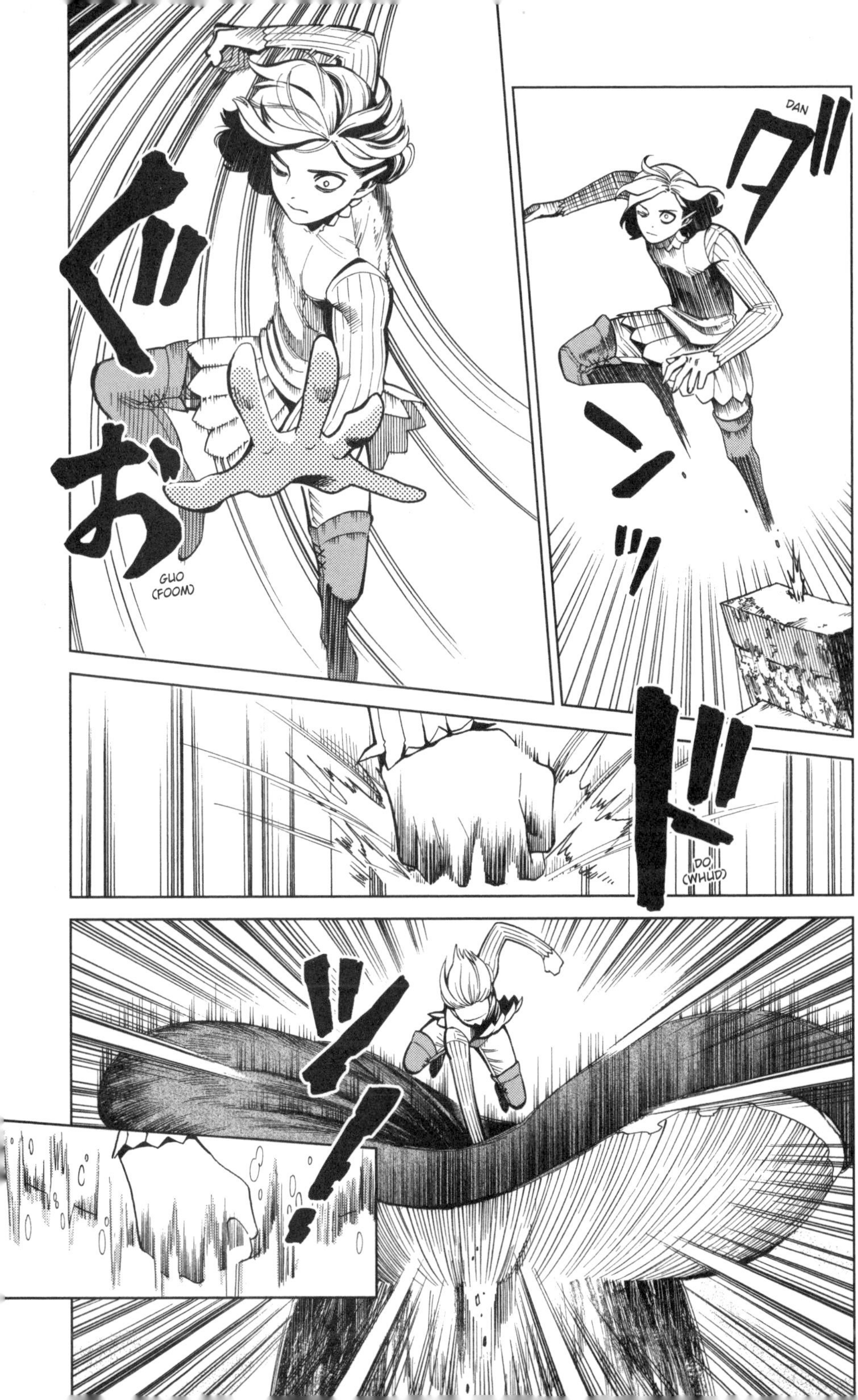
DAN
GUO
(FOOM)
DO
(WHUD)

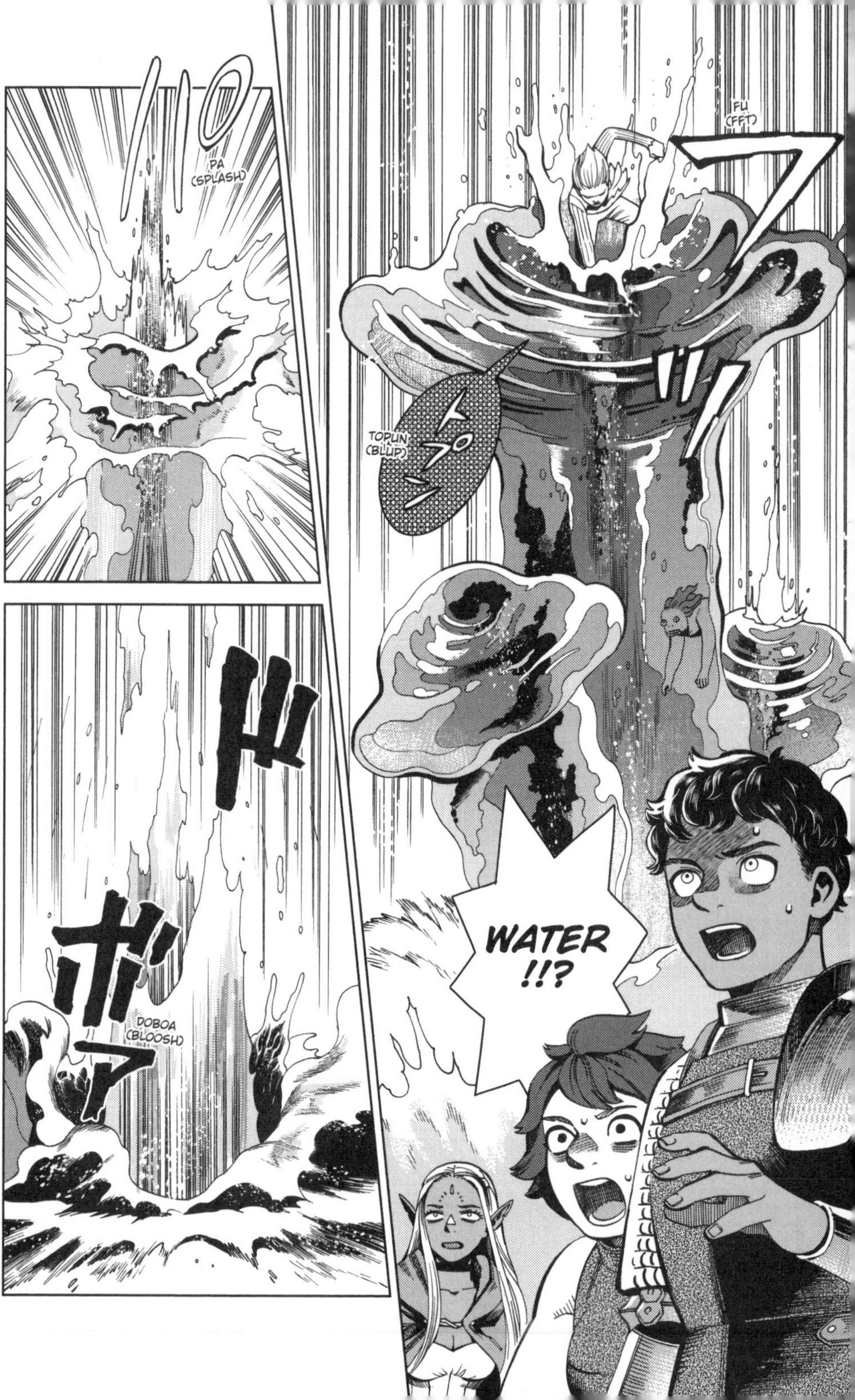
FU (FFT)
TOPUN (BLUP)
WATER !!?
PA (SPLASH)
DOBOA (BLOOSH)

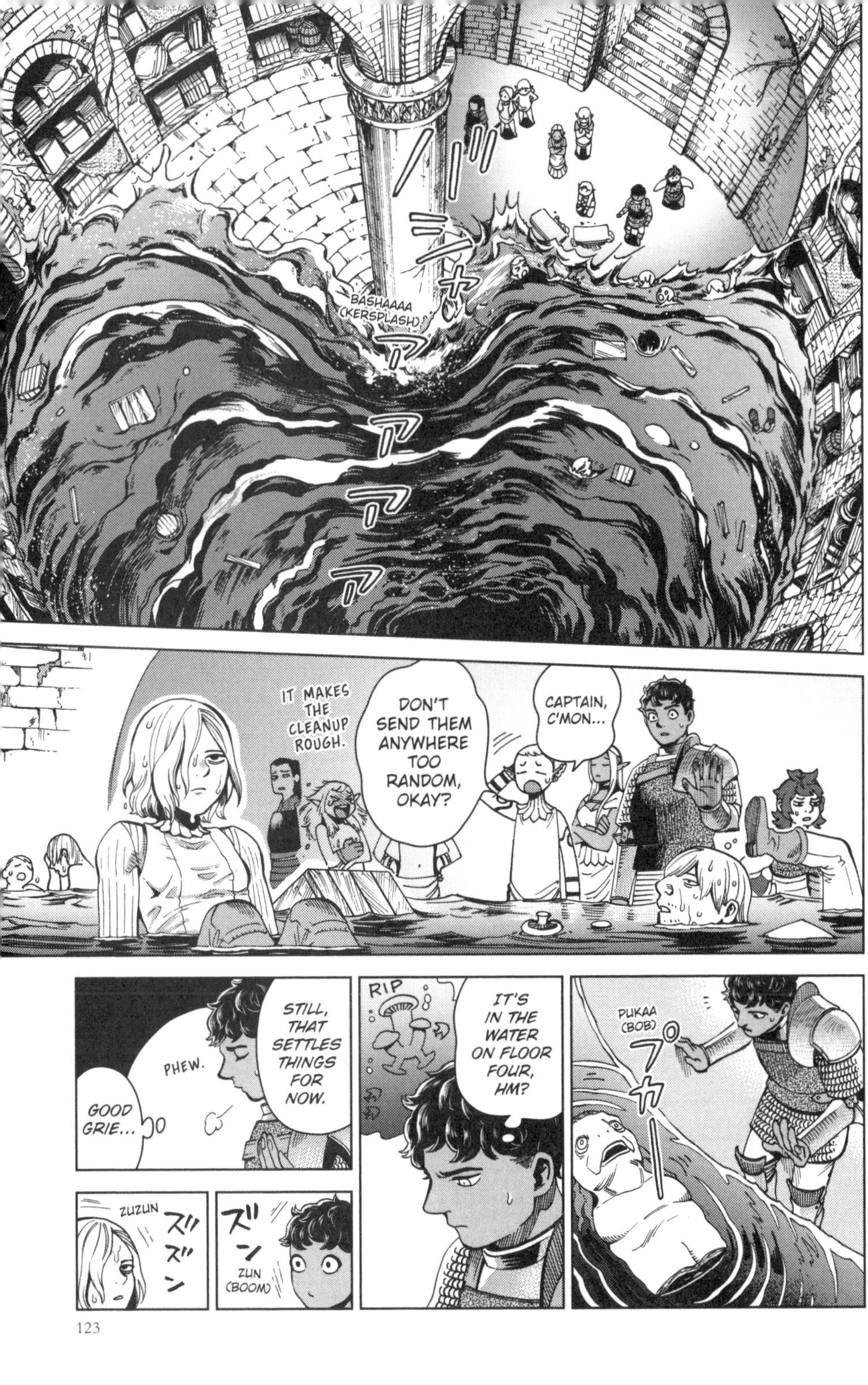
BASHAAAA (KERSPLASH)
CAPTAIN, C'MON...
DON'T SEND THEM ANYWHERE TOO RANDOM, OKAY?
IT MAKES THE CLEANUP ROUGH.
PUKAA (BOB)
RIP
IT'S IN THE WATER ON FLOOR FOUR, HM?
STILL, THAT SETTLES THINGS FOR NOW.
PHEW.
GOOD GRIE...
ZUN (BOOM)
ZUZUN

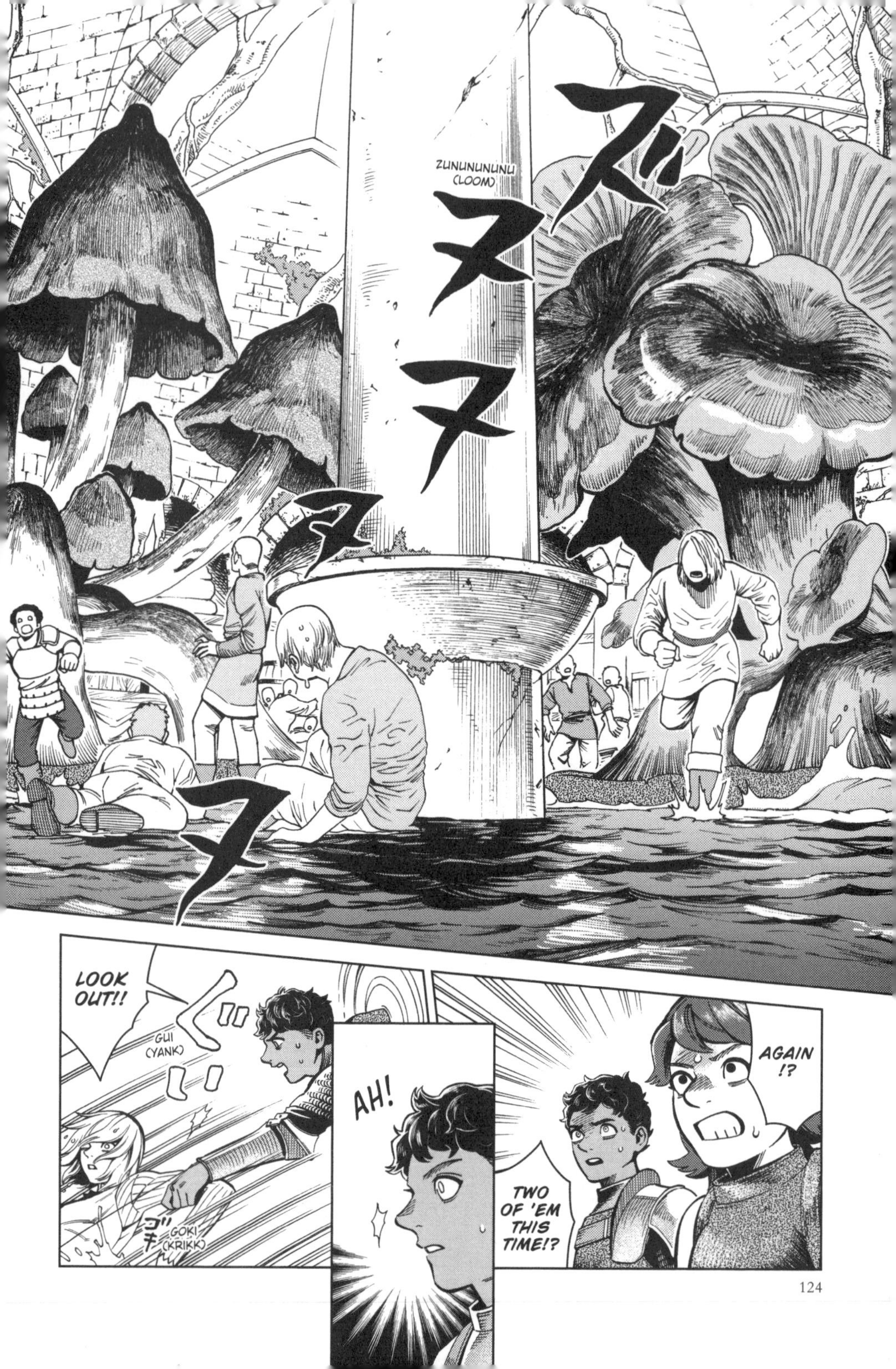
ZUNUNUNUNU
(LOOM)
AGAIN!?
TWO OF 'EM THIS TIME!?
AH!
LOOK OUT!!
ぐいっ
GUI (YANK)
ゴキ
GOKI (KRIKK)

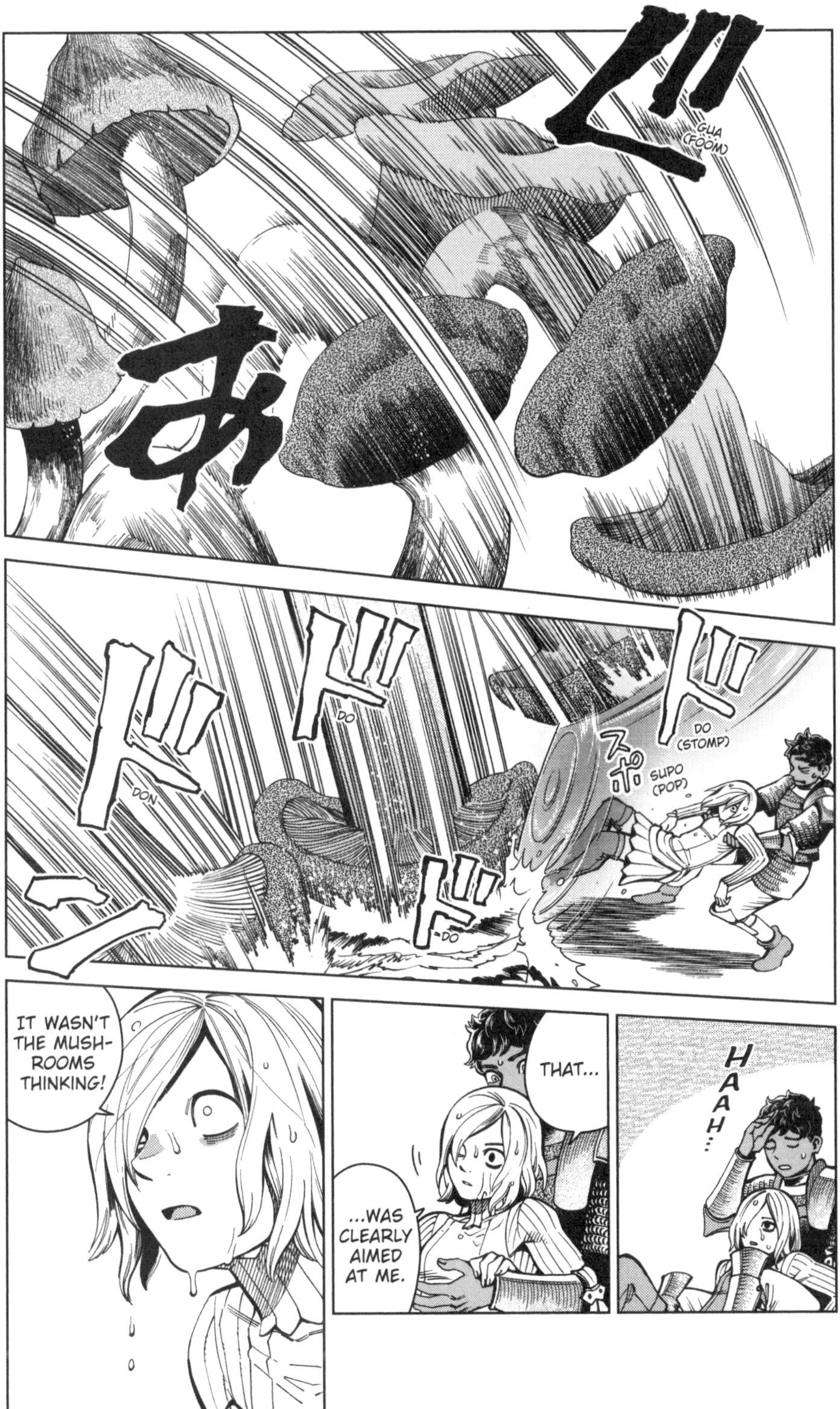

ぐ
GUA (FOOM)
あ
ドッ
DO (STOMP)
スポ
SUPO (POP)
ドッ
DO
ドッ
DON
ドッ
DO
HAAH...
THAT...
...WAS CLEARLY AIMED AT ME.
IT WASN'T THE MUSH-ROOMS THINKING!

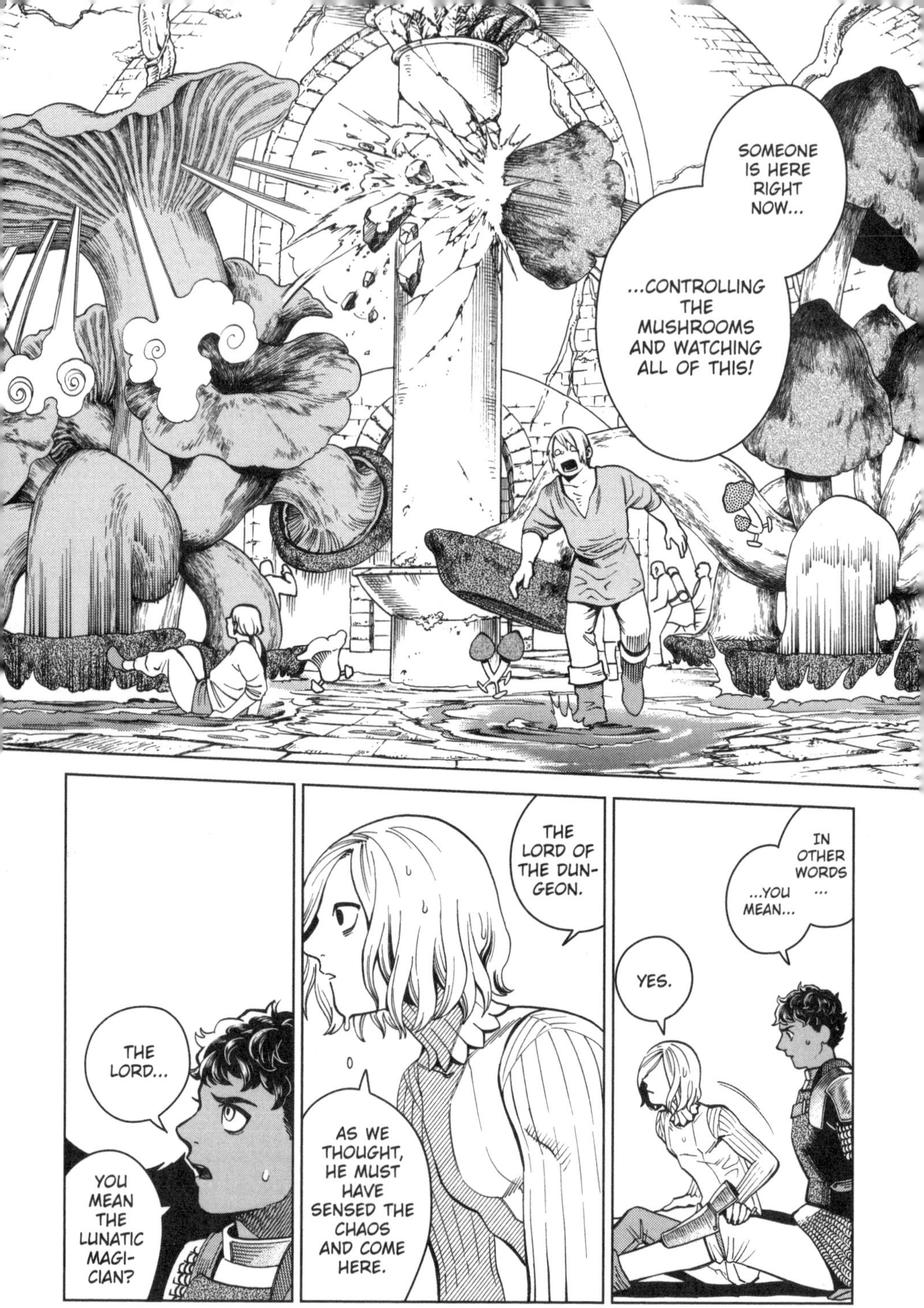
SOMEONE IS HERE RIGHT NOW...
...CONTROLLING THE MUSHROOMS AND WATCHING ALL OF THIS!
IN OTHER WORDS...
...YOU MEAN...
YES.
THE LORD OF THE DUNGEON.
AS WE THOUGHT, HE MUST HAVE SENSED THE CHAOS AND COME HERE.
THE LORD...
YOU MEAN THE LUNATIC MAGICIAN?

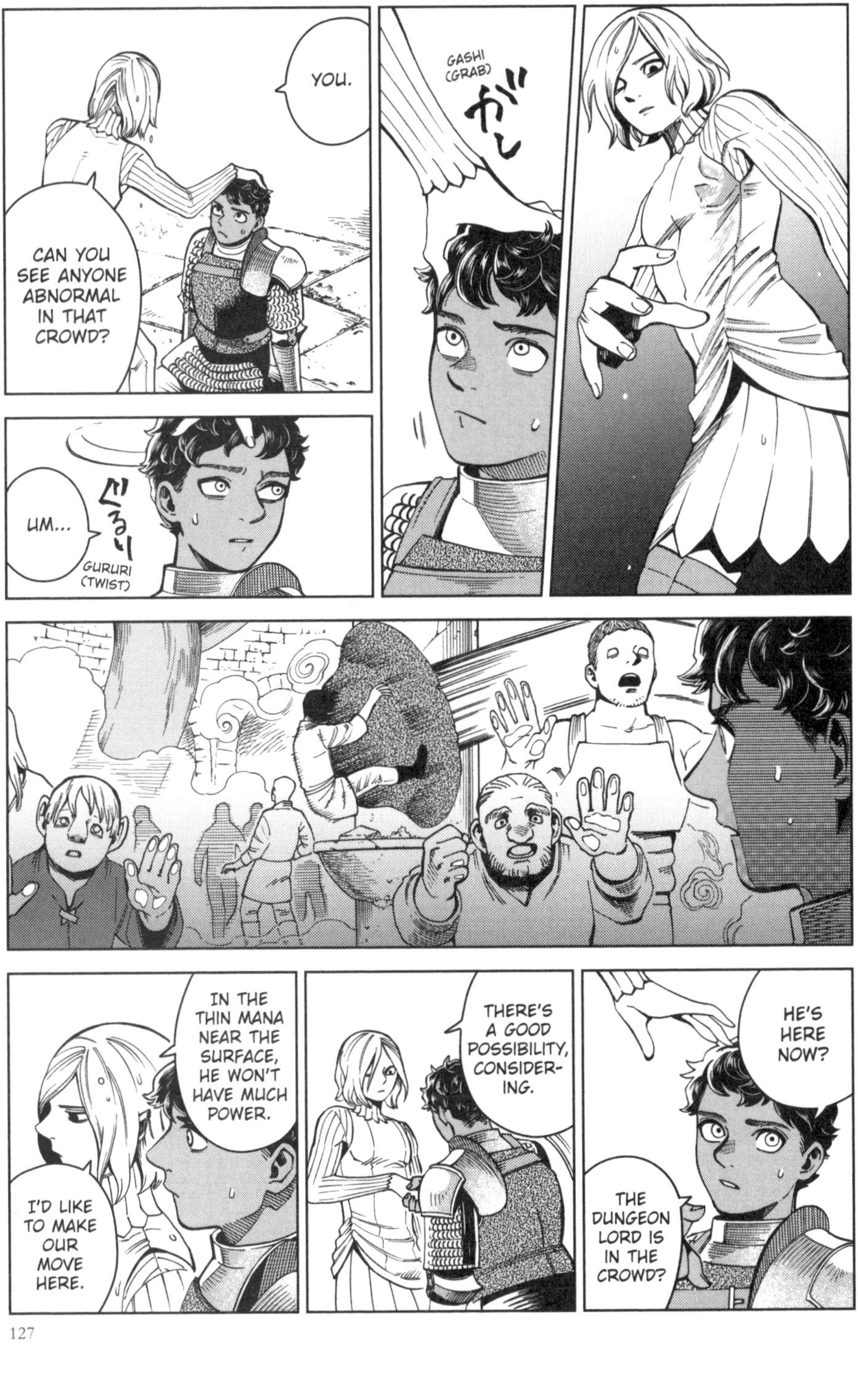
GASHI (GRAB)
がし
YOU.
CAN YOU SEE ANYONE ABNORMAL IN THAT CROWD?
UM...
ぐるり
GURURI (TWIST)
HE'S HERE NOW?
THE DUNGEON LORD IS IN THE CROWD?
THERE'S A GOOD POSSIBILITY, CONSIDER-ING.
IN THE THIN MANA NEAR THE SURFACE, HE WON'T HAVE MUCH POWER.
I'D LIKE TO MAKE OUR MOVE HERE.

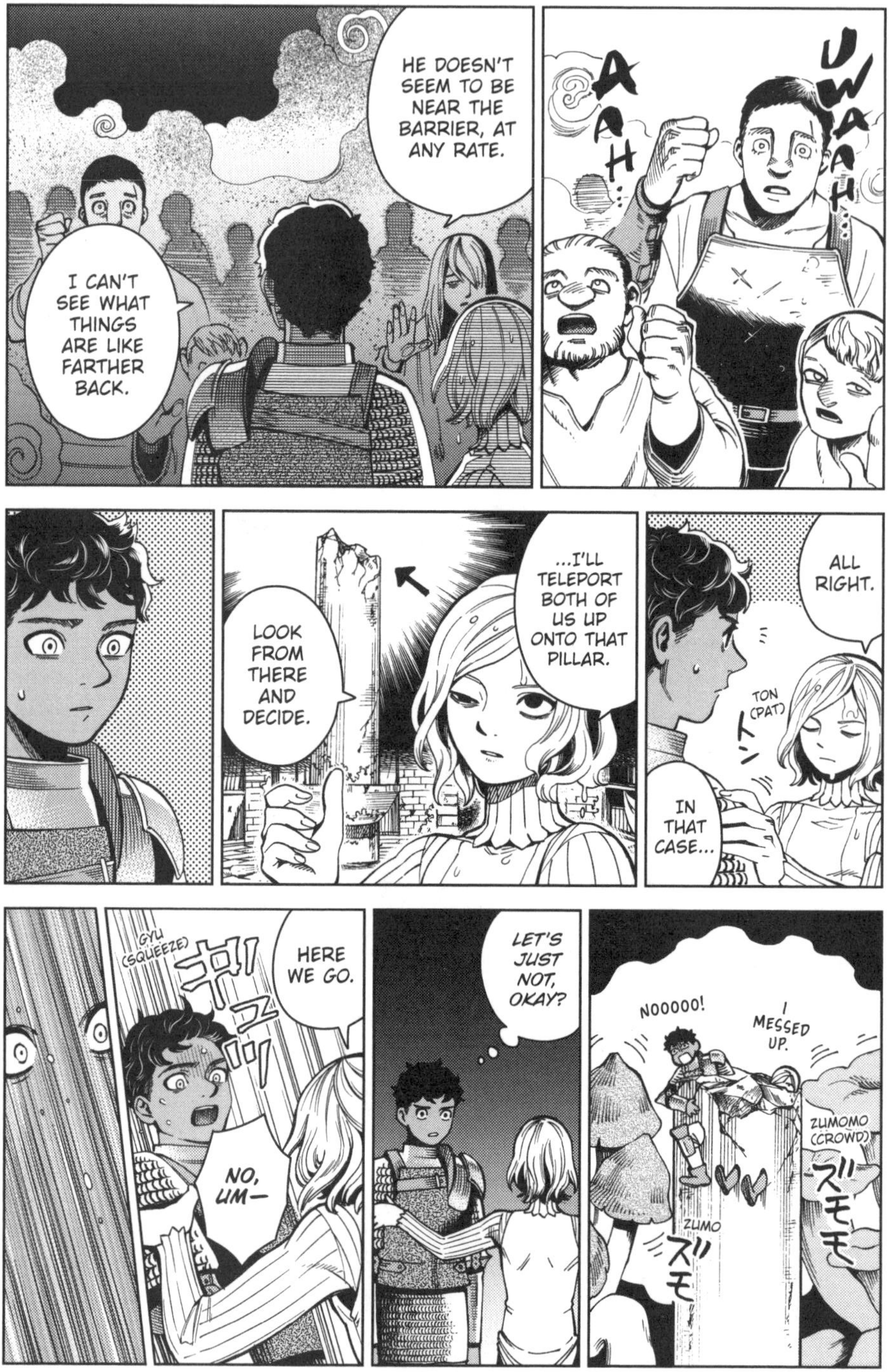
UWAAH...
AAH...
HE DOESN'T SEEM TO BE NEAR THE BARRIER, AT ANY RATE.
I CAN'T SEE WHAT THINGS ARE LIKE FARTHER BACK.
ALL RIGHT.
TON (PAT)
IN THAT CASE...
...I'LL TELEPORT BOTH OF US UP ONTO THAT PILLAR.
LOOK FROM THERE AND DECIDE.
I MESSED UP.
NOOOOO!
ZUMOMO (CROWD)
ZUMO
LET'S JUST NOT, OKAY?
HERE WE GO.
GYU (SQUEEZE)
NO, UM—

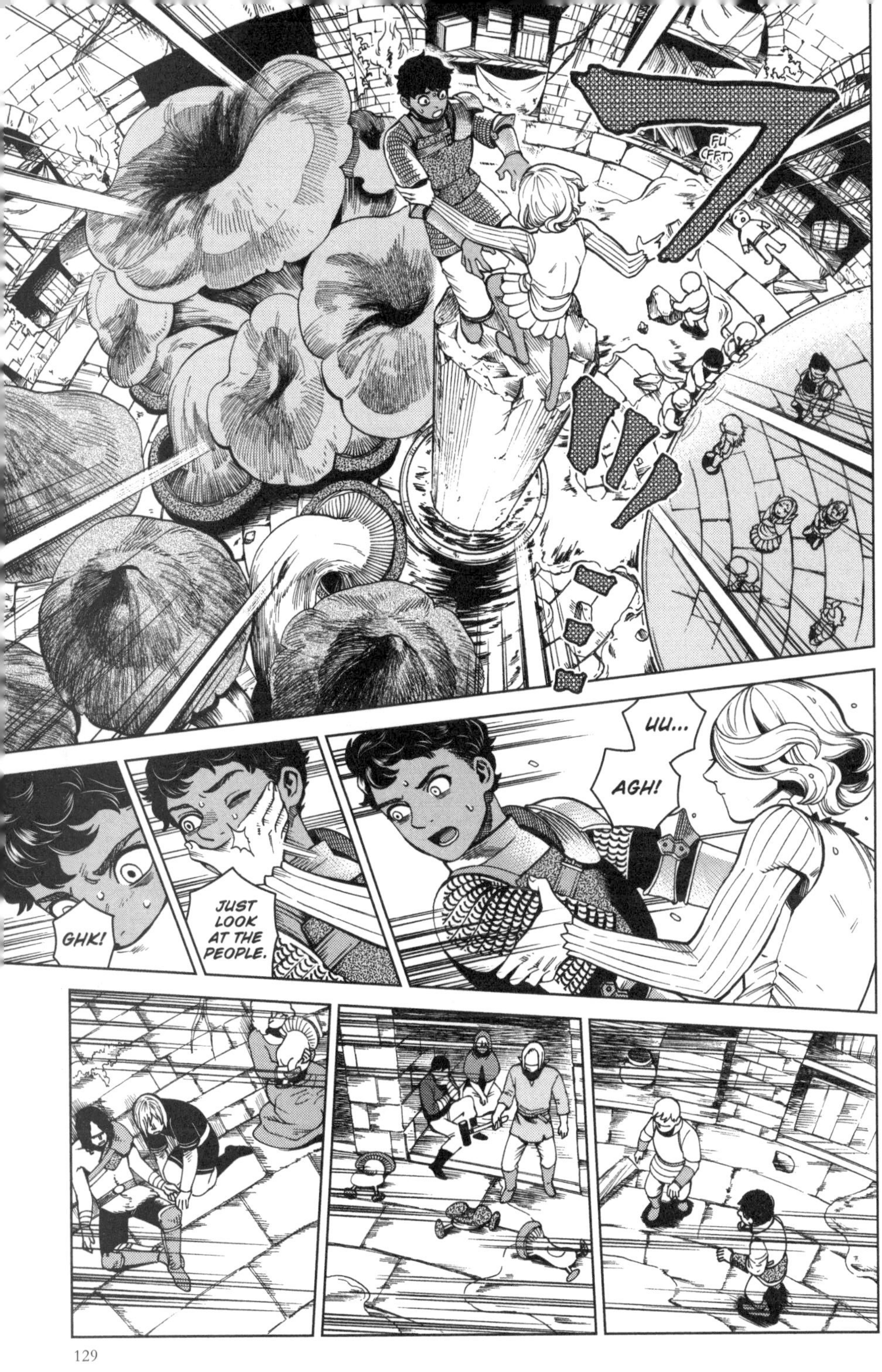
FU (FFT)
UU...
AGH!
JUST LOOK AT THE PEOPLE.
GHK!

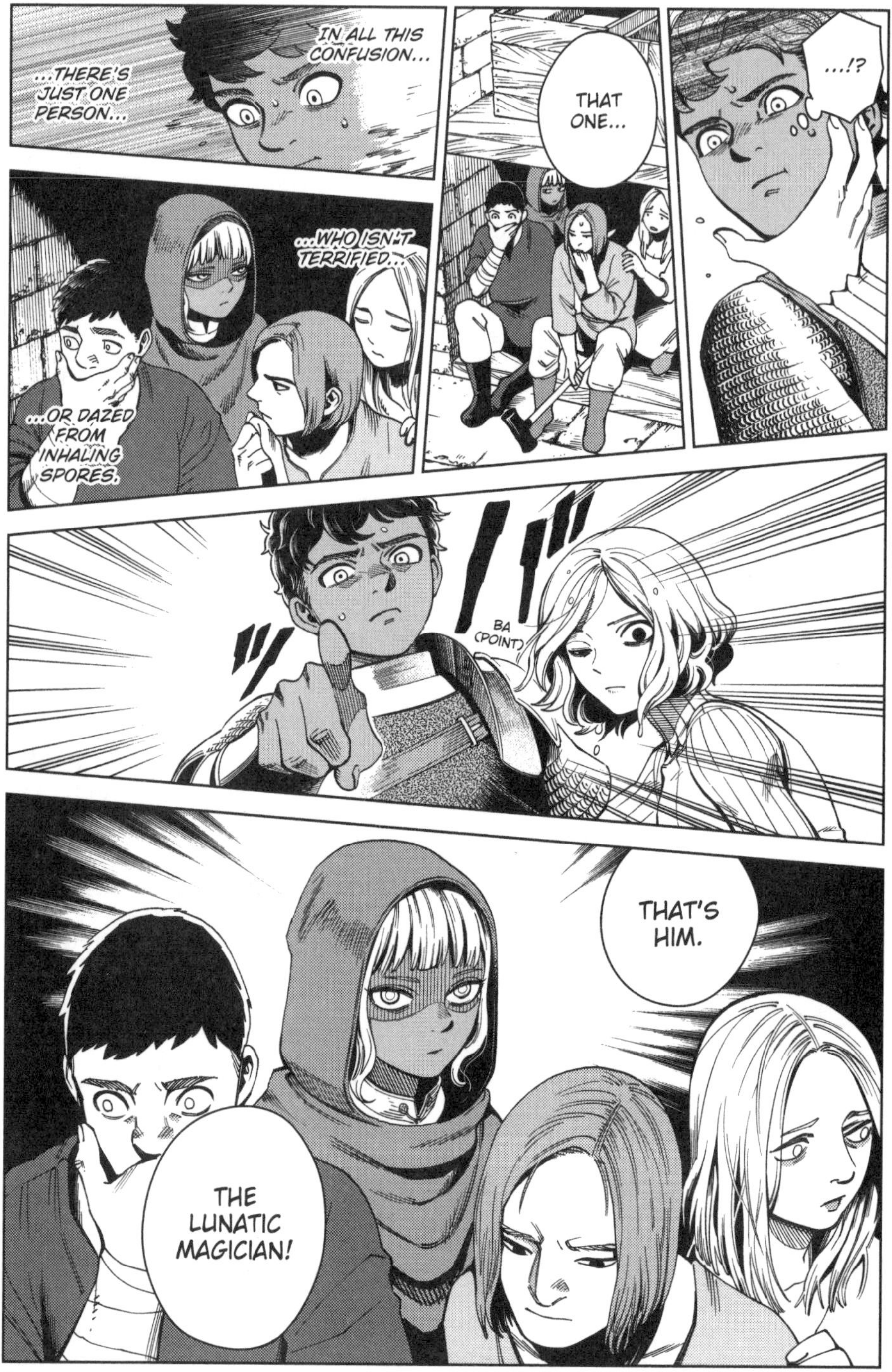
...!?
THAT ONE...
IN ALL THIS CONFUSION...
...THERE'S JUST ONE PERSON...
...WHO ISN'T TERRIFIED...
...OR DAZED FROM INHALING SPORES.
BA (POINT)
THAT'S HIM.
THE LUNATIC MAGICIAN!

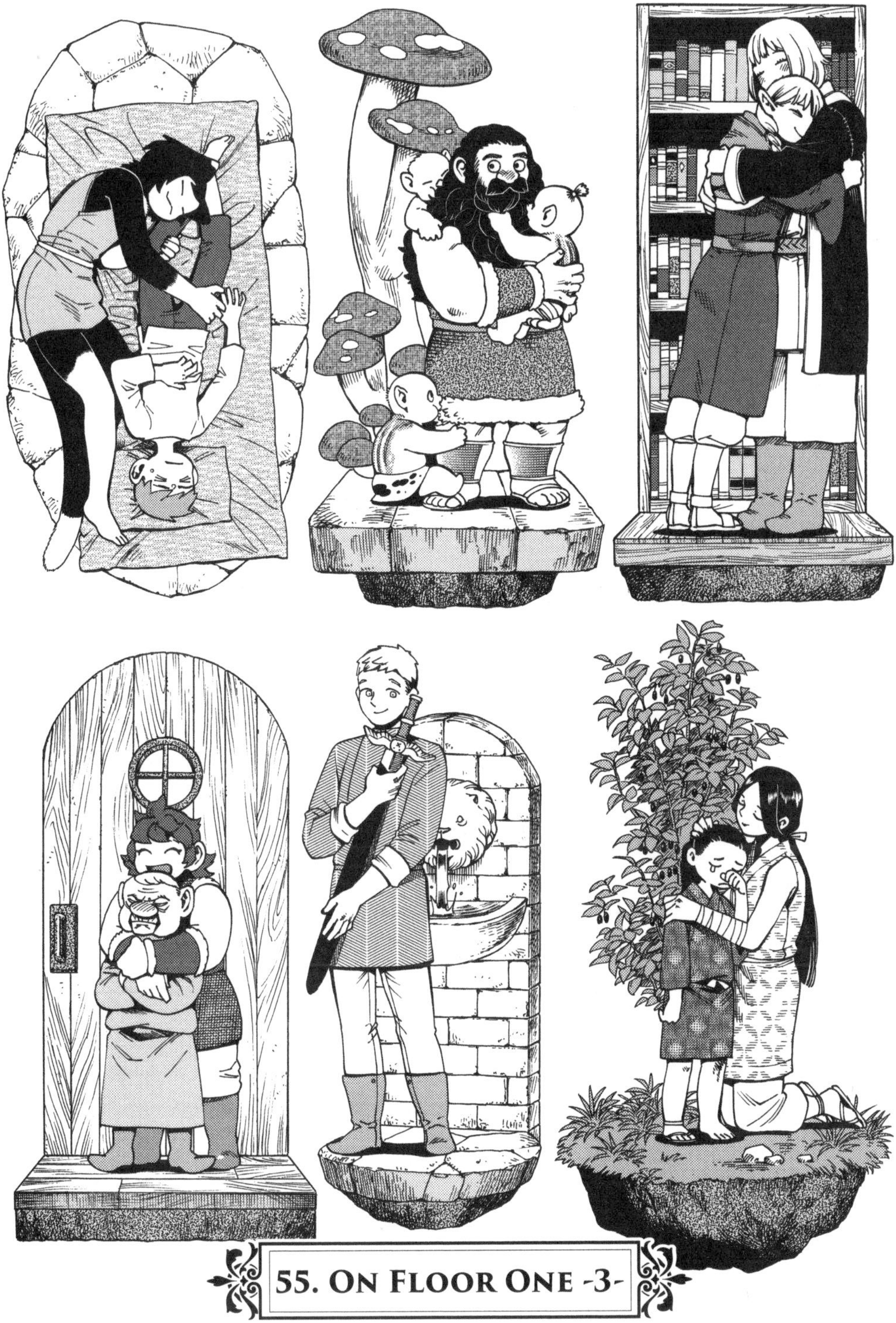

55. On Floor One -3-

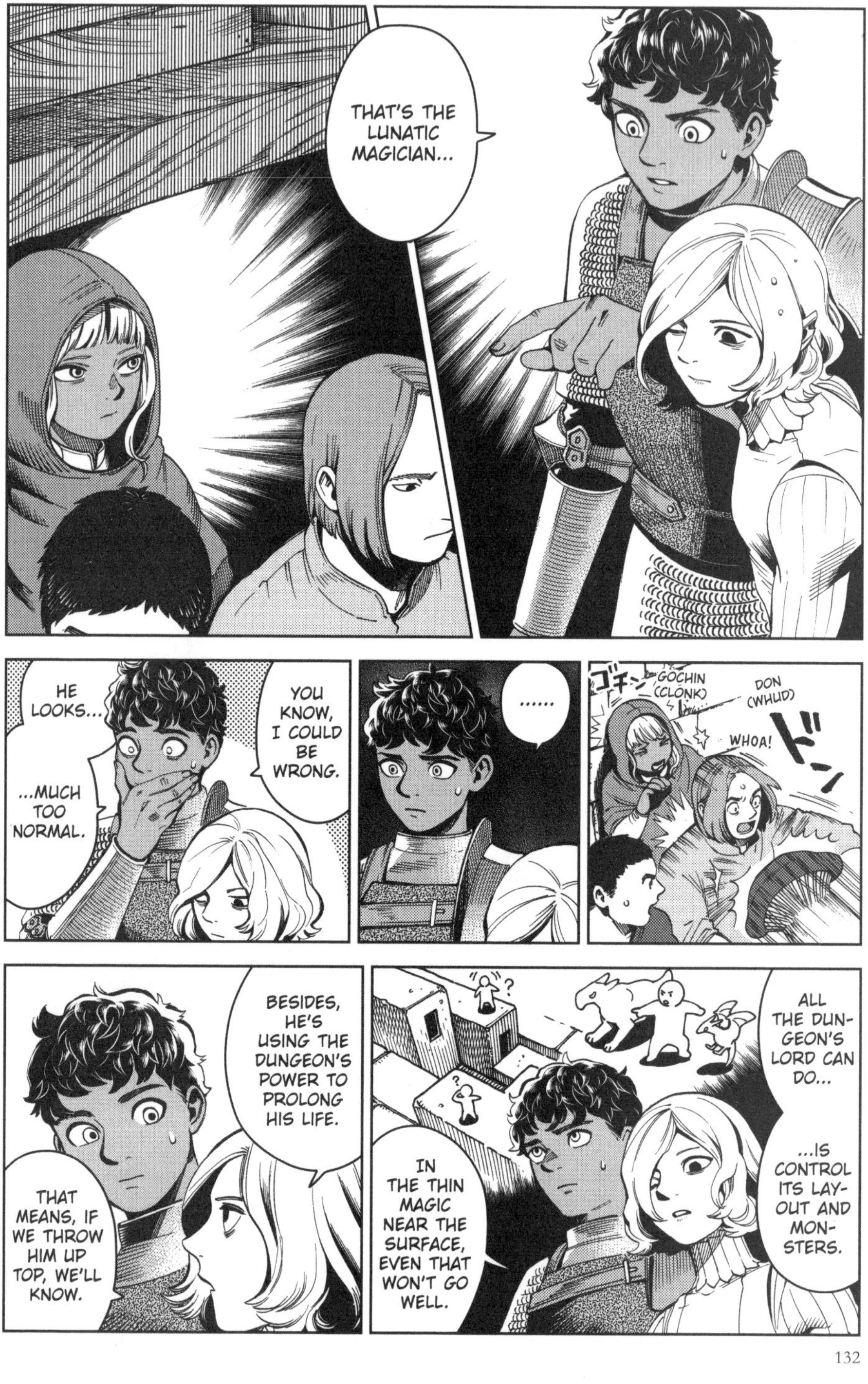
THAT'S THE LUNATIC MAGICIAN...
ゴチン
GOCHIN (CLONK)
DON (WHUD)
ドン
WHOA!
......
YOU KNOW, I COULD BE WRONG.
HE LOOKS...
...MUCH TOO NORMAL.
ALL THE DUNGEON'S LORD CAN DO...
...IS CONTROL ITS LAYOUT AND MONSTERS.
IN THE THIN MAGIC NEAR THE SURFACE, EVEN THAT WON'T GO WELL.
BESIDES, HE'S USING THE DUNGEON'S POWER TO PROLONG HIS LIFE.
THAT MEANS, IF WE THROW HIM UP TOP, WE'LL KNOW.

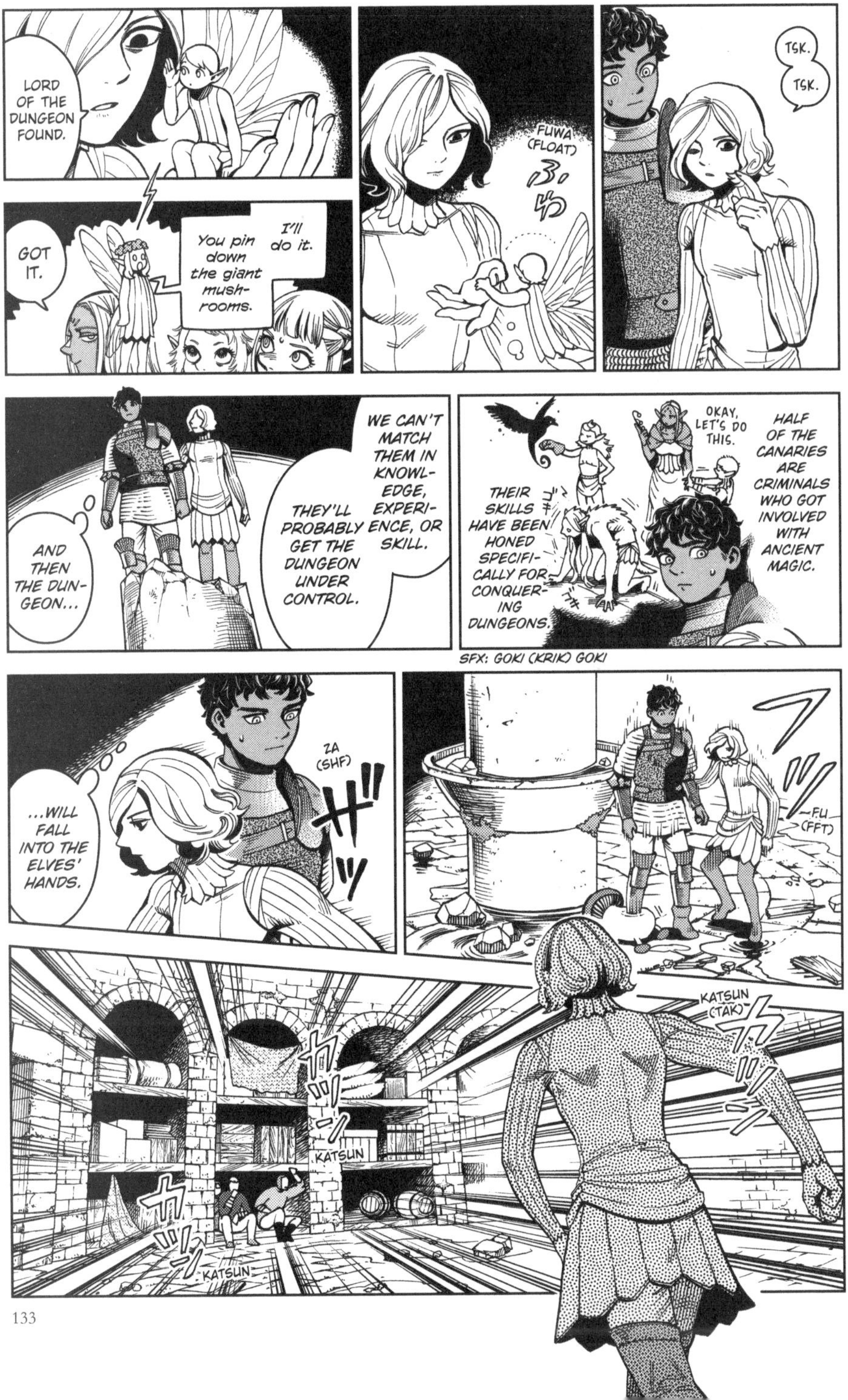
TSK. TSK.
FUWA (FLOAT)
LORD OF THE DUNGEON FOUND.
I'll do it.
You pin down the giant mushrooms.
GOT IT.
HALF OF THE CANARIES ARE CRIMINALS WHO GOT INVOLVED WITH ANCIENT MAGIC.
OKAY, LET'S DO THIS.
THEIR SKILLS HAVE BEEN HONED SPECIFICALLY FOR CONQUERING DUNGEONS.
SFX: GOKI (KRIK) GOKI
WE CAN'T MATCH THEM IN KNOWLEDGE, EXPERIENCE, OR SKILL.
THEY'LL PROBABLY GET THE DUNGEON UNDER CONTROL.
AND THEN THE DUNGEON...
FU (FFT)
ZA (SHF)
...WILL FALL INTO THE ELVES' HANDS.
KATSUN (TAK)
KATSUN
KATSUN

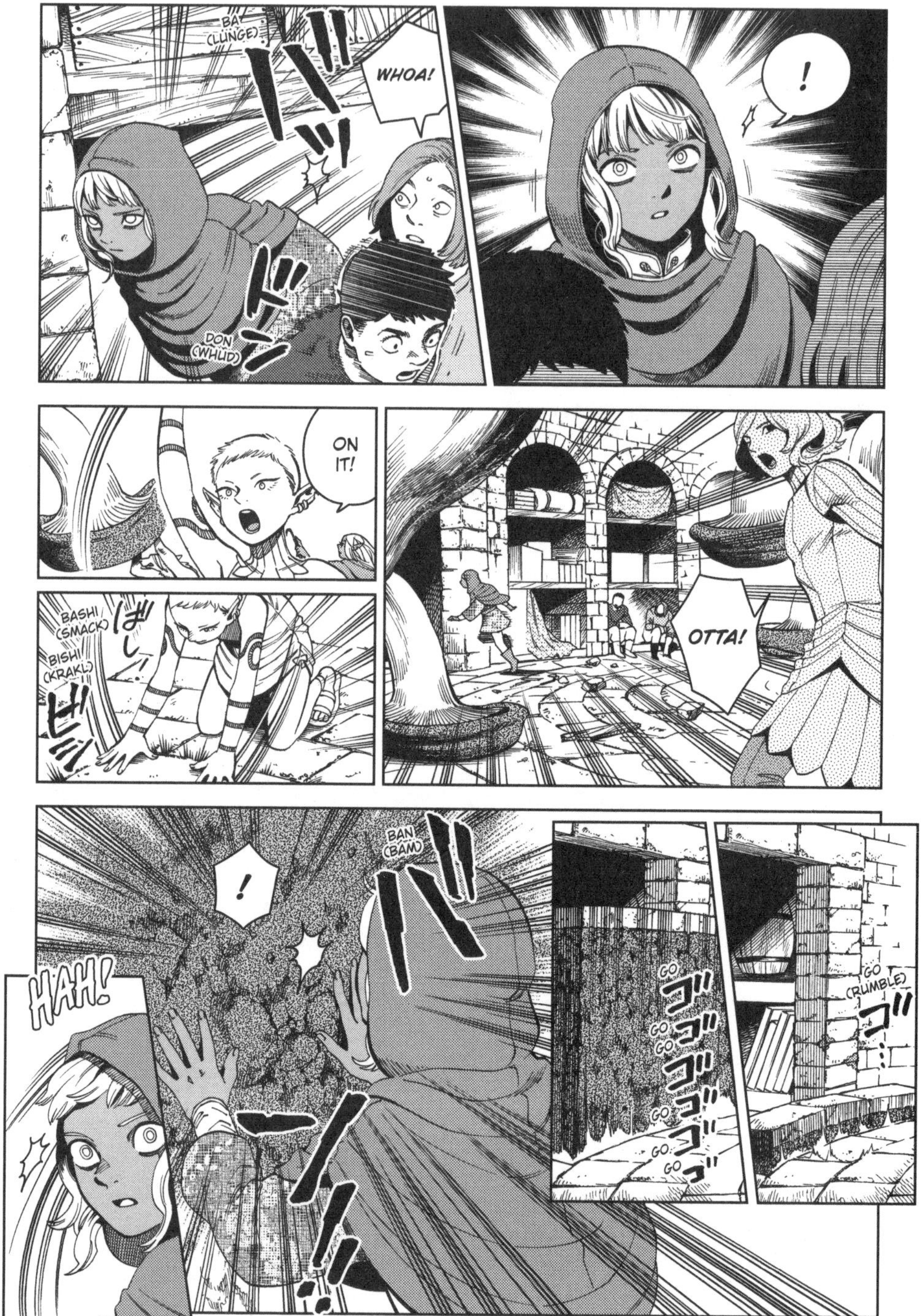
!
WHOA!
BA (LUNGE)
DON (WHUD)
OTTA!
ON IT!
BASHI (SMACK)
BISHI (KRAKL)
GO (RUMBLE)
GO GO GO GO GO GO
BAN (BAM)
!
HAH!

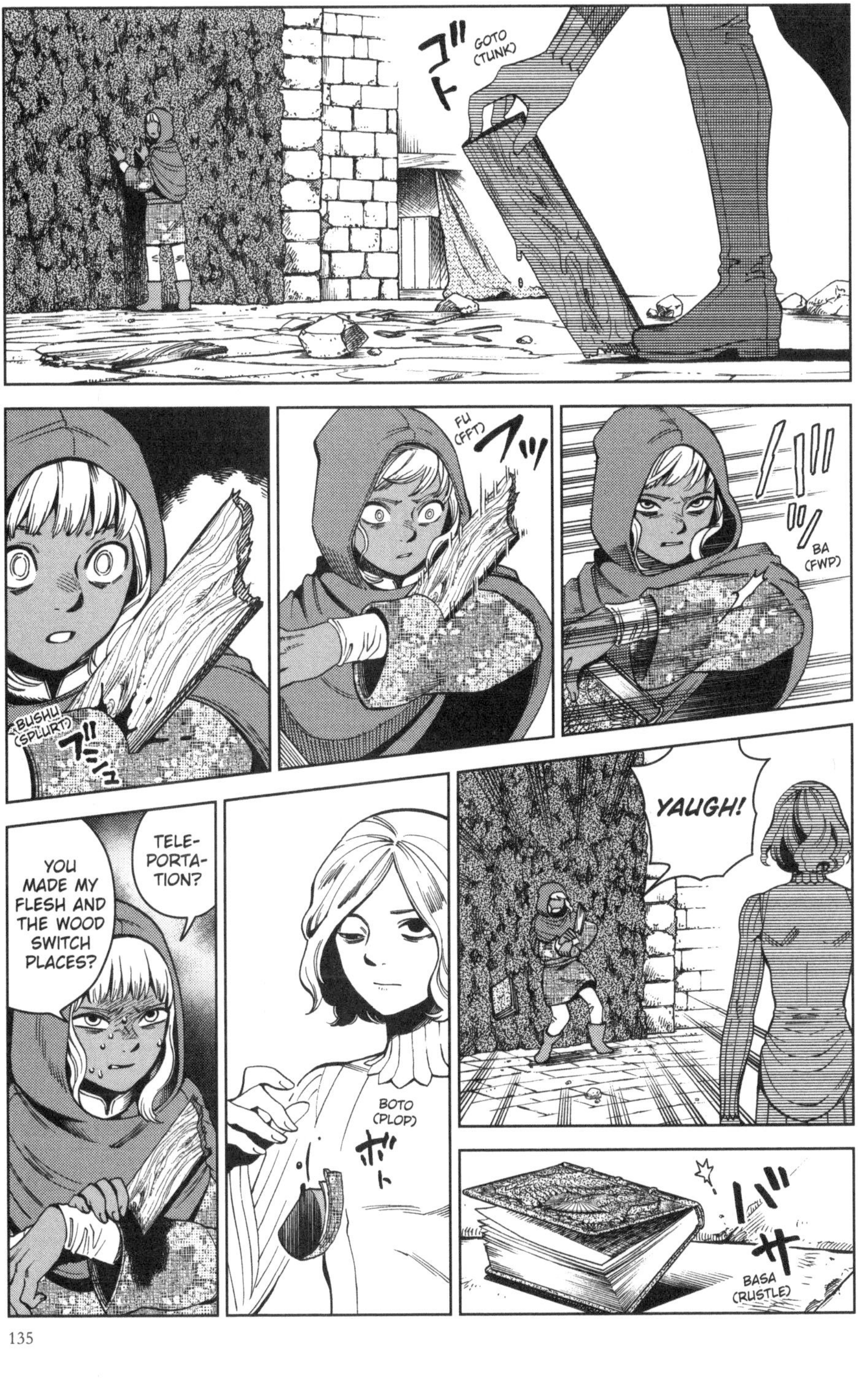

ゴト
GOTO (TUNK)
BA (FWP)
フッ
FU (FFT)
BUSHU (SPLURT)
ブシュ
YAUGH!
バサ
BASA (RUSTLE)
BOTO (PLOP)
ボト
TELE-PORTATION?
YOU MADE MY FLESH AND THE WOOD SWITCH PLACES?

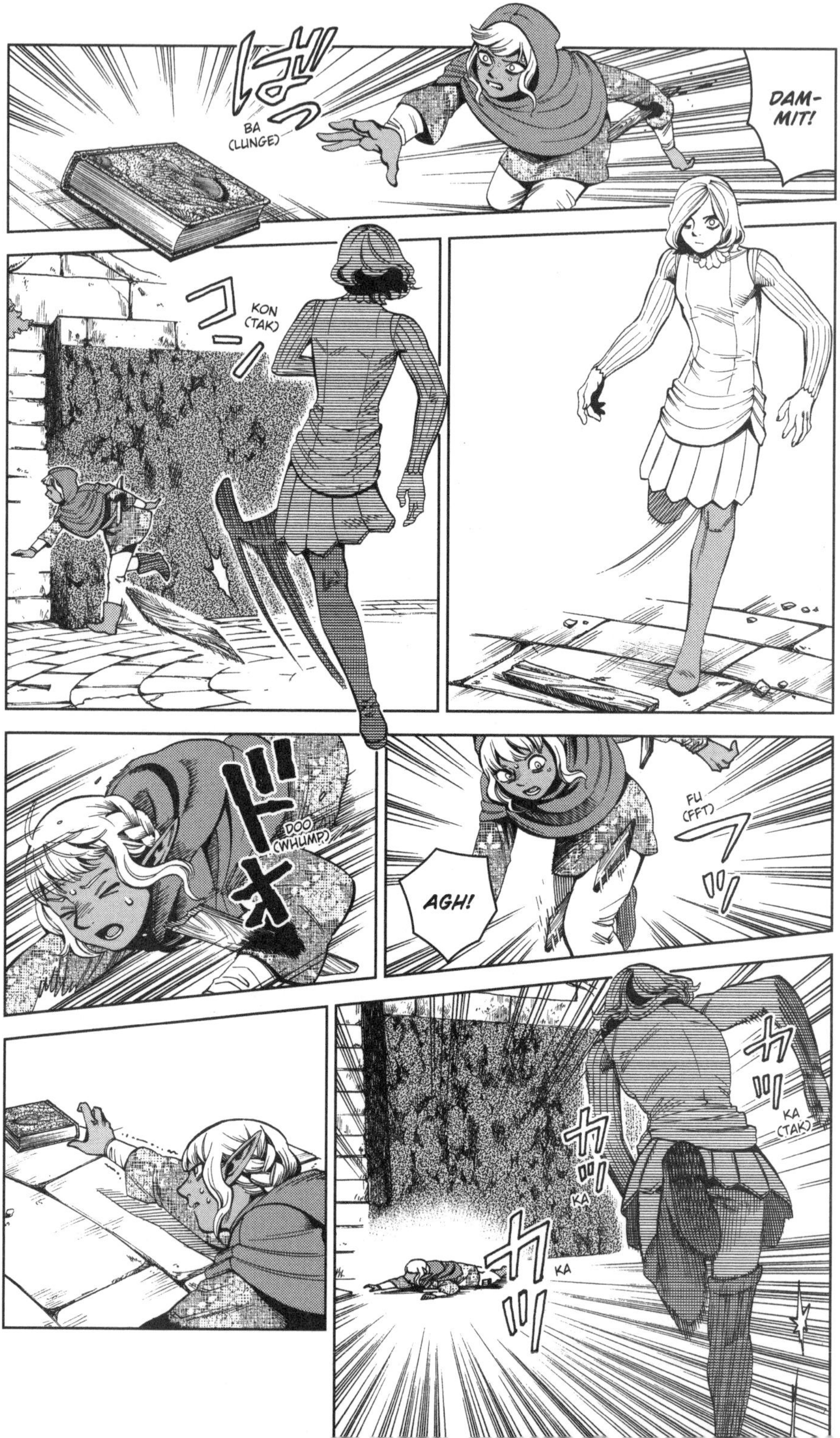
DAM-MIT!
ばっ
BA (LUNGE)
コーン
KON (TAK)
AGH!
フッ
FU (FFFT)
ドオ
DOO (WHUMP)
カッ
KA (TAK)
カッ
KA
カッ
KA

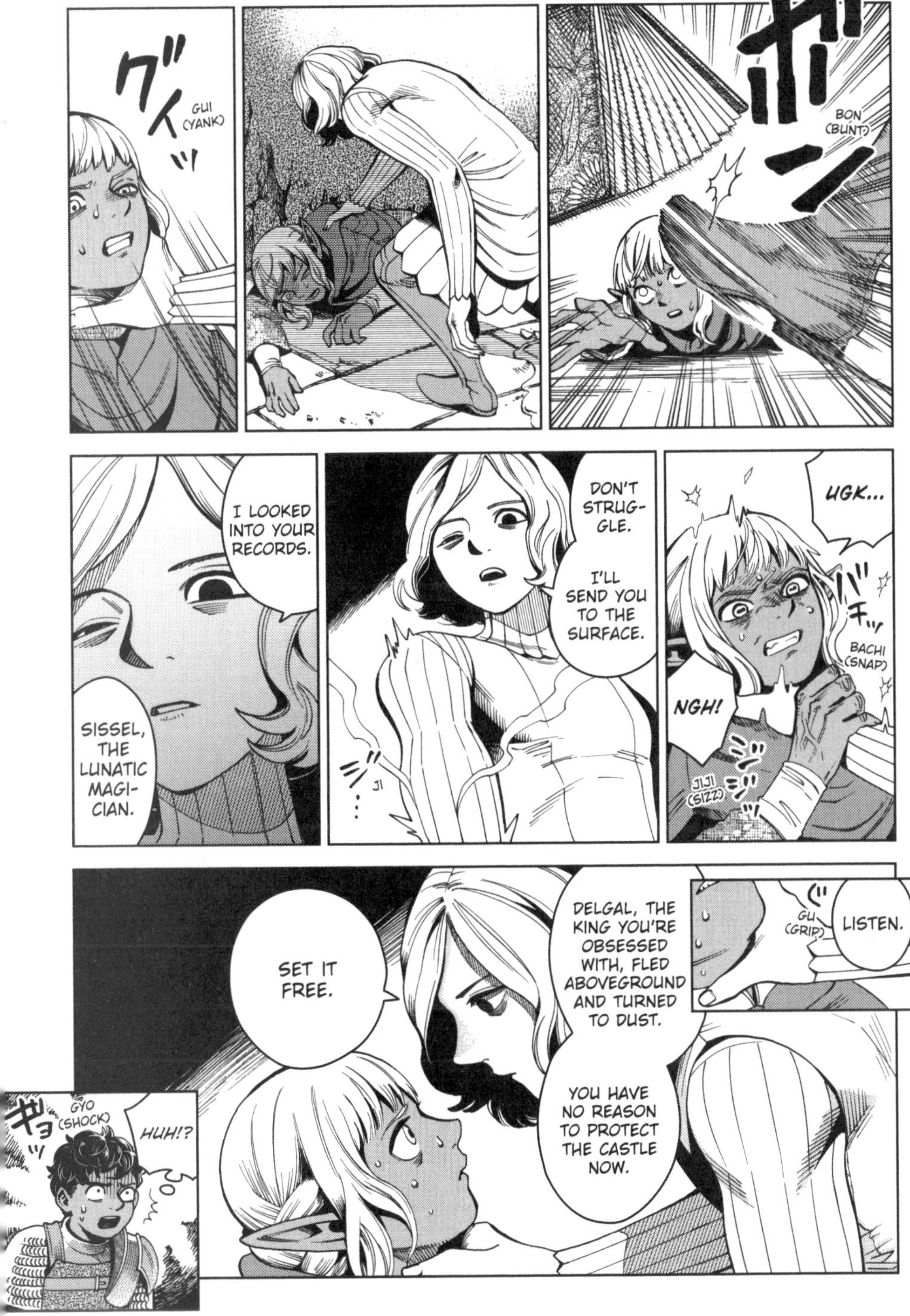
BON (BUNT)
GUI (YANK)
UGK...
BACHI (SNAP)
NGH!
JIJI (SIZZ)
DON'T STRUG-GLE.
I'LL SEND YOU TO THE SURFACE.
JI
I LOOKED INTO YOUR RECORDS.
SISSEL, THE LUNATIC MAGI-CIAN.
GU (GRIP)
LISTEN.
DELGAL, THE KING YOU'RE OBSESSED WITH, FLED ABOVEGROUND AND TURNED TO DUST.
YOU HAVE NO REASON TO PROTECT THE CASTLE NOW.
SET IT FREE.
GYO (SHOCK)
HUH!?

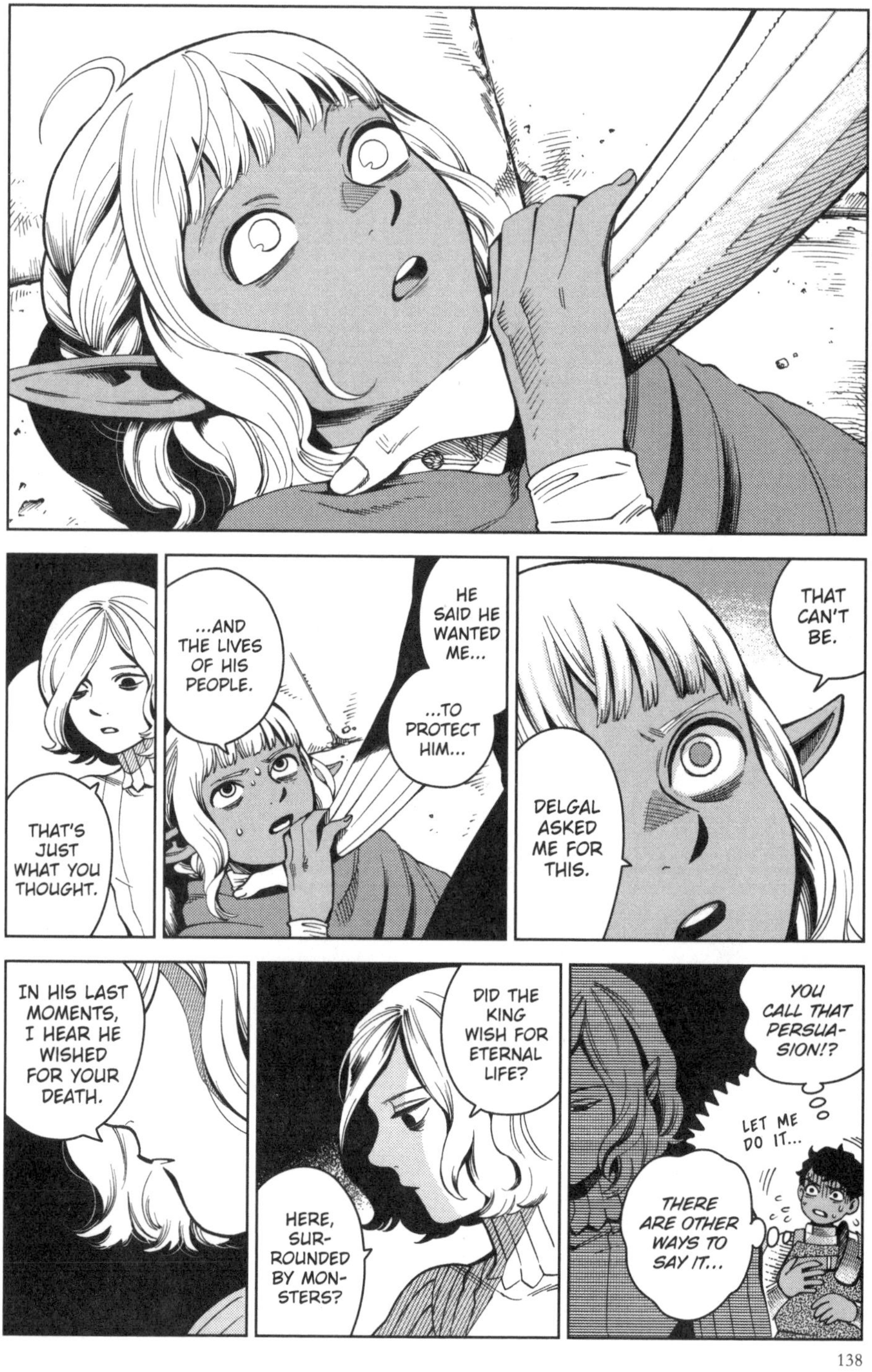
THAT CAN'T BE.
DELGAL ASKED ME FOR THIS.
HE SAID HE WANTED ME...
...TO PROTECT HIM...
...AND THE LIVES OF HIS PEOPLE.
THAT'S JUST WHAT YOU THOUGHT.
YOU CALL THAT PERSUASION!?
LET ME DO IT...
THERE ARE OTHER WAYS TO SAY IT...
DID THE KING WISH FOR ETERNAL LIFE?
HERE, SURROUNDED BY MONSTERS?
IN HIS LAST MOMENTS, I HEAR HE WISHED FOR YOUR DEATH.

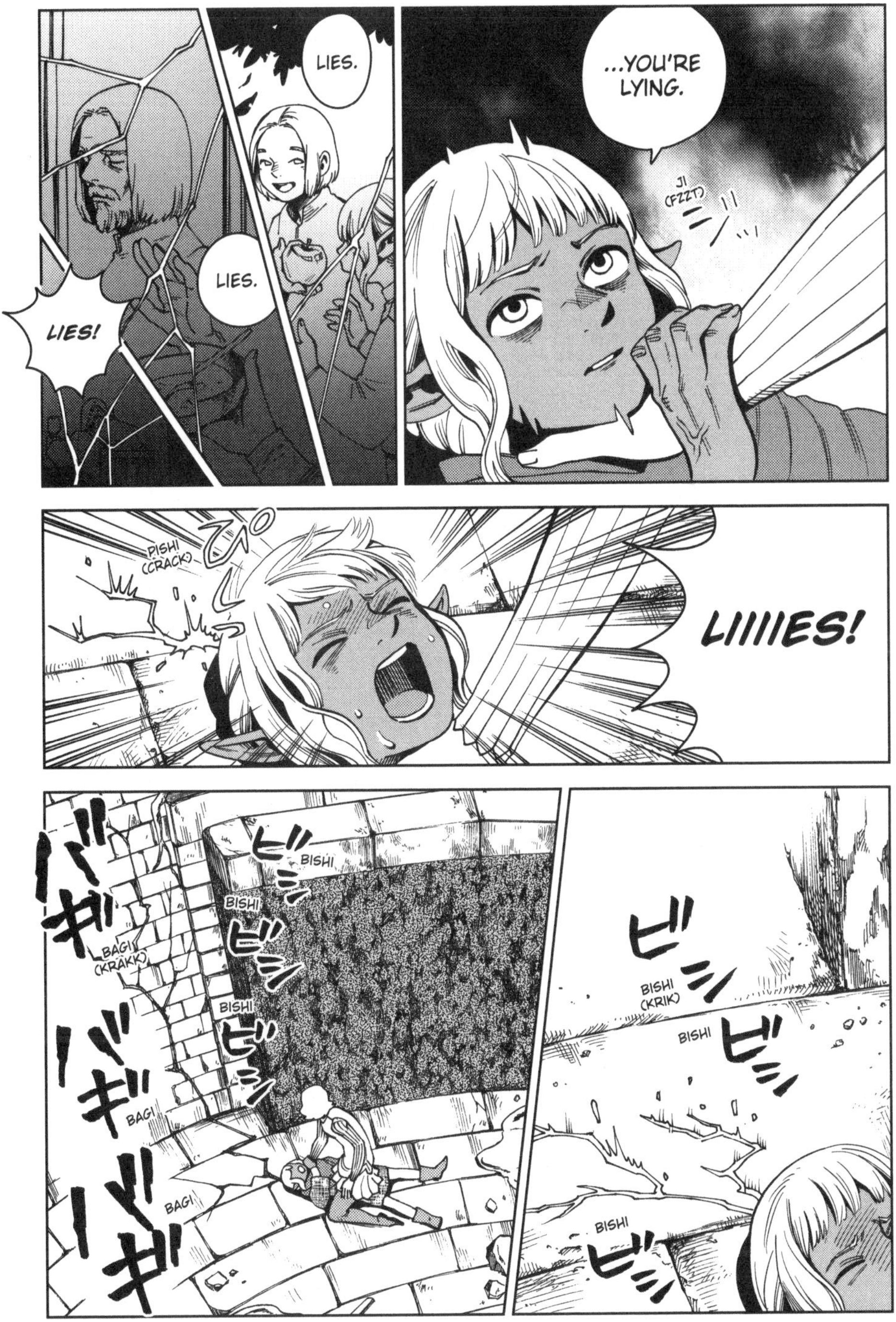
...YOU'RE LYING.
JI (FZZT)
LIES.
LIES.
LIES!
LIIIIES!
PISHI (CRACK)
BISHI (KRIK)
BISHI
BISHI
BISHI
BISHI
BAGI (KRÄKK)
BISHI
BAGI
BAGI

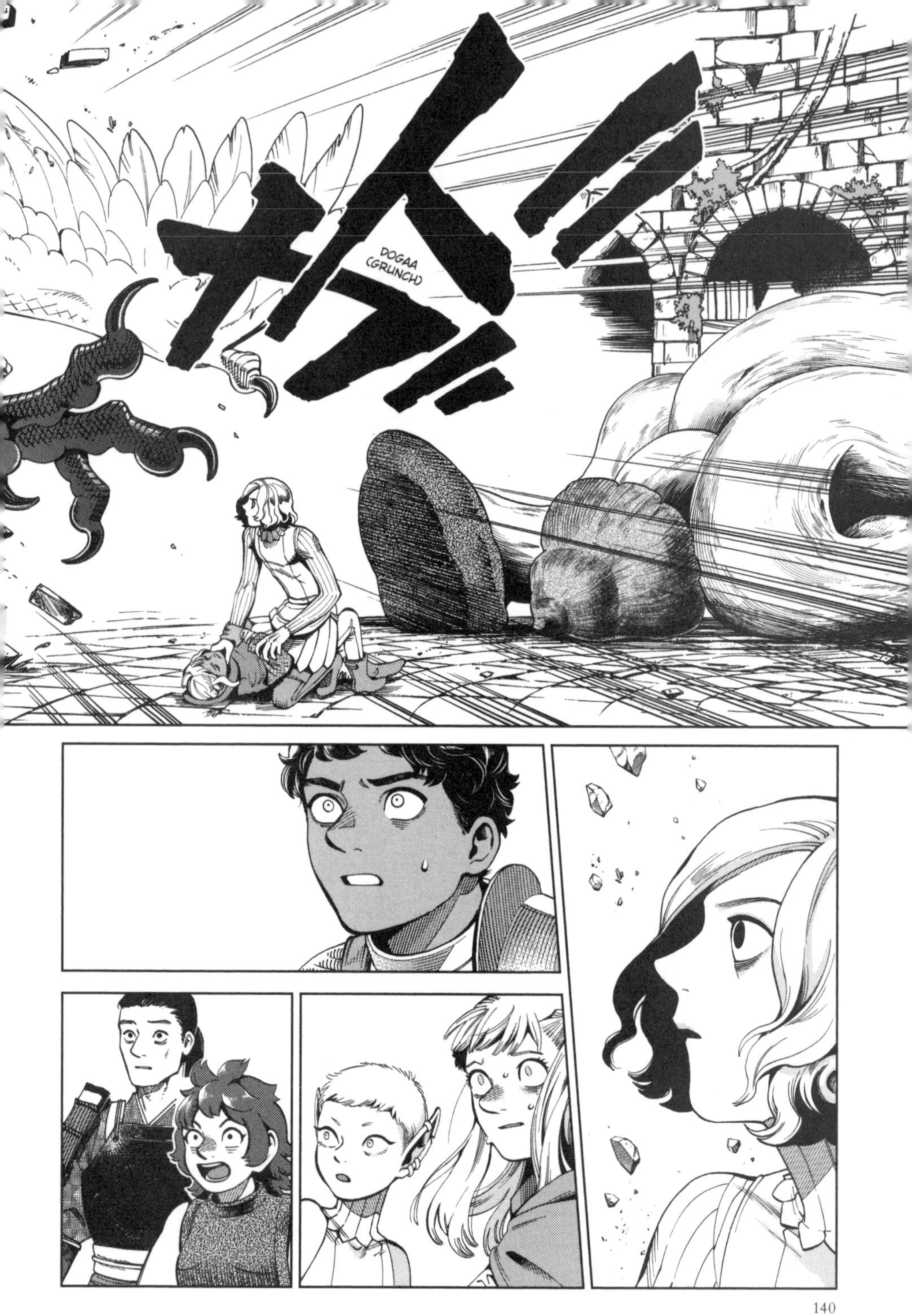
DOGAA
(GRUNCH)

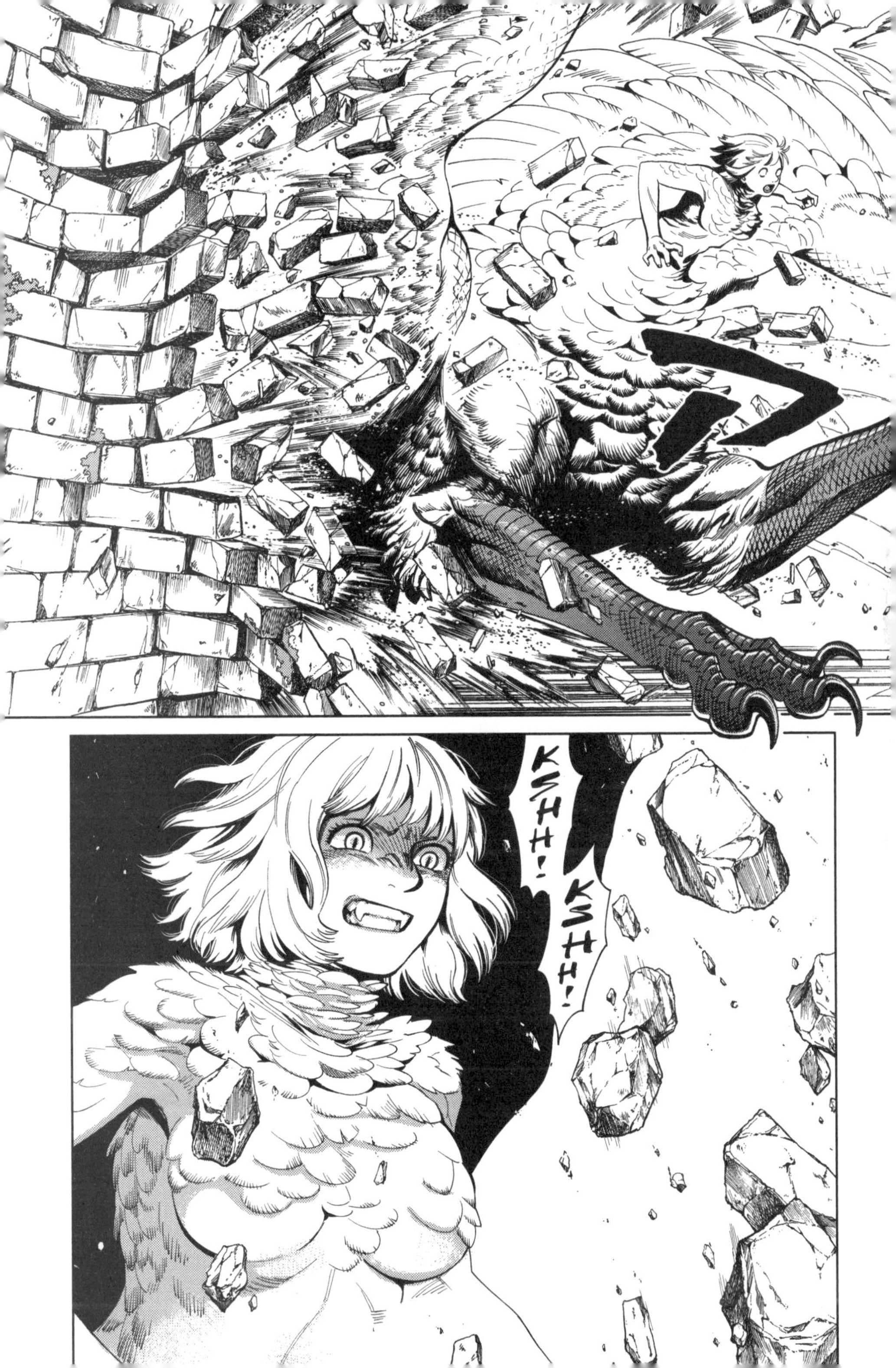
KSHH!
KSHH!

DON
(WHUD)

FU
(FFT)

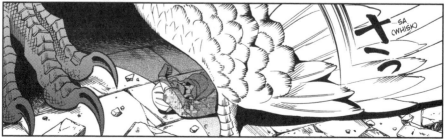

SA
(WHISK)

142

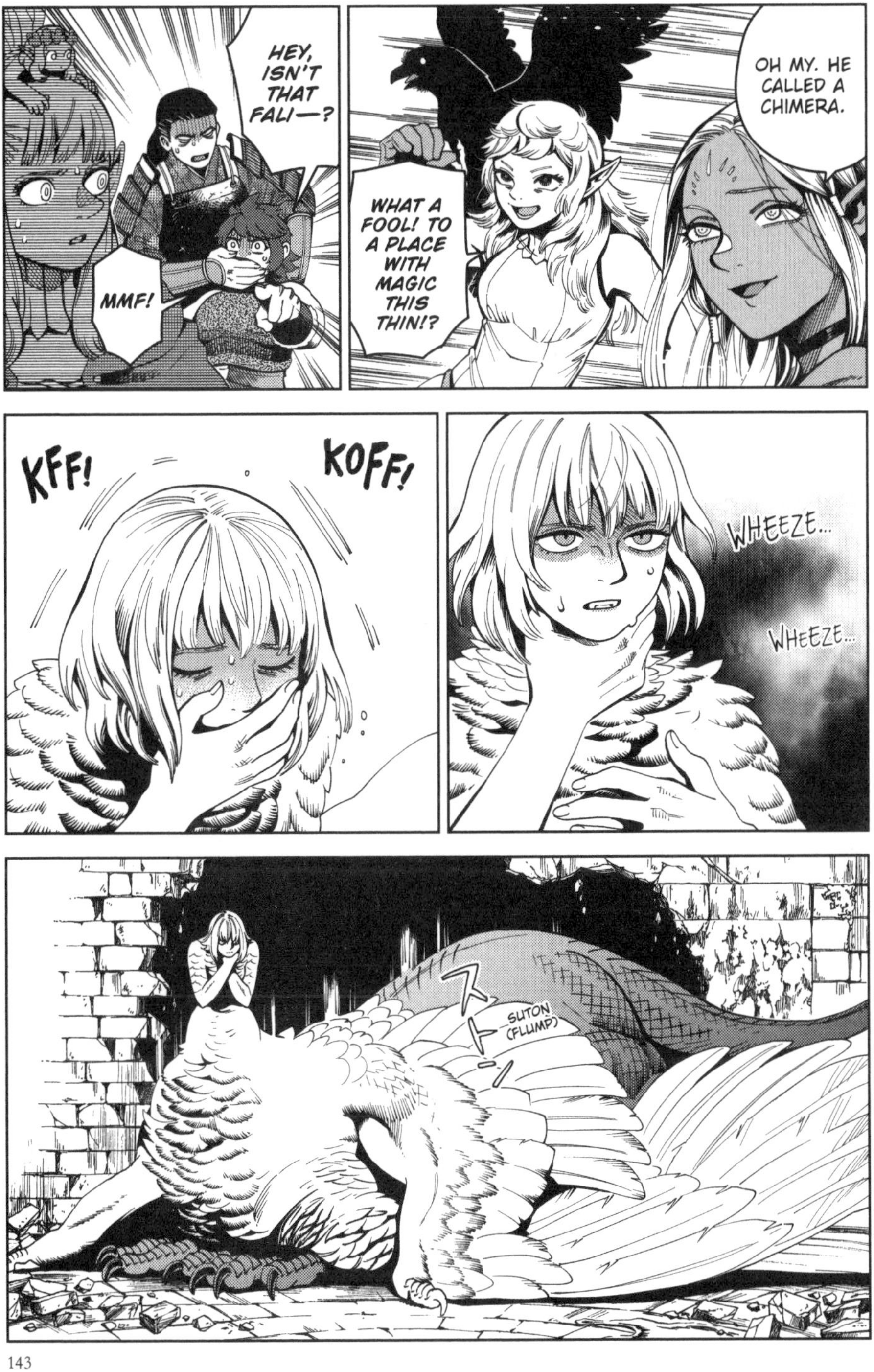
OH MY. HE CALLED A CHIMERA.
WHAT A FOOL! TO A PLACE WITH MAGIC THIS THIN!?
HEY, ISN'T THAT FALI—?
MMF!
WHEEZE...
WHEEZE...
KOFF!
KFF!
SUTON (FLUMP)

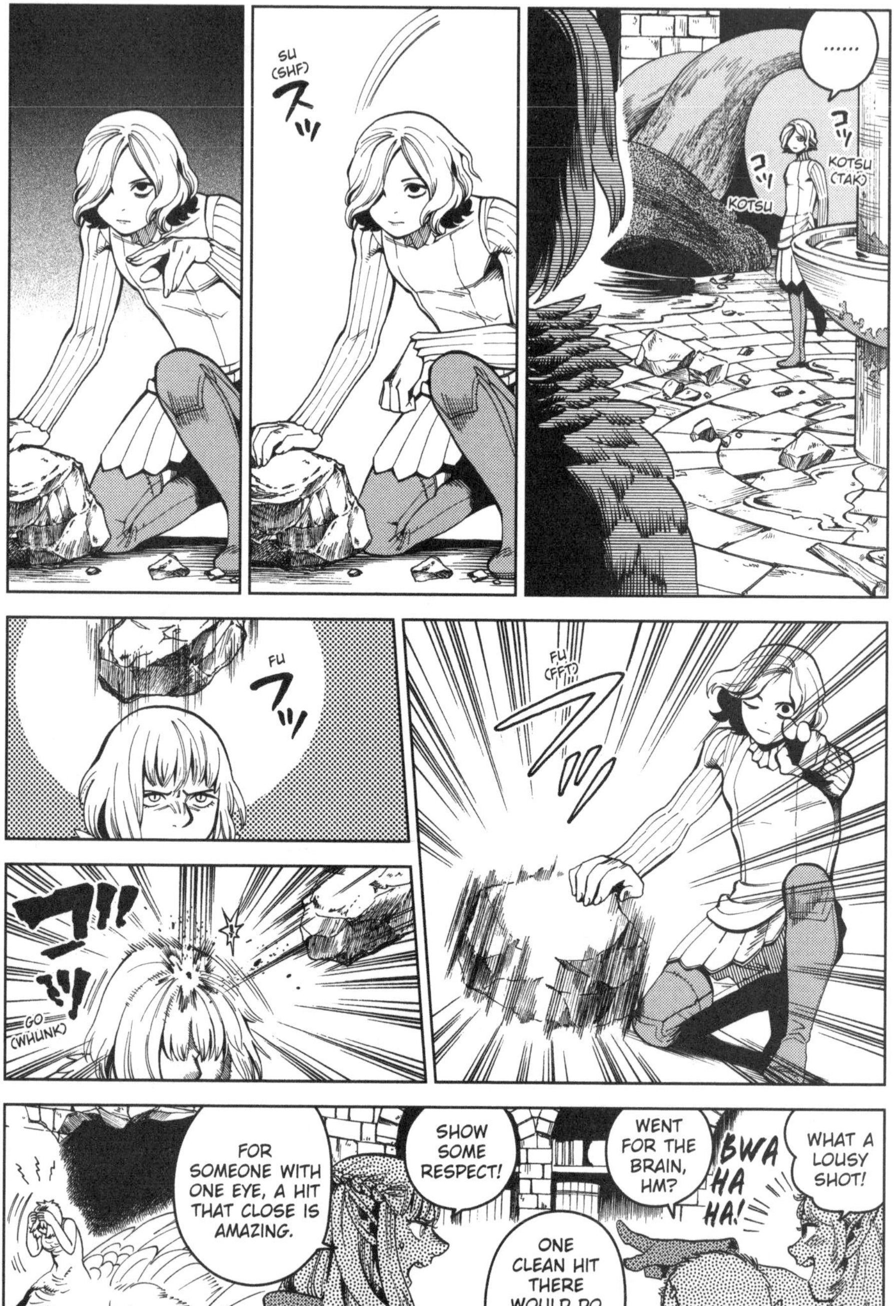

......
コツ
KOTSU (TAK)
コツ
KOTSU
SU (SHF)
スッ
FU (FFT)
フッ
FU
フッ
ゴッ!!
GO (WHUNK)
WHAT A LOUSY SHOT!
BWA HA HA!
WENT FOR THE BRAIN, HM?
ONE CLEAN HIT THERE WOULD DO IT, BUT I DUNNO...
SHOW SOME RESPECT!
FOR SOMEONE WITH ONE EYE, A HIT THAT CLOSE IS AMAZING.

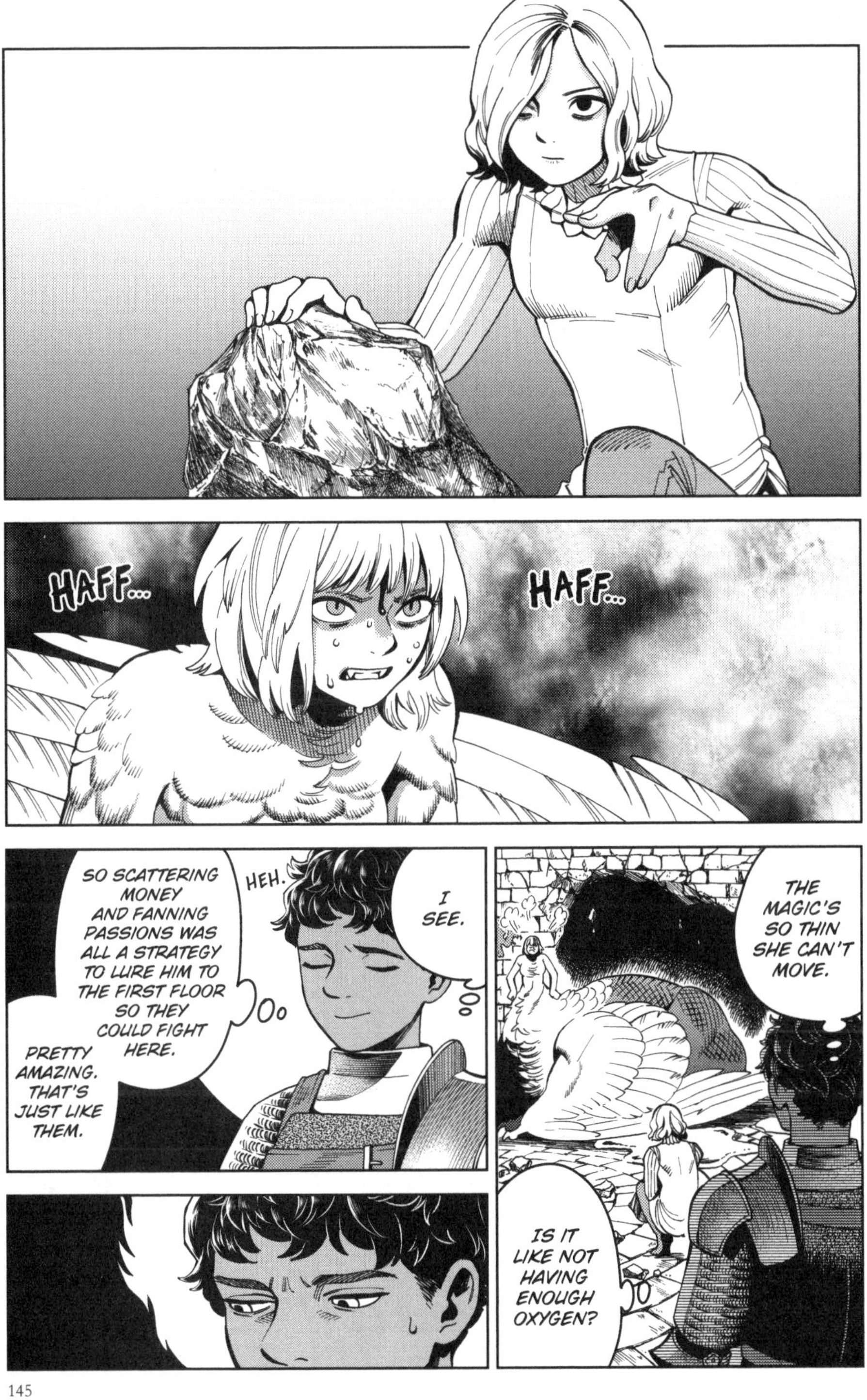
HAFF...
HAFF...
THE MAGIC'S SO THIN SHE CAN'T MOVE.
IS IT LIKE NOT HAVING ENOUGH OXYGEN?
I SEE.
HEH.
SO SCATTERING MONEY AND FANNING PASSIONS WAS ALL A STRATEGY TO LURE HIM TO THE FIRST FLOOR SO THEY COULD FIGHT HERE.
PRETTY AMAZING. THAT'S JUST LIKE THEM.

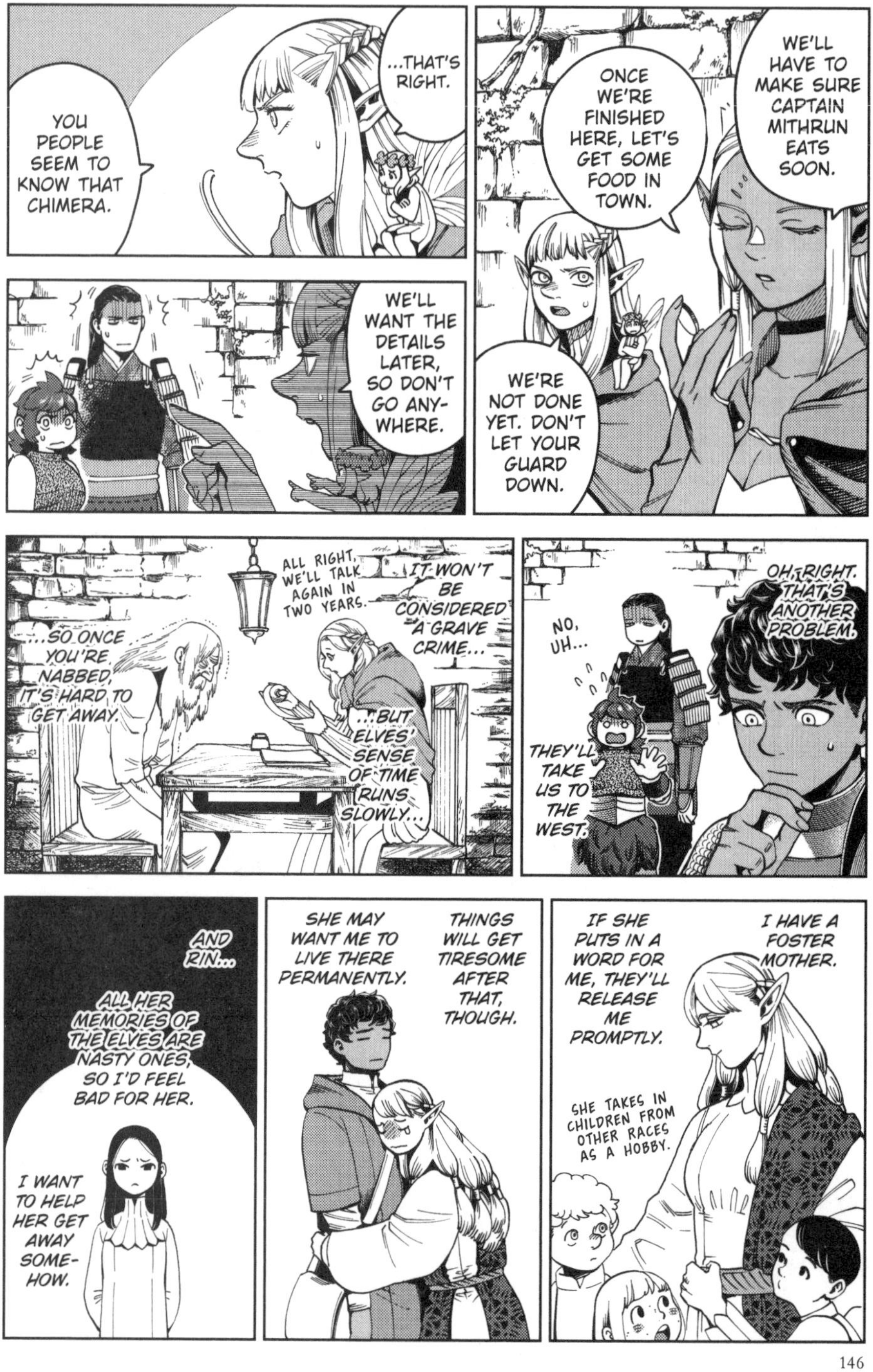
WE'LL HAVE TO MAKE SURE CAPTAIN MITHRUN EATS SOON.
ONCE WE'RE FINISHED HERE, LET'S GET SOME FOOD IN TOWN.
WE'RE NOT DONE YET. DON'T LET YOUR GUARD DOWN.
YOU PEOPLE SEEM TO KNOW THAT CHIMERA.
...THAT'S RIGHT.
WE'LL WANT THE DETAILS LATER, SO DON'T GO ANY-WHERE.
OH, RIGHT. THAT'S ANOTHER PROBLEM.
NO, UH...
THEY'LL TAKE US TO THE WEST.
IT WON'T BE CONSIDERED A GRAVE CRIME...
...BUT ELVES' SENSE OF TIME RUNS SLOWLY...
ALL RIGHT, WE'LL TALK AGAIN IN TWO YEARS.
...SO ONCE YOU'RE NABBED, IT'S HARD TO GET AWAY.
I HAVE A FOSTER MOTHER.
IF SHE PUTS IN A WORD FOR ME, THEY'LL RELEASE ME PROMPTLY.
SHE TAKES IN CHILDREN FROM OTHER RACES AS A HOBBY.
SHE MAY WANT ME TO LIVE THERE PERMANENTLY.
THINGS WILL GET TIRESOME AFTER THAT, THOUGH.
AND RIN...
ALL HER MEMORIES OF THE ELVES ARE NASTY ONES, SO I'D FEEL BAD FOR HER.
I WANT TO HELP HER GET AWAY SOME-HOW.

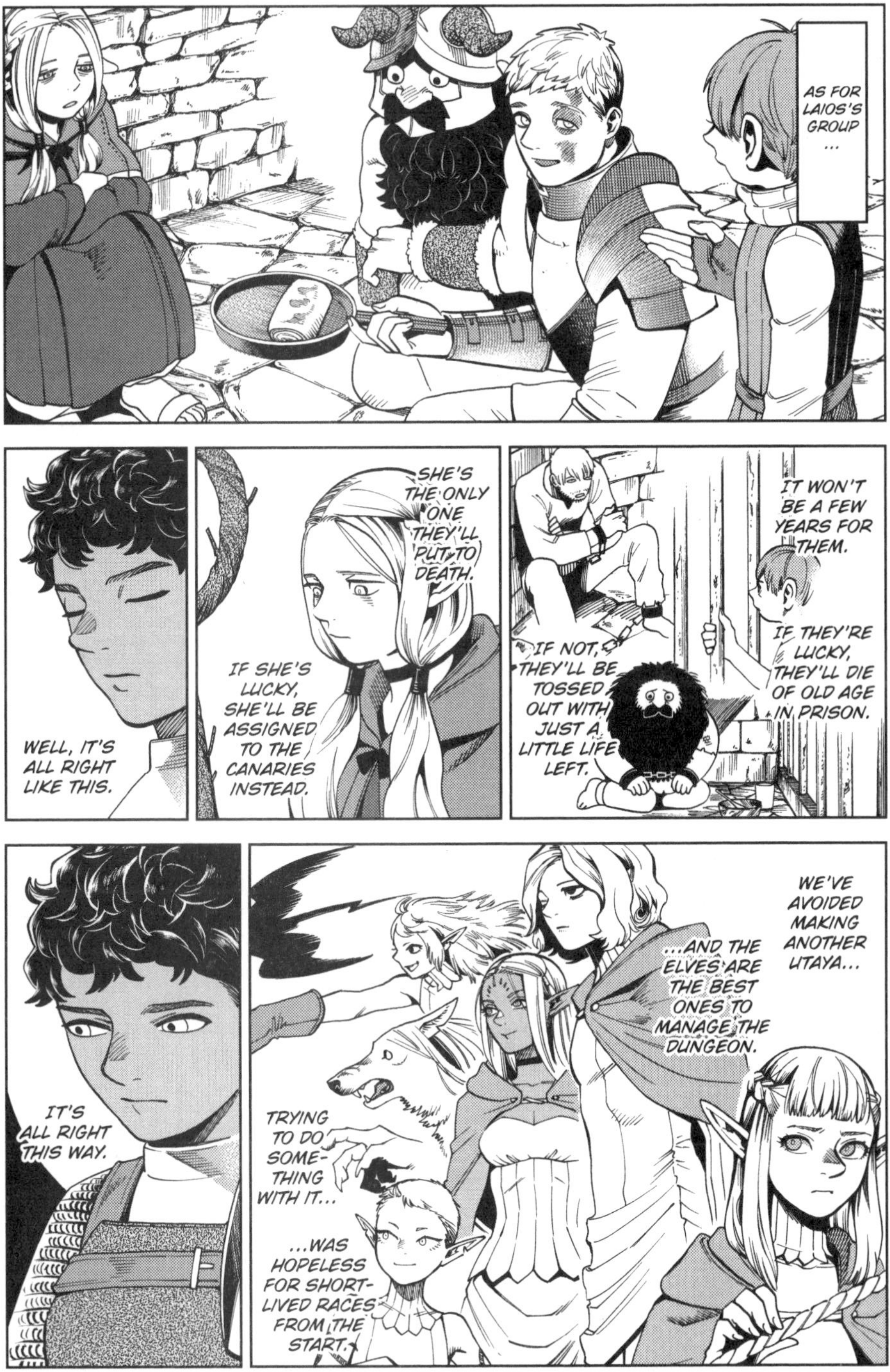
AS FOR LAIOS'S GROUP ...
IT WON'T BE A FEW YEARS FOR THEM.
IF THEY'RE LUCKY, THEY'LL DIE OF OLD AGE IN PRISON.
IF NOT, THEY'LL BE TOSSED OUT WITH JUST A LITTLE LIFE LEFT.
SHE'S THE ONLY ONE THEY'LL PUT TO DEATH.
IF SHE'S LUCKY, SHE'LL BE ASSIGNED TO THE CANARIES INSTEAD.
WELL, IT'S ALL RIGHT LIKE THIS.
WE'VE AVOIDED MAKING ANOTHER UTAYA...
...AND THE ELVES ARE THE BEST ONES TO MANAGE THE DUNGEON.
TRYING TO DO SOME-THING WITH IT...
...WAS HOPELESS FOR SHORT-LIVED RACES FROM THE START.
IT'S ALL RIGHT THIS WAY.

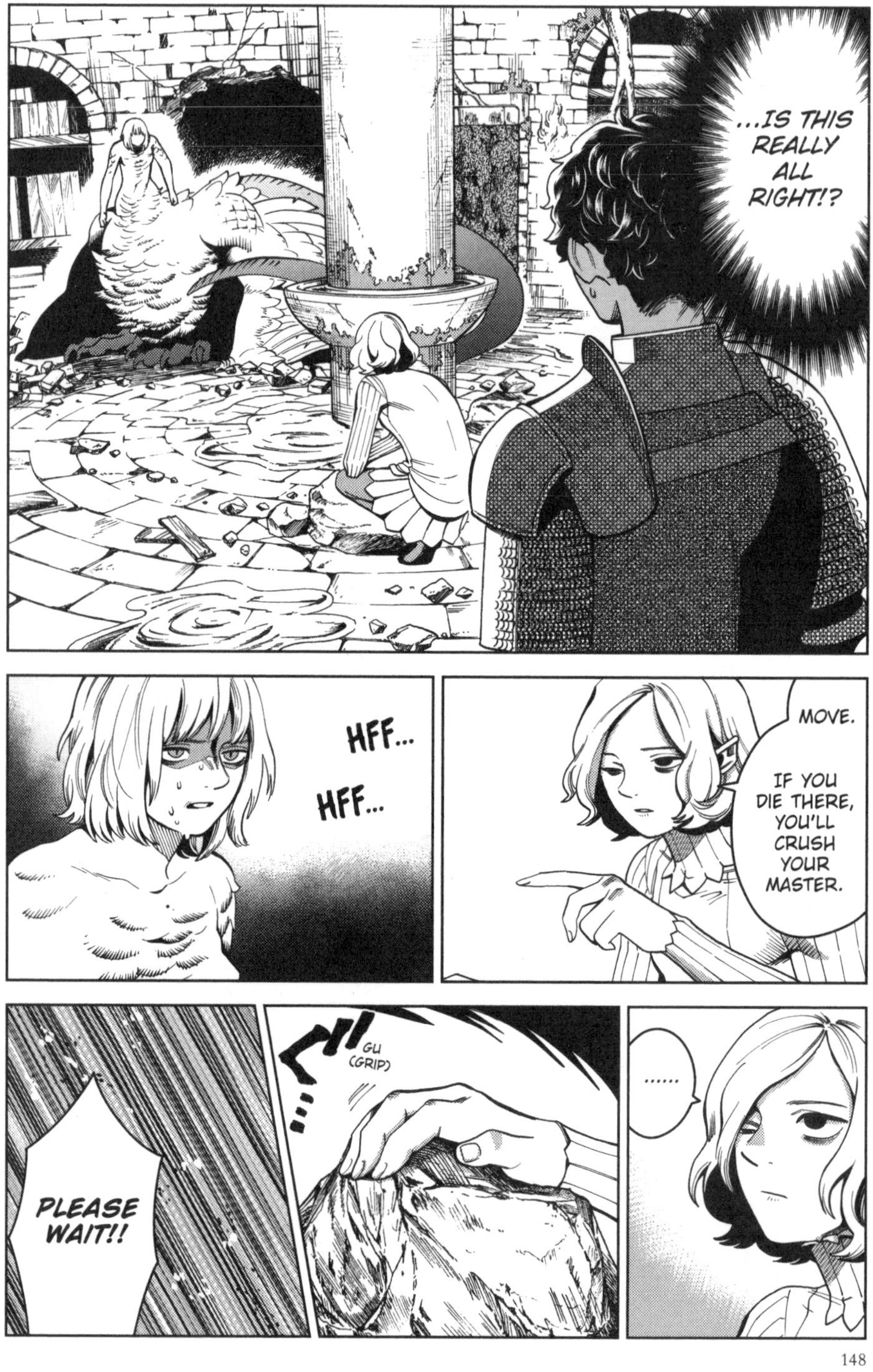
...IS THIS REALLY ALL RIGHT!?
MOVE.
IF YOU DIE THERE, YOU'LL CRUSH YOUR MASTER.
HFF...
HFF...
......
GU (GRIP)
PLEASE WAIT!!

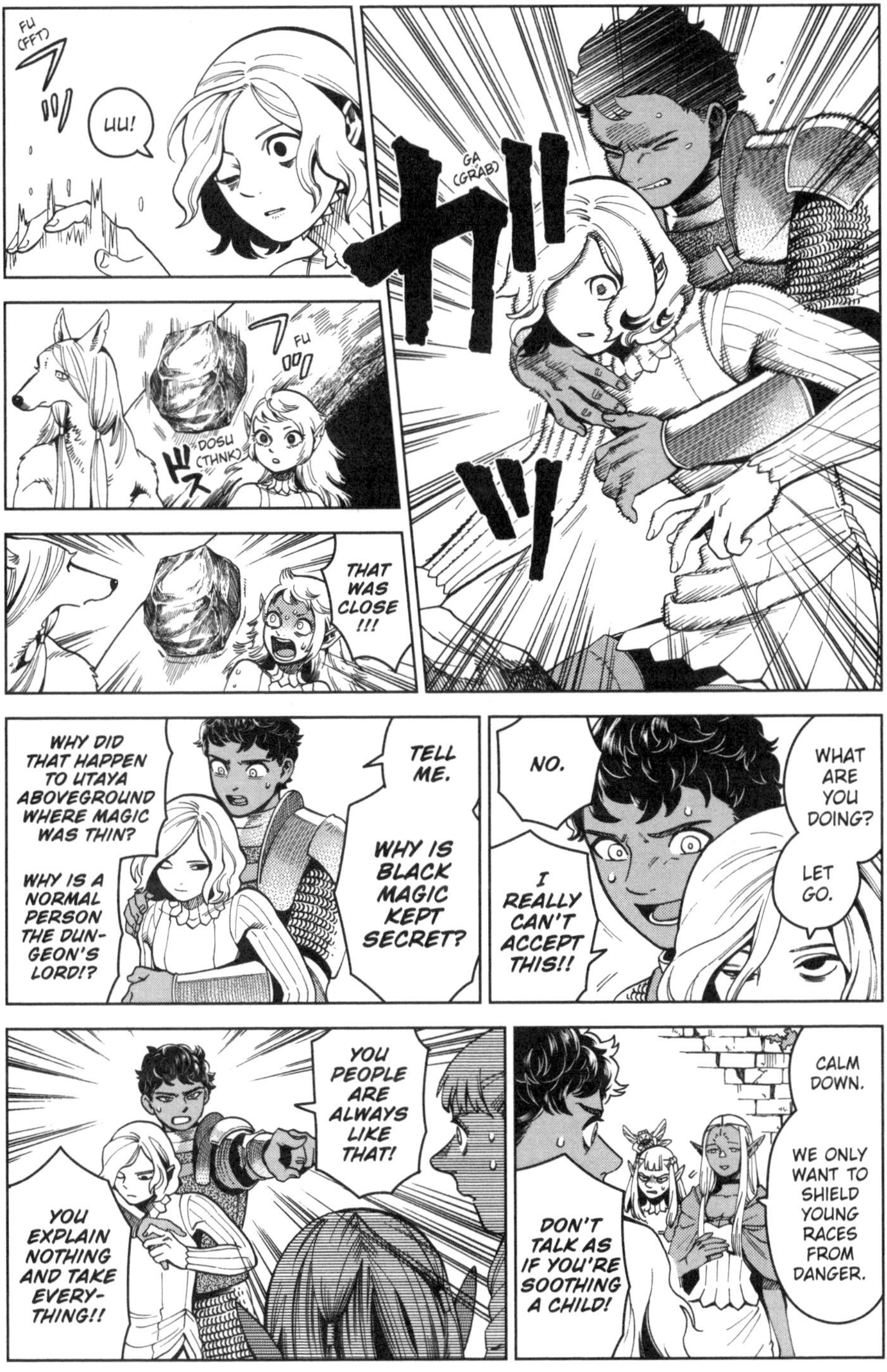
FU (FFT)
UU!
GA (GRAB)
FU
DOSU (THNK)
THAT WAS CLOSE !!!
WHAT ARE YOU DOING?
LET GO.
NO.
I REALLY CAN'T ACCEPT THIS!!
TELL ME.
WHY DID THAT HAPPEN TO UTAYA ABOVEGROUND WHERE MAGIC WAS THIN?
WHY IS BLACK MAGIC KEPT SECRET?
WHY IS A NORMAL PERSON THE DUNGEON'S LORD!?
CALM DOWN.
WE ONLY WANT TO SHIELD YOUNG RACES FROM DANGER.
DON'T TALK AS IF YOU'RE SOOTHING A CHILD!
YOU PEOPLE ARE ALWAYS LIKE THAT!
YOU EXPLAIN NOTHING AND TAKE EVERYTHING!!

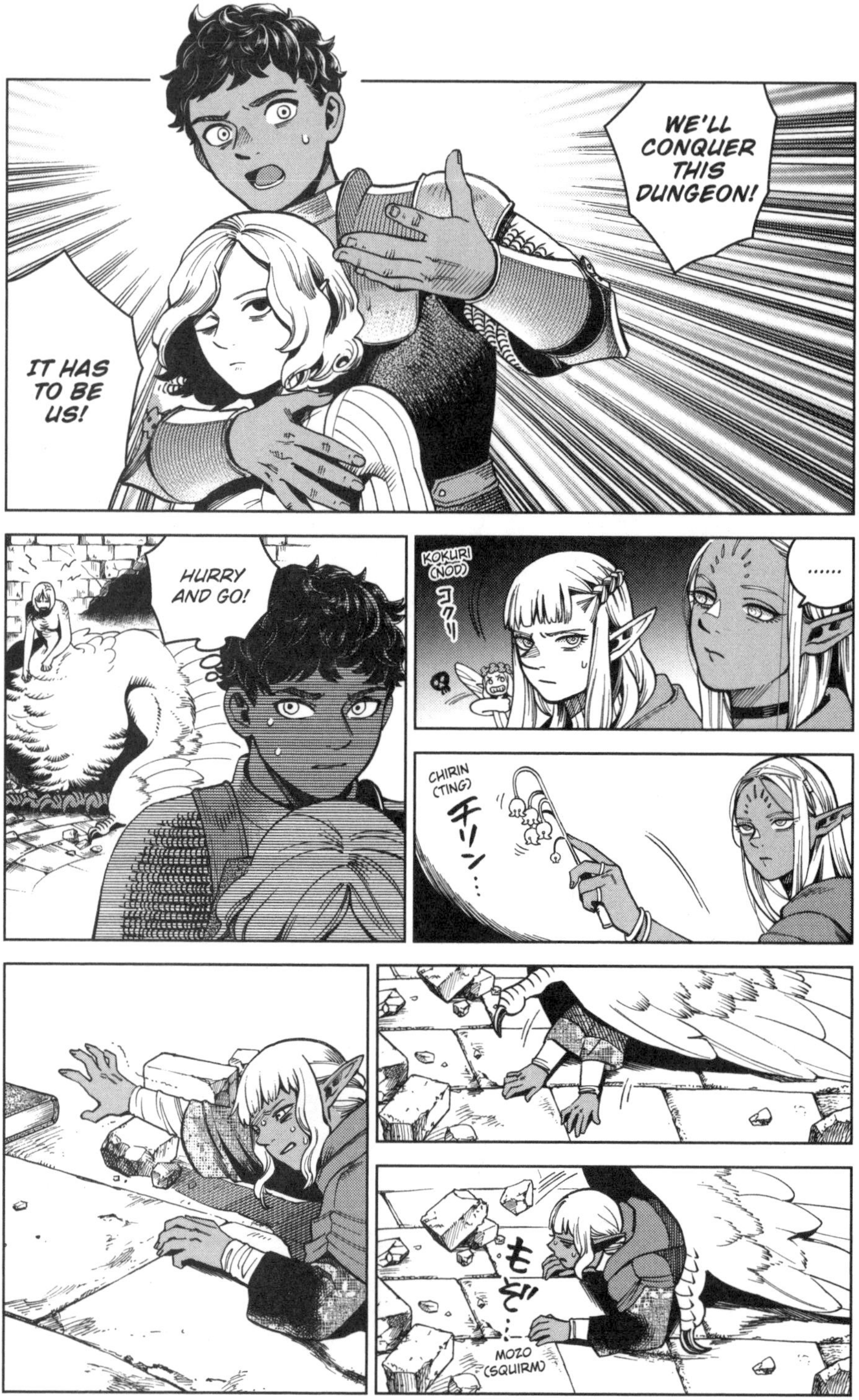
WE'LL CONQUER THIS DUNGEON!
IT HAS TO BE US!
KOKURI (NOD)
コクリ
......
CHIRIN (TING)
チリン…
HURRY AND GO!
もぞ…
MOZO (SQUIRM)

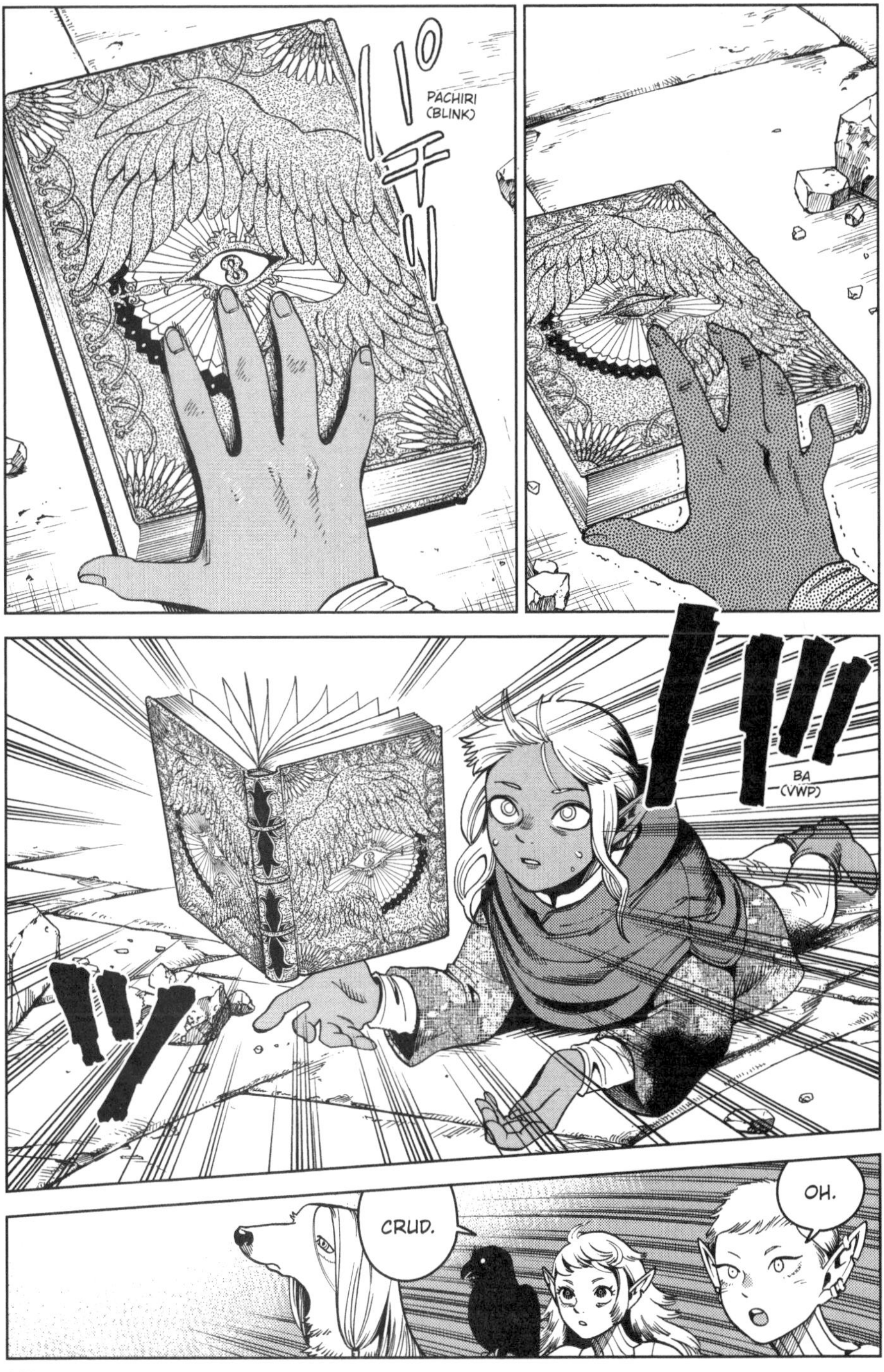
PACHIRI (BLINK)
BA (VWP)
OH.
CRUD.

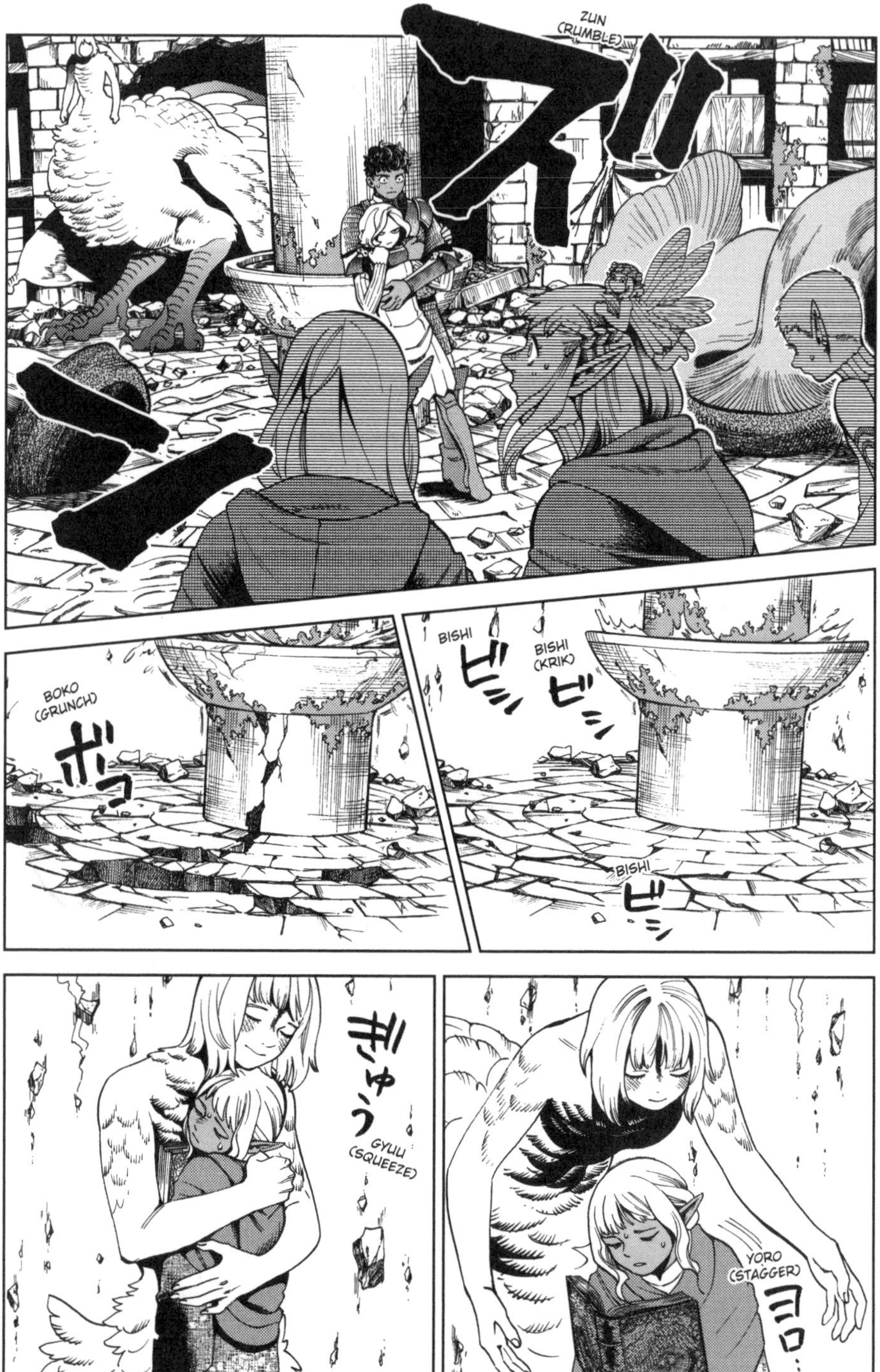
ZUN (RUMBLE)
ズン
BISHI
ビシ
BISHI (KRIK)
ビシ
BISHI
ビシ
BOKO (GRUNCH)
ボコ
YORO (STAGGER)
ヨロ‥
ぎゅう
GYUU (SQUEEZE)

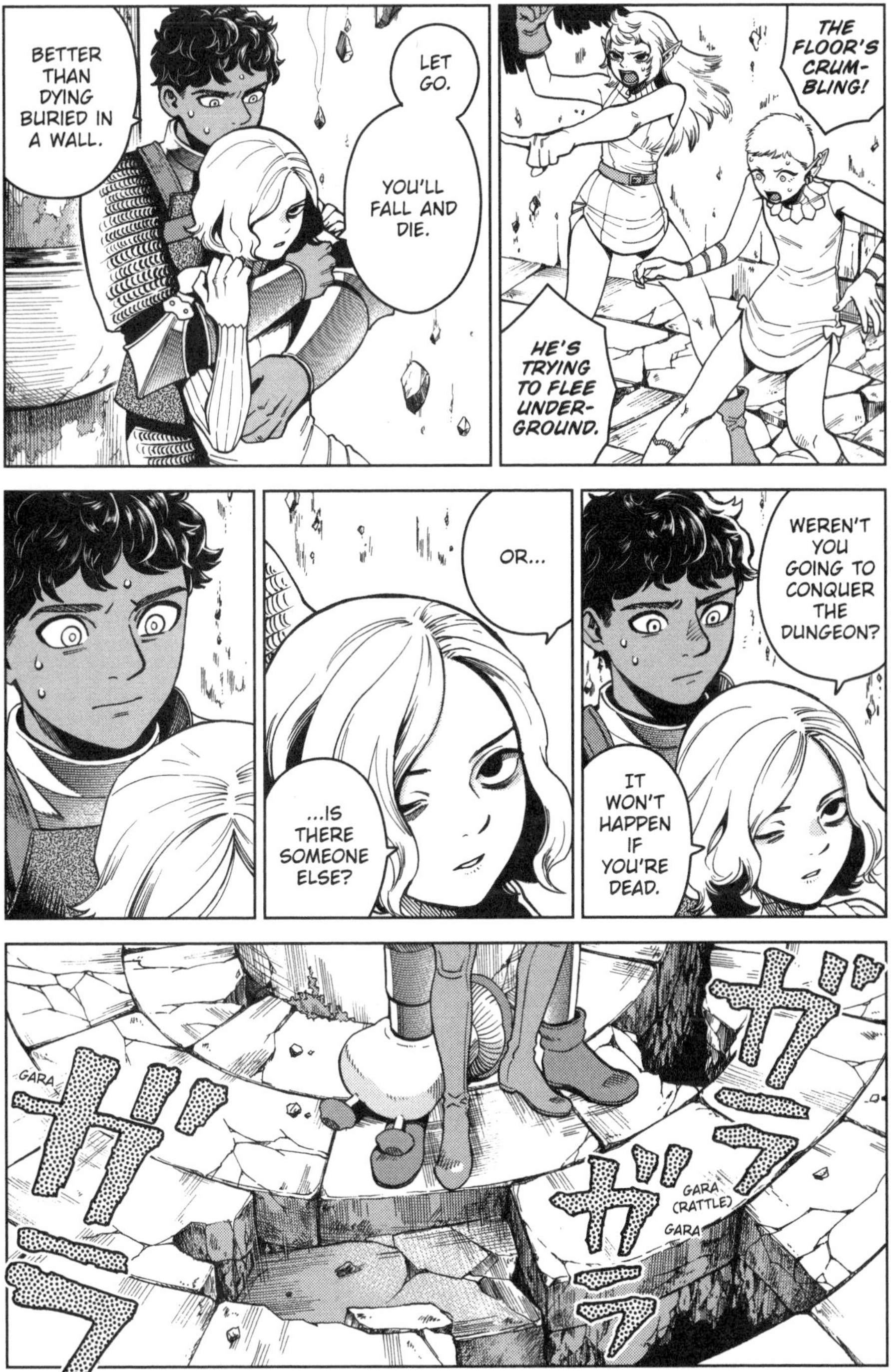
THE FLOOR'S CRUMBLING!
HE'S TRYING TO FLEE UNDERGROUND.
LET GO.
YOU'LL FALL AND DIE.
BETTER THAN DYING BURIED IN A WALL.
WEREN'T YOU GOING TO CONQUER THE DUNGEON?
IT WON'T HAPPEN IF YOU'RE DEAD.
OR...
...IS THERE SOMEONE ELSE?
ガラ
ガラ
GARA (RATTLE)
GARA
ガラ
GARA

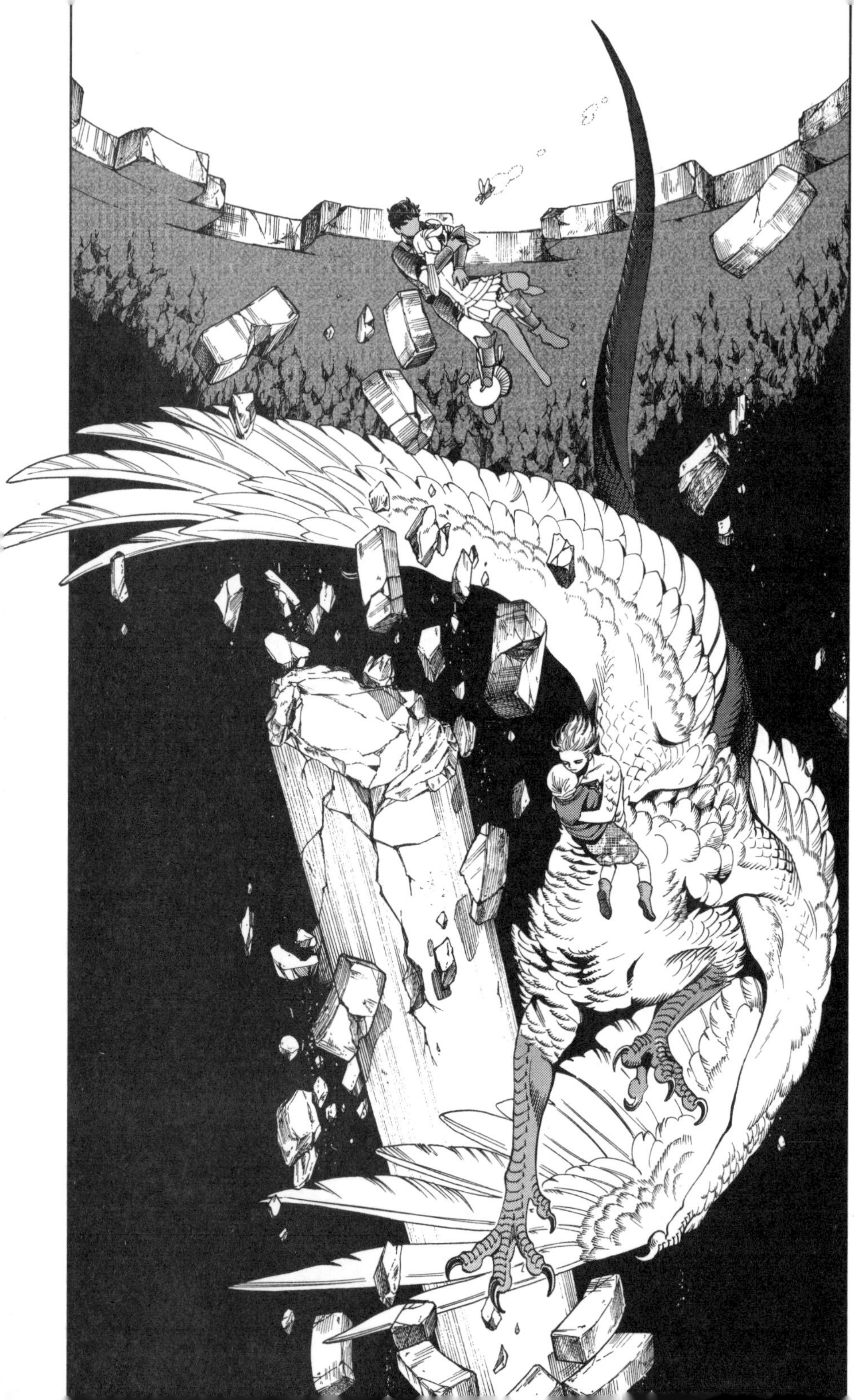

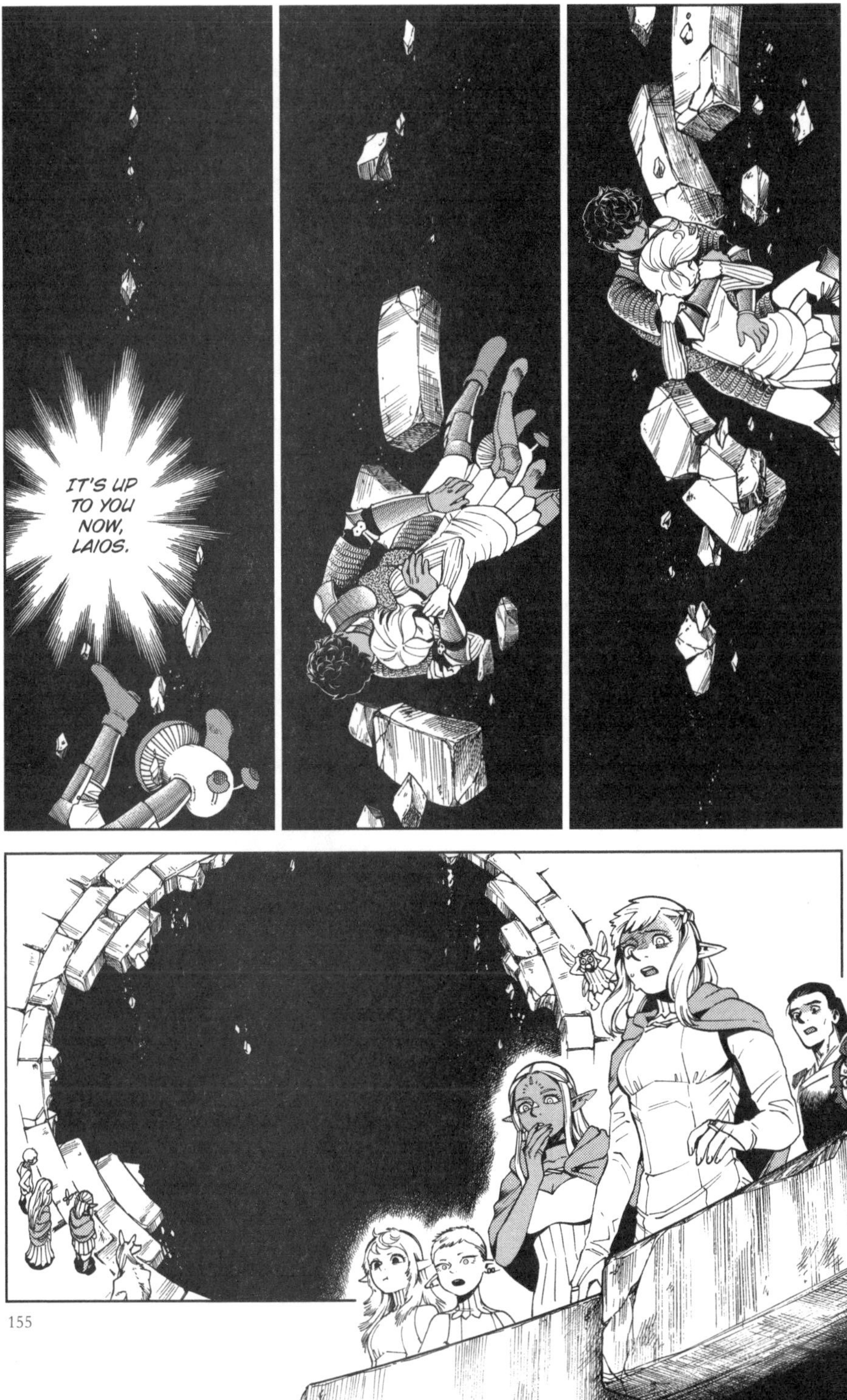
IT'S UP TO YOU NOW, LAIOS.

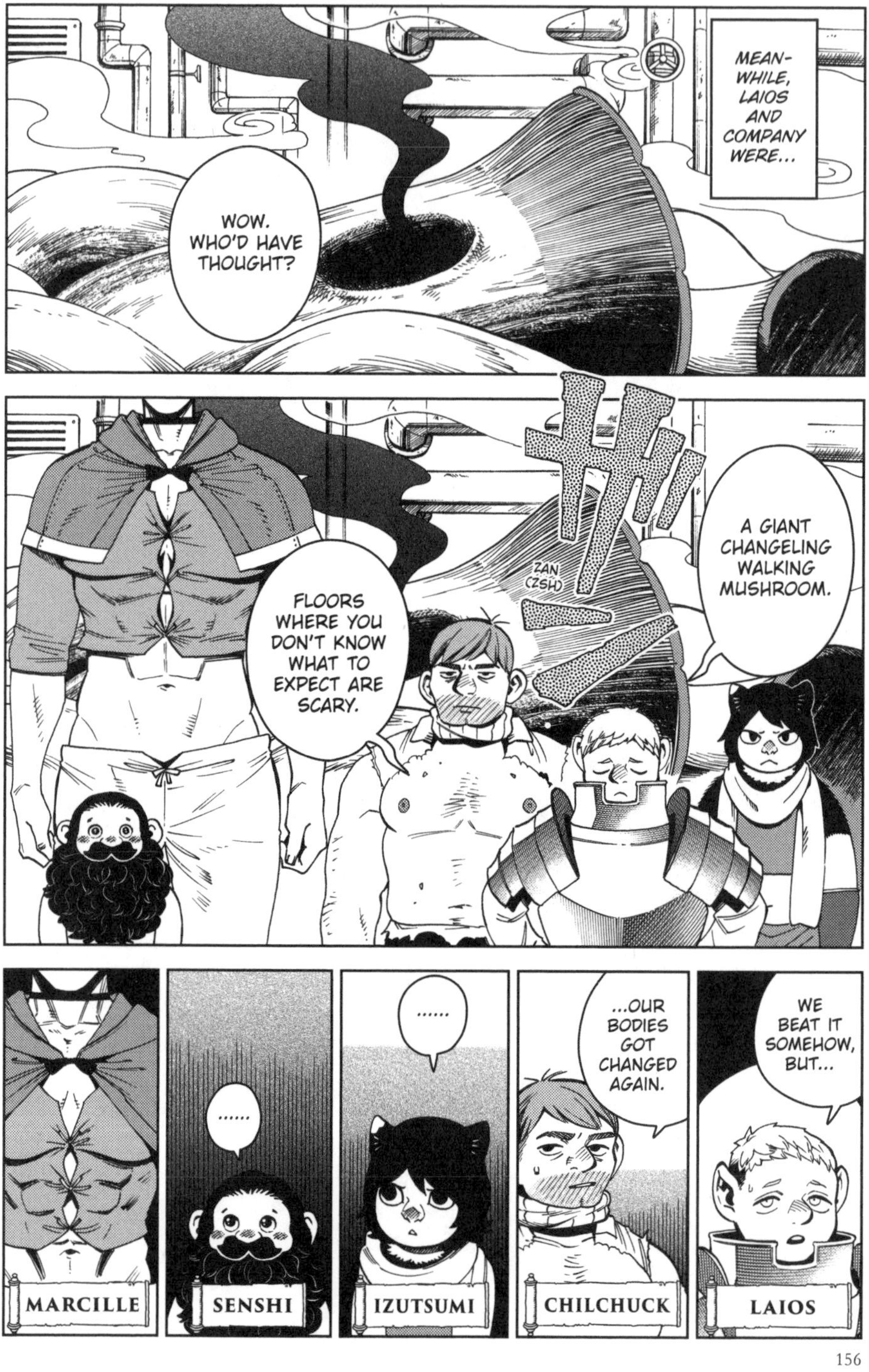
MEAN-WHILE, LAIOS AND COMPANY WERE...
WOW. WHO'D HAVE THOUGHT?
A GIANT CHANGELING WALKING MUSHROOM.
ZAN (ZSH)
FLOORS WHERE YOU DON'T KNOW WHAT TO EXPECT ARE SCARY.
WE BEAT IT SOMEHOW, BUT...
LAIOS
...OUR BODIES GOT CHANGED AGAIN.
CHILCHUCK
......
IZUTSUMI
......
SENSHI
MARCILLE

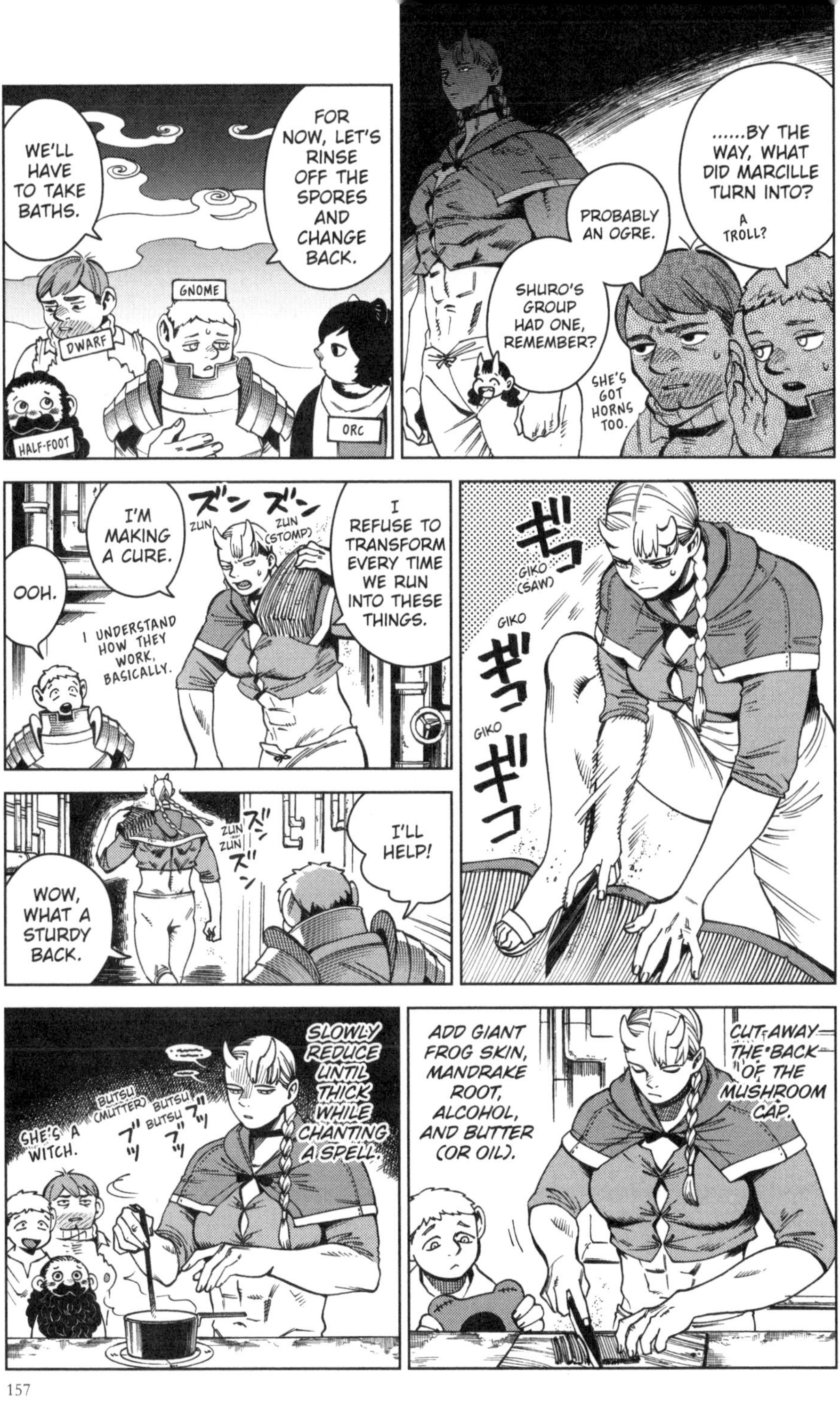
......BY THE WAY, WHAT DID MARCILLE TURN INTO?
A TROLL?
PROBABLY AN OGRE.
SHURO'S GROUP HAD ONE, REMEMBER?
SHE'S GOT HORNS TOO.
FOR NOW, LET'S RINSE OFF THE SPORES AND CHANGE BACK.
WE'LL HAVE TO TAKE BATHS.
GNOME
DWARF
ORC
HALF-FOOT
ギコ
GIKO (SAW)
GIKO
ギコ
GIKO
ギコ
I REFUSE TO TRANSFORM EVERY TIME WE RUN INTO THESE THINGS.
ズン ズン
ZUN ZUN (STOMP)
I'M MAKING A CURE.
OOH.
I UNDERSTAND HOW THEY WORK, BASICALLY.
I'LL HELP!
ズン ズン
ZUN ZUN
WOW, WHAT A STURDY BACK.
CUT AWAY THE BACK OF THE MUSHROOM CAP.
ADD GIANT FROG SKIN, MANDRAKE ROOT, ALCOHOL, AND BUTTER (OR OIL).
SLOWLY REDUCE UNTIL THICK WHILE CHANTING A SPELL.
ブツ ブツ
BUTSU (MUTTER) BUTSU
SHE'S A WITCH.

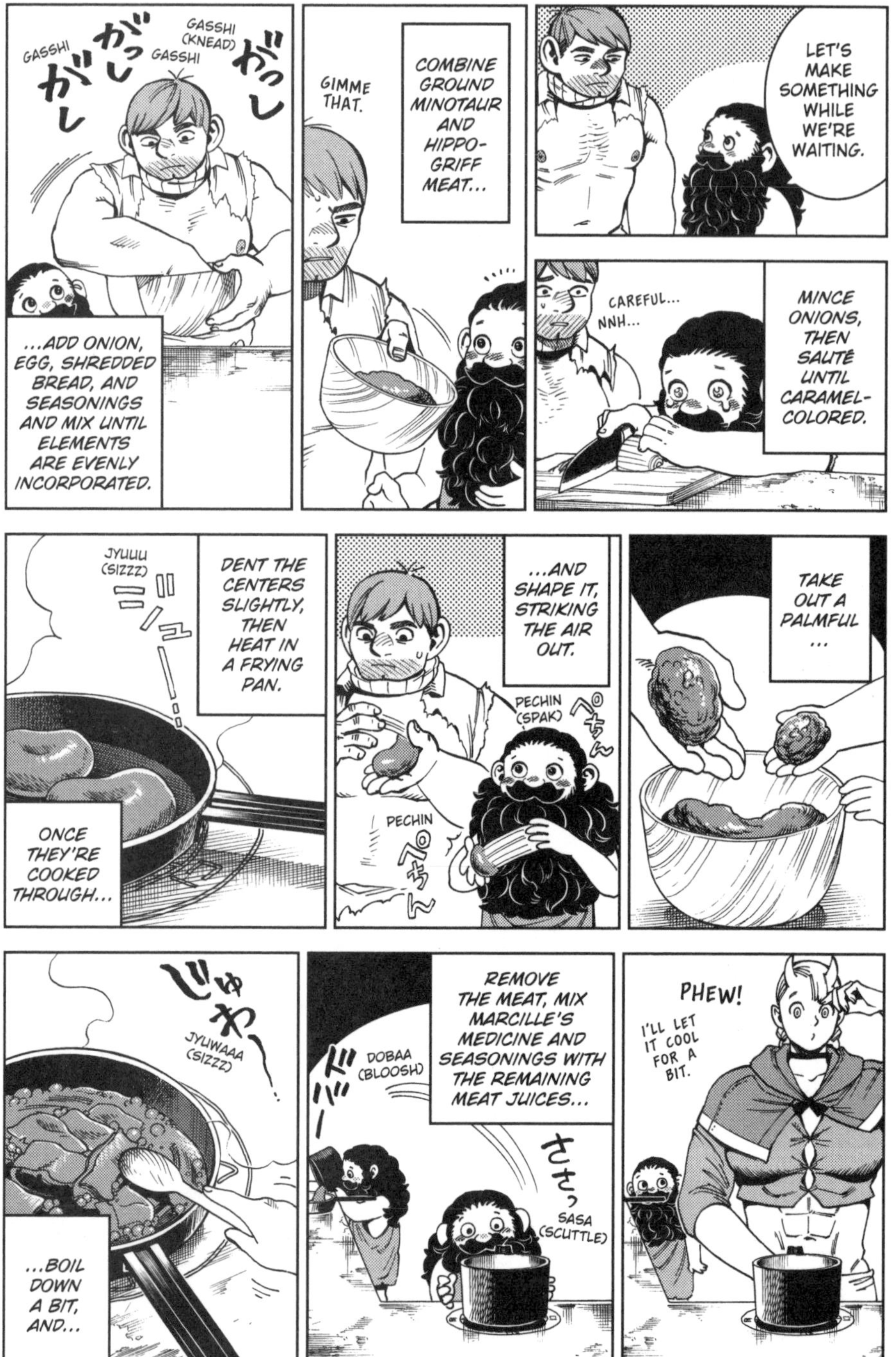
LET'S MAKE SOMETHING WHILE WE'RE WAITING.
MINCE ONIONS, THEN SAUTÉ UNTIL CARAMEL-COLORED.
CAREFUL... NNH...
COMBINE GROUND MINOTAUR AND HIPPO-GRIFF MEAT...
GIMME THAT.
がっし
GASSHI (KNEAD)
がっし
GASSHI
がし
GASSHI
...ADD ONION, EGG, SHREDDED BREAD, AND SEASONINGS AND MIX UNTIL ELEMENTS ARE EVENLY INCORPORATED.
TAKE OUT A PALMFUL...
...AND SHAPE IT, STRIKING THE AIR OUT.
ぺちん
PECHIN (SPAK)
ぺちん
PECHIN
DENT THE CENTERS SLIGHTLY, THEN HEAT IN A FRYING PAN.
ジュー!!
JYUUU (SIZZZ)
ONCE THEY'RE COOKED THROUGH...
PHEW!
I'LL LET IT COOL FOR A BIT.
REMOVE THE MEAT, MIX MARCILLE'S MEDICINE AND SEASONINGS WITH THE REMAINING MEAT JUICES...
ドバー
DOBAA (BLOOSH)
ささっ
SASA (SCUTTLE)
じゅわ～
JYUWAAA (SIZZZ)
...BOIL DOWN A BIT, AND...

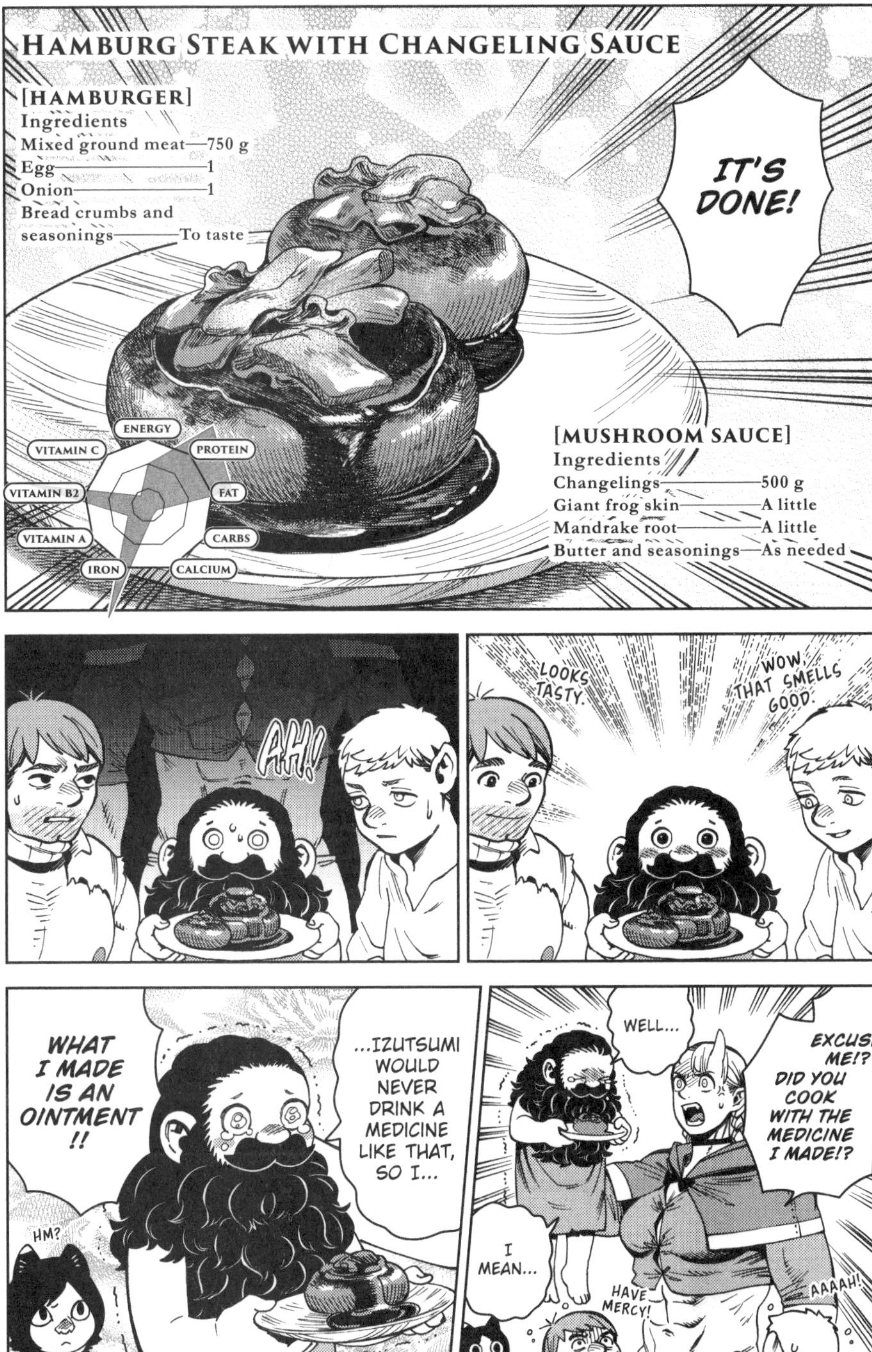

HAMBURG STEAK WITH CHANGELING SAUCE
IT'S DONE!
[HAMBURGER]
Ingredients
Mixed ground meat—750 g
Egg—1
Onion—1
Bread crumbs and seasonings—To taste
ENERGY
PROTEIN
FAT
CARBS
CALCIUM
IRON
VITAMIN A
VITAMIN B2
VITAMIN C
[MUSHROOM SAUCE]
Ingredients
Changelings—500 g
Giant frog skin—A little
Mandrake root—A little
Butter and seasonings—As needed
WOW THAT SMELLS GOOD.
LOOKS TASTY.
AH!
EXCUSE ME!? DID YOU COOK WITH THE MEDICINE I MADE!?
WELL...
I MEAN...
AAAAH!
HAVE MERCY!
...IZUTSUMI WOULD NEVER DRINK A MEDICINE LIKE THAT, SO I...
WHAT I MADE IS AN OINTMENT !!
HM?

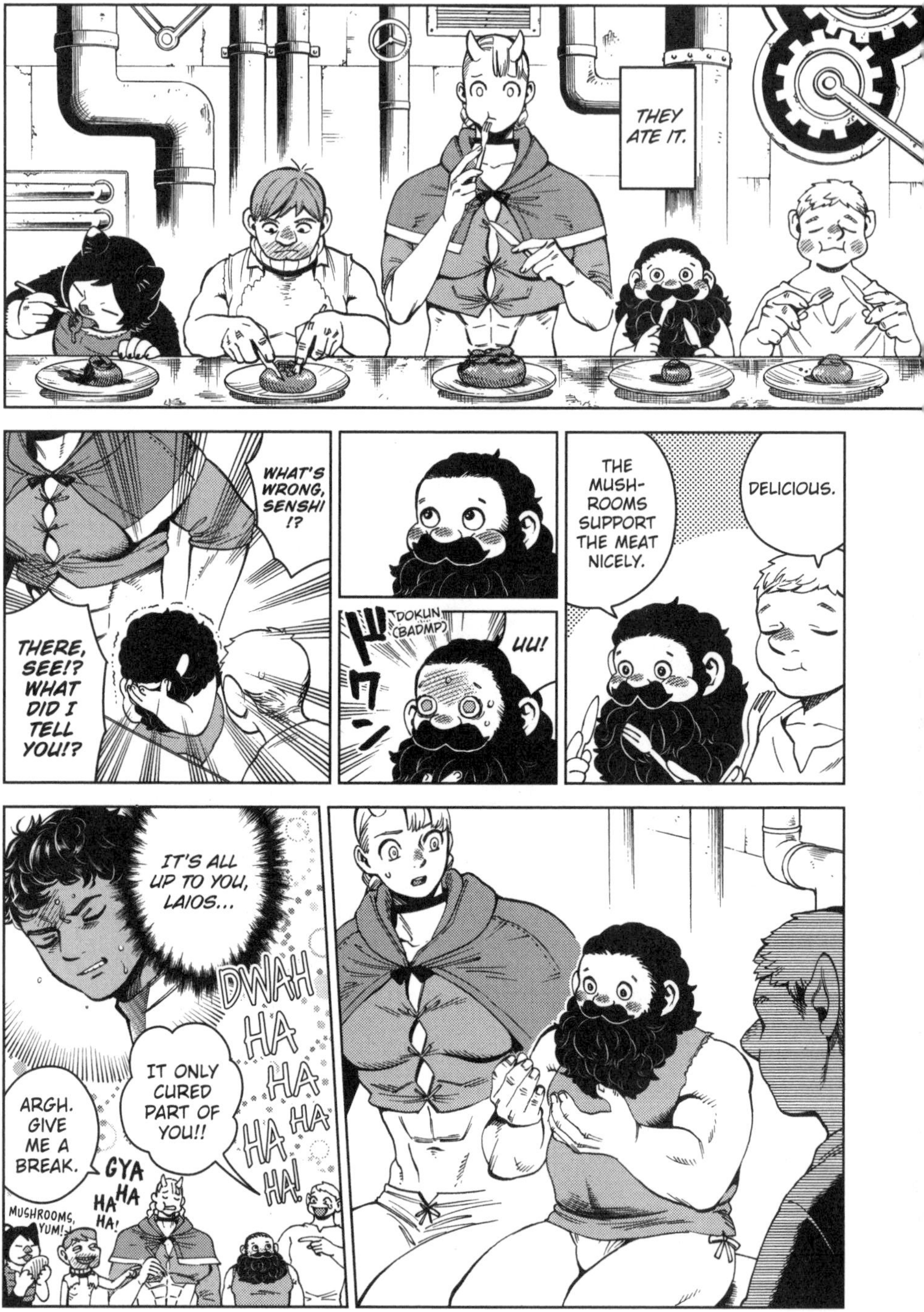
THEY ATE IT.
DELICIOUS.
THE MUSHROOMS SUPPORT THE MEAT NICELY.
DOKUN (BADMP)
UU!
WHAT'S WRONG, SENSHI!?
THERE, SEE!? WHAT DID I TELL YOU!?
IT'S ALL UP TO YOU, LAIOS...
DWAH HA HA HA HA HA HA!
IT ONLY CURED PART OF YOU!!
ARGH. GIVE ME A BREAK.
GYA HA HA HA!
MUSHROOMS, YUM!

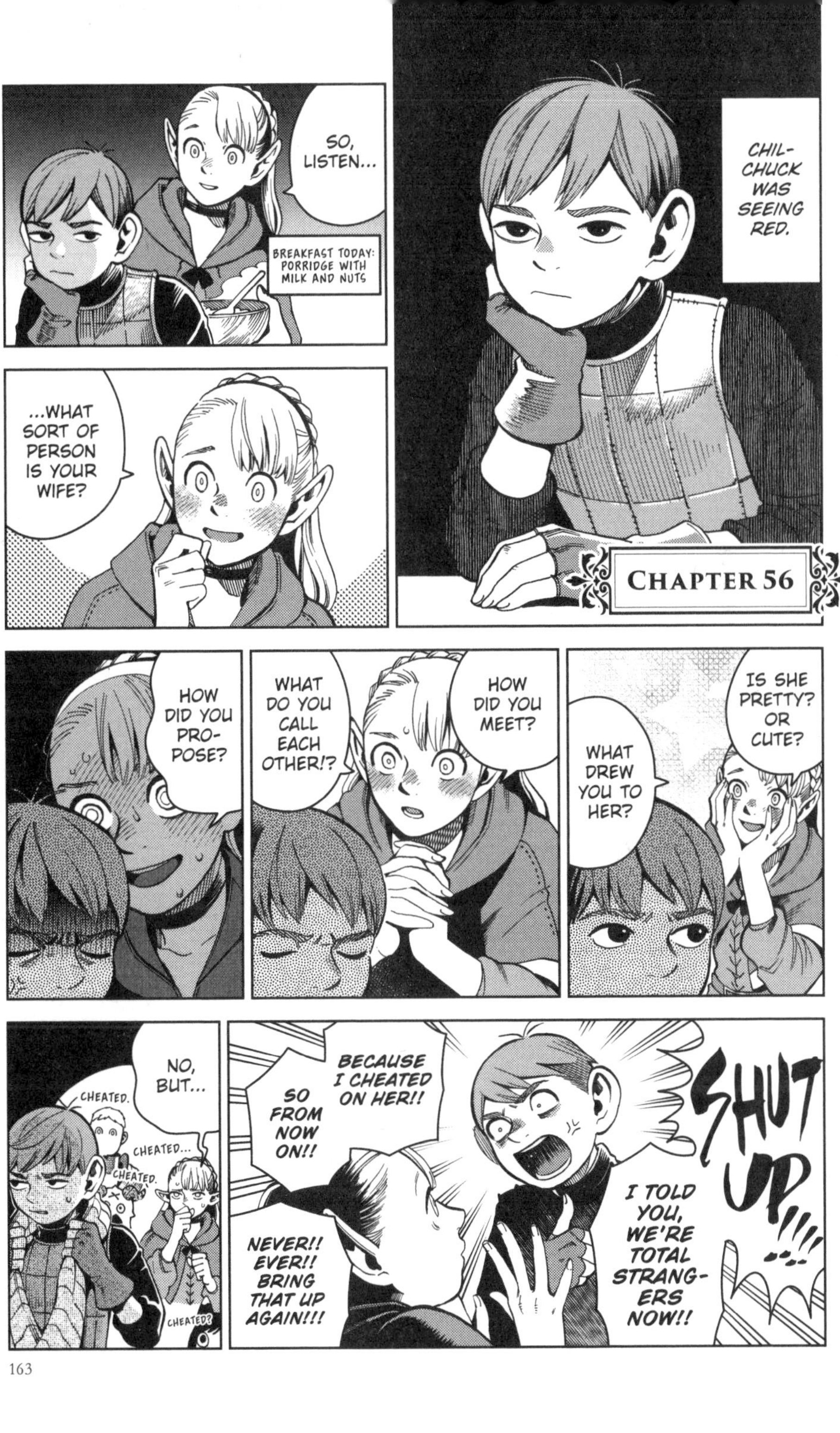
CHIL-CHUCK WAS SEEING RED.
CHAPTER 56
SO, LISTEN...
BREAKFAST TODAY: PORRIDGE WITH MILK AND NUTS
...WHAT SORT OF PERSON IS YOUR WIFE?
IS SHE PRETTY? OR CUTE?
WHAT DREW YOU TO HER?
HOW DID YOU MEET?
WHAT DO YOU CALL EACH OTHER!?
HOW DID YOU PRO-POSE?
SHUT UP!!!
I TOLD YOU, WE'RE TOTAL STRANG-ERS NOW!!
BECAUSE I CHEATED ON HER!!
SO FROM NOW ON!!
NEVER!! EVER!! BRING THAT UP AGAIN!!!
NO, BUT...
CHEATED.
CHEATED...
CHEATED.
CHEATED?

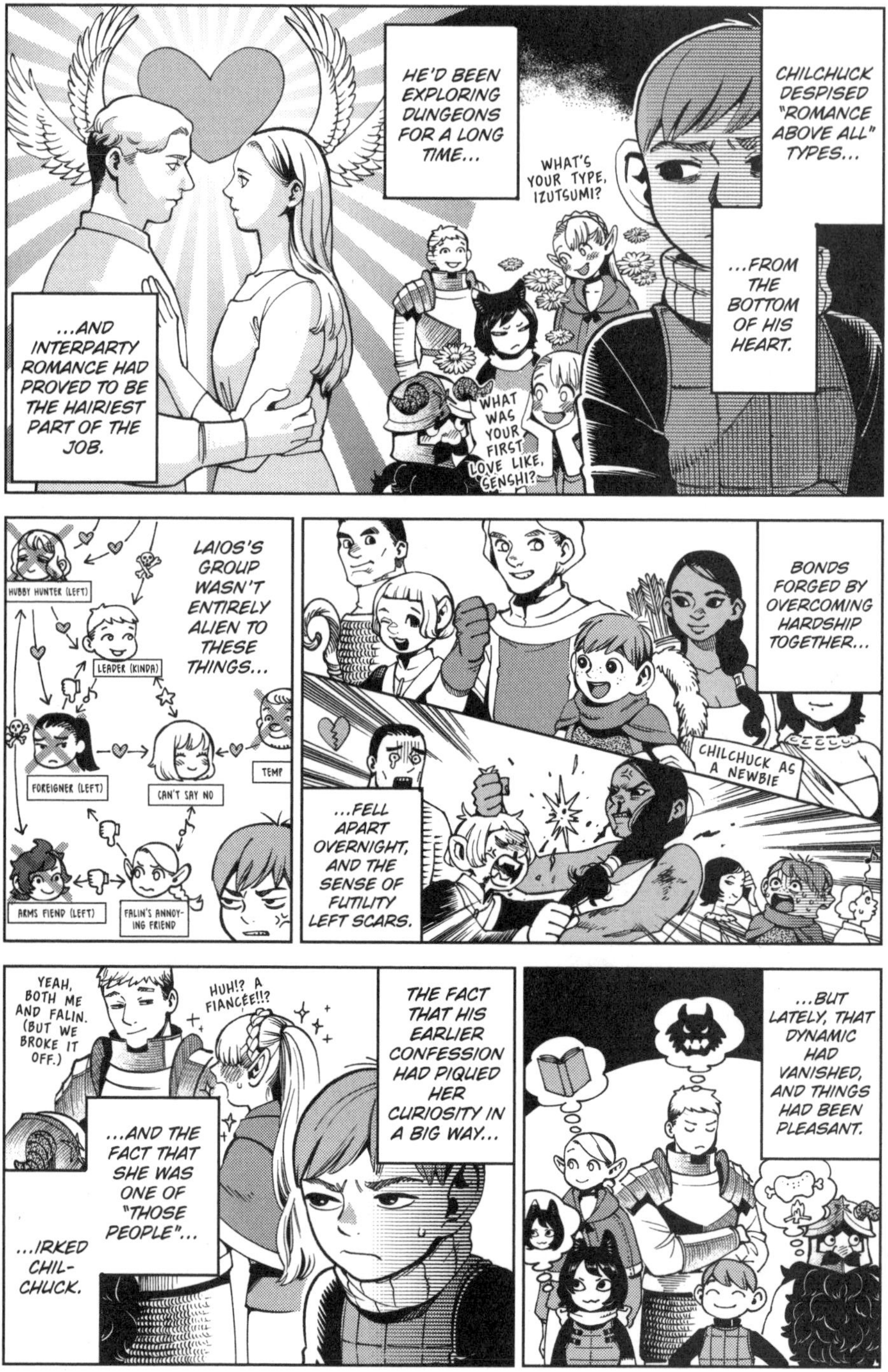
CHILCHUCK DESPISED "ROMANCE ABOVE ALL" TYPES...
...FROM THE BOTTOM OF HIS HEART.
WHAT'S YOUR TYPE, IZUTSUMI?
HE'D BEEN EXPLORING DUNGEONS FOR A LONG TIME...
WHAT WAS YOUR FIRST LOVE LIKE, SENSHI?
...AND INTERPARTY ROMANCE HAD PROVED TO BE THE HAIRIEST PART OF THE JOB.
BONDS FORGED BY OVERCOMING HARDSHIP TOGETHER...
CHILCHUCK AS A NEWBIE
...FELL APART OVERNIGHT, AND THE SENSE OF FUTILITY LEFT SCARS.
LAIOS'S GROUP WASN'T ENTIRELY ALIEN TO THESE THINGS...
HUBBY HUNTER (LEFT)
LEADER (KINDA)
TEMP
FOREIGNER (LEFT)
CAN'T SAY NO
ARMS FIEND (LEFT)
FALIN'S ANNOYING FRIEND
...BUT LATELY, THAT DYNAMIC HAD VANISHED, AND THINGS HAD BEEN PLEASANT.
THE FACT THAT HIS EARLIER CONFESSION HAD PIQUED HER CURIOSITY IN A BIG WAY...
HUH!? A FIANCÉE!!?
YEAH, BOTH ME AND FALIN. (BUT WE BROKE IT OFF.)
...AND THE FACT THAT SHE WAS ONE OF "THOSE PEOPLE"...
...IRKED CHIL-CHUCK.

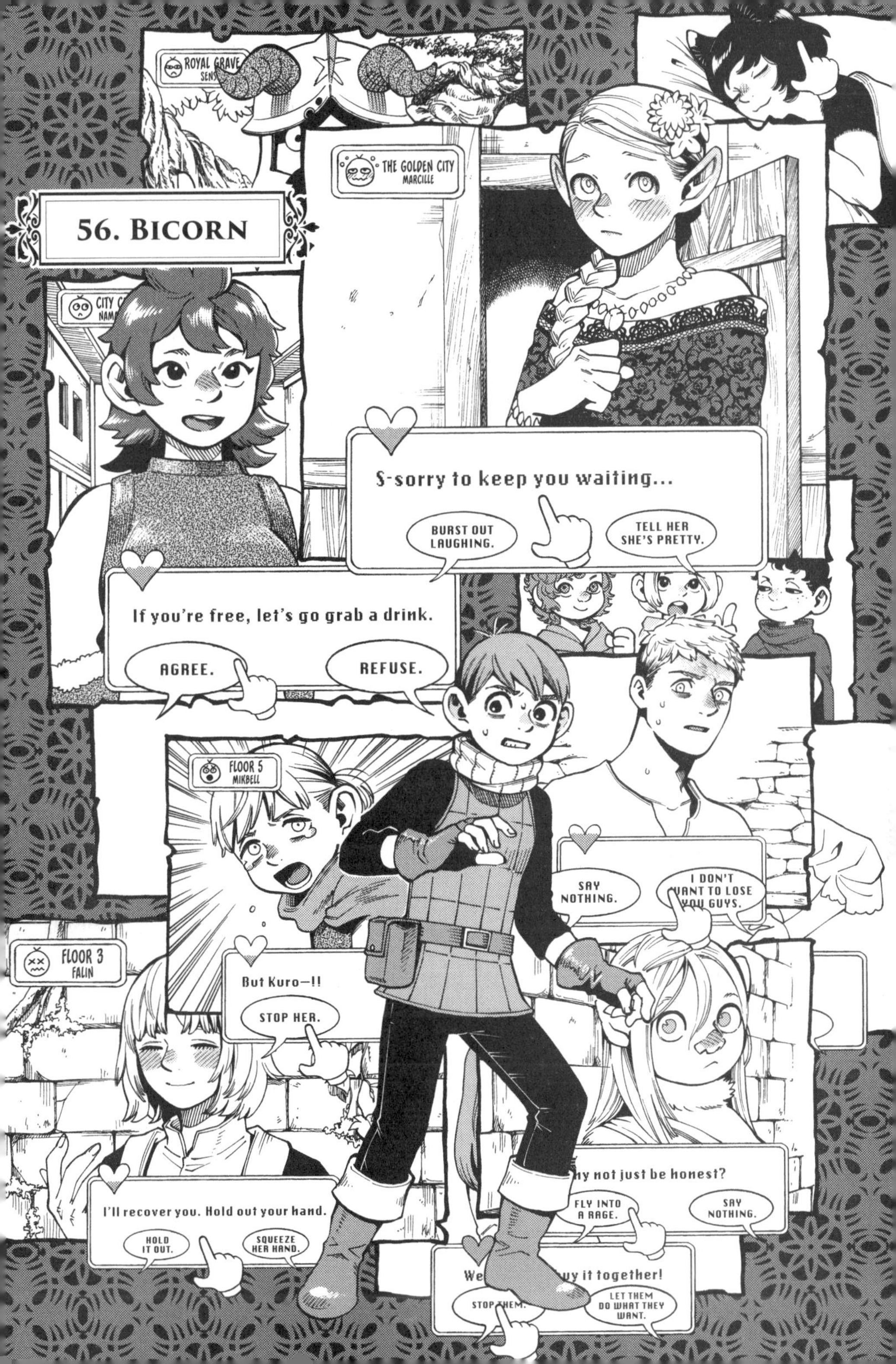
THE GOLDEN CITY
MARCILLE
S-sorry to keep you waiting...
BURST OUT LAUGHING.
TELL HER SHE'S PRETTY.
ROYAL GRAVE
56. Bicorn
If you're free, let's go grab a drink.
AGREE.
REFUSE.
SAY NOTHING.
I DON'T WANT TO LOSE YOU GUYS.
FLOOR 5
MIKBELL
But Kuro—!!
STOP HER.
hy not just be honest?
FLY INTO A RAGE.
SAY NOTHING.
FLOOR 3
FALIN
I'll recover you. Hold out your hand.
HOLD IT OUT.
SQUEEZE HER HAND.
uy it together!
STOP THEM.
LET THEM DO WHAT THEY WANT.

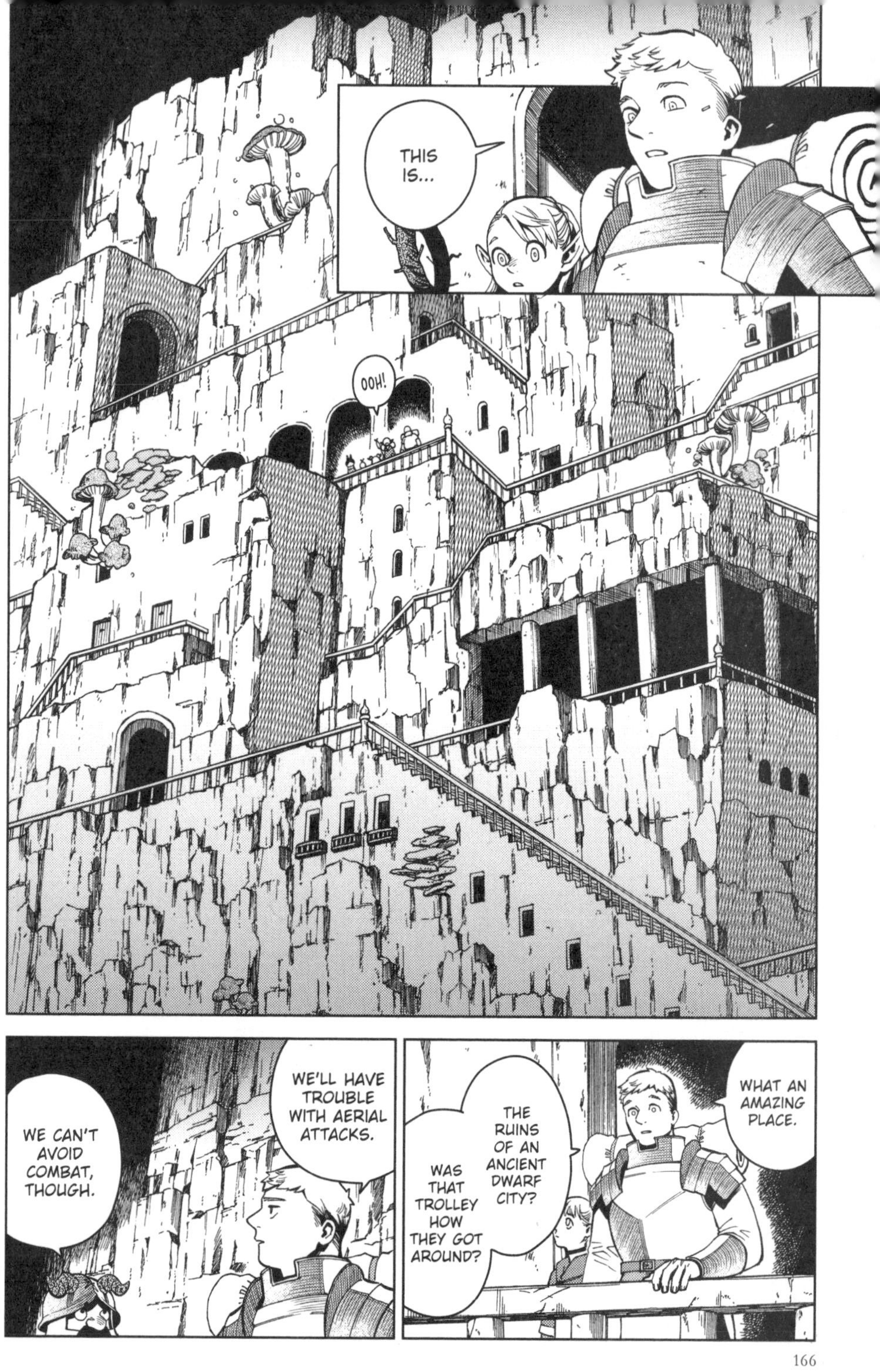
THIS IS...
OOH!
WHAT AN AMAZING PLACE.
THE RUINS OF AN ANCIENT DWARF CITY?
WAS THAT TROLLEY HOW THEY GOT AROUND?
WE'LL HAVE TROUBLE WITH AERIAL ATTACKS.
WE CAN'T AVOID COMBAT, THOUGH.

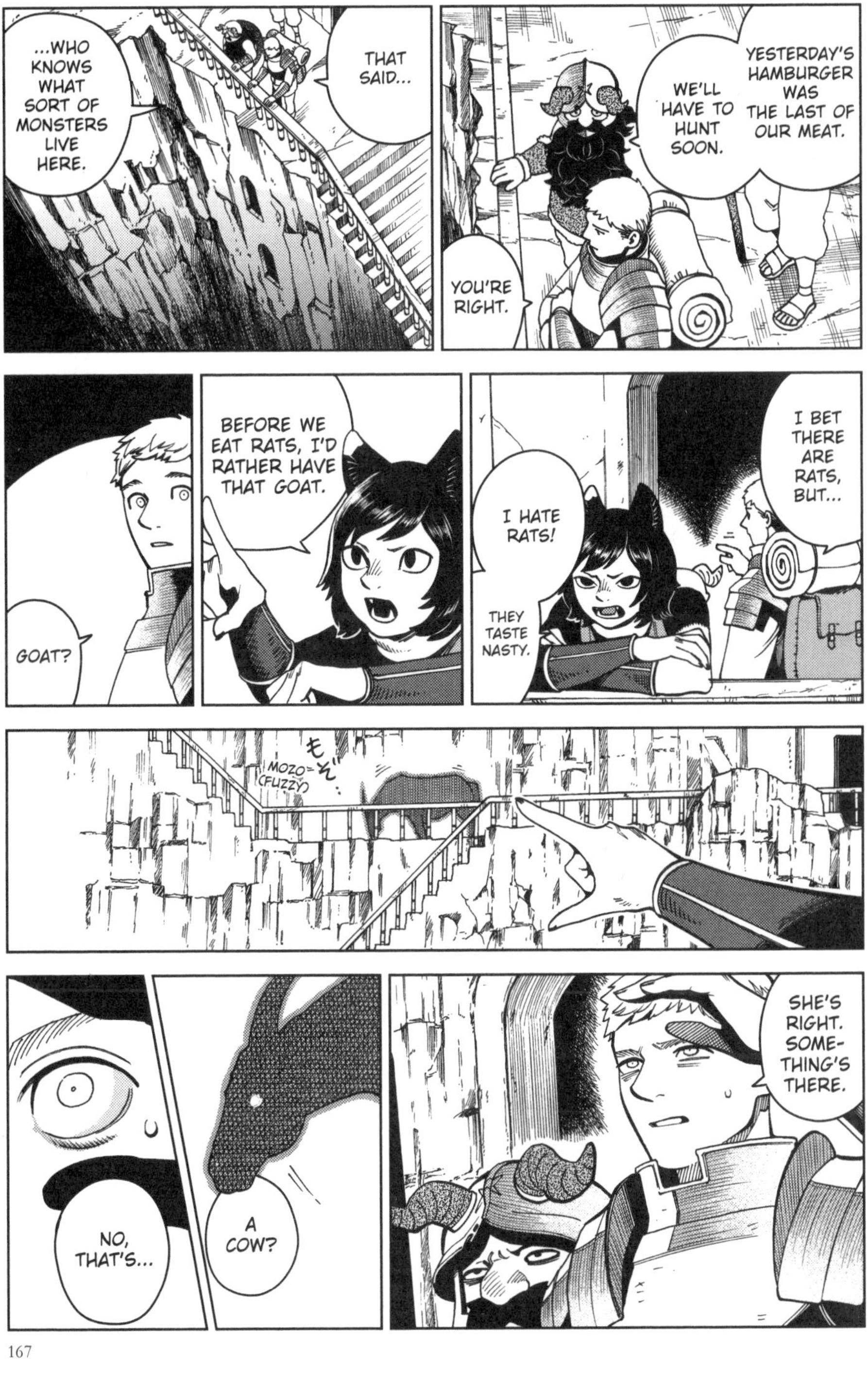
YESTERDAY'S HAMBURGER WAS THE LAST OF OUR MEAT.
WE'LL HAVE TO HUNT SOON.
YOU'RE RIGHT.
THAT SAID...
...WHO KNOWS WHAT SORT OF MONSTERS LIVE HERE.
I BET THERE ARE RATS, BUT...
I HATE RATS!
THEY TASTE NASTY.
BEFORE WE EAT RATS, I'D RATHER HAVE THAT GOAT.
GOAT?
もぞ…
MOZO (FUZZY)
SHE'S RIGHT. SOME-THING'S THERE.
A COW?
NO, THAT'S...

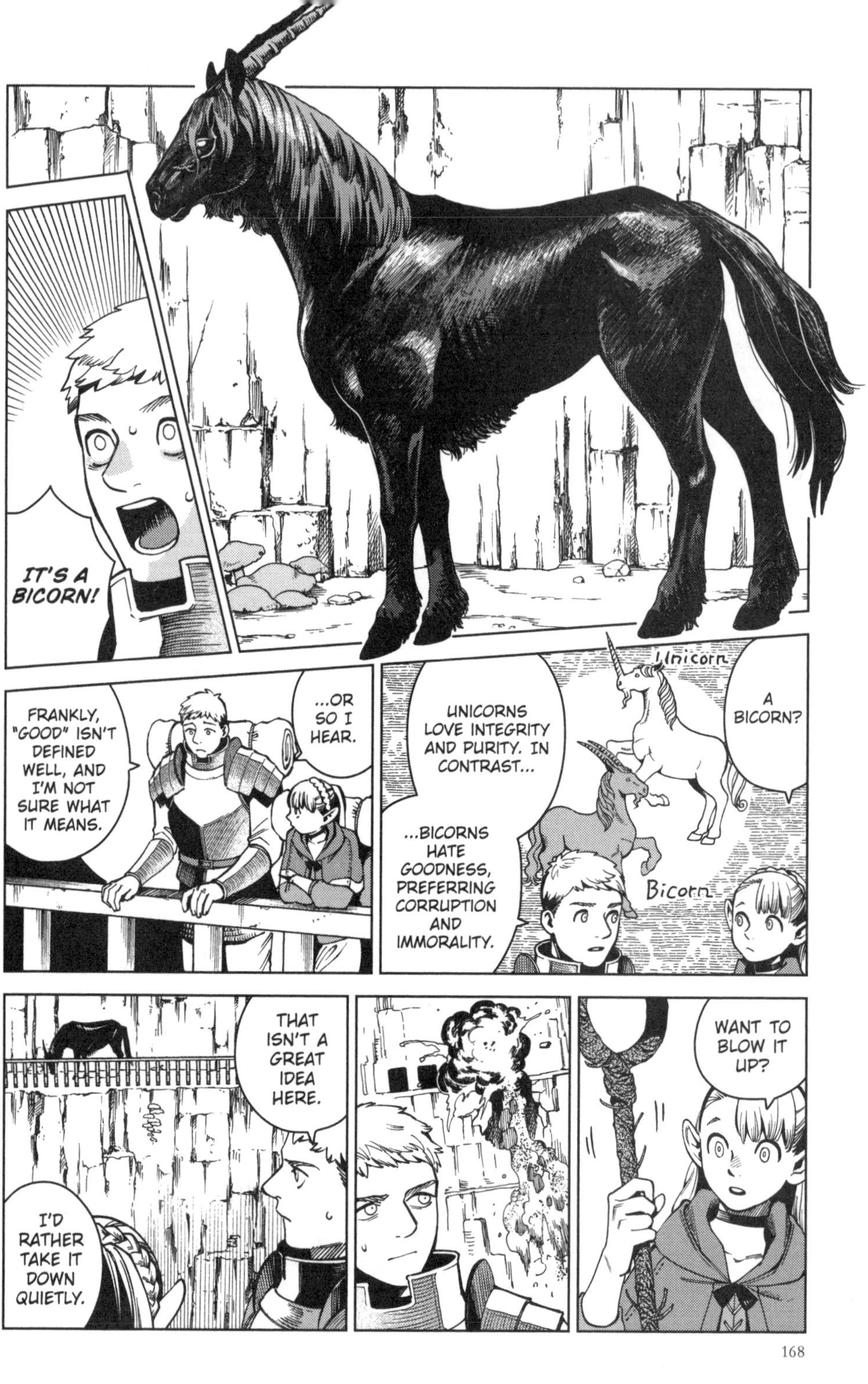
IT'S A BICORN!
A BICORN?
Unicorn
UNICORNS LOVE INTEGRITY AND PURITY. IN CONTRAST...
Bicorn
...BICORNS HATE GOODNESS, PREFERRING CORRUPTION AND IMMORALITY.
...OR SO I HEAR.
FRANKLY, "GOOD" ISN'T DEFINED WELL, AND I'M NOT SURE WHAT IT MEANS.
WANT TO BLOW IT UP?
THAT ISN'T A GREAT IDEA HERE.
I'D RATHER TAKE IT DOWN QUIETLY.

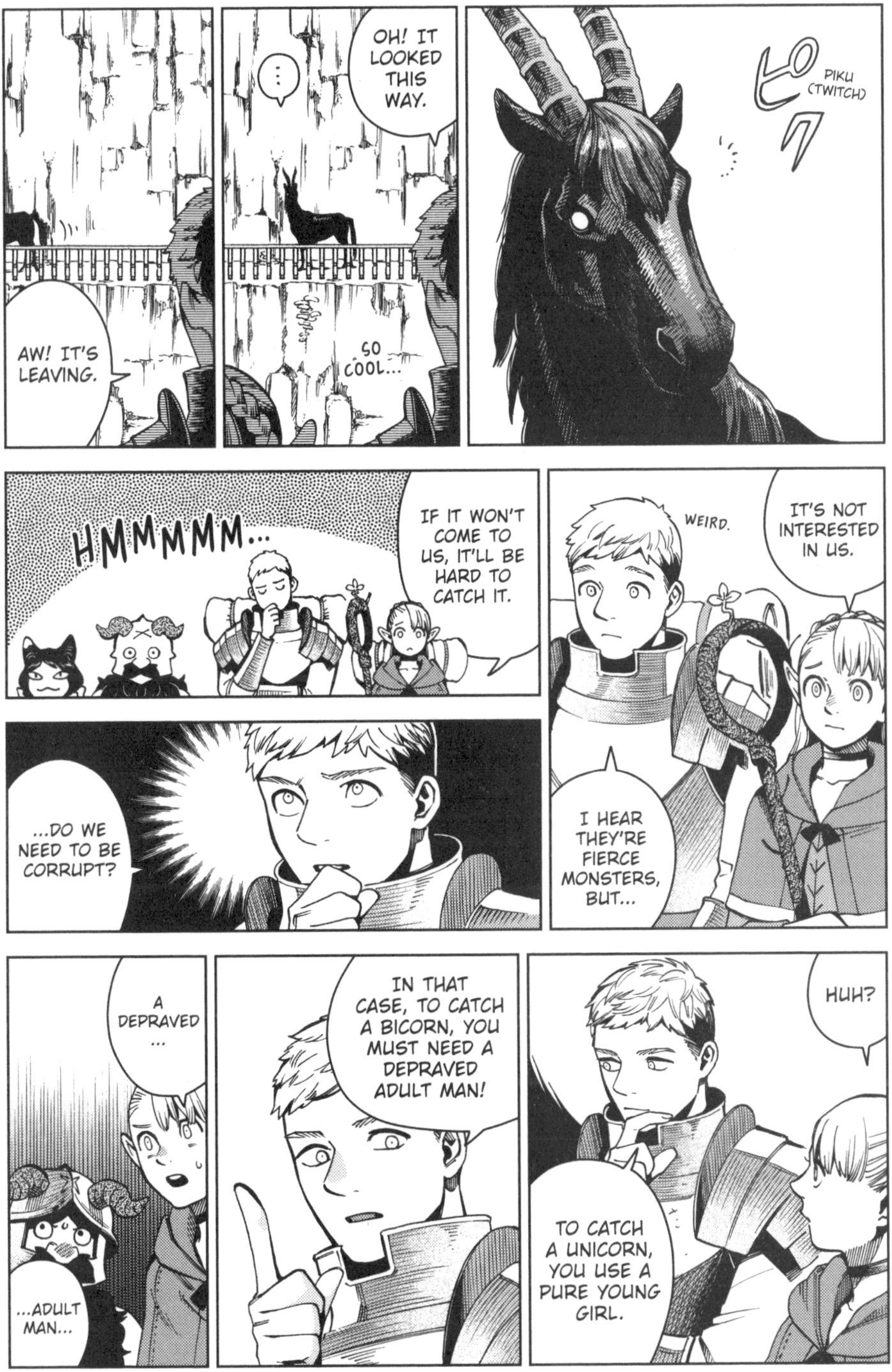
ピク
PIKU (TWITCH)
OH! IT LOOKED THIS WAY.
...
SO COOL...
AW! IT'S LEAVING.
IT'S NOT INTERESTED IN US.
WEIRD.
I HEAR THEY'RE FIERCE MONSTERS, BUT...
IF IT WON'T COME TO US, IT'LL BE HARD TO CATCH IT.
HMMMMM...
...DO WE NEED TO BE CORRUPT?
HUH?
TO CATCH A UNICORN, YOU USE A PURE YOUNG GIRL.
IN THAT CASE, TO CATCH A BICORN, YOU MUST NEED A DEPRAVED ADULT MAN!
A DEPRAVED ...
...ADULT MAN...

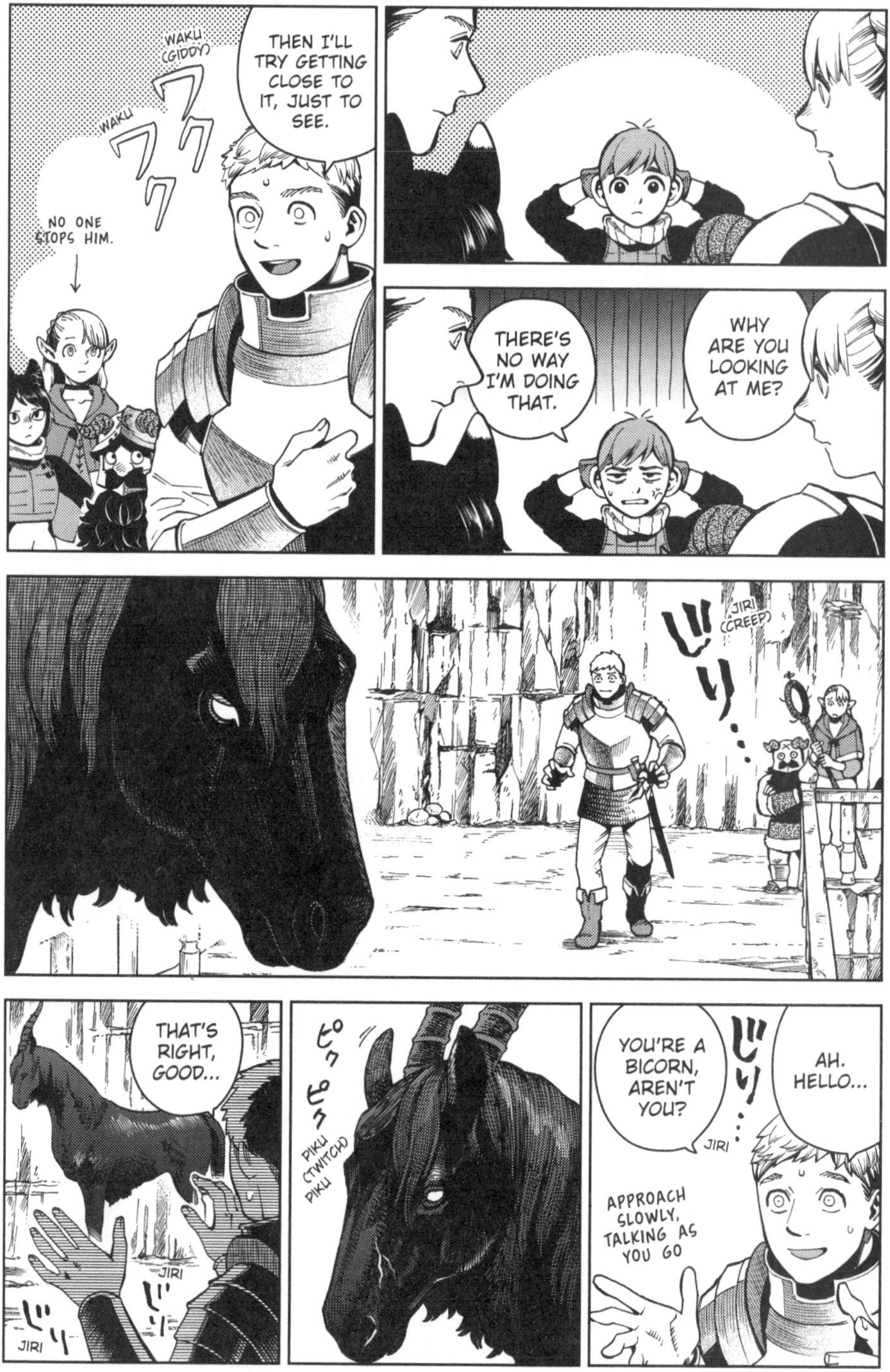
WHY ARE YOU LOOKING AT ME?
THERE'S NO WAY I'M DOING THAT.
THEN I'LL TRY GETTING CLOSE TO IT, JUST TO SEE.
WAKU (GIDDY)
WAKU
NO ONE STOPS HIM.
JIRI (CREEP)
AH. HELLO...
YOU'RE A BICORN, AREN'T YOU?
JIRI
APPROACH SLOWLY, TALKING AS YOU GO
PIKU (TWITCH) PIKU
THAT'S RIGHT, GOOD...
JIRI
JIRI

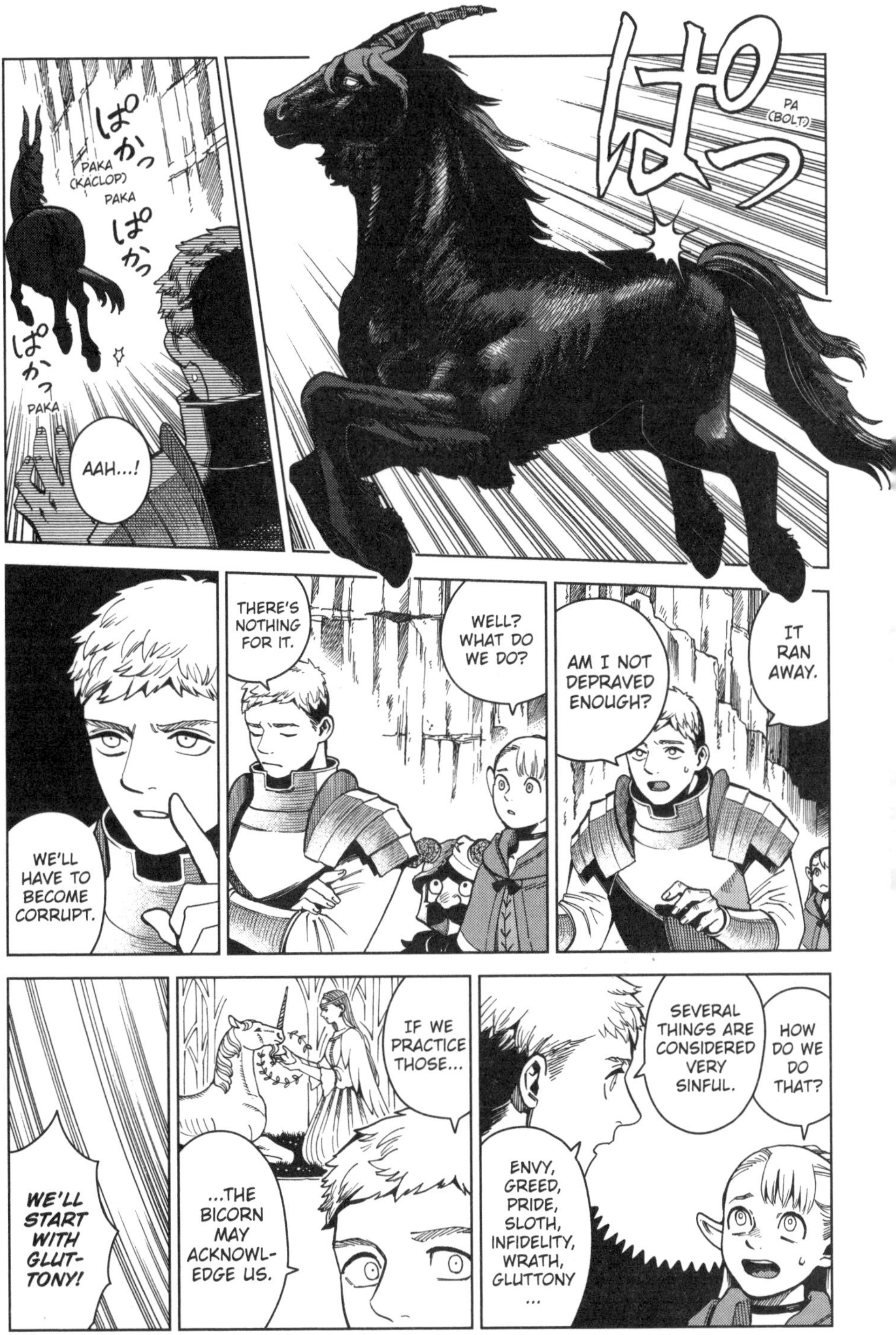
ぱっ
PA (BOLT!)
ぱかっ
PAKA (KACLOP)
PAKA
ぱかっ
ぱかっ
PAKA
AAH...!
IT RAN AWAY.
AM I NOT DEPRAVED ENOUGH?
WELL? WHAT DO WE DO?
THERE'S NOTHING FOR IT.
WE'LL HAVE TO BECOME CORRUPT.
HOW DO WE DO THAT?
SEVERAL THINGS ARE CONSIDERED VERY SINFUL.
ENVY, GREED, PRIDE, SLOTH, INFIDELITY, WRATH, GLUTTONY ...
IF WE PRACTICE THOSE...
...THE BICORN MAY ACKNOWL-EDGE US.
WE'LL START WITH GLUT-TONY!

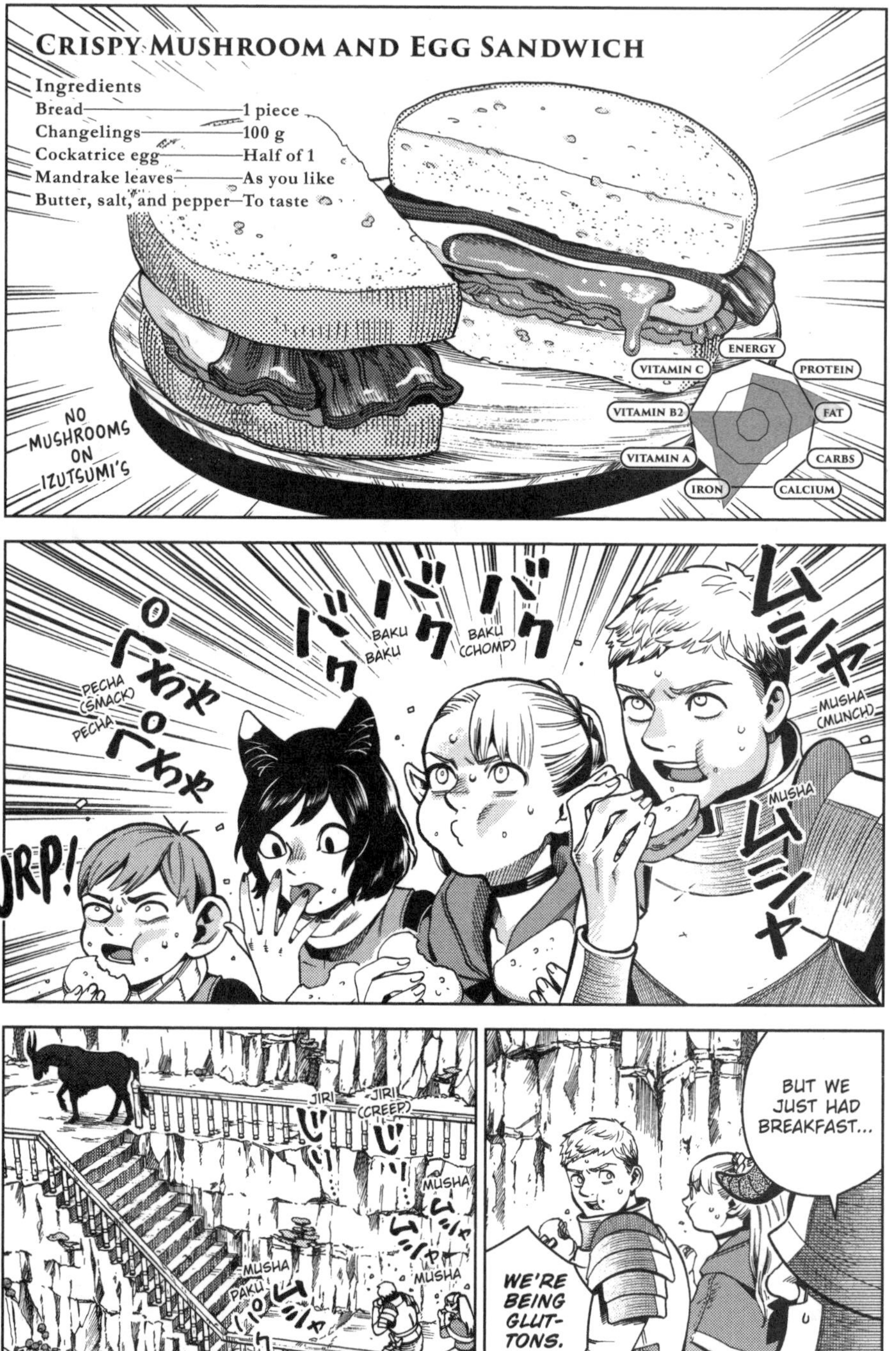
CRISPY MUSHROOM AND EGG SANDWICH
Ingredients
Bread—1 piece
Changelings—100 g
Cockatrice egg—Half of 1
Mandrake leaves—As you like
Butter, salt, and pepper—To taste
ENERGY
PROTEIN
FAT
CARBS
CALCIUM
IRON
VITAMIN A
VITAMIN B2
VITAMIN C
NO MUSHROOMS ON IZUTSUMI'S
ムシャ
MUSHA (MUNCH)
ムシャ
MUSHA
バク
BAKU (CHOMP)
バク
BAKU BAKU
ぺちゃ
PECHA (SMACK)
ぺちゃ
PECHA
URP!
BUT WE JUST HAD BREAKFAST...
WE'RE BEING GLUT-TONS.
じり
JIRI (CREEP)
じり
JIRI
ムシャ
MUSHA
ムシャ
MUSHA
ムシャ
MUSHA
パク
PAKU

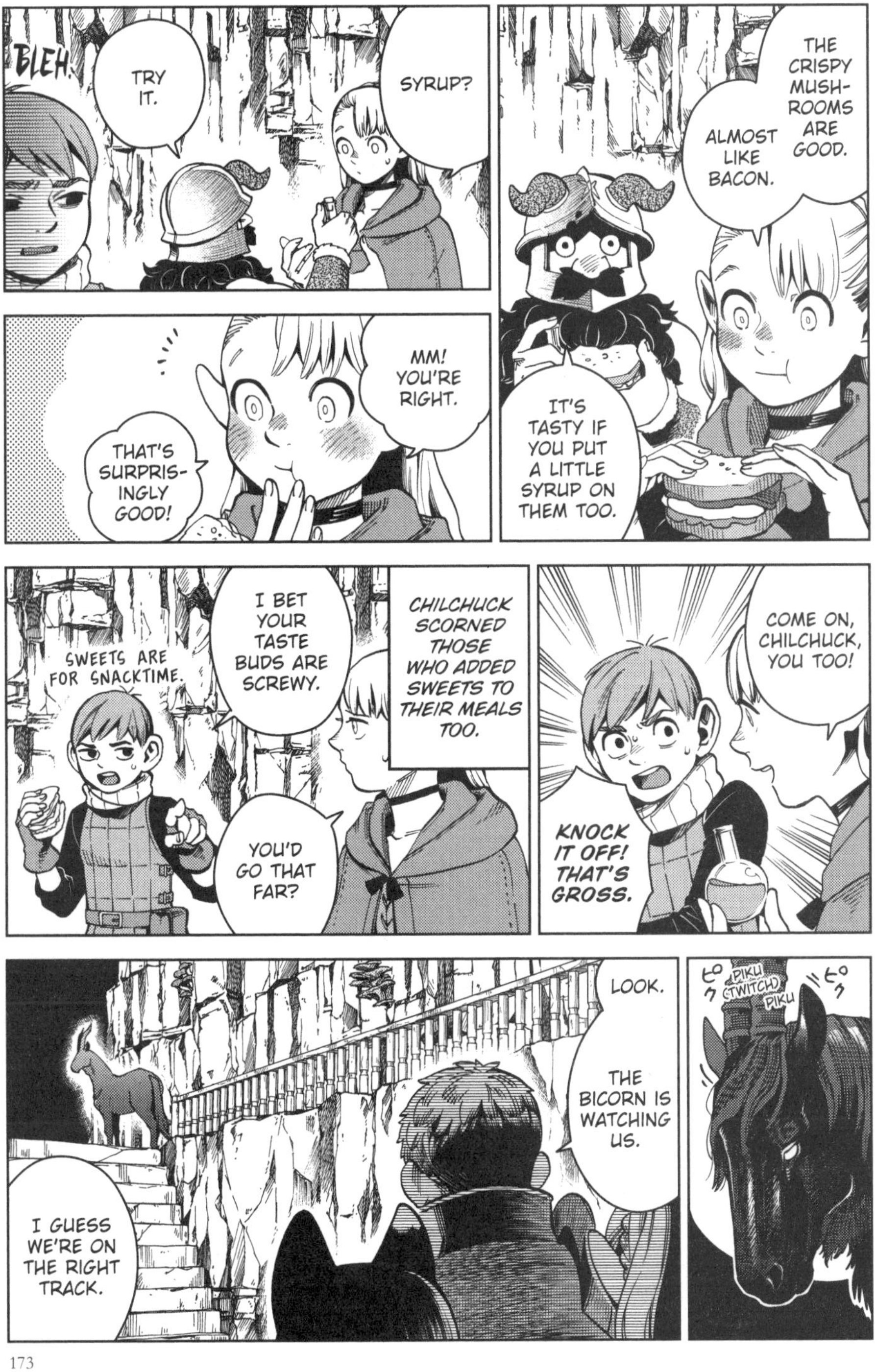
THE CRISPY MUSHROOMS ARE GOOD.
ALMOST LIKE BACON.
IT'S TASTY IF YOU PUT A LITTLE SYRUP ON THEM TOO.
SYRUP?
TRY IT.
BLEH!
MM! YOU'RE RIGHT.
THAT'S SURPRISINGLY GOOD!
COME ON, CHILCHUCK, YOU TOO!
KNOCK IT OFF! THAT'S GROSS.
CHILCHUCK SCORNED THOSE WHO ADDED SWEETS TO THEIR MEALS TOO.
I BET YOUR TASTE BUDS ARE SCREWY.
SWEETS ARE FOR SNACKTIME.
YOU'D GO THAT FAR?
ピク PIKU
(TWITCH)
ピク PIKU
LOOK.
THE BICORN IS WATCHING US.
I GUESS WE'RE ON THE RIGHT TRACK.

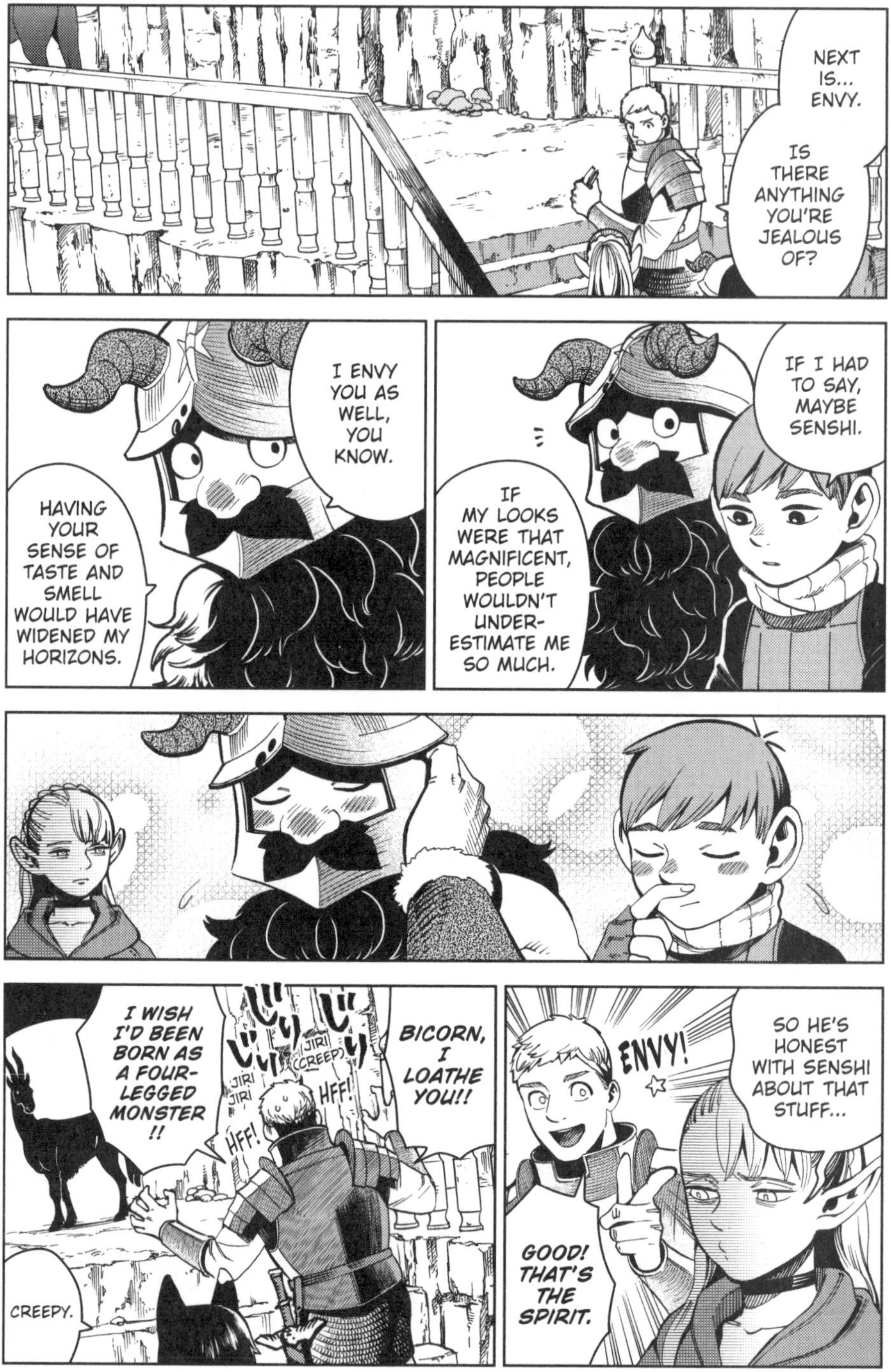

NEXT IS... ENVY.
IS THERE ANYTHING YOU'RE JEALOUS OF?
IF I HAD TO SAY, MAYBE SENSHI.
IF MY LOOKS WERE THAT MAGNIFICENT, PEOPLE WOULDN'T UNDER-ESTIMATE ME SO MUCH.
I ENVY YOU AS WELL, YOU KNOW.
HAVING YOUR SENSE OF TASTE AND SMELL WOULD HAVE WIDENED MY HORIZONS.
SO HE'S HONEST WITH SENSHI ABOUT THAT STUFF...
ENVY!
GOOD! THAT'S THE SPIRIT.
BICORN, I LOATHE YOU!!
JIRI (CREEP)
JIRI JIRI
HFF!
HFF!
I WISH I'D BEEN BORN AS A FOUR-LEGGED MONSTER!!
CREEPY.

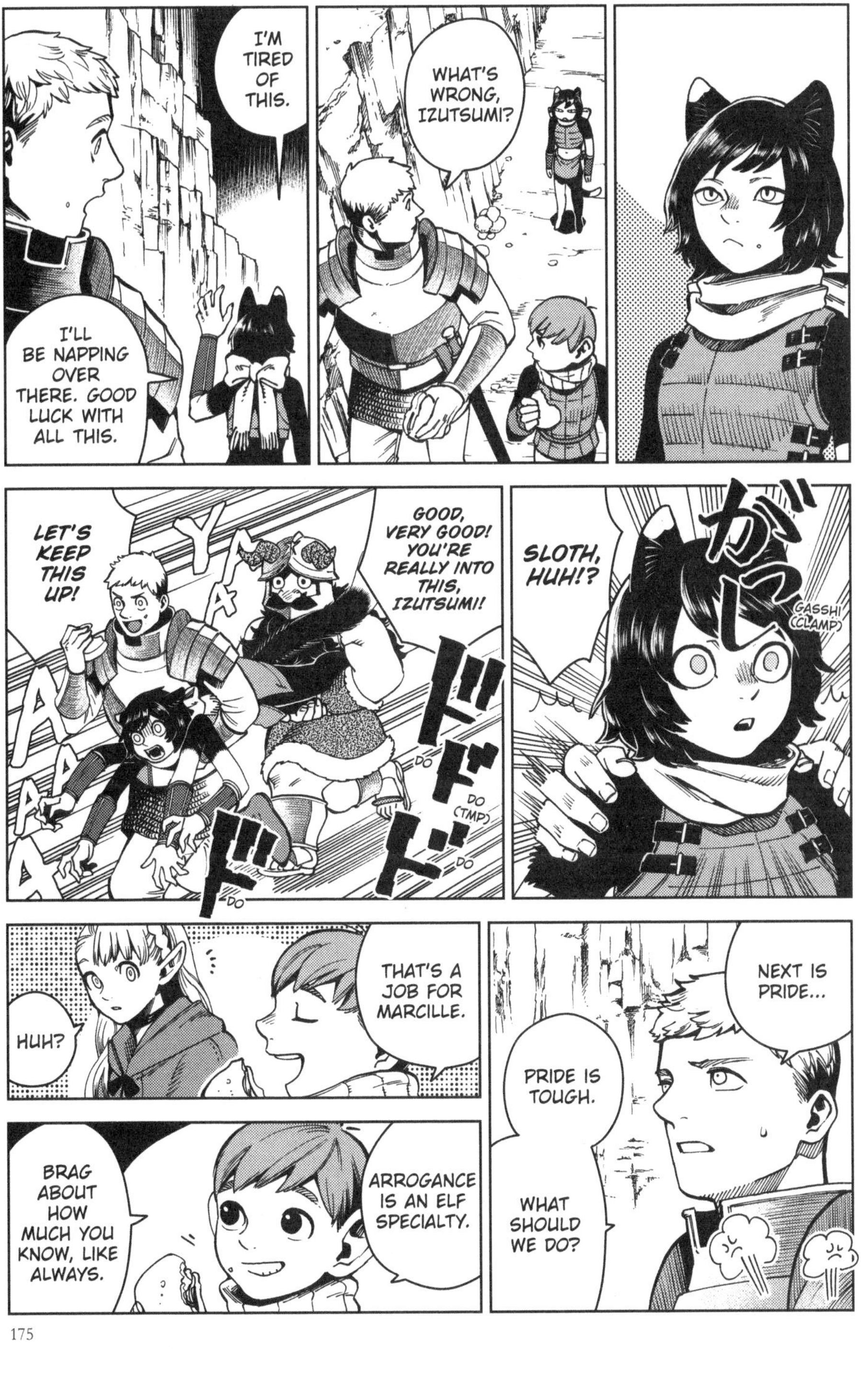
WHAT'S WRONG, IZUTSUMI?
I'M TIRED OF THIS.
I'LL BE NAPPING OVER THERE. GOOD LUCK WITH ALL THIS.
SLOTH, HUH!?
がっし
GASSHI (CLAMP)
GOOD, VERY GOOD! YOU'RE REALLY INTO THIS, IZUTSUMI!
LET'S KEEP THIS UP!
YAAAAAA
ドドドド
DO
DO (TMP)
DO
DO
NEXT IS PRIDE...
PRIDE IS TOUGH.
WHAT SHOULD WE DO?
THAT'S A JOB FOR MARCILLE.
HUH?
ARROGANCE IS AN ELF SPECIALTY.
BRAG ABOUT HOW MUCH YOU KNOW, LIKE ALWAYS.

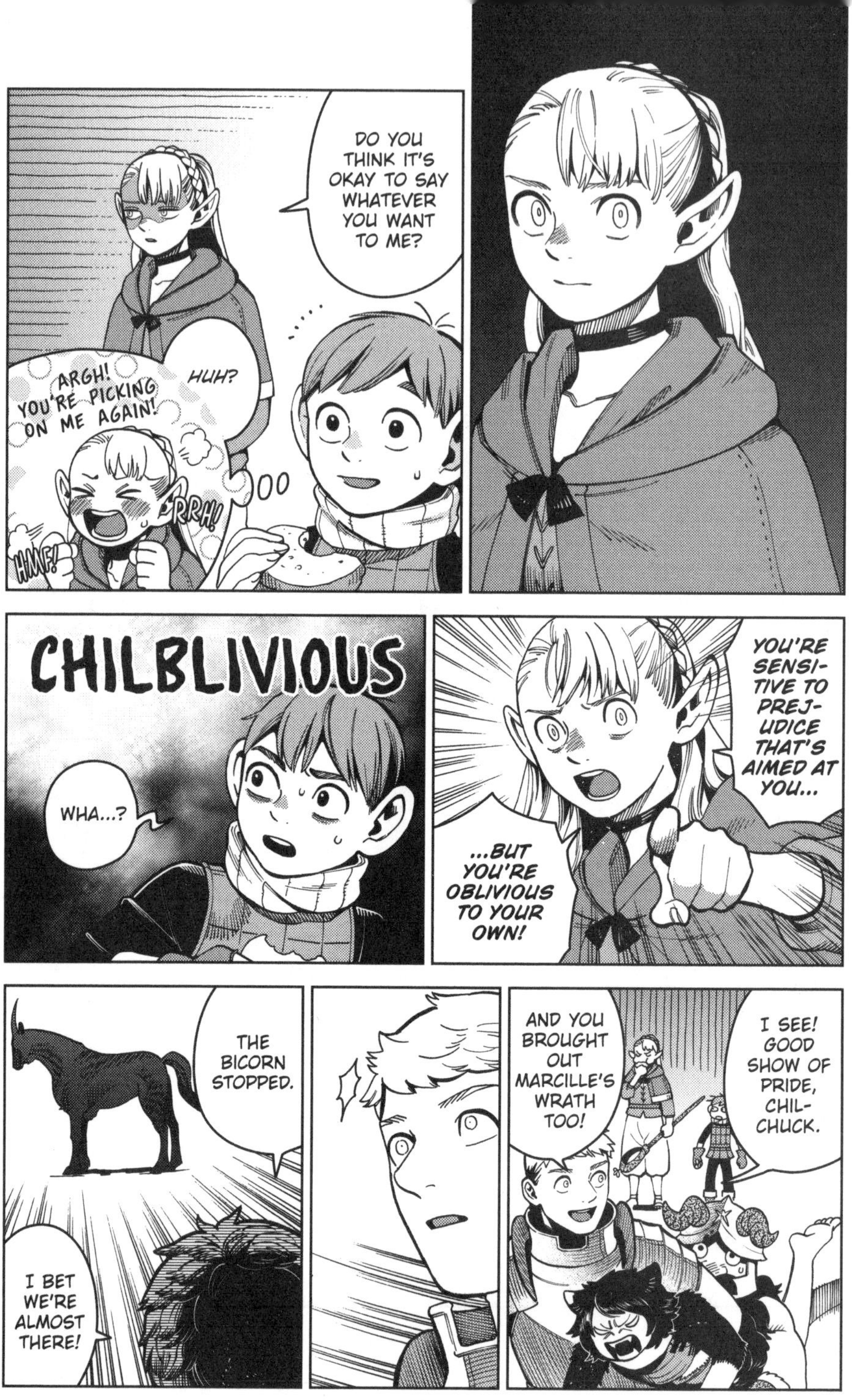

DO YOU THINK IT'S OKAY TO SAY WHATEVER YOU WANT TO ME?
......
HUH?
ARGH! YOU'RE PICKING ON ME AGAIN!
RRH!
HMF!
YOU'RE SENSITIVE TO PREJUDICE THAT'S AIMED AT YOU...
...BUT YOU'RE OBLIVIOUS TO YOUR OWN!
CHILBLIVIOUS
WHA...?
I SEE! GOOD SHOW OF PRIDE, CHILCHUCK.
AND YOU BROUGHT OUT MARCILLE'S WRATH TOO!
THE BICORN STOPPED.
I BET WE'RE ALMOST THERE!

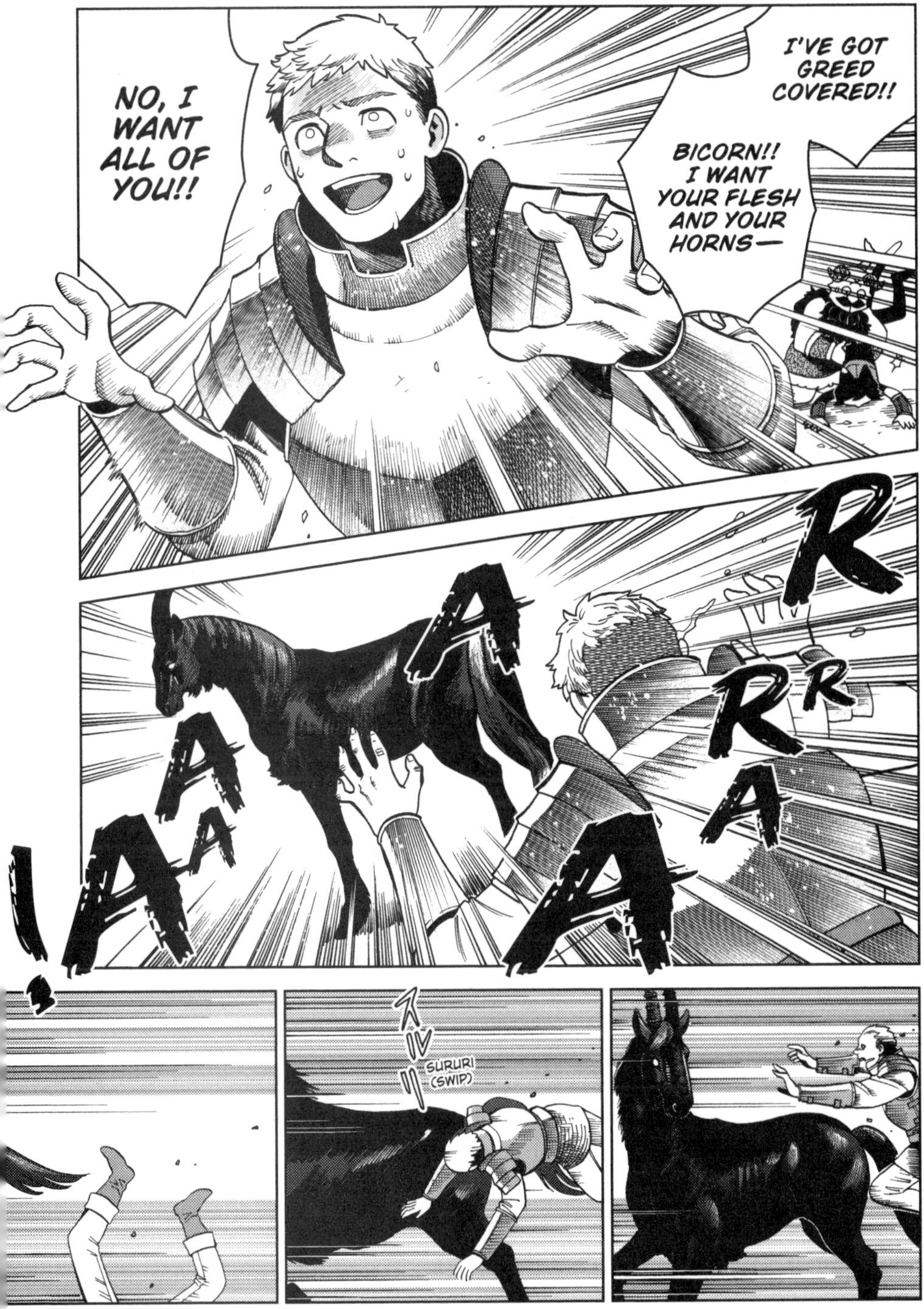
I'VE GOT GREED COVERED!!
BICORN!! I WANT YOUR FLESH AND YOUR HORNS—
NO, I WANT ALL OF YOU!!
IAAAAAAARRRR
スルリ
SURURI (SWIP)

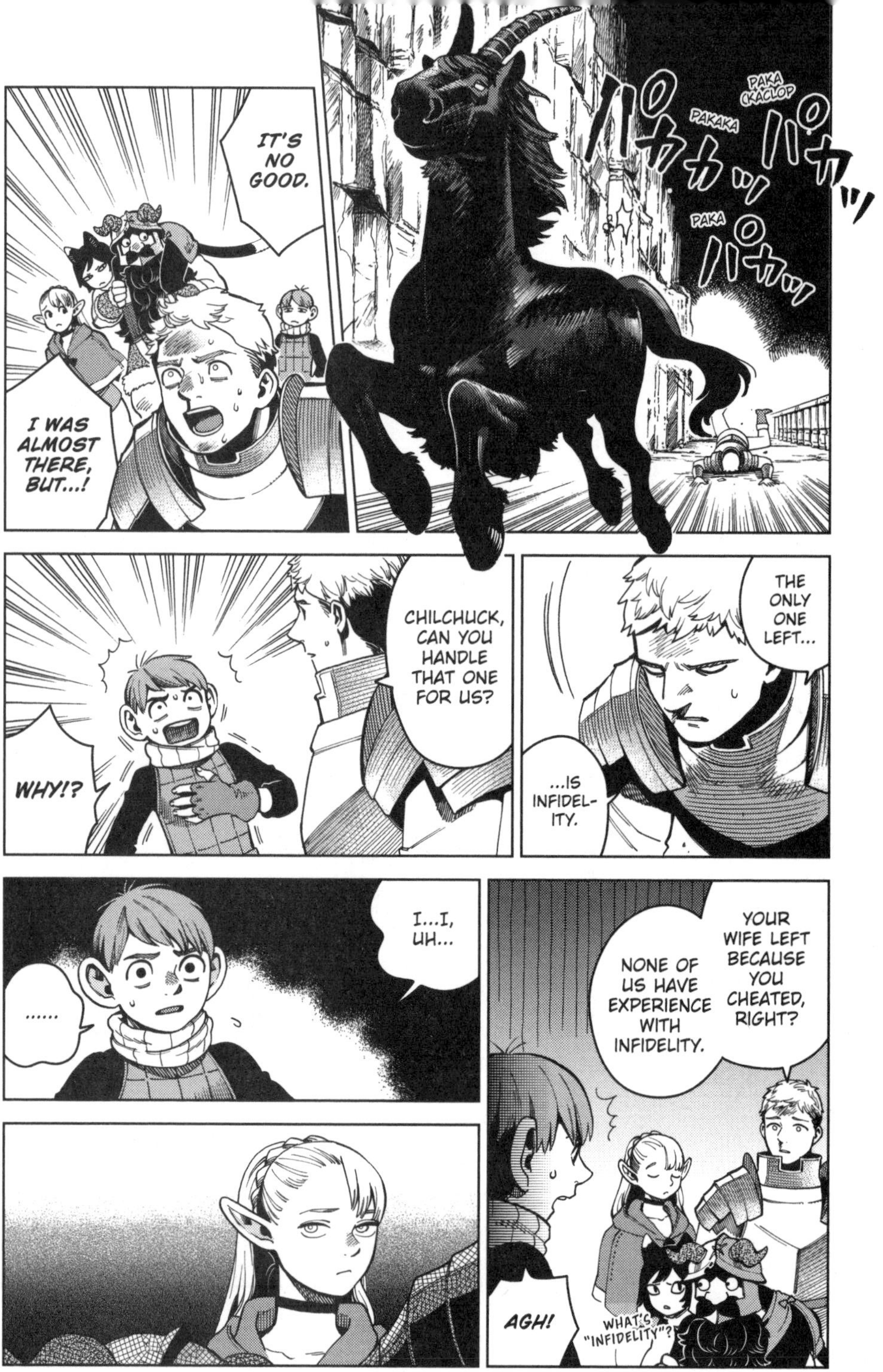
パカッ
PAKA CKACLOP
パカカッ
PAKAKA
パカッ
PAKA
IT'S NO GOOD.
I WAS ALMOST THERE, BUT...!
THE ONLY ONE LEFT...
...IS INFIDELITY.
CHILCHUCK, CAN YOU HANDLE THAT ONE FOR US?
WHY!?
YOUR WIFE LEFT BECAUSE YOU CHEATED, RIGHT?
NONE OF US HAVE EXPERIENCE WITH INFIDELITY.
AGH!
WHAT'S "INFIDELITY"?
I...I, UH...
......

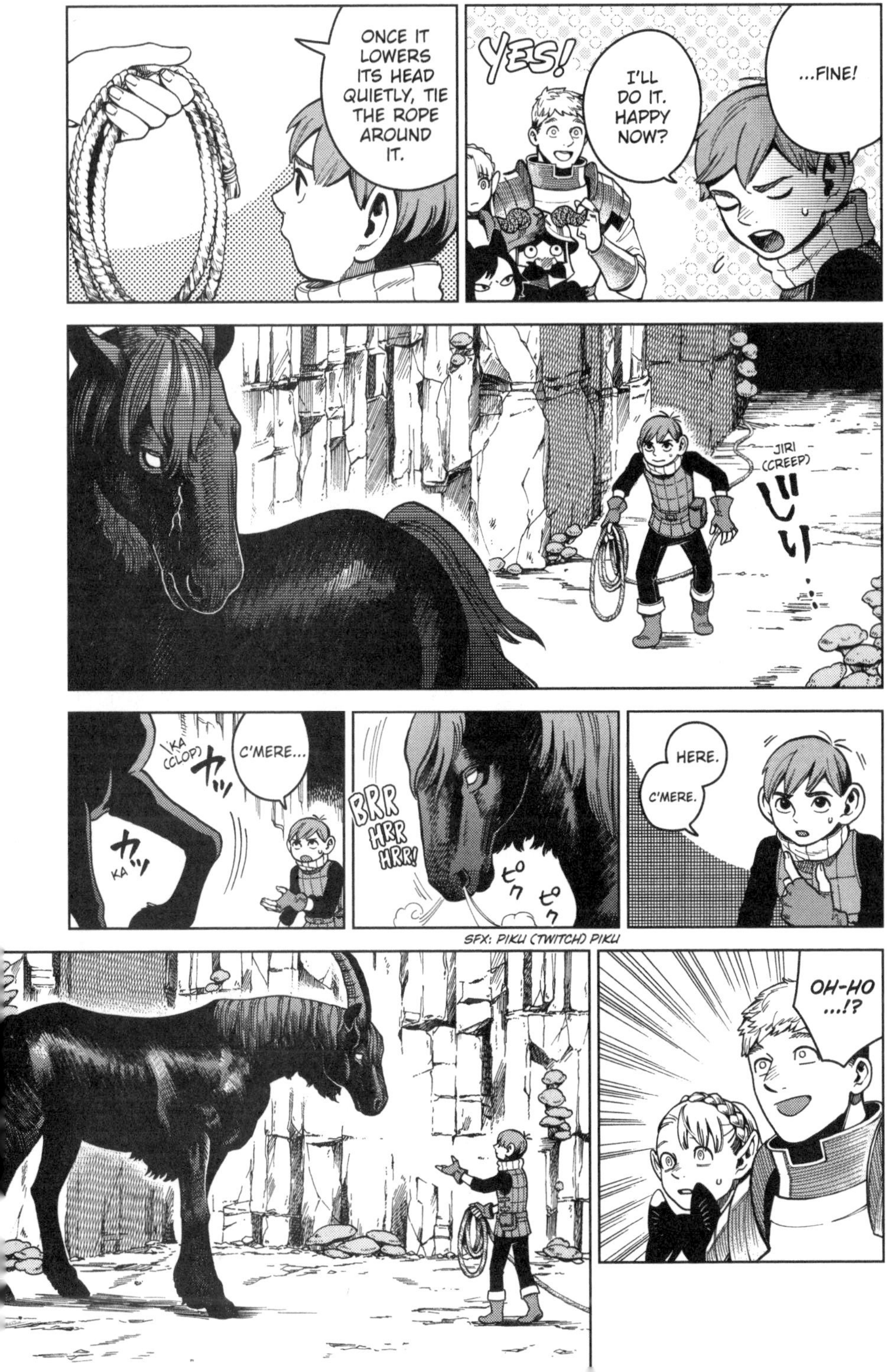
...FINE!
I'LL DO IT. HAPPY NOW?
YES!
ONCE IT LOWERS ITS HEAD QUIETLY, TIE THE ROPE AROUND IT.
JIRI (CREEP)
じり…
HERE.
C'MERE.
BRR HRR HRR!
ピク ピク
KA (CLOP)
カッ
C'MERE...
カッ
KA
SFX: PIKU (TWITCH) PIKU
OH-HO ...!?

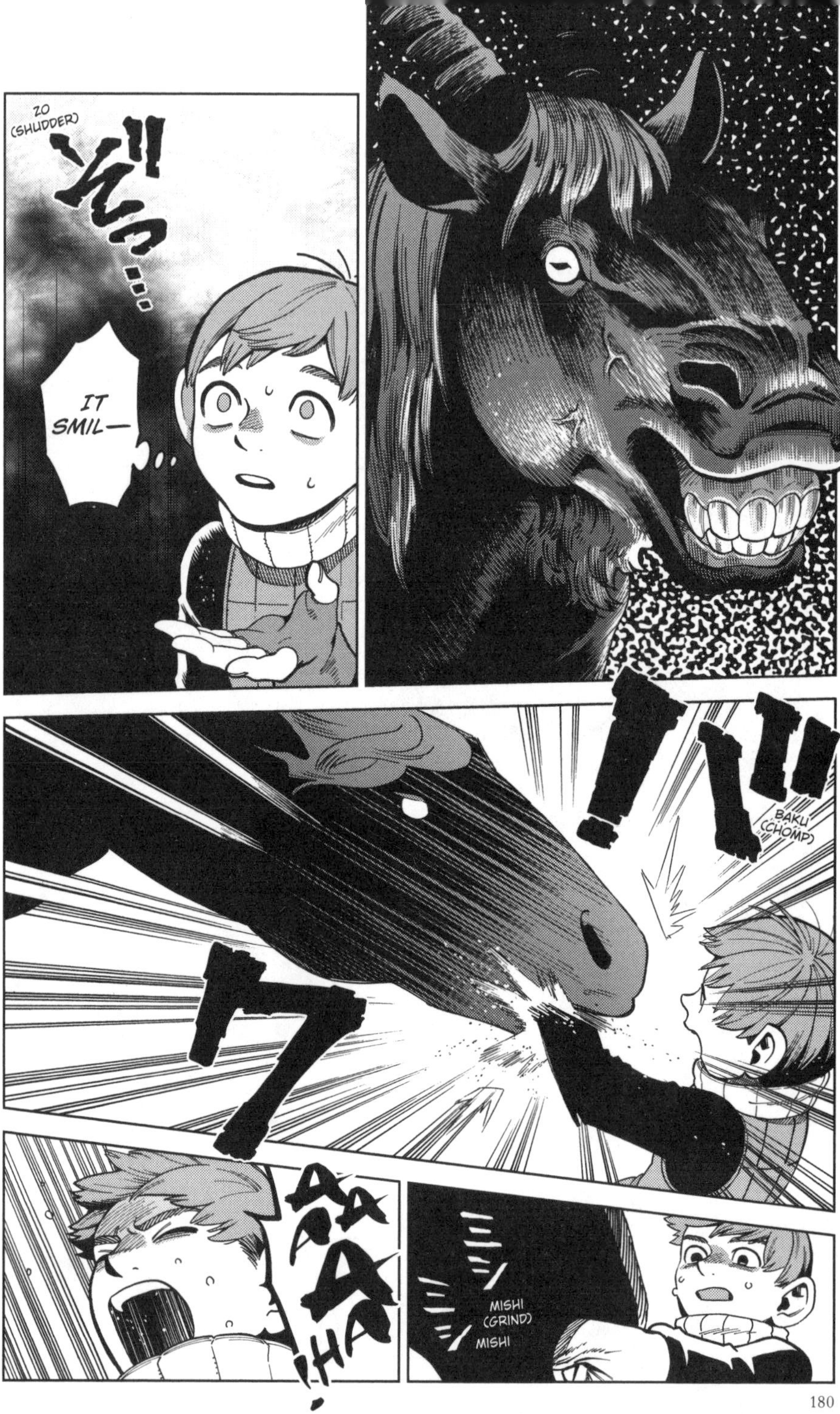
ZO
(SHUDDER)
IT SMIL—
BAKU
(CHOMP)
MISHI
(GRIND)
MISHI
AAAAAAH!

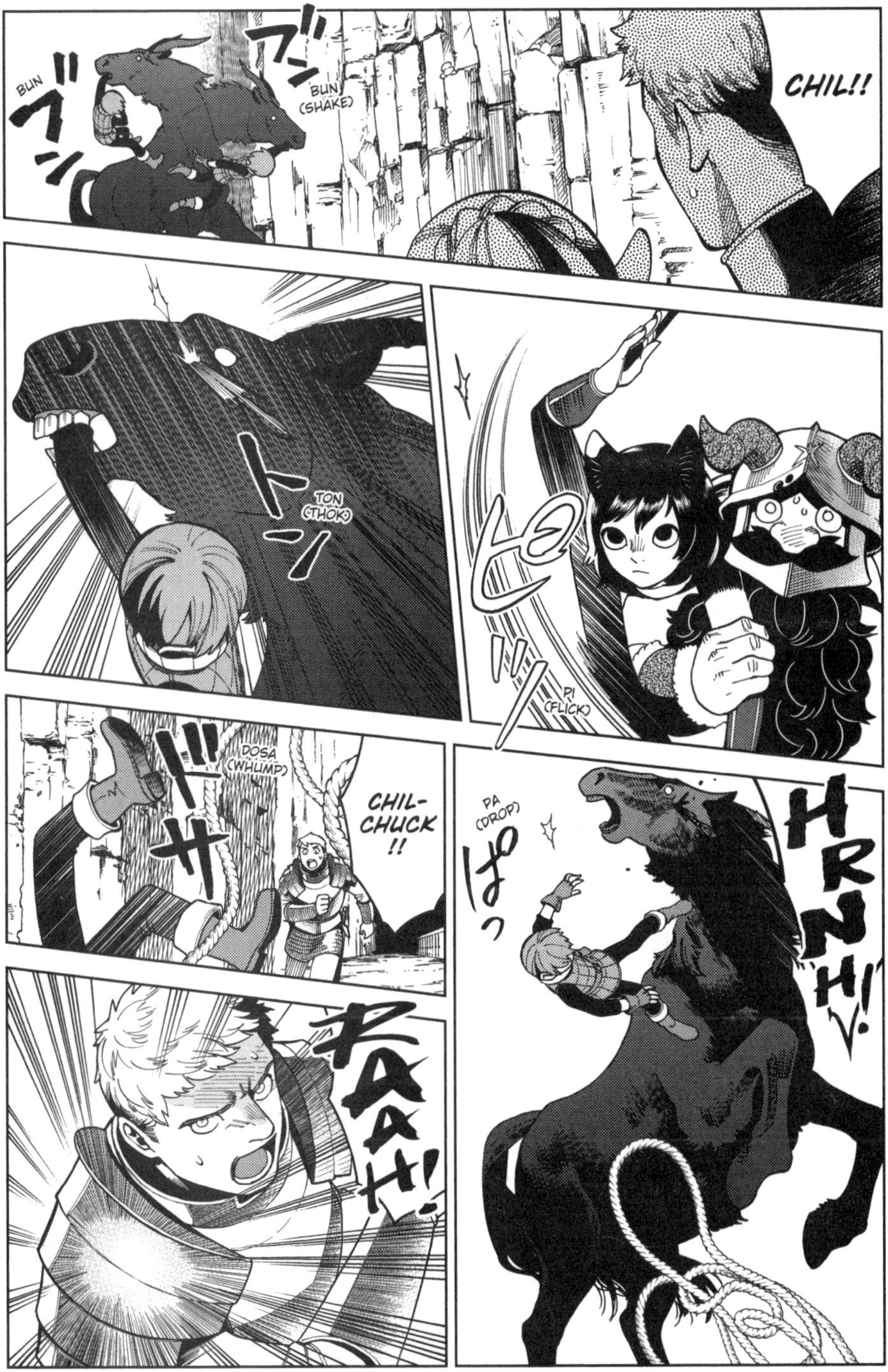
CHIL!!
BUN (SHAKE)
BUN
PI (FLICK)
TON (THOK)
HRNH!
PA (DROP)
CHIL-CHUCK!!
DOSA (WHUMP)
RAAH!

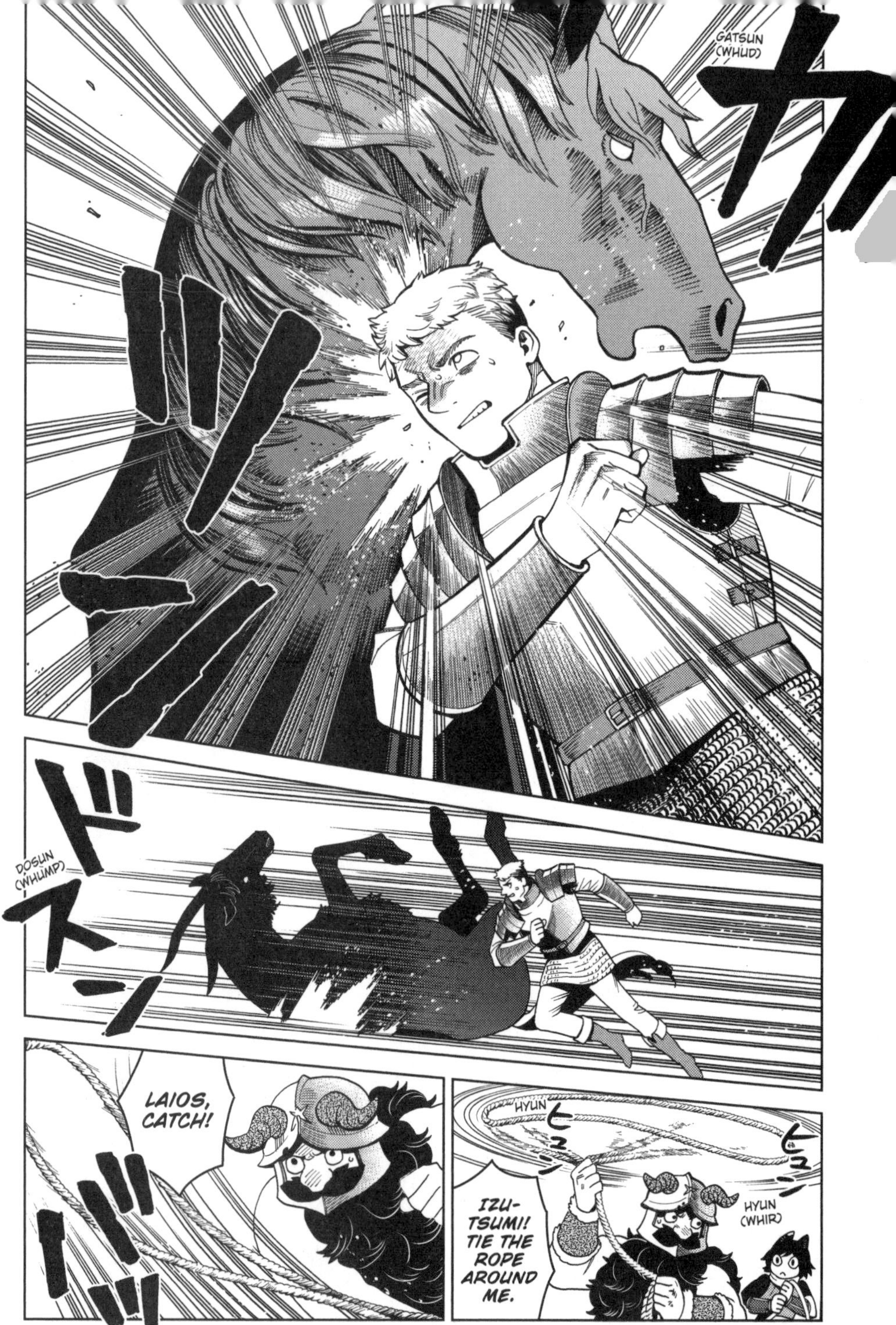
GATSUN (WHUD)
DOSUN (WHUMP)
HYUN
HYUN (WHIR)
IZU-TSUMI! TIE THE ROPE AROUND ME.
LAIOS, CATCH!
BA (FLING)

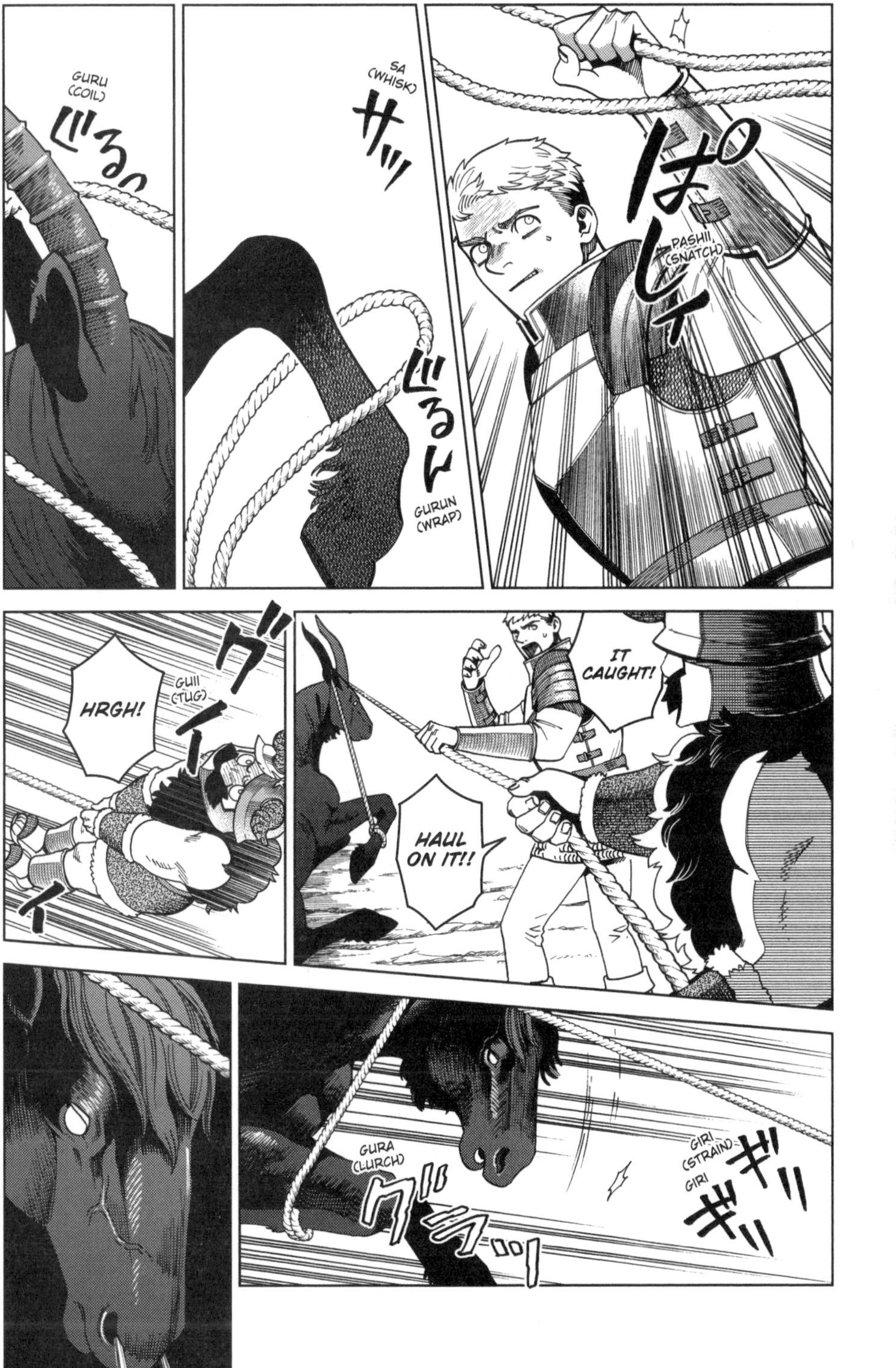
ぱしィ
PASHII (SNATCH)
サッ
SA (WHISK)
ぐるん
GURUN (WRAP)
ぐるっ
GURU (COIL)
IT CAUGHT!
HAUL ON IT!!
グイー
GUII (TUG)
HRGH!
ギリ ギリ
GIRI (STRAIN) GIRI
グラッ
GURA (LURCH)
DO!

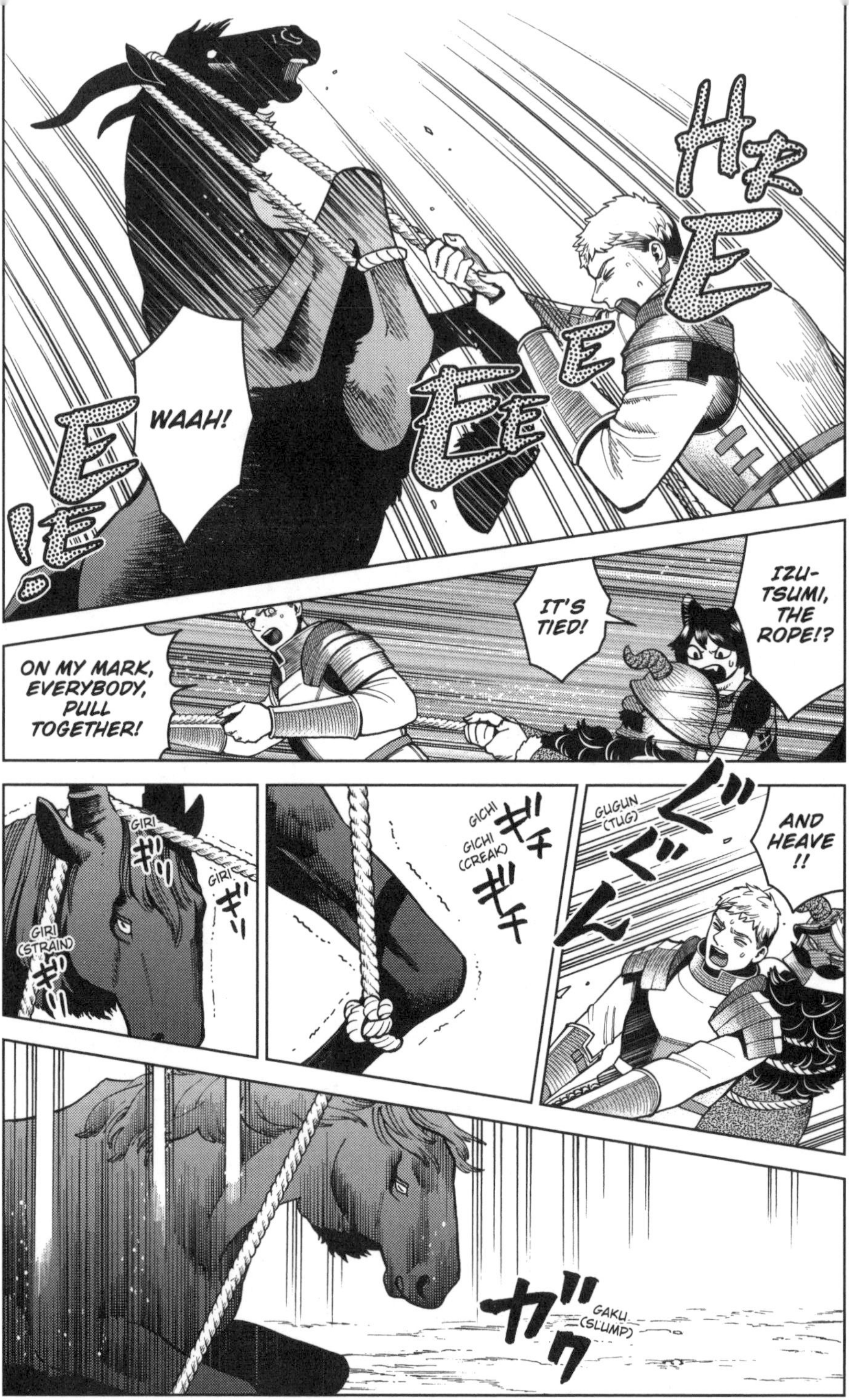
WAAH!
IZU-TSUMI, THE ROPE!?
IT'S TIED!
ON MY MARK, EVERYBODY, PULL TOGETHER!
AND HEAVE !!
GUGUN (TUG)
ぐぐん
GICHI GICHI (CREAK)
ギチギチ
GIRI GIRI GIRI (STRAIN)
ギリギリギリ
GAKU (SLUMP)
ガク

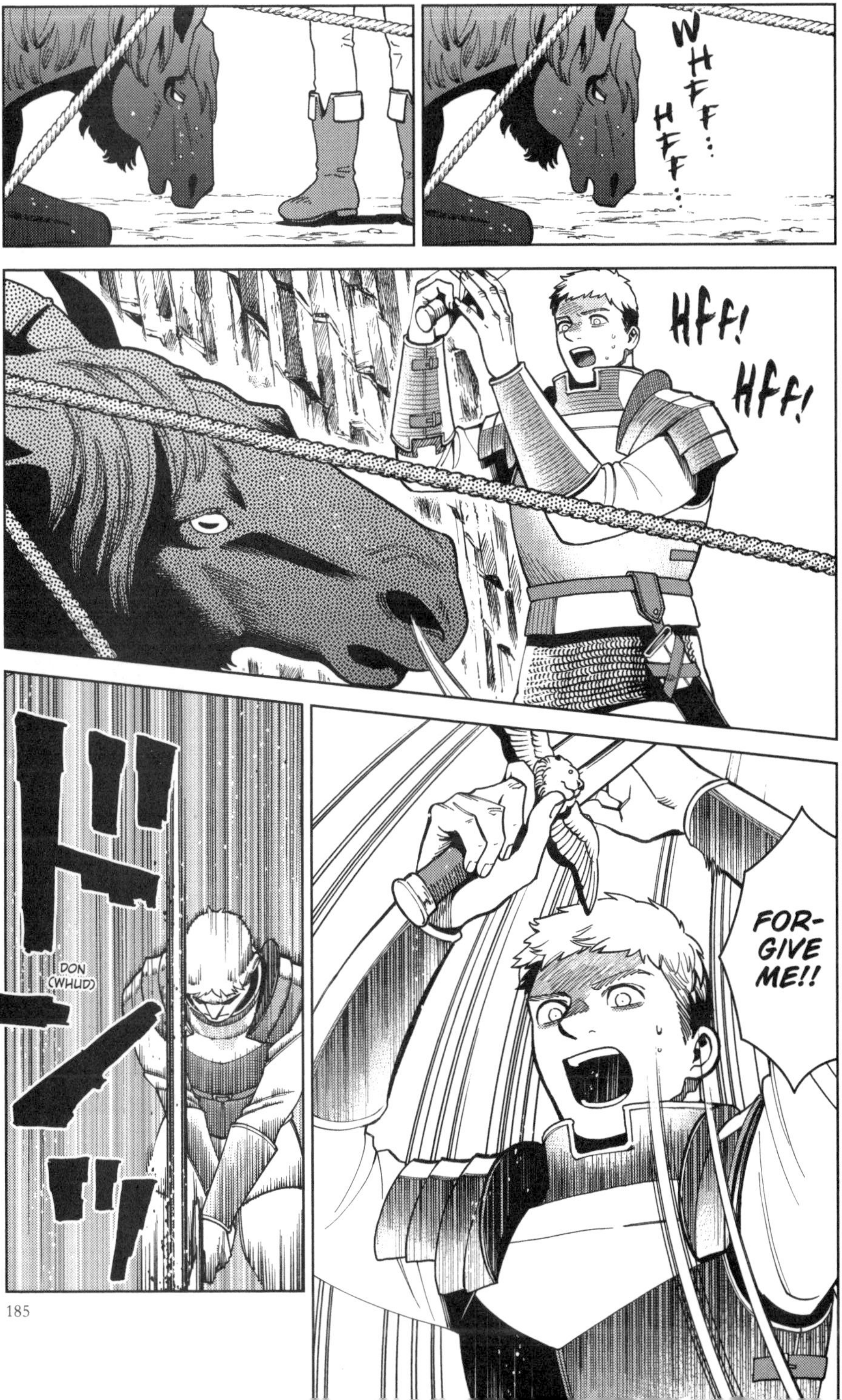
WHFF...
HFF...
HFF!
HFF!
FOR-GIVE ME!!
DON (WHUD)

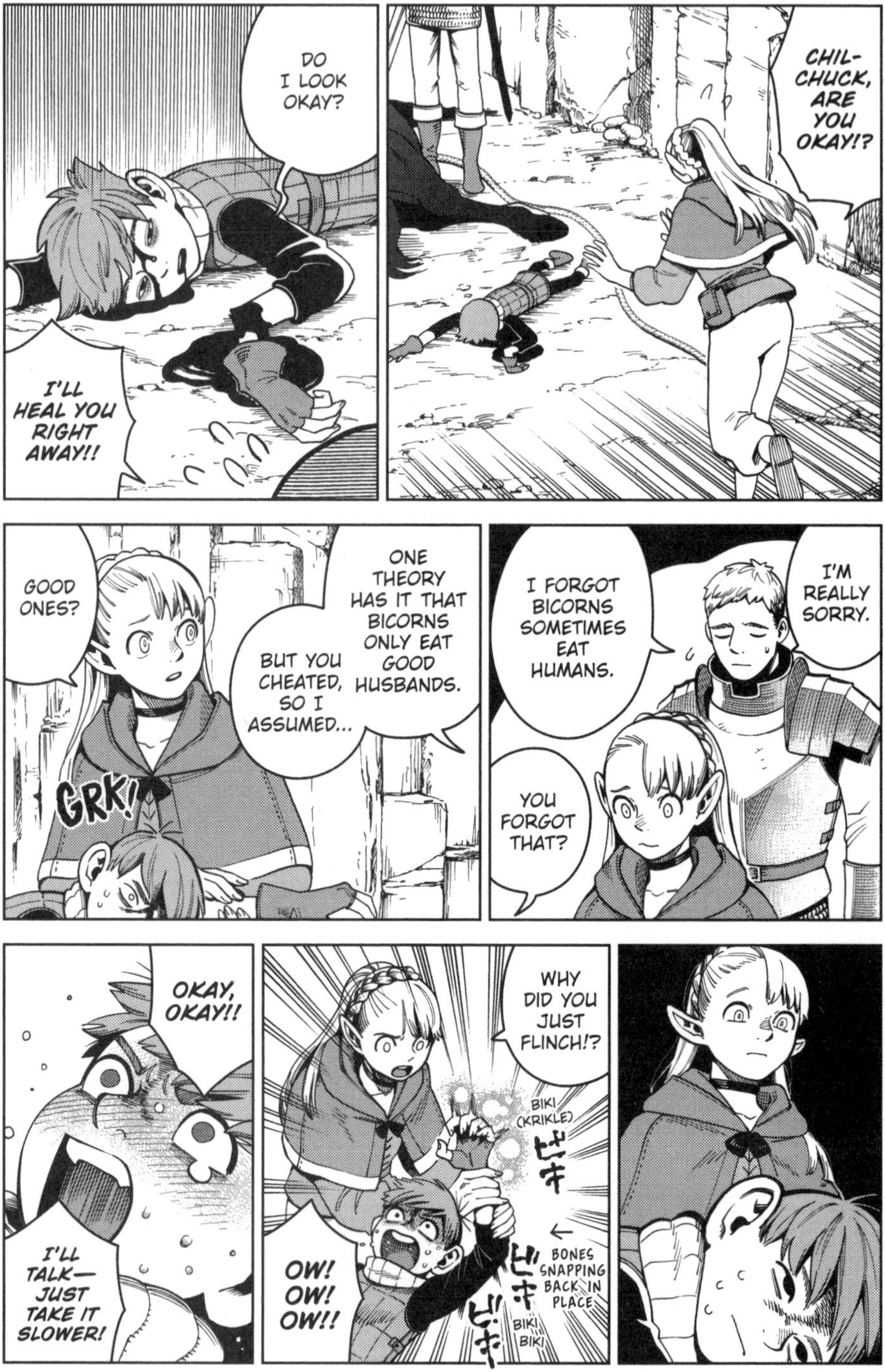
CHIL-CHUCK, ARE YOU OKAY!?
DO I LOOK OKAY?
I'LL HEAL YOU RIGHT AWAY!!
I'M REALLY SORRY.
I FORGOT BICORNS SOMETIMES EAT HUMANS.
YOU FORGOT THAT?
ONE THEORY HAS IT THAT BICORNS ONLY EAT GOOD HUSBANDS.
BUT YOU CHEATED, SO I ASSUMED...
GOOD ONES?
GRK!
WHY DID YOU JUST FLINCH!?
BIKI (KRIKLE)
ビキ
← BONES SNAPPING BACK IN PLACE
ビキ
ビキ
BIKI BIKI
OW! OW! OW!!
OKAY, OKAY!!
I'LL TALK—JUST TAKE IT SLOWER!

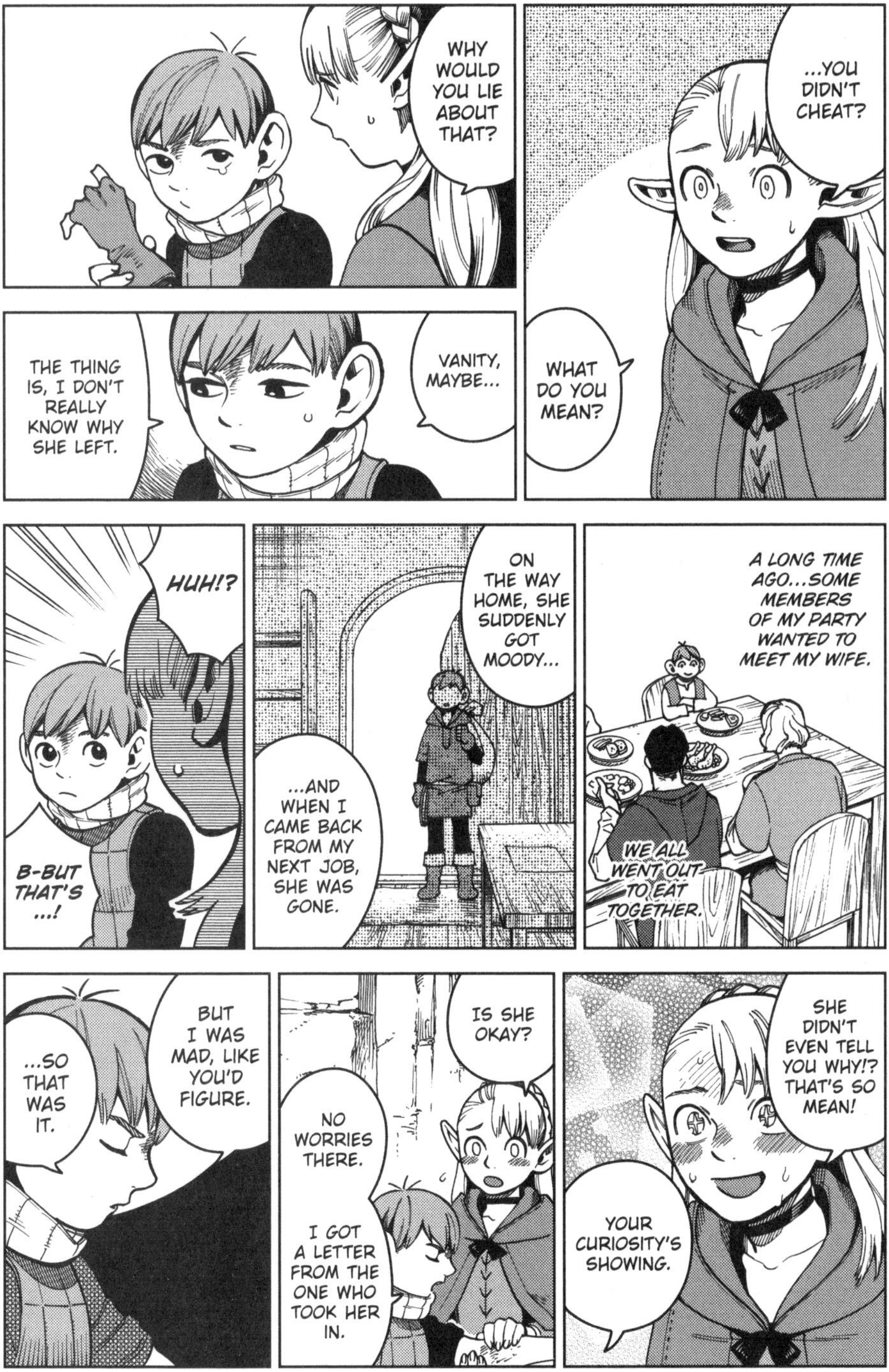
...YOU DIDN'T CHEAT?
WHAT DO YOU MEAN?
WHY WOULD YOU LIE ABOUT THAT?
VANITY, MAYBE...
THE THING IS, I DON'T REALLY KNOW WHY SHE LEFT.
A LONG TIME AGO...SOME MEMBERS OF MY PARTY WANTED TO MEET MY WIFE.
WE ALL WENT OUT TO EAT TOGETHER.
ON THE WAY HOME, SHE SUDDENLY GOT MOODY...
...AND WHEN I CAME BACK FROM MY NEXT JOB, SHE WAS GONE.
HUH!?
B-BUT THAT'S ...!
SHE DIDN'T EVEN TELL YOU WHY!? THAT'S SO MEAN!
YOUR CURIOSITY'S SHOWING.
IS SHE OKAY?
NO WORRIES THERE.
I GOT A LETTER FROM THE ONE WHO TOOK HER IN.
BUT I WAS MAD, LIKE YOU'D FIGURE.
...SO THAT WAS IT.

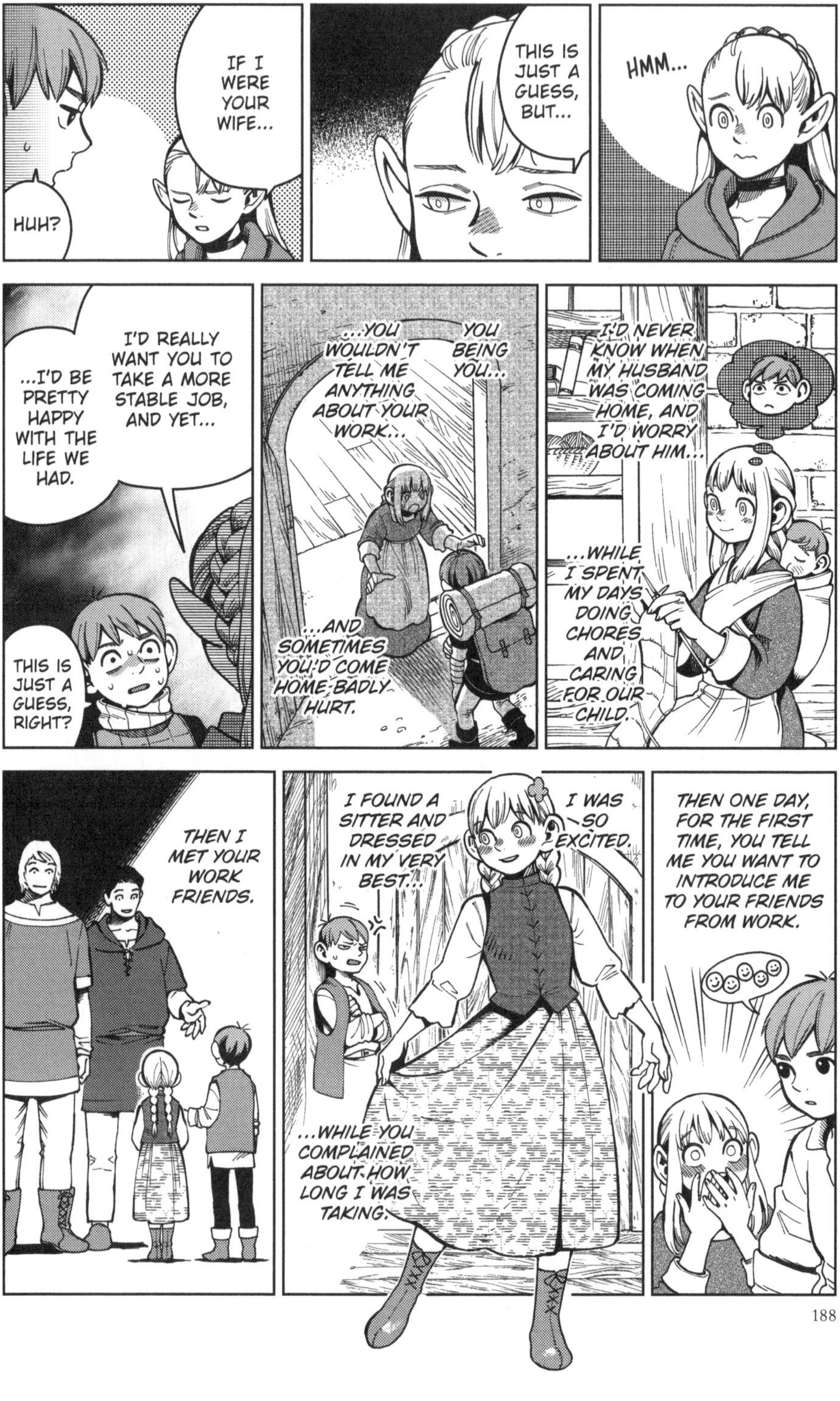
HMM...
THIS IS JUST A GUESS, BUT...
IF I WERE YOUR WIFE...
HUH?
I'D NEVER KNOW WHEN MY HUSBAND WAS COMING HOME, AND I'D WORRY ABOUT HIM...
...WHILE I SPENT MY DAYS DOING CHORES AND CARING FOR OUR CHILD.
YOU BEING YOU...
...YOU WOULDN'T TELL ME ANYTHING ABOUT YOUR WORK...
...AND SOMETIMES YOU'D COME HOME BADLY HURT.
I'D REALLY WANT YOU TO TAKE A MORE STABLE JOB, AND YET...
...I'D BE PRETTY HAPPY WITH THE LIFE WE HAD.
THIS IS JUST A GUESS, RIGHT?
THEN ONE DAY, FOR THE FIRST TIME, YOU TELL ME YOU WANT TO INTRODUCE ME TO YOUR FRIENDS FROM WORK.
I WAS SO EXCITED.
I FOUND A SITTER AND DRESSED IN MY VERY BEST...
...WHILE YOU COMPLAINED ABOUT HOW LONG I WAS TAKING.
THEN I MET YOUR WORK FRIENDS.

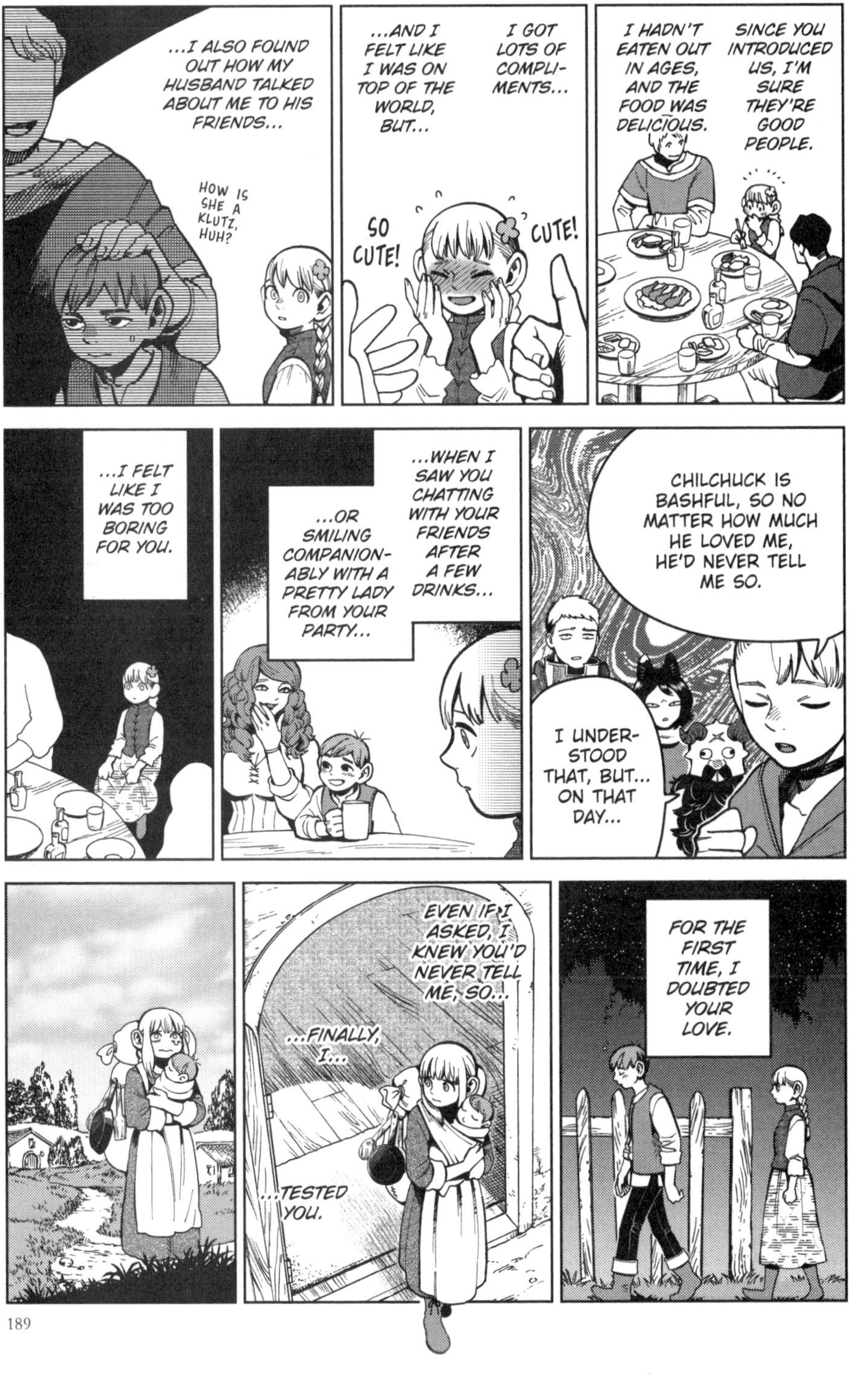
SINCE YOU INTRODUCED US, I'M SURE THEY'RE GOOD PEOPLE.
I HADN'T EATEN OUT IN AGES, AND THE FOOD WAS DELICIOUS.
I GOT LOTS OF COMPLIMENTS...
...AND I FELT LIKE I WAS ON TOP OF THE WORLD, BUT...
CUTE!
SO CUTE!
...I ALSO FOUND OUT HOW MY HUSBAND TALKED ABOUT ME TO HIS FRIENDS...
HOW IS SHE A KLUTZ, HUH?
CHILCHUCK IS BASHFUL, SO NO MATTER HOW MUCH HE LOVED ME, HE'D NEVER TELL ME SO.
I UNDERSTOOD THAT, BUT... ON THAT DAY...
...WHEN I SAW YOU CHATTING WITH YOUR FRIENDS AFTER A FEW DRINKS...
...OR SMILING COMPANIONABLY WITH A PRETTY LADY FROM YOUR PARTY...
...I FELT LIKE I WAS TOO BORING FOR YOU.
FOR THE FIRST TIME, I DOUBTED YOUR LOVE.
EVEN IF I ASKED, I KNEW YOU'D NEVER TELL ME, SO...
...FINALLY, I...
...TESTED YOU.

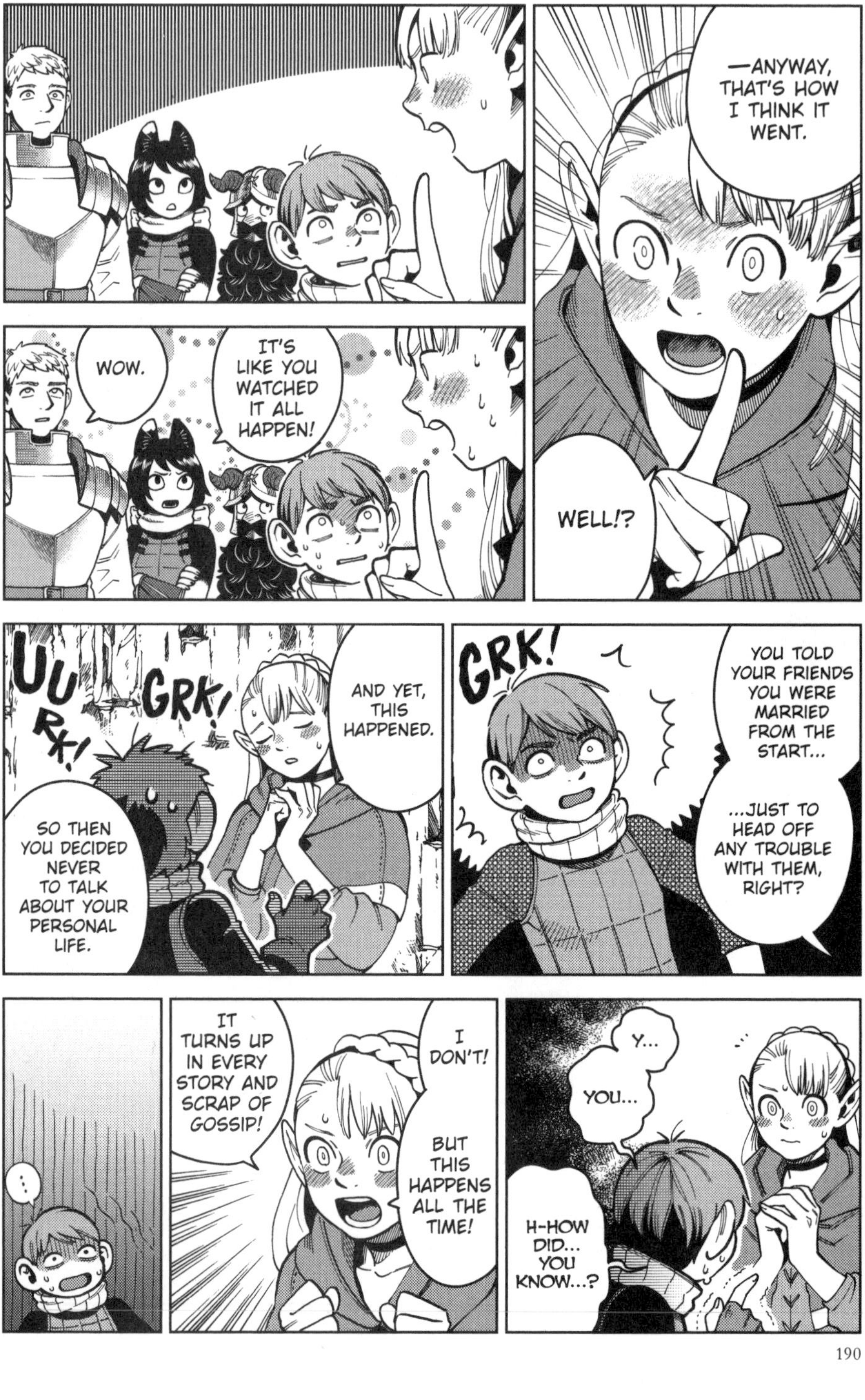
—ANYWAY, THAT'S HOW I THINK IT WENT.
WELL!?
IT'S LIKE YOU WATCHED IT ALL HAPPEN!
WOW.
YOU TOLD YOUR FRIENDS YOU WERE MARRIED FROM THE START...
GRK!
...JUST TO HEAD OFF ANY TROUBLE WITH THEM, RIGHT?
AND YET, THIS HAPPENED.
GRK!
UURK!
SO THEN YOU DECIDED NEVER TO TALK ABOUT YOUR PERSONAL LIFE.
Y...
YOU...
H-HOW DID... YOU KNOW...?
I DON'T!
BUT THIS HAPPENS ALL THE TIME!
IT TURNS UP IN EVERY STORY AND SCRAP OF GOSSIP!
...

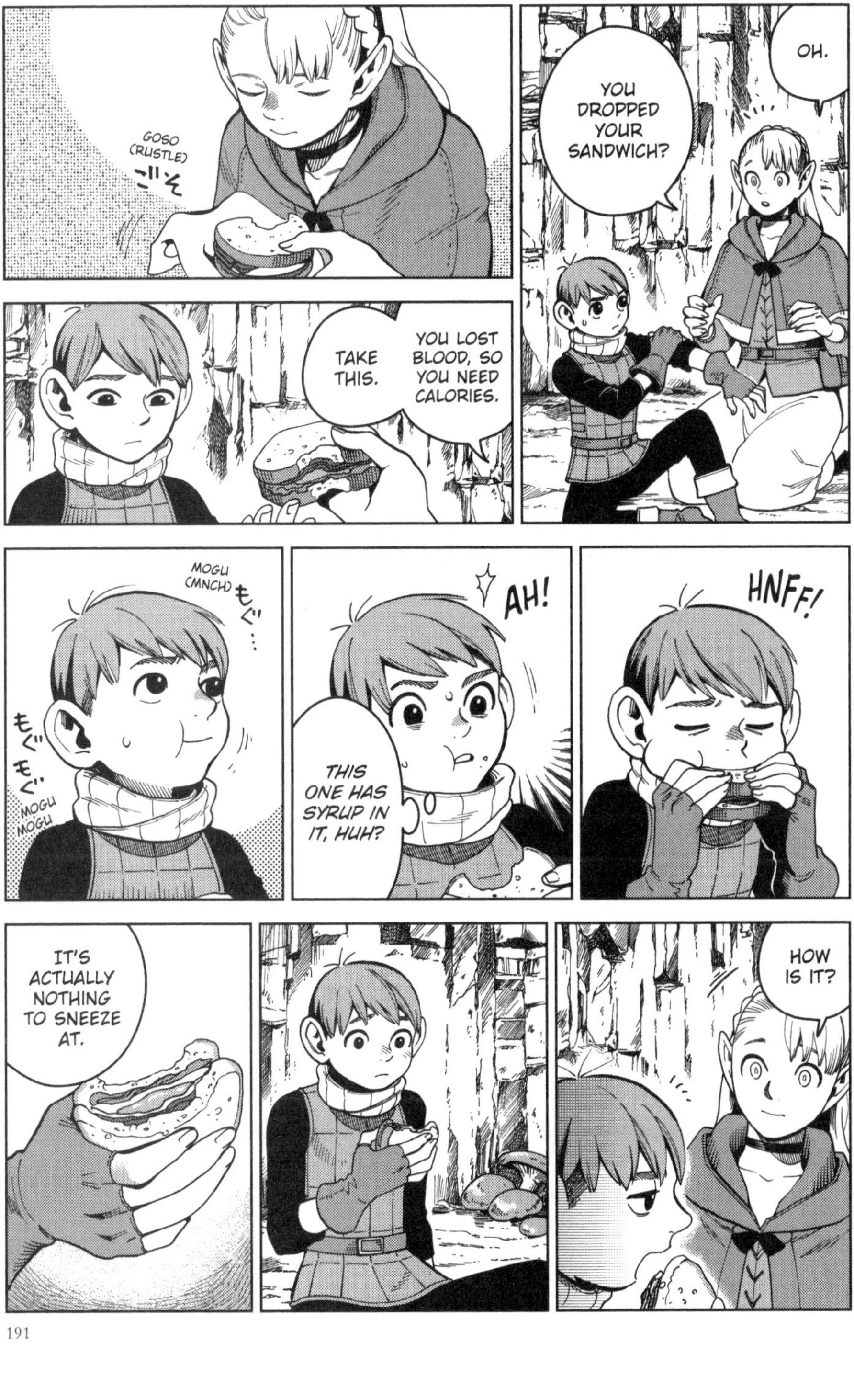
OH.
YOU DROPPED YOUR SANDWICH?
GOSO (RUSTLE) ごそ
YOU LOST BLOOD, SO YOU NEED CALORIES.
TAKE THIS.
HNFF!
AH!
THIS ONE HAS SYRUP IN IT, HUH?
MOGU (MNCH) もぐ…
もぐもぐ MOGU MOGU
HOW IS IT?
IT'S ACTUALLY NOTHING TO SNEEZE AT.

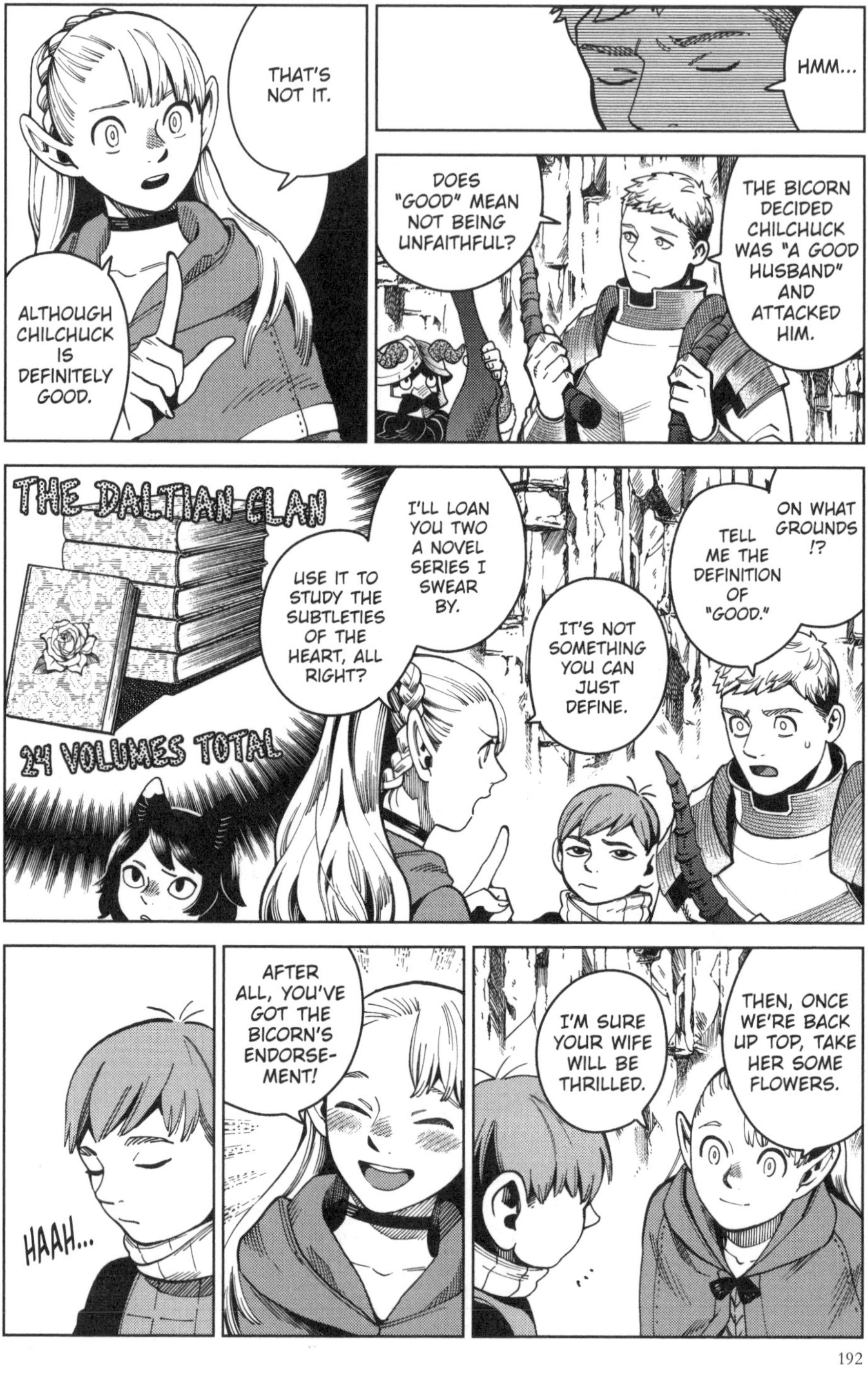
HMM...
THE BICORN DECIDED CHILCHUCK WAS "A GOOD HUSBAND" AND ATTACKED HIM.
DOES "GOOD" MEAN NOT BEING UNFAITHFUL?
THAT'S NOT IT.
ALTHOUGH CHILCHUCK IS DEFINITELY GOOD.
ON WHAT GROUNDS!?
TELL ME THE DEFINITION OF "GOOD."
IT'S NOT SOMETHING YOU CAN JUST DEFINE.
I'LL LOAN YOU TWO A NOVEL SERIES I SWEAR BY.
USE IT TO STUDY THE SUBTLETIES OF THE HEART, ALL RIGHT?
THE DALTIAN CLAN
24 VOLUMES TOTAL
THEN, ONCE WE'RE BACK UP TOP, TAKE HER SOME FLOWERS.
I'M SURE YOUR WIFE WILL BE THRILLED.
...
AFTER ALL, YOU'VE GOT THE BICORN'S ENDORSE-MENT!
HAAH...

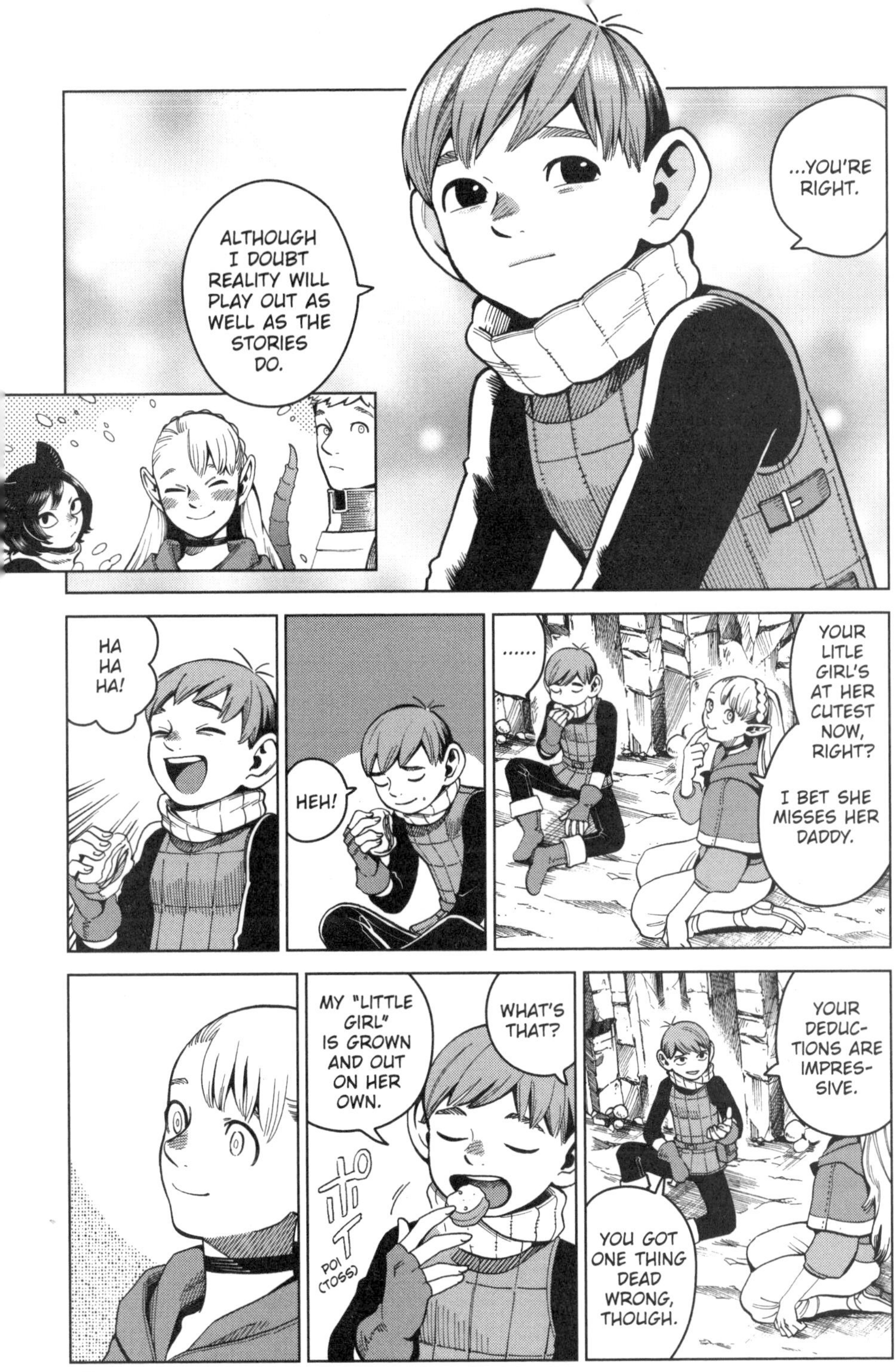
...YOU'RE RIGHT.
ALTHOUGH I DOUBT REALITY WILL PLAY OUT AS WELL AS THE STORIES DO.
YOUR LITTLE GIRL'S AT HER CUTEST NOW, RIGHT?
I BET SHE MISSES HER DADDY.
......
HEH!
HA HA HA!
YOUR DEDUC-TIONS ARE IMPRES-SIVE.
YOU GOT ONE THING DEAD WRONG, THOUGH.
WHAT'S THAT?
MY "LITTLE GIRL" IS GROWN AND OUT ON HER OWN.
ポイ
POI (TOSS)

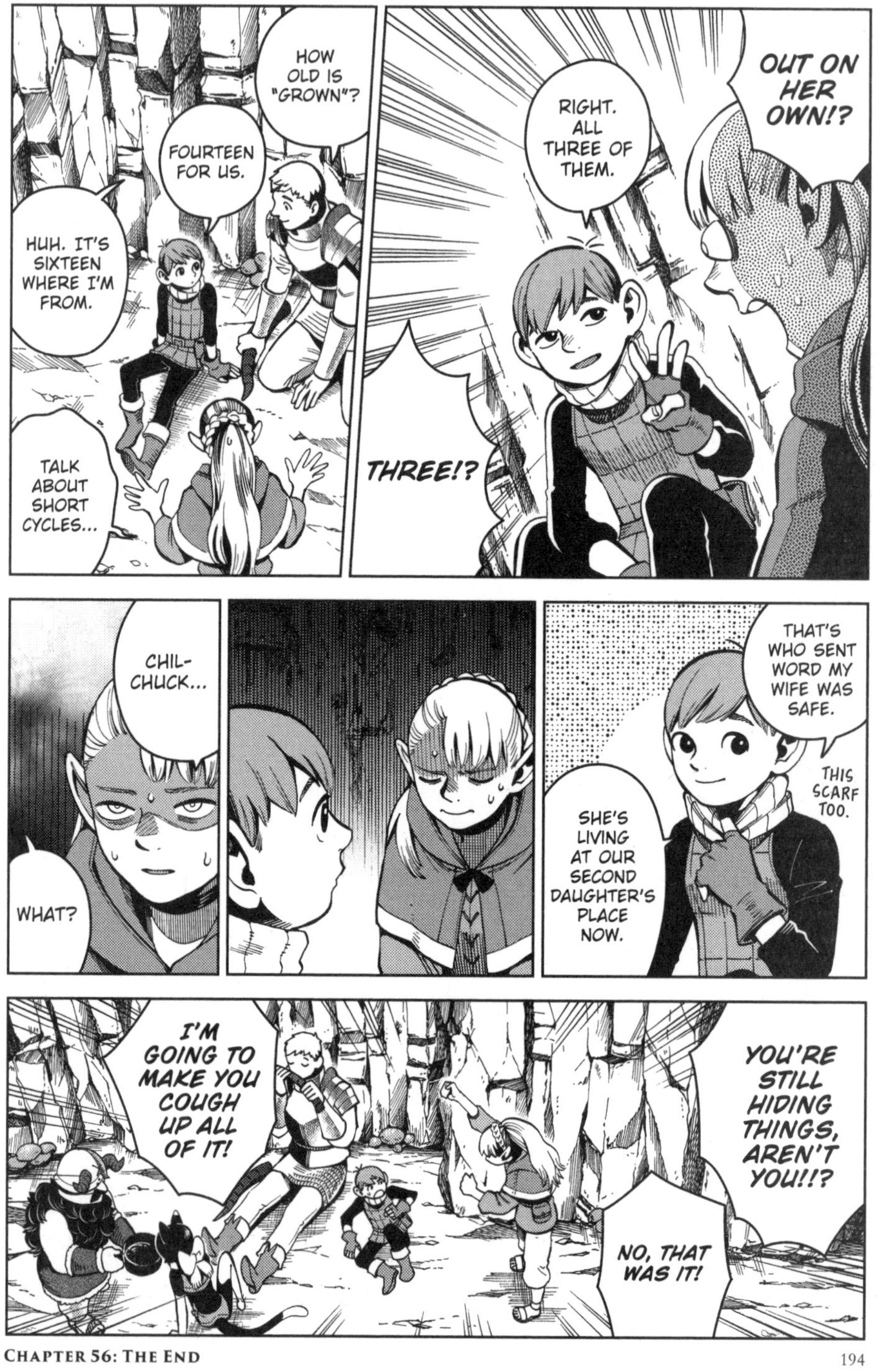
OUT ON HER OWN!?
RIGHT. ALL THREE OF THEM.
THREE!?
HOW OLD IS "GROWN"?
FOURTEEN FOR US.
HUH. IT'S SIXTEEN WHERE I'M FROM.
TALK ABOUT SHORT CYCLES...
THAT'S WHO SENT WORD MY WIFE WAS SAFE.
THIS SCARF TOO.
SHE'S LIVING AT OUR SECOND DAUGHTER'S PLACE NOW.
CHIL-CHUCK...
WHAT?
YOU'RE STILL HIDING THINGS, AREN'T YOU!!?
I'M GOING TO MAKE YOU COUGH UP ALL OF IT!
NO, THAT WAS IT!

To be continued...

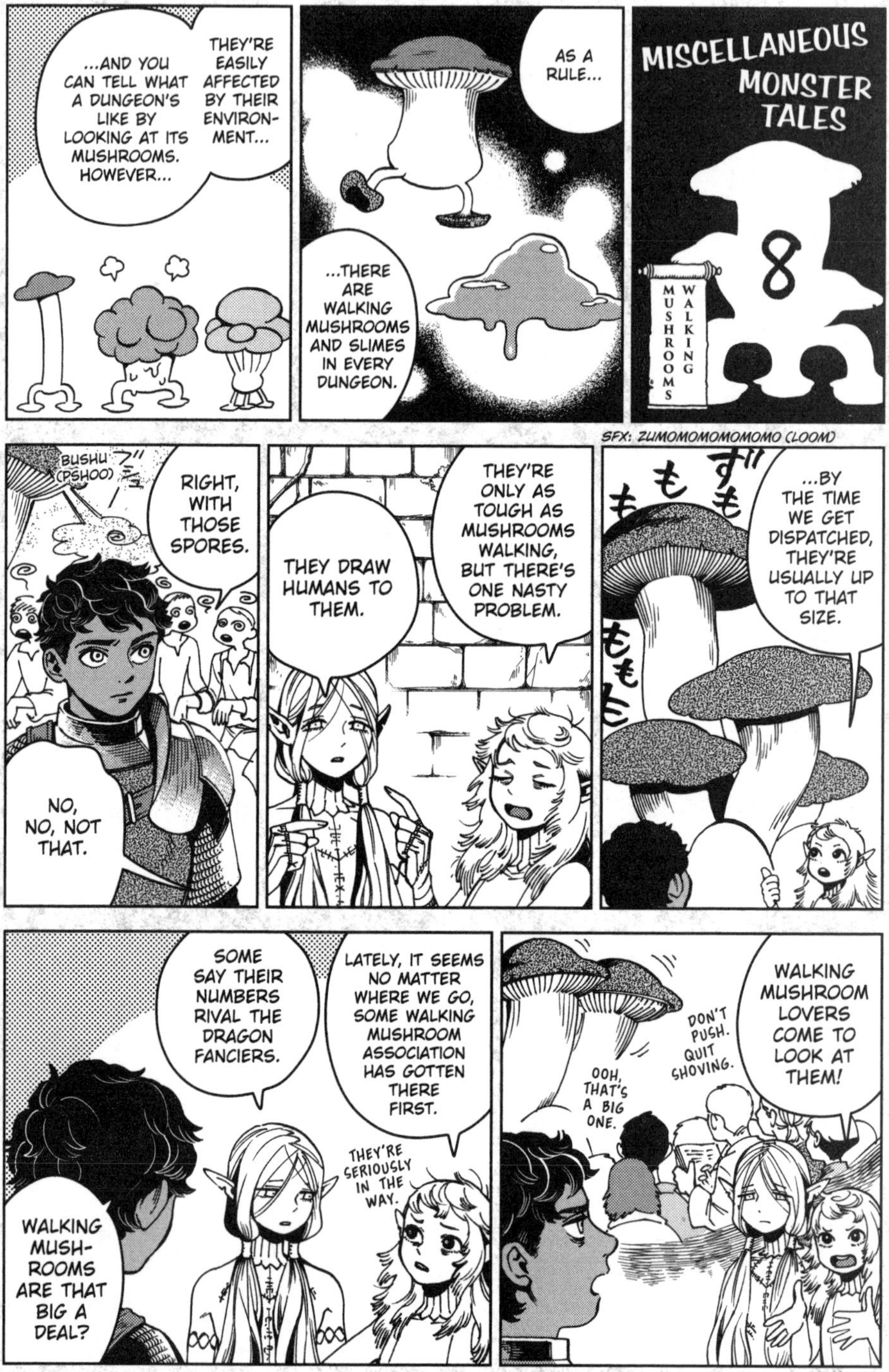
MISCELLANEOUS MONSTER TALES
8
WALKING MUSHROOMS
AS A RULE...
...THERE ARE WALKING MUSHROOMS AND SLIMES IN EVERY DUNGEON.
THEY'RE EASILY AFFECTED BY THEIR ENVIRONMENT...
...AND YOU CAN TELL WHAT A DUNGEON'S LIKE BY LOOKING AT ITS MUSHROOMS. HOWEVER...
SFX: ZUMOMOMOMOMOMO (LOOM)
...BY THE TIME WE GET DISPATCHED, THEY'RE USUALLY UP TO THAT SIZE.
THEY'RE ONLY AS TOUGH AS MUSHROOMS WALKING, BUT THERE'S ONE NASTY PROBLEM.
THEY DRAW HUMANS TO THEM.
BUSHU (PSHOO)
RIGHT, WITH THOSE SPORES.
NO, NO, NOT THAT.
WALKING MUSHROOM LOVERS COME TO LOOK AT THEM!
DON'T PUSH. QUIT SHOVING.
OOH, THAT'S A BIG ONE.
LATELY, IT SEEMS NO MATTER WHERE WE GO, SOME WALKING MUSHROOM ASSOCIATION HAS GOTTEN THERE FIRST.
SOME SAY THEIR NUMBERS RIVAL THE DRAGON FANCIERS.
THEY'RE SERIOUSLY IN THE WAY.
WALKING MUSH-ROOMS ARE THAT BIG A DEAL?

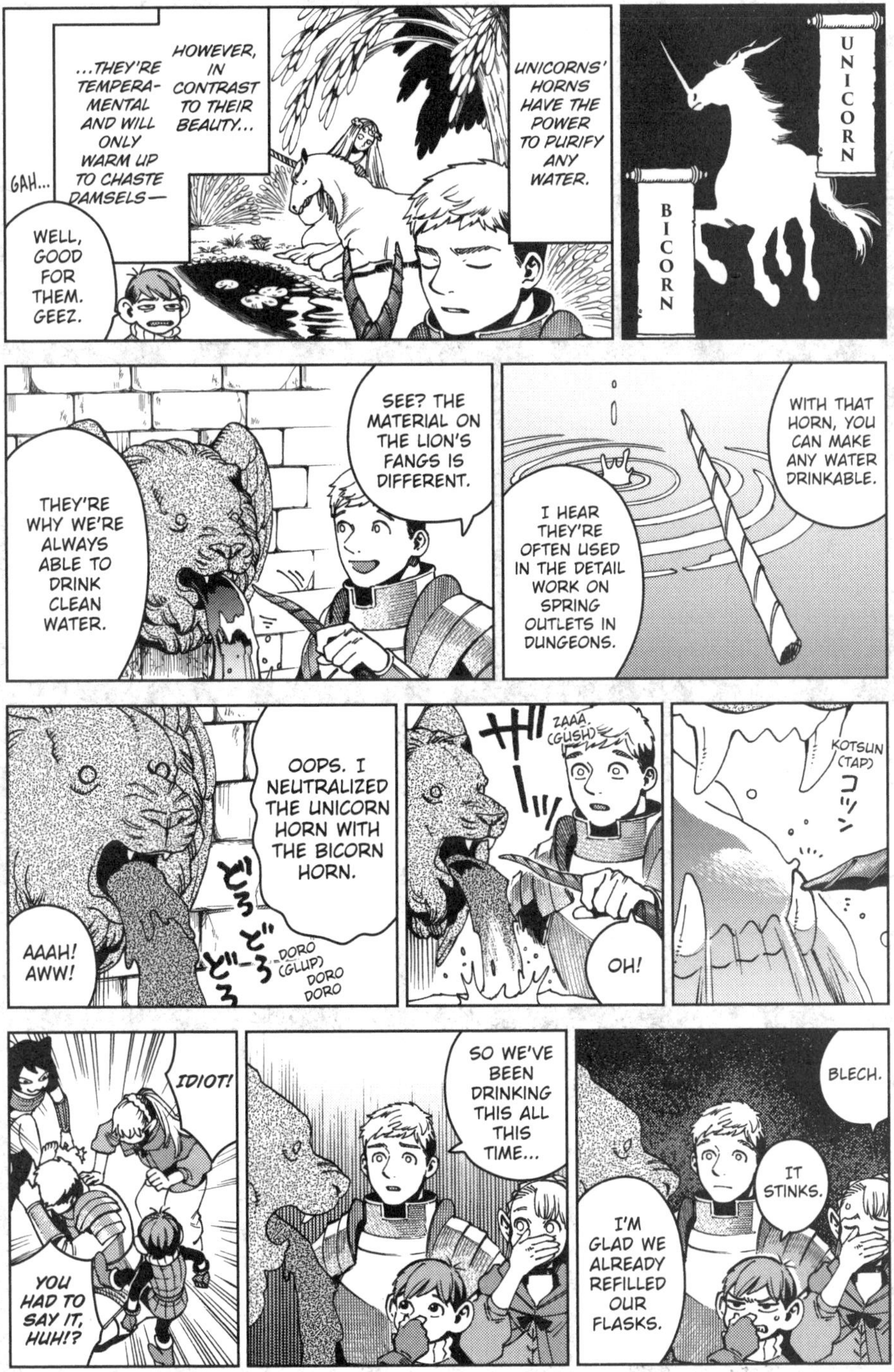
UNICORN
BICORN
UNICORNS' HORNS HAVE THE POWER TO PURIFY ANY WATER.
HOWEVER, IN CONTRAST TO THEIR BEAUTY...
...THEY'RE TEMPERAMENTAL AND WILL ONLY WARM UP TO CHASTE DAMSELS—
GAH...
WELL, GOOD FOR THEM. GEEZ.
WITH THAT HORN, YOU CAN MAKE ANY WATER DRINKABLE.
I HEAR THEY'RE OFTEN USED IN THE DETAIL WORK ON SPRING OUTLETS IN DUNGEONS.
SEE? THE MATERIAL ON THE LION'S FANGS IS DIFFERENT.
THEY'RE WHY WE'RE ALWAYS ABLE TO DRINK CLEAN WATER.
KOTSUN (TAP)
コツン
ZAAA (GUSH)
ザーッ
OH!
OOPS. I NEUTRALIZED THE UNICORN HORN WITH THE BICORN HORN.
AAAH! AWW!
DORO (GLUP) DORO DORO
どろどろどろ
BLECH.
IT STINKS.
I'M GLAD WE ALREADY REFILLED OUR FLASKS.
SO WE'VE BEEN DRINKING THIS ALL THIS TIME...
IDIOT!
YOU HAD TO SAY IT, HUH!?

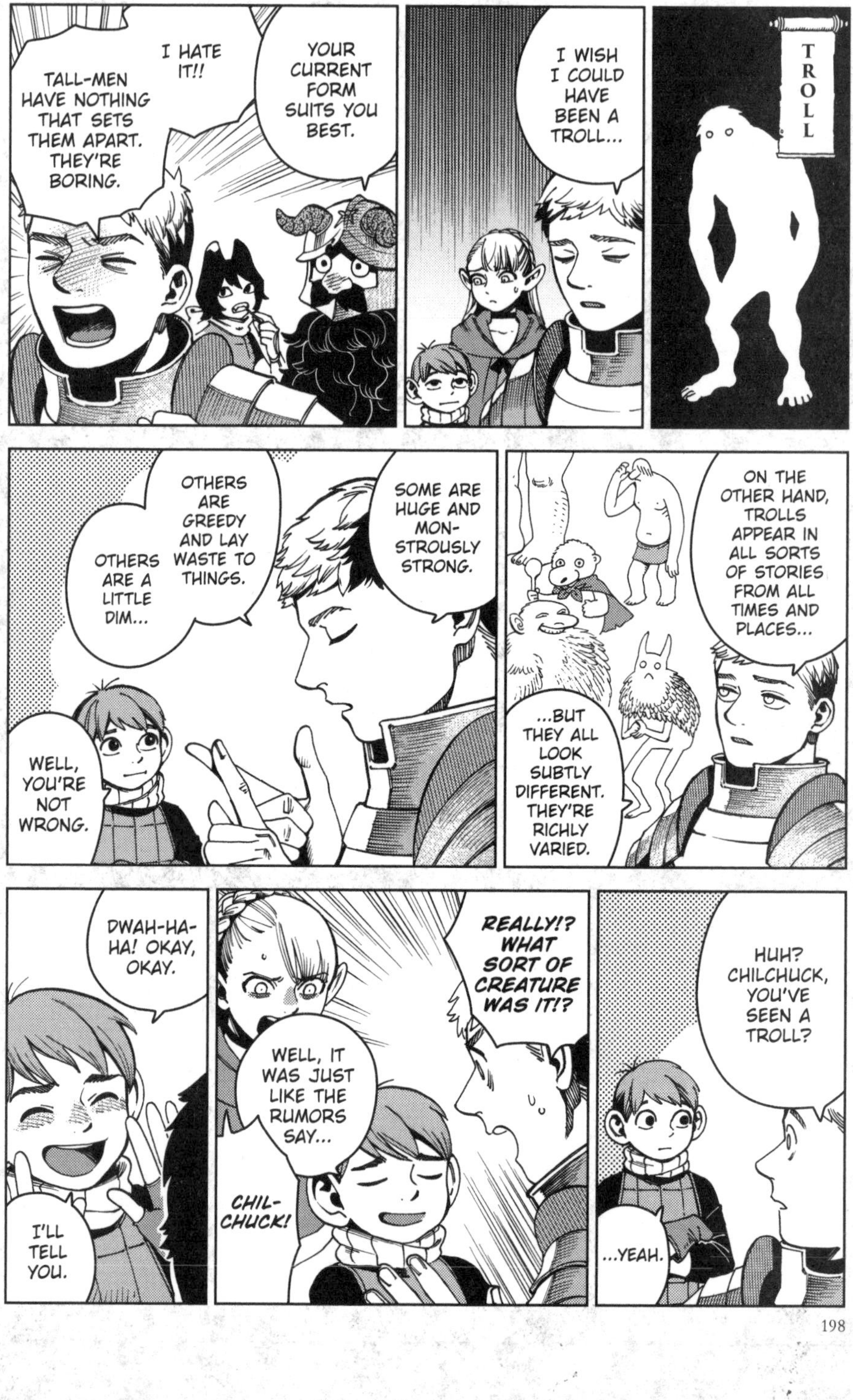
TROLL
I WISH I COULD HAVE BEEN A TROLL...
YOUR CURRENT FORM SUITS YOU BEST.
I HATE IT!!
TALL-MEN HAVE NOTHING THAT SETS THEM APART. THEY'RE BORING.
ON THE OTHER HAND, TROLLS APPEAR IN ALL SORTS OF STORIES FROM ALL TIMES AND PLACES...
...BUT THEY ALL LOOK SUBTLY DIFFERENT. THEY'RE RICHLY VARIED.
SOME ARE HUGE AND MON-STROUSLY STRONG.
OTHERS ARE GREEDY AND LAY WASTE TO THINGS.
OTHERS ARE A LITTLE DIM...
WELL, YOU'RE NOT WRONG.
HUH? CHILCHUCK, YOU'VE SEEN A TROLL?
...YEAH.
REALLY!? WHAT SORT OF CREATURE WAS IT!?
WELL, IT WAS JUST LIKE THE RUMORS SAY...
CHIL-CHUCK!
DWAH-HA-HA! OKAY, OKAY.
I'LL TELL YOU.

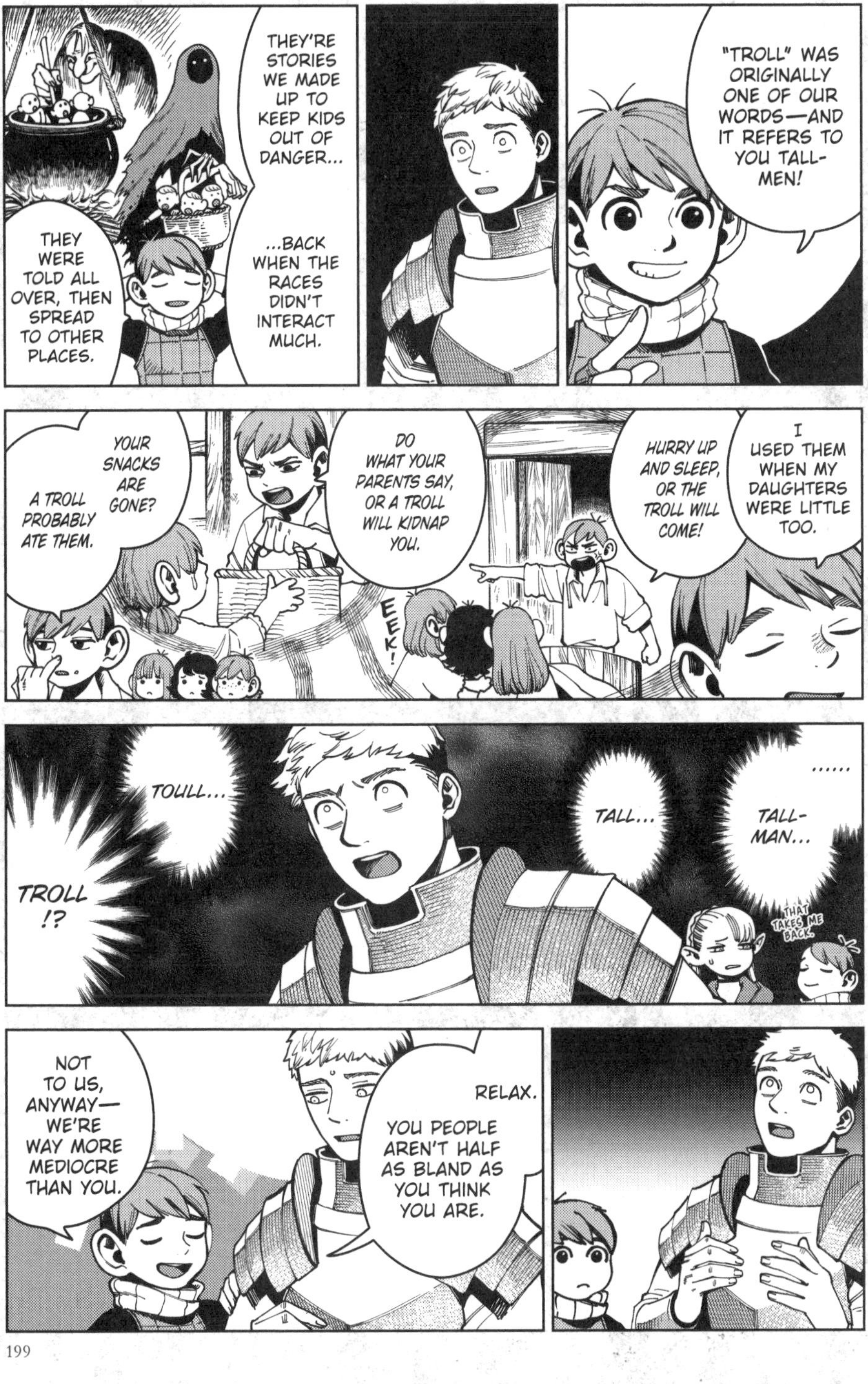
"TROLL" WAS ORIGINALLY ONE OF OUR WORDS—AND IT REFERS TO YOU TALL-MEN!
THEY'RE STORIES WE MADE UP TO KEEP KIDS OUT OF DANGER...
...BACK WHEN THE RACES DIDN'T INTERACT MUCH.
THEY WERE TOLD ALL OVER, THEN SPREAD TO OTHER PLACES.
I USED THEM WHEN MY DAUGHTERS WERE LITTLE TOO.
HURRY UP AND SLEEP, OR THE TROLL WILL COME!
EEK!
DO WHAT YOUR PARENTS SAY, OR A TROLL WILL KIDNAP YOU.
YOUR SNACKS ARE GONE?
A TROLL PROBABLY ATE THEM.
......
TALL-MAN...
TALL...
THAT TAKES ME BACK.
TOULL...
TROLL!?
RELAX.
YOU PEOPLE AREN'T HALF AS BLAND AS YOU THINK YOU ARE.
NOT TO US, ANYWAY—WE'RE WAY MORE MEDIOCRE THAN YOU.

TRANSLATION NOTES

Page 32
In Japan, having a "cat's tongue" means you're extra-sensitive to the temperature of your food and have a hard time eating or drinking hot things. The phrase isn't usually applied to actual cats.

Page 41
The mushkhushshu is a creature from Mesopotamian mythology said to have scales, hind legs like an eagle's, the forelimbs of a lion, a long neck and tail, horns, a snake-like tongue, and a crest. Images of this beast adorn the reconstructed Ishtar Gate, a famous entryway in the ancient city of Babylon.

Page 59
The gargoyle's transformation is a send-up of the famous *Manneken Pis* statue in Brussels, Belgium. The current statue was put in place in 1618 or 1619 (original installation is unknown) and actually was intended to produce potable water for public consumption.

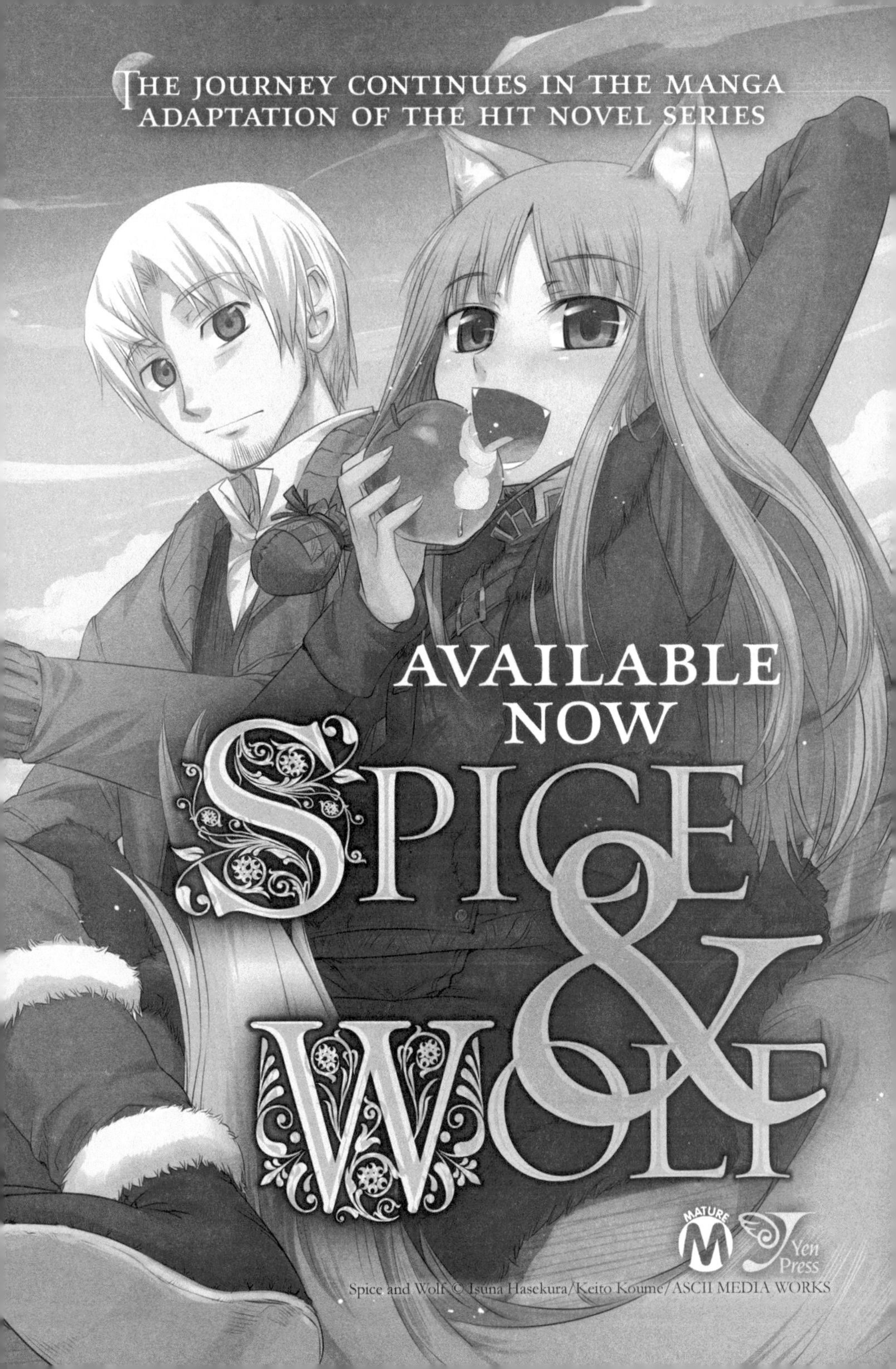
THE JOURNEY CONTINUES IN THE MANGA
ADAPTATION OF THE HIT NOVEL SERIES
AVAILABLE
NOW
SPICE & WOLF
MATURE
M
Yen
Press
Spice and Wolf © Isuna Hasekura/Keito Koume/ASCII MEDIA WORKS

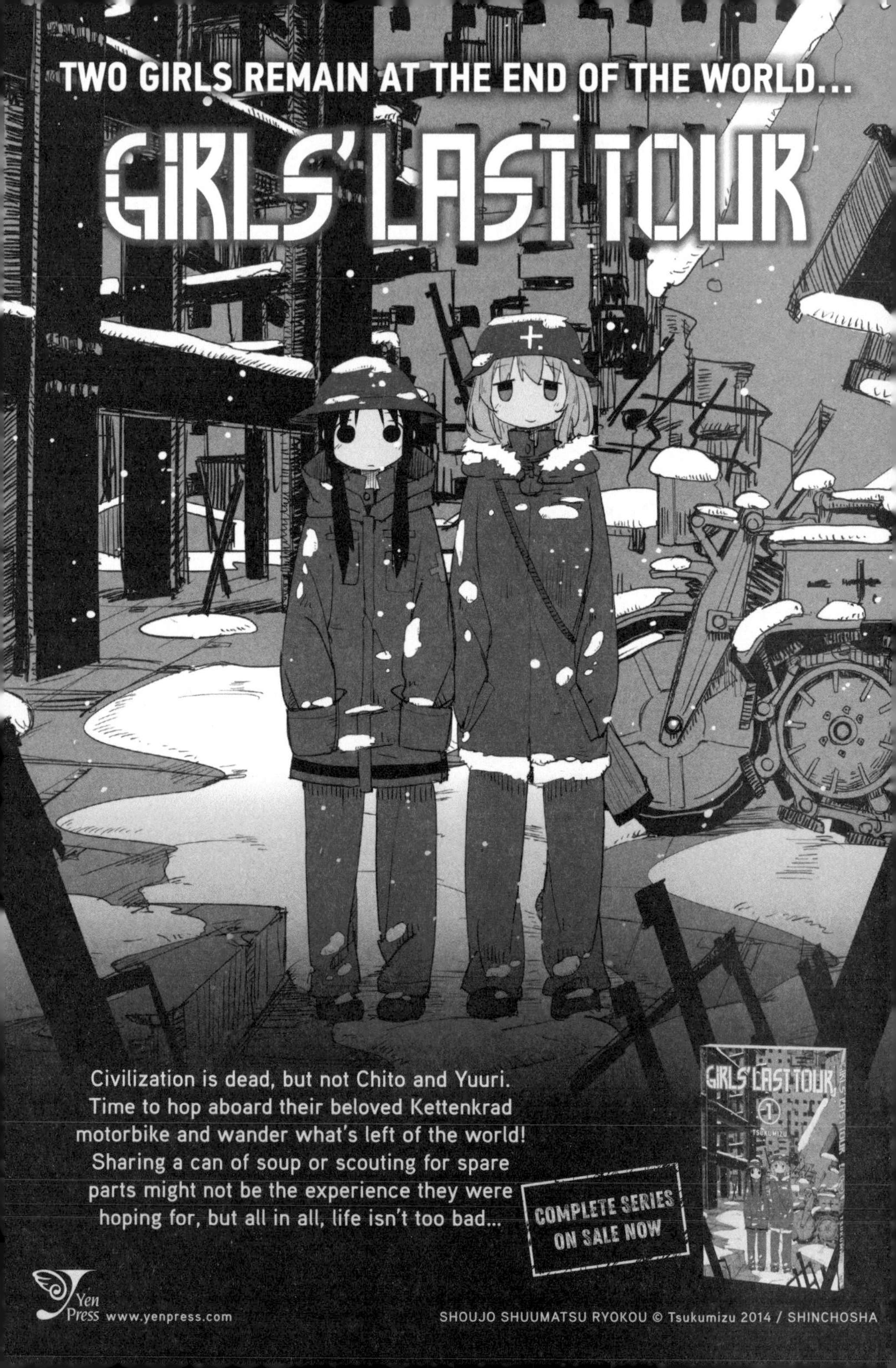
TWO GIRLS REMAIN AT THE END OF THE WORLD...
GIRLS' LAST TOUR
Civilization is dead, but not Chito and Yuuri. Time to hop aboard their beloved Kettenkrad motorbike and wander what's left of the world! Sharing a can of soup or scouting for spare parts might not be the experience they were hoping for, but all in all, life isn't too bad...
COMPLETE SERIES ON SALE NOW
GIRLS' LAST TOUR 1 TSUKUMIZU
Yen Press www.yenpress.com
SHOUJO SHUUMATSU RYOKOU © Tsukumizu 2014 / SHINCHOSHA

Two girls, a new school, and the beginning of a beautiful friendship.

Kiss & White Lily for My Dearest Girl

In middle school, Ayaka Shiramine was the perfect student: hard-working, with excellent grades and a great personality to match. As Ayaka enters high school she expects to still be on top, but one thing she didn't account for is her new classmate, the lazy yet genuine genius Yurine Kurosawa. What's in store for Ayaka and Yurine as they go through high school...together?

8

DELICIOUS IN DUNGEON
RYOKO KUI

Translation: Taylor Engel   **Lettering: Abigail Blackman**

This book is a work of fiction. Names, characters, places, and incidents are the product of the author's imagination or are used fictitiously. Any resemblance to actual events, locales, or persons, living or dead, is coincidental.

DUNGEON MESHI Volume 8 © Ryoko Kui 2019
First published in Japan in 2019 by **KADOKAWA CORPORATION**, Tokyo. English translation rights arranged with **KADOKAWA CORPORATION**, Tokyo through Tuttle-Mori Agency, Inc., Tokyo.

English translation © 2020 by Yen Press, LLC

Yen Press
150 West 30th Street, 19th Floor
New York, NY 10001

Visit us at yenpress.com
facebook.com/yenpress
twitter.com/yenpress
yenpress.tumblr.com
instagram.com/yenpress

First Yen Press Edition: March 2020

Yen Press is an imprint of Yen Press, LLC.
The Yen Press name and logo are trademarks of Yen Press, LLC.

The publisher is not responsible for websites (or their content) that are not owned by the publisher.

Library of Congress Control Number: 2017932141

ISBNs: 978-1-9753-9940-5 (paperback)
       978-1-9753-0864-3 (ebook)

10 9 8 7 6 5 4 3 2

WOR

Printed in the United States of America